Westside

JESUS IS RISEN

JESUS IS RISEN

RISEN

PAUL AND THE **EARLY CHURCH**

DAVID LIMBAUGH

REGNERY
PUBLISHING
A Division of Salem Media Group

Cataloging-in-Publication data on file with the Library of Congress

ISBN 978-1-62157-704-1
ebook ISBN 978-1-62157-759-1

Published in the United States by
Regnery Publishing
A Division of Salem Media Group
300 New Jersey Ave NW
Washington, DC 20001
www.Regnery.com

Manufactured in the United States of America

10 9 8 7 6 5 4 3 2

Books are available in quantity for promotional or premium use. For information on discounts and terms, please visit our website: www.Regnery.com.

*To Christen and Sam—May God
richly bless your marriage.*

CONTENTS

Introduction   ix

CHAPTER 1
How a Trip to Damascus Changed the World   1

CHAPTER 2
Acts 1-7: A Church Is Born   21

CHAPTER 3
Acts 8-13: An Equal Opportunity Faith   45

CHAPTER 4
Acts 14-20: Suffering and Success While Spreading the Word   71

CHAPTER 5
Acts 21-28: Arrest of an Apostle   97

CHAPTER 6
Galatians: Freedom in Christ   125

CHAPTER 7
1 Thessalonians and 2 Thessalonians: Christ's Return and
the Day of the Lord   143

CHAPTER 8
1 Corinthians 1–8: A Call for Unity in the Church   167

CHAPTER 9
1 Corinthians 9–16: The Primacy of Love, and a
Spiritual Gift for Every Believer   195

CHAPTER 10
2 Corinthians: Strength in Weakness   225

CHAPTER 11
Romans 1–7: Righteousness through Faith   259

CHAPTER 12
Romans 8–16: Christ: The Hope of Jews and Gentiles   289

Conclusion   319
Acknowledgments   321
Notes   325
Index   409

INTRODUCTION

This is my fourth Christian-themed book, and I get more enthused about the subject matter with each one. In my first one, *Jesus On Trial*, I recounted my personal faith journey from skeptic to believer and laid out the reasons I came to believe that Jesus Christ is the Son of God and gave His life for the redemption of all who put their trust in Him. Next was *The Emmaus Code*, in which I detailed the countless ways the Old Testament points to Jesus Christ.

Then in *The True Jesus* I presented the Gospels in one unified narrative in chronological order. I went through nearly every verse in all four books, sometimes quoting verbatim and other times paraphrasing, though always striving to remain true to the text. Throughout the narrative, I interlaced commentary and insights—my own and those of reliable scholars and commentators. My aim was to introduce readers—both inexperienced and advanced—to the flow of the Gospels and to help them better understand the material. My ultimate goals, as with all these books, were to whet the readers' appetite to read the words of Scripture itself, instill a passion for the Bible, and encourage people to make reading and studying it a lifelong commitment.

When I began *The True Jesus*, I had the ambitious goal of covering the entire New Testament. As I sunk my teeth into the project, however, I realized I could not cover all the material in sufficient depth. So I decided to cover the Gospels alone and complete the remaining New Testament books, with the possible exception of the Book of Revelation, in one or more additional books.

To briefly review, the New Testament contains twenty-seven books, which fit into three categories: history, doctrine, and prophecy. The first five books—the four Gospels and Acts—are historical books: the Gospels are accounts of Jesus' life, death, and resurrection, while Acts is the history of the early Church. The following twenty-one books are epistles—letters written mostly by apostles[1] to churches or individuals. They sometimes address specific problems in local churches, but also expound Christian doctrine for the instruction of all Christians generally. The letters were substitute communications from the apostles when they could not deliver their messages to the churches personally.[2] Validated by the apostles' authority, the epistles provided a reliable body of truth and a consistent set of principles for Christian living, which grounded the early Church in its faith.[3]

The epistles are generally divided into two categories. The Apostle Paul wrote thirteen of them, which are called "the Pauline epistles." The other eight are Catholic or General Epistles, sometimes called the "non-Pauline epistles," most of which are not addressed to any particular church or individual.[4] Of the Pauline epistles, nine are addressed to Gentile churches in Galatia, Thessalonica, Corinth, Rome, Colossae, Ephesus, and Philippi, and four to individuals: Timothy, Titus, and Philemon.[5] Of the General Epistles, John wrote three, Peter two, and Jesus' brothers James and Jude wrote one each, with the authorship of the Book of Hebrews being unknown.[6] Revelation is the last book of the Bible and in its own category—apocalypse, prophecy, or revelation. Comprising John's vision, it is a revelation of how God will consummate His plan of redemption and salvation for mankind. Irving Jensen aptly calls Revelation "the climax of God's Book, the last chapter of world history."

Readers seemed to enjoy my chronological narrative of the Gospels in *The True Jesus*, so it seemed fitting to structure *Jesus Is Risen* the same way. I initially planned for this book to cover the Book of Acts and the thirteen Pauline epistles, but once again, when I began to write I discovered my original plan was unrealistic. So I decided to cover only Paul's six so-called missionary epistles—Galatians, 1 & 2 Thessalonians, 1 & 2 Corinthians, and Romans—which are believed to have been written before his other seven epistles. This has worked out nicely, as Luke provides an illuminating picture of the early Church in Acts, including Paul's tireless activities spreading the Gospel. Then in the six epistles, Paul covers some of the historical material chronicled in Acts and addresses issues related to the early Church and Christian doctrine.

I pray that readers will get a flavor for the history of the early Church and how Christianity spread so rapidly throughout the Roman Empire during the first century AD following its founding. As in *The True Jesus*, I paraphrase the biblical text or quote it verbatim while providing an ongoing commentary designed to aid the reader's understanding of the action and theology in the corresponding Scripture. When I do paraphrase, I make every effort to remain absolutely true to the text, which I firmly believe is the inspired Word of God.

The Gospels are where we meet Jesus in person—His words and actions come alive, His character jumps from the pages, and His love and goodness permeate every verse. While we learn Christianity through encountering the Person of Jesus in the Gospels, we see Him and His message from a different perspective in Acts and the epistles, the former showing the apostles' fervor for Christ, honoring His Great Commission to spread the Gospel through the power of the Holy Spirit, and the latter setting forth Christian doctrine and instructions for the early Church. It's exciting and powerful stuff.

Since I first began reading the Bible, Paul has been my favorite biblical figure and writer. After his conversion, he becomes a tireless evangelist and literally "writes the book" on spreading and teaching the Gospel. The richness of his theology and his practical advice to churches is unparalleled in Scripture. He wears his heart on his sleeve, and his theology springs from his prolific pen. In terms of understanding the spiritual message and implications of the Gospel, there is no substitute for reading Paul's writings.

I hope that with this chronological arrangement, you will learn the historical context for the robust activities of the early Church and the genuine challenges the apostles confront as they doggedly preach the Word throughout the Roman Empire. I earnestly pray the book's framework will enhance your perspective of the events as they unfold and your understanding of Paul's writings in the setting and mindset in which he writes them. It is riveting to experience the explosion of Christianity through Paul's eyes and those of other Church leaders. You will stand side by side with them as they square off against ruthless opponents and grow through adversity.

Paul expounds the Gospel message like no one else, especially the notion of salvation by grace through faith in Jesus Christ. That's why preeminent Biblical scholar F. F. Bruce called him "the preacher of free grace." "Paul's pre-eminent contribution to the world has been his presentation of the good news of free grace—as he himself would have put it (rightly), his re-presentation of the good news explicit in Jesus' teaching and embodied in his life and work," writes Bruce. "The free grace of God which Paul proclaimed is free grace in more senses than one— free in the sense that it is sovereign and unfettered, free in the sense that it is held forth to men and women for their acceptance by faith alone, and free in the sense that it is the source and principle of their liberation from all kinds of inward and spiritual bondage, including the bondage of legalism and the bondage of moral anarchy."[7]

Paul explains the role, activities, and indispensability of the Holy Spirit to the Christian's life in Christ. In his letters (and through Luke's account in Acts) we see Paul's deeply human side and his spirituality like no other biblical figure apart from Christ. He leaves no stone unturned as he unapologetically defends his positions and ministry against fraudulent opponents who would have destroyed the Gospel in its infancy.

Throughout Paul's writings, what stands out to me as much as his profoundly logical mind and his love for Christ is his raw genuineness as a human being. His professed agony over the fate of his beloved Jewish brothers tugs at our heart strings. His stubborn and abiding love for his people persists to the very end, which has not yet been written. If

Christianity's greatest evangelist and theologian is unafraid to share his own weaknesses and shortcomings with the world, then as lesser mortals we must be truly encouraged when we face our own struggles in the faith.

Paul imparts clear instructions on how to live life in the Spirit and to become free from sin's reign as we grow more Christ-like. Through Paul we learn the true meaning of Christian liberty. Free in Christ from the bondage of sin and the strict requirements of the Law, we must hold ourselves to a higher standard—not as a matter of following rules and regulations, but voluntarily, out of our love for Christ. With the exception of Christ, there is no greater teacher than Paul, and we owe it to ourselves to sit at his feet as we watch him in action and read his words of instruction, which have been divinely preserved for our edification in Christ. Contrary to certain skeptics, Paul's teachings are wholly consistent with those of Christ. The message is clear: through His mercy and grace, God forgives sinners who place their faith in Jesus. Christ's righteousness is imputed to believers, and God maintains His standard of perfect righteousness and justice. It's too marvelous for words!

As I strive to remain true to the biblical text, you will sometimes notice Paul repeating ideas or stories for varying emphases. Instead of brushing aside such restatements, please savor them, knowing Paul regarded them as especially important. As you read these summaries of Acts and Paul's six missionary epistles, remember that the people about whom Luke and Paul are writing are human beings, no different from you and me. They actually existed in human history, and critics who suggest otherwise are contradicted by a mountain of evidence, much like other skeptics who have failed throughout the centuries to discredit this wonderful, God-breathed account of the early Church and these magnificent, inspired epistles. Try to imagine yourself present with Peter, Paul, and the other apostles and early Christians as they forge the path for the most prolific spread of any religion in history and open the door, under the power of the Holy Spirit, to our salvation through faith in Jesus Christ.

CHAPTER ONE

HOW A TRIP TO DAMASCUS CHANGED THE WORLD

[Saul] hated the name of Jesus. So much so, he became a self-avowed, violent aggressor, persecuting and killing Christians in allegiance to the God of heaven. Shocking though it may seem, we must never forget the pit from which he came. The better we understand the darkness of his past, the more we will understand his gratitude for grace.

—CHUCK SWINDOLL[1]

A PROVIDENTIAL LIFE

P aul, probably even more than Peter, is the prominent leader of the early Christian Church. The central figure in the Book of Acts, Paul writes more New Testament books than any other apostle, though Luke's books contain more words and verses.[2]

To understand Paul, we must study both his life and writings. We can glean much about his life from Luke's detailed and often firsthand accounts in Acts and from Paul's remarkably candid epistles. New Testament scholar F. F. Bruce observes, "Of all the New Testament authors, Paul is the one who has stamped his own personality most unmistakably on his writings."[3] As the earliest datable Christian documents, the epistles are our primary source on the beginnings of the faith. Many were likely written just eighteen to thirty years after Jesus' death,[4] which is earlier than some of the Gospels, though the Gospels appear before them in the New Testament.

Certain biblical critics argue that the Paul of Acts is fundamentally different from the Paul of his letters, but I disagree, and not just because I believe in the inerrancy of Scripture. Having intensely studied the Book of Acts and the epistles in my research for this book, I am convinced this complex man is accurately and compositely portrayed in these complementary sources. Any dissimilarities in the accounts are differences we would expect between a person's self-portrait and one that another painted of him. Acts is an independent and historically reliable source for events in Paul's life, providing an invaluable framework for his main epistles.[5]

As doctrinally prolific and influential as Paul is, he's an equally energetic and consequential evangelist. Astonishingly, and principally because of his own efforts, Christianity becomes a Gentile religion within a generation of his death even though its Founder and His disciples were Jews who began the new religion in Judea. Though born Jewish, Paul spreads the Good News throughout the Roman Empire from Syria to Italy in the three short decades following his conversion. He is so confident in the churches he establishes that he plans missionary tours much farther west without fear they will dissolve when he leaves.[6]

Paul, more than anyone else, clarifies the Christian message as predominantly about grace and not works—that sinners can find forgiveness and redemption in Christ not as a result of their own efforts, but solely based on His finished work on the cross. Contrary to skeptics' claims, Paul's message is wholly consistent with the teachings and actions of Christ, Who repeatedly forgave repentant sinners without abandoning His standard of perfect righteousness, as shown in His parable of the prodigal son (Luke 15:11–32). Throughout the Gospel accounts Christ preached salvation by faith alone (John 3:16), and nowhere is that principle more clearly demonstrated than in His promise of salvation to the thief on the cross (Luke 23:43). Christian grace is aptly described as free—a gift to those who accept it by faith alone—but it was anything but free for our holy Benefactor, Who gave everything in His life and death to purchase our salvation. This grace is not only free but also freeing, as it liberates human beings from the bondage of their sin.[7]

Crucially, Paul's Gospel of "free grace" does not contradict the Law of Moses. Christ affirmed that He came not to abolish but to fulfill the

Law (Matt. 5:17), which Jesus summarized as the duty to love God and one's neighbors, as embodied in the first two commandments (Matt. 22:40). Accordingly, Paul pronounces love as "the fulfilling of the law" (Romans 13:10) and emphasizes that the Gospel of faith and grace does not "overthrow the law," but upholds it (Romans 3:31).[8]

It is fitting that Paul is known as the "apostle of grace" because at the time of his conversion, no one is less deserving of the gift. He becomes the consummate preacher of grace because he is its greatest and most grateful beneficiary. Prior to his conversion, Paul hates Christ and His followers and dedicates his life to persecuting these heretics. He delights in the stoning of the martyr Stephen, who refuses to renounce Christ, and like his Master, Stephen prays for his killers at the very moment they execute him. Paul's conversion from such seemingly irredeemable depths moves him to appreciate grace in direct proportion to his unworthiness. This is why Paul "understood and explained grace better than any of his contemporaries," writes Chuck Swindoll. "He never got over his own gratitude as a recipient of it. God's unmerited favor, His super-abounding grace, reached down to him in all his self-righteous zeal, crushed his pride, drove him to his knees, softened his heart, and transformed this once-violent aggressor into a powerful spokesman for Christ."[9]

By all appearances, Paul is the least likely person to become Christianity's premiere evangelist. He is a Jew, born "Saul," in Tarsus (Acts 21:39, 22:3), a city in Asia Minor in the province of Cilicia, close to Syria.[10] He is raised and educated in Jerusalem under Gamaliel, a highly respected rabbi and Jewish scholar who mentors him on the "strict manner of the law of our fathers" (Acts 22:3). In his epistle to the Philippians Paul expands on his Jewish bona fides, declaring, "If anyone else thinks he has reason for confidence in the flesh, I have more: circumcised on the eighth day, of the people of Israel, of the tribe of Benjamin, a Hebrew of Hebrews; as to the law, a Pharisee; as to zeal, a persecutor of the church; as to righteousness under the law, blameless" (3:4–6).

No one is more avidly devoted to Jewish Law. Paul is of pure Jewish lineage and of the honored tribe of Benjamin, from which came Israel's first king, Saul (1 Samuel 9:1–2).[11] As a Pharisee, he obeys the Law's precepts to the letter and zealously torments Christians for ostensibly corrupting his religion. Yet upon his conversion, he happily abandons all these boasting rights and discards his credentials, counting them as rubbish "because of the surpassing worth of knowing Christ Jesus my Lord" (Philip. 3:8). Given his background, who could better understand the futility of seeking salvation through works? Paul has few peers in "the accomplishments of the flesh"—few who achieved so much by their own deeds. He once had great pride in these "achievements" but ultimately comes to regard them as valueless, realizing that by himself he is utterly unworthy—as "all our righteous deeds are like filthy rags" (Isaiah 64:6 NIV). Paul understands that all glory belongs to Christ—"not having a righteousness of my own that comes from the law, but that which comes through faith in Christ, the righteousness from God that depends on faith" (Philip. 3:9).

Also qualifying Paul for his mission to the Gentiles are his fluency in Greek and his familiarity with Hellenistic culture, which help him relate to Gentiles (Greek was the lingua franca at that time),[12] and his Roman citizenship from birth (Acts 22:28).[13] Alister McGrath notes that whereas Jesus spoke mainly to rural Palestinian people, Paul evangelizes in Greek-speaking cities of the Roman Empire, employing images that are intelligible to his urban audience. The Christian apologist "needs to know his or her audience, speak its language, and share its common flow of life."[14]

Roman citizenship is profoundly important, as citizens are part of the social elite. While such status was originally limited to freeborn natives of the city of Rome, citizenship expanded as the empire grew. It's not entirely clear who in Paul's lineage first gained citizenship, but it's possible one of his immediate ancestors acquired it in exchange for his services to Rome.[15] Cicero plainly expresses the benefits Roman citizens like Paul derived from their status: "To bind a Roman citizen is a crime, to flog him an abomination, and to slay him is almost an act of murder."[16] Indeed, Paul's citizenship facilitates his evangelistic work in hostile climates in the empire, as the authorities recoil in fear when Paul invokes it: "So those who were about to examine him withdrew from him immediately, and the tribune also was afraid, for he realized that Paul was a Roman citizen and that he had bound him" (Acts 22:29).

Providentially, Paul possesses the ideal attributes to become Christianity's greatest evangelist—personality traits that he exhibits, ironically, in his dark record of persecuting the Church. That God molds Paul into such a masterful messenger accentuates the gloriousness of the unmerited grace he is commissioned to preach. He is not only the Gospel's fiercest advocate, but his writings are the most thorough biblical formulations of Christian theology.[17]

PAUL'S ZEAL

As noted, Paul admits having been a zealous persecutor of the Church. But why? The answer can be found in his passion for his religion. He believes it's his duty to purge impurities, admitting that he even executes fellow Jews for violating God's special covenant with Israel (Acts 26:10). This new sect is especially dangerous because its adherents aren't just disobeying God but corrupting his religion at its core.

Theologian Lyman Abbott asks us to imagine what is going through Paul's mind as Christian churches spring up everywhere and many people, including those he had been close to, are betraying the cause he has always lived for, thereby dishonoring the living God of the universe.[18] This is an instructive exercise that illuminates why so many Jews at this time reject Jesus as the Messiah.

The Jewish people had suffered throughout history, having been ruled and enslaved by successive world powers, and they longed for their liberation and triumph. They were expecting their Messiah to be a political and military leader who would deliver Israel from Roman oppression and make Israel the dominant world power.

Paul's conversion was early—perhaps within five years of Christ's resurrection—so he probably learned about Jesus from eyewitnesses, possibly from Jesus' followers as well as his enemies. There were still no written Gospels or apostles' writings, so by word of mouth Paul likely learned a disturbing version of these events—one that would upset anyone with half his devotion to the God he served.

Consider the facts as they were likely presented to Paul. This imposter Messiah was born out of wedlock, attracted a motley group of misfit followers with no qualifying credentials, cavorted with overt sinners, and demeaned those learned in the true religion and the Law. Despite

His interloping corruption, Jesus reportedly healed people, performed other miracles, and adding insult to injury, violated the Sabbath and flouted other sacred laws. Defying the most respected members of the Sanhedrin—the Jewish high council—He challenged and ridiculed the revered Pharisees, and rather than deferring to their holiness, denounced them as whitewashed tombs with an outward appearance of righteousness but full of hypocrisy and lawlessness (Matt. 23:27). He presumed to discard God's sacrificial system and inserted Himself as the proper medium to forgive people's sins. Not only did He contradict the Jews' messianic expectations, He predicted that Jerusalem, instead of becoming the capital of a newly inaugurated messianic empire, would be annihilated and the Temple would be reduced to abject ruins. On top of all this, this faux liberator wholly failed to bring the Jews their long awaited victory and emancipation, instead ending His life in utter defeat, hanged on a "tree" and thus, according to Old Testament Law, accursed by God (Deut. 21:23).

All this might have been tolerable had this disgraceful fellow's blasphemies died along with Him, but His death and rumored resurrection resulted in an explosion of the cult. Once Jesus had been crucified and entombed the religious authorities surely assumed this would be the end of the movement, especially because its leader suffered such an ignominious defeat. After all, Jesus' followers cowered into the darkness when He was arrested, so the authorities reasonably assumed they would hear nothing further from them. But everything changed days later when Jesus rose from the dead and "presented himself alive to them after his suffering by many proofs, appearing to them during forty days and speaking about the kingdom of God" (Acts 1:3). Even Jesus' close family members who had been skeptics thereafter became ardent believers. The movement was expanding at an alarming pace and the authorities knew they had to quash it before it spun out of control.[19]

We must view Paul's persecution of the Church in the context of this mindset. Renegade heretics are trying to turn his entire world upside down—not just his world, but God's. He has to do everything in his power to nip this upstart movement in the bud. Even killing some of them won't be enough; they must be humiliated and all their dangerous ideas defeated. He admits in his letter to the Galatians, "For you have heard of my former life in Judaism, how I persecuted the church of God violently and tried to destroy it" (1:13).

But Paul grasps that the two systems—the rigorous, legalistic system of the religious authorities and the new Gospel of grace—are incompatible. With our New Testament hindsight today, we see how Christianity is a logical extension and fulfillment of the Jewish religion—but Paul, before his conversion, sees it differently. He views the new system as an affront to the laws God gave Moses and the customs based on them. The authorities acknowledge as much, and it is just as the martyr Stephen is beginning to deliver his fateful sermon that some "false witnesses" declare, "This man never ceases to speak words against this holy place and the law, for we have heard him say that this Jesus of Nazareth will destroy this place and will change the customs that Moses delivered to us" (Acts 6:13–14).

Even if Jesus' newly offered system were somehow acceptable to Paul, which is impossible barring some divine intervention, he could still never abide the preposterous notion that Jesus was the Messiah for the reasons we've already addressed. Consequently, he is on a mission to destroy the new Church. "Everything that was of value in Judaism [was] imperiled by the disciples' activity and teaching," F. F. Bruce notes. "Here was a malignant growth which called for drastic surgery."[20] Paul lives for his God as he understands Him, and he is determined to eradicate this tumor.

This is Paul's mindset as he sets out from Jerusalem to persecute Christians in Damascus, but he may be more deeply conflicted. No one honors God with more vigor, yet his obedience and holiness aren't calming his soul. He is extraordinarily restless for one so certain of the righteousness of his cause. Perhaps he is tormented by the difficulty of reconciling his commitment to his loving God with his mission to obliterate religious dissenters. As Abbott observes of Paul on his way to Damascus,

> He was left to himself, and he found himself a very uncomfortable companion. The kindliness in his heart was always great, and there marched in the way before him the shadowy forms of those whom he had put to death. He was always

courageous, and the boldness of the men who stood for their own convictions unto death stirred him with a new, strange pain. The problem of his own life came up again before him, and he remembered that though he had been blameless in the law, he had never had that peace which the Psalmist and the prophets promised to the man who has the blessing of the Almighty.[21]

A VISIT FROM GOD

The biblical account is unambiguous—the event leading to Paul's conversion is sudden, unexpected, and dramatic. Rev. D. J. Burrell describes it as "truly one of the most momentous of history."[22] A. C. Gaebelein writes that the "conversion of this great persecutor and his call by the risen and glorified Lord to be the Apostle to the Gentiles ... is the greatest event recorded in Acts next to the outpouring of the Holy Spirit on the day of Pentecost."[23] It isn't just life changing for Paul but for Christianity itself. Paul will be that important. "We believe it would be impossible to come up with another conversion," writes Rev. John G. Butler, "that has so affected in a positive way the growth, development, and history of the church."[24]

The Book of Acts records Paul's conversion three times. The first and main account is in verses 9:1–19, which is in the middle of a section that describes the expansion of the early Church beyond Judea and into Gentile lands. Some commentators believe Luke places the story here to highlight that Paul is Christ's chosen missionary to the Gentiles, just before Luke begins to describe this mission in chapter 13.[25] The other two accounts appear in Paul's speeches defending himself, first to a Jewish mob (22:3–16) and then to King Agrippa (26:4–18).

Paul's conversion has always had immense apologetic value because no one is a less likely candidate for such a radical transformation. George Lyttelton argues that "the conversion and apostleship of St. Paul alone, duly considered, was of itself a demonstration sufficient to prove Christianity to be a divine revelation."[26] Paul begins toward Damascus planning to capture dangerous Christian heretics and return them to

Jerusalem. He even volunteers for the privilege. In Burrell's words, "He went out a bitter antagonist of Christianity; he came back a Christian. A miracle had happened. Saul had seen the dead, risen, and now glorified Christit. . . . Such is the only explanation admissible, considering the quality of Saul's mind."[27]

Paul repeatedly testifies to the event. "Am I not free?" he asks in his first letter to the Corinthians. "Am I not an apostle? Have I not seen Jesus our Lord?" (9:1). He affirms his personal, physical encounter with Jesus later in the epistle: "Last of all, as to one untimely born, he appeared also to me" (15:8). Though Paul does not satisfy the apostolic credentials specified in Acts 1:21–22—as he was not with Jesus during his earthly ministry and did not witness His resurrection prior to His Ascension—Christ commissions him directly, and he becomes a vitally important witness to the risen Christ. Further, Luke refers to Paul as an apostle in Acts 14:14, and Luke's conversion accounts portray Paul's upcoming missionary work as being based on the work of the risen Christ (9:3–5; 22:6–8; 26:12–18).[28] Paul himself also frequently asserts that his apostleship is grounded in Christ calling Him (Rom. 1:1; 1 Cor. 1:1; Gal. 1:1; 15; 2 Cor. 1:1; Eph. 1:1; Col. 1:1; 1 Tim. 1:1; 2 Tim. 1:1; Titus 1:1).[29]

Finally, it's important to recognize that in his previous frenzy to persecute the burgeoning Church, Paul was not merely brutalizing human beings. He was also, and much more significantly, persecuting the Lord, as Christ elucidates in His exchange with Paul during the Damascus Road encounter. As Paul falls to the ground under blinding light, Jesus asks him, "Saul, Saul, why are you persecuting me?" Paul replies, "Who are you, Lord?" Christ says, "I am Jesus, whom you are persecuting" (Acts 9:4–5). Nothing more convicting can be imagined in this life.

Before Damascus Road, Paul was on a mission to imprison and punish heretics and destroy the Church. He was "breathing threats and murder against the disciples of the Lord" (Acts 9:1) and "was ravaging the church, and entering house after house, he dragged off men and women and committed them to prison" (Acts 8:3). Paul later admits, "I persecuted this Way to the death, binding and delivering to prison both men and women, as the high priest and the whole council of elders can bear me witness. From them I received letters to the brothers, and I journeyed toward Damascus to take those also who were there and bring them in bonds to Jerusalem to be punished" (Acts 22:4–5). Notably, when the Lord tells Ananias to look for Saul in Damascus following his conversion, Ananias protests, "Lord, I have heard from many about this man, how much evil he has done to your saints at Jerusalem" (Acts 9:13).

In a marvelous outworking of His sovereign will, however, God produces a wondrous silver lining from Paul's persecutions. To escape this unspeakable abuse, believers—except for the apostles—fled from Jerusalem "throughout the regions of Judea and Samaria" (Acts 8:1). In an ironic twist, this fanning out of believers resulted in the preaching of the Gospel in areas outside Jerusalem, causing the Gospel to spread like wildfire.[30] Even before his conversion Paul was an unconscious instrument of God, unwittingly laying the foundation for obeying Christ's command to the Apostles, "You will be my witnesses in Jerusalem and in all Judea and Samaria, and to the end of the earth" (Acts 1:8). How exquisitely God works His sovereign will, using Paul's unique passion and intensity to spread the Good News, both in Paul's persecution phase and in his signature work as history's foremost Christian missionary!

FINDING STRENGTH IN WEAKNESS

Paul's background is instrumental in informing his epistles. Who else would have proclaimed, "For I am not ashamed of the gospel" (Romans 1:16)? But it makes perfect sense since he dedicated years to attacking the Gospel. Who else would have declared, "For Jews demand signs and Greeks seek wisdom, but we preach Christ crucified, a stumbling block to Jews and folly to Gentiles, but to those who are called, both Jews and Greeks, Christ the power of God and the wisdom of God. For the foolishness of God is wiser than men, and the weakness of God is stronger than men" (1 Cor. 1:22–25)? Clearly, Paul witnessed firsthand the counterintuitive nature of the Gospel. God showed His strength through Christ's "weakness" on the cross; He proved His wisdom by orchestrating a salvation scheme that seemed completely foolish to men.

Paul comes to see Christ's voluntary submission to the evil authorities not as weakness and defeat but as strength and victory. He then appropriates Christ's example of "weakness" in his own relationship with God and commends it to all believers. Pride, he knows, is faith's worst enemy and the devil's best friend. It keeps us from God. In his second letter to the Corinthians, Paul writes, "But he said to me, 'My grace is sufficient for you, for my power is made perfect in weakness.' Therefore, I will boast all the more gladly of my weaknesses, so that the power of Christ may rest upon me. . . . For he was crucified in weakness, but lives by the power of God. For we also are weak in him, but in dealing with you we will live with him by the power of God" (2 Cor. 12:9, 13:4). How far Paul has come from railing against Christ's weakness to adopting it as fundamental to Christian living! He intimately understands that God's salvation plan for mankind can be achieved only through Christ's sacrificial death, which represents strength and victory, not weakness and defeat, because it completed God's triumph over Satan, sin, and death. And while Christ hadn't yet restored King David's throne, He would do so in His second coming. God reveals Himself to Paul, transforming him into a confirmed believer who uniquely embraces this theological paradox of weakness as strength. Thereafter Paul redirects his zeal to the cause of Christ, enduring sacrificial suffering on His behalf and on behalf of those to whom he presents the Gospel.

THE BOOK OF ACTS: A BRIDGE BETWEEN THE GOSPELS AND THE EPISTLES

The Book of Acts is a history of the early Church beginning with Christ's resurrection. It is not a comprehensive history of this period but, like other historical sections of the Bible, is part of God's salvation history that includes only those events pertinent to God's redemptive plan for mankind.

Acts ends with Paul in his home in Rome under guard, welcoming and preaching the Kingdom of God to all who visit him, without describing what subsequently happened to the great evangelist. Pastor Ray Stedman notes that the book is deliberately unfinished because it is really a story about the unfinished work of Jesus Christ. "The book of Acts continues to be written today in the lives of men and women in the living body of Christ, the church," writes Stedman. "Even though Jesus has been taken up in the clouds, His body life goes on! It goes on in your life. It goes on in my life. . . . You and I are still writing the book of Acts today because it is an account of what the Holy Spirit continues to do through us today, all around the world."[31]

Acts is a bridge between the Gospels and the epistles. It shows the apostles continuing Christ's work, provides the historical backdrop for the epistles, and offers insight into the churches to which Paul directs his epistles. The book is summarized neatly in one of its beginning verses, which records the risen Christ's charge to His apostles: "But you will receive power when the Holy Spirit has come upon you, and you will be my witnesses in Jerusalem and in all Judea and Samaria, and to the end of the earth" (Acts 1:8).

Acts is crucially important, for if the book were not part of the biblical canon, meaning Paul's epistles would immediately follow the Gospels, we would have no idea why this new apostle appeared and would have far less historical context for his many epistles.[32] J. Vernon McGee, in his famous series *Thru the Bible*, remarks that it contains much information found nowhere else in the Bible—unlike the Gospels and epistles, which include much overlapping information. Illustrating the continuity between the Gospels and Acts, the last recorded events in each of the Gospels are also recorded in Acts (Matthew [and the other Gospels]: the Resurrection; Mark: the Ascension;[33] Luke: the promise of the Holy Spirit; and John: the second coming of Christ.) "It is as if the four Gospels had been poured into a funnel," writes McGee, "and they all come down into this jug of the first chapter of the Book of Acts." In short, Acts confirms Christ's Great Commission to the apostles to spread the Gospel to the ends of the earth.[34]

Commentators debate whose acts are referenced in the book's title, depending on whom they believe is the book's lead character. Most say the title refers to the activities of the apostles, who take the Gospel message to the world. Many say the book describes the work of the Holy Spirit, Who empowered the apostles for their work. "It is impossible to read the Acts," says nineteenth and early twentieth century minister Joseph Exell, "without seeing that the Holy Spirit was the acting Guide of all the sayings and actions of the first teachers of Christianity."[35]

Theologian R. C. Sproul favors the title, "The History of the Acts of the Holy Spirit" because the Holy Spirit inspired the book, which is a record of the Spirit's outpouring on the apostolic Church and its ministry.[36] Admittedly, references to the Holy Spirit in Acts are, says Ben Witherington, too numerous to list.[37] Still others argue that the main actor is "the risen and glorified Christ through the apostles."[38]

This strikes me as a false choice. All three are correct. We must recognize the apostles' obedience in carrying out their mission, honor the Holy Spirit for His indwelling power that enables their work, and glorify Jesus Christ, Who sacrificed His life for us, fulfilled His promise to send the Holy Spirit following His death and resurrection, and continues His work through the apostles, empowered by the Spirit. Theologian John Stott notes that Luke "implies that the acts and words he reports are those of the ascended Christ working through the Holy Spirit who, as Luke knows, is, 'the Spirit of Jesus' (Acts 16:7)."[39] Stott therefore suggests the title, "The Continuing Words and Deeds of Jesus by his Spirit through his Apostles."[40]

Indeed, while all three are vital—Christ, the Holy Spirit, and the apostles—Christ is the central figure of all salvation history. "It is not enough to say that while the Gospels contain the history of the Master's ministry, the Acts record that of the apostles," writes Exell. "Both alike narrate the work of the Lord: the Gospels what He did in Person, the Acts what He did by His chosen witnesses. . . . His incarnation [and] death ... were only the foundation. In the Acts He rears a lofty temple on that foundation."[41]

There is sovereign continuity in all of God's salvation history throughout which Christ is the Prime Mover. Before Christ's birth, God prepared the way for Christ. The Gospels record Christ's acts and teachings. The Book of Acts records His further actions and teachings through the apostles empowered by the Holy Spirit. But His saving activities didn't end with the death of the apostles. He has been acting and teaching ever since, through the Holy Spirit and His Word. Exell observes that Luke, in his two-part story, describes Christ's model of doing and teaching. Exell nicely summarizes the balance that we must bring to our evangelism and exhorts us to incorporate both elements in our Christian living. "If we do, but fail to teach, we shall be but barren puzzles," he observes. "If we teach, but fail to do, we may incur the just imputation of being theorists and fanatics, or devotional sentimentalists."[42] As Charles Foster Kent comments, "While the book of Acts is excellent history, it is more than history, it is the epic of conquering Christianity; it is the pragmatic proof of the invincible power of the spirit and teachings of Jesus."[43]

FACTS YOU CAN COUNT ON

Though the text does not identify the author by name, Church tradition and most scholars hold that Luke, the author of the third Gospel, wrote Acts as the second part of his two-part record.[44] It's possible that the two books became separated because of an early Church practice of setting apart the four Gospels for studying and praying.[45] Luke addresses his Gospel to his friend Theophilus, and Luke acknowledges him again in the first verse of Acts, in which he refers to "the first book." Acts, then, continues where the Gospel of Luke ends and details how the apostles obey the risen Christ's command to preach the Gospel throughout the world (Acts 1:8). Specifically, Luke begins by affirming Christ's sacrificial death, His numerous resurrection appearances over forty days, His promise that He would soon send the Holy Spirit to His apostles, and His ascension, which had to precede the coming of the Spirit.

Scholars differ widely on when Acts was written, but many believe it significant that it ends abruptly with two of early Christianity's key leaders, Paul and James, the brother of Jesus, still living. Clement of Rome and other early Church fathers report that Paul was executed during Nero's reign, which ended in 68 AD, and Jewish historian Josephus writes that James was killed in 62 AD, so it is reasonable to assume the book was written in or before 62.[46]

In the opening verses of his Gospel, Luke expresses his driving passion for presenting an accurate account of the Gospel and the history of the early Church. These are among my favorite Bible verses because each time I read them, I am moved by Luke's heartfelt commitment to presenting a meticulously researched and authentic historical account to assure his readers that these momentous events actually occurred. This flies in the face of cynics who dismiss the Gospels as sloppy compilations of orally passed-down stories. Luke writes, "Inasmuch as many have undertaken to compile a narrative of the things that have been accomplished among us, just as those who from the beginning were eyewitnesses and ministers of the word have delivered them to us, it seemed good to me also, having followed all things closely for some time past, to write an orderly account for you, most excellent Theophilus, that you may have certainty concerning the things you have been taught."

Though nineteenth-century liberal scholars panned the book as historically unreliable, many archaeologists and scholars persuasively defended the factual accuracy of Luke's record. Scottish archaeologist Sir William Ramsay began as a skeptic, accepting the liberal Tubingen school theory that Luke's writings should be dated in the second century. But after his extensive studies in Asia Minor, he became an ardent believer in the accuracy of Luke's historical account.[47] "Luke's history is unsurpassed in respect of its trustworthiness," writes Ramsay.[48] "Luke is a historian of the first rank; not merely are his statements of fact trustworthy; he is possessed of the true historical sense; he fixes his mind on the idea and plan that rules in the evolution of history, and proportions the scale of his treatment of the importance of each incident. He seizes the important and critical events and shows their true nature at greater length, while he touches lightly or omits entirely much that was valueless for his purpose. In short, this author should be placed along with the very greatest of historians."[49]

Similarly, classical Roman historian A. N. Sherwin-White declares, "For the New Testament book of Acts, the confirmation of historicity is overwhelming. . . . Any attempt to reject its basic historicity, even in matters of detail must now appear absurd. Roman historians have long taken it for granted."[50]

Luke demonstrates his intricate familiarity with the geography and titles of the time, such as precisely identifying the various Roman provinces and the particular titles of government officials. His references to persons and events from other sources are easily corroborated. He proves his detailed knowledge of the Roman judicial system in his recounting of Paul's trials, such as in Acts 22–26.[51] J. B. Lightfoot shows that Acts is unique among New Testament books in its quantity of historically verifiable events. He concludes, "No ancient work affords so many tests of veracity; for no other has such numerous points of contact in all directions with contemporary history, politics, and topography, whether Jewish, Greek or Roman."[52]

Norman Geisler and Frank Turek note that Luke cites eighty-four details from Acts 13–28 that could have only been derived from an eyewitness.[53] Admittedly, some conservative scholars acknowledge certain questionable passages in the historical record put forward by Luke, but they have plausible explanations. In 1999, Brian Janeway examined and compared the critical scholarship and concluded, "The Book of Acts is not without difficult passages, yet when compared to Josephus' well-documented biases and tendencies to exaggerate, Luke's careful accounting of events, people and their speeches is even more apparent. . . . In the final analysis, we must conclude that the Book of Acts is historically reliable."[54]

"ALL THE RESIDENTS OF ASIA HEARD OF THE WORD OF THE LORD"

In his narrative, as noted, Luke often provides summaries of the condition of the early Church at different times.[55] He reports that following Pentecost, the believers are devoted to teaching, fellowship, breaking bread, and prayers. They are awestruck by the apostles' many signs and wonders, and they act as a tight-knit community, selling their possessions and distributing the proceeds to the needy. Each day they attend the Temple together, socialize in their homes, display happy and generous hearts, and praise God. More people become believers every day (2:42–47). Again in verses 4:32–35, Luke describes the extraordinary communion and generosity among believers and the ongoing power of the apostles' testimony to Christ's resurrection. In verses 5:12–16, he recapitulates how believers hold the apostles in high esteem as they perform many signs and wonders in Jerusalem, including healings, which draw many afflicted people from surrounding towns. And in verse 19:10, we find a brief description of Paul's extended ministry in Ephesus: "This continued for two years, so that all the residents of Asia heard of the word of the Lord, both Jews and Greeks."[56]

Acts prominently features numerous important speeches, including three from Peter (to Jews in Jerusalem [2:14–36 and 3:11–26] and in Cornelius's household [10:34–43]); one from Stephen (to Jews in Jerusalem, leading to his execution [7:1–53]); and six from Paul (to Jews in Pisidian Antioch [13:16–47]; to Greeks in Athens [17:22–31]; to Church elders in Ephesus [20:18–35]; to Jews in Jerusalem [22:1–21]; to Felix and his court [24:10–21]; and to Agrippa and his court [26:1–29]).[57] There are also shorter speeches throughout Acts. Constituting some thirty percent of the book,[58] these addresses center on the proclamation of the Gospel, emphasizing Christ's fulfillment of God's Old Testament promises, His messiahship, His works (the crucifixion, resurrection, and His promised return and judgment), and the call to repent and be baptized.[59]

The powerful speeches demonstrate the unity of scripture and how Christ fulfills the Old Testament prophecies and consummates God's salvation plan. Ralph Martin aptly observes that these sermons splice together "in one narrative thread the past, present, and future of God's salvific activity."[60] They show that Christianity neither distorts nor departs from Judaism but is its legitimate fulfillment. The Church is shown as including both Jews and Gentiles, which further demonstrates Christianity's continuity with the Old Testament.[61] In that sense, the book presupposes a unified picture of salvation divided into three major sequential and interconnected epochs: the history of Israel during Old Testament times (the time of the Law and prophecy); the earthly ministry of Jesus; and the Church era, in which the Church, empowered by Holy Spirit, spreads the Gospel throughout the world.[62]

The sheer volume of recorded speeches in the book might suggest Luke is fascinated with the power of words, but the speeches convey voluminous information showing "All that God had done with them" (14:27). The speeches report actions and are also an important part of the action—the spreading of God's Word.[63]

Another dominant theme is the indispensability of the Christian witness to Jesus.[64] Considering Christ's charge to the apostles to be His witnesses in Jerusalem and throughout the world, it is significant that these speeches are made by witnesses and that in recording them, Luke is giving further witness in a more permanent form. The witnessing is worldwide and to all groups—Jews, Gentiles, Samaritans, the infirm, the pagans, jailers, philosophers, governors, and kings. The witnesses boldly testify to their faith in Christ in obedience to the Great Commission, persevering despite fierce opposition, threats, and other challenges.[65]

Luke shows that the Gospel is intended for the Gentiles as well as the Jews, pointing to Old Testament passages foretelling this development (Luke 24:27; Acts 13:47; 15:15–18; 28:25–28).[66] A salient confirmation of the universality of the Gospel occurs in Acts 2, when at Pentecost the Holy Spirit is poured out on Jews from all over the empire, who begin to speak in other tongues (Acts 2:4). We tend to focus on the supernatural aspects of this event, as each person speaks a language unknown to him, yet others present hear and understand the people in their own language. Some are so astonished they accuse the speakers of being drunk on wine. But we must recognize the symbolic import of this miraculous enabling of Jews from many nations to hear the Gospel in their native languages, illustrating that the Gospel is for people of all tongues and nations, but for the Jews first.[67]

OUTLINES

Scholars outline the book in various ways, including the biographical outline, which divides the book into the works of Peter (Chapters 1–12) and Paul (Chapters 13–28), respectively.[68] "It is one of the most striking features about Acts that it says so little about the other apostles and so much about Peter and Paul," writes Donald Guthrie.[69] He suggests this might be because Peter is chief apostle to the Jews and Paul chief apostle to the Gentiles, and because there are certain notable parallels between their works.[70] The *New Testament in Antiquity* highlights some of these parallels in a comparative chart:

- Peter delivers a sermon in Jerusalem (2:22–36) and Paul delivers one in Pisidian Antioch (13:26–41);
- Peter and Paul both heal a lame man (3:1–10, 14:8–11);
- They are both filled with the Spirit (4:8, 13:9);

- They both perform extraordinary healings (5:15, 19:12);
- They both lay their hands on people to enable them to receive the Spirit (8:17, 19:6);
- They both have a conflict with a magician (8:18–24, 13:6–11);
- Empowered by the Spirit, both raise people from the dead (Peter with Tabitha [9:36–41] and Paul with Eutychus [20:9–12]);
- Both are miraculously released from jail (12:6–11, 16:25–40).[71]

Another approach is the summary statements outline, which divides the book into six sections based on thematic statements Luke makes at the end of each section summarizing what he has just described.[72] The six sections and their accompanying summaries are as follows:

1. The beginning Church in Jerusalem (1:1–6:7): "And the word of God continued to increase, and the number of the disciples multiplied greatly in Jerusalem, and a great many of the priests became obedient to the faith."[73]
2. The Church expands into Judea and Samaria (6:8–9:31): "So the church throughout all Judea and Galilee and Samaria had peace and was being built up. And walking in the fear of the Lord and in the comfort of the Holy Spirit, it multiplied."
3. Spreading of the Gospel to the Gentiles (9:32–12:24): "But the word of God increased and multiplied."
4. The Gospel spreads into Asia on Gentile missions (12:25–16:5): "So the churches were strengthened in the faith, and they increased in numbers daily."
5. Further expansion of the Gospel into the Gentile world (16:6–19:20): "So the word of the Lord continued to increase and prevail mightily."
6. The Gospel moves into Rome (19:21–28:31): Paul for two years is "proclaiming the kingdom of God and teaching

about the Lord Jesus Christ with all boldness and without
hindrance."[74]

I believe the most useful way to organize the book, however, is the
geographical outline, which is framed around Luke's thematic summary
of the book in verse 1:8, in which Jesus tells His disciples they will receive
power from the Holy Spirit and then commands them to be His witnesses
in Jerusalem, in all Judea and Samaria, and to the end of the earth. The
disciples dutifully obey, and the book follows a natural structure corresponding to the missions.[75] Following the prologue (1:1–8), Acts is
outlined according to the locations of the missions:

1. The witness to Jerusalem (1:9–8:3);
2. The witness to Judea and Samaria (8:4–12:25);
3. The witness to the ends of the earth (13:1–28:31).[76]

This geographical outline reflects the sequence in which the Gospel
is preached: first to the Jews and then to the Gentiles, as Paul explains
(Romans 1:16). As noted, Peter is considered the main evangelist to the
Jews, and Paul the head of the Gentile mission.[77]

In the next chapter, we'll be looking over the shoulders of the apostles as they lead the explosive growth of the Church through persecution
and hardship. The inspiring history of the early Church is recorded with
meticulous detail by Luke, a medical doctor, who actually joins Paul on
missionary journeys all over the ancient world. But Luke will start us in
Jerusalem with Jesus.

CHAPTER TWO

ACTS 1–7
A CHURCH IS BORN

*TWENTY-EIGHT thrilling chapters lie before us! Any
one of them we can read a dozen times, only to find
its fascination growing with each reading. . . . [The
Acts of the Apostles] is the sequel to the mighty events
of the Gospels, and the gateway to the glorious doc-
trines of the Epistles. It marks, in fact, one of the greatest turning-points in history, as we shall soon see.*

—J. SIDLOW BAXTER[1]

CHAPTER 1

L uke begins Acts with a brief prologue addressing the book to
Theophilus,[2] noting that in his Gospel he chronicled Jesus' acts
and teachings until His ascension. Jesus made numerous appearances to His apostles over forty days, preaching the kingdom of God
and giving instructions from the Holy Spirit. Jesus' selection of His
apostles authorized them to "preach, teach, direct the Church, and preserve the record of His life and teaching."[3] His instructions represented
a transition from His earthly ministry to His ministry through them.[4]
Luke mentions that Christ's instructions were through the Holy Spirit
to introduce the Holy Spirit's central role in forming and growing the
Church and in the lives of all believers.

Luke demonstrates the continuity between the ministries of Jesus
and the apostles, as the Spirit who rested upon and empowered Jesus in

His earthly ministry now empowers the apostles for their witness. During Jesus' earthly ministry, the apostles experienced the Spirit through Jesus' presence; but after Pentecost, they experience Christ through the Spirit's presence.[5] Had Jesus stayed on earth, His physical presence would have inhibited the rapid spread of the Gospel because, in His human form, He could be in only one place at a time. After His ascension, however, He would be with them everywhere, through the Spirit.[6] "He who was born into our humanity, lived our life, died for our sins, rose from the dead and ascended into heaven," writes John Stott, "now sent his Spirit to his people to constitute them his body and to work out in them what he had won for them."[7]

Jesus commanded the apostles to wait in Jerusalem for the Holy Spirit (cf. Luke 24:49), reaffirming His promise at the Last Supper: "And I will ask the Father, and he will give you another Helper, to be with you forever, even the Spirit of truth, whom the world cannot receive, because it neither sees him nor knows him. You know him, for he dwells with you and will be in you" (John 14:16–17). Jesus assured them about the Holy Spirit's role: "But the Helper, the Holy Spirit, whom the Father will send in my name, he will teach you all things and bring to your remembrance all that I have said to you" (John 14:26).

Jesus told the apostles that "not many days from now," they would be baptized with the Holy Spirit—as distinguished from the water baptism that John the Baptist had administered. John had humbly admitted that his baptism was only with water and was a baptism of repentance, merely preparatory for their later baptism with the Holy Spirit and with fire (Matt. 3:11: Luke 3:16). Paul describes baptism of the Holy Spirit as the process whereby the Spirit unites believers with Jesus upon their conversion, and they become part of the body of Christ (His Church) (1 Cor. 12:13; cf. Romans 8:9). At the moment of conversion, believers are indwelt by the Spirit—"your body is a temple of the Holy Spirit within you" (1 Cor. 6:19)—and thereafter empowered by Him for service to Christ, to resist sin, and to become more Christ-like. Jesus had said earlier that believers would not receive the Spirit until He had ascended (John 7:38–39).

The Holy Spirit in the believer is what distinguishes him from the nonbeliever (1 Cor. 2:10–14) and makes him a child of God (Romans

8:14–17). Receiving the Spirit begins one's Christian life (Gal. 3:2–3)[8] and empowers him for discipleship, witnessing, understanding the things freely given him by God (salvation in Jesus Christ)[9] (1 Cor. 2: 12), understanding God's Word and His will (1 Cor. 2:14, 15; 1 John 2:27), praying when we don't know what we ought to pray for (Romans 8:26), and overcoming sin on a daily basis (Romans 5:5; 6:1–14, 8:13; 1 Cor. 6:11; 2 Cor. 3:18; Gal. 5:22–23; 2 Thess. 2:13; 1 Peter 1:2). The Spirit glorifies Christ (John 16:14) and convicts the world concerning sin, righteousness, and judgment (John 16:8).

The Spirit, as one of the three persons of the Triune Godhead, has existed forever. He was at work in Old Testament times, as the Old Testament records and the New Testament confirms (Acts 7:51; 2 Peter. 1:21). He was involved in the planning (Isaiah 40:12–14) and creation of the universe (Gen. 1:2; Job 26:13; 27:3; 33:4; Psalms 33:6; 104:30; Isaiah 40:12–14), and the earth (Gen. 1:2). He revealed God's messages to man just as He would in New Testament times.[10] But in Old Testament times, the Spirit only directly interacted with specific individuals—and only temporarily—to serve God's purposes (Exodus 31:3; Judges 14:6; 1 Samuel 16:13),[11] as opposed to His permanent indwelling of New Testament believers (John 14:16). "The Old Testament witness to the Spirit anticipates a coming time when the ministry of the Spirit is to be more complete," writes Millard Erickson.[12]

Before Jesus ascended, the apostles asked Him if He was about to restore the kingdom to Israel, and He said it wasn't for them to know when this would occur. They should focus instead on the power they were about to receive from the Holy Spirit and their charge, thereupon, to be His witnesses "in Jerusalem and in all Judea and Samaria, and to the end of the earth" (Acts 1:8). Jesus then ascended and as the apostles watched, two angels in white robes appeared and told them Jesus would return to earth (at His second coming) in the same way He left, namely, He would come with power and great glory (Luke 21:27; Matt. 24:30; Mark 13:26), defeating Satan and evil to establish His eternal reign. At that time, there would be no doubt as to His identity.[13]

Returning to Jerusalem, the apostles go to the upper room where they are staying. Along with others (120 people altogether), they join in prayer and cast lots to determine God's will on whether Barsabbas or

Matthias should replace Judas Iscariot as an apostle. The lot falls on Matthias (cf. Prov. 16:33).

Notice two things about this event. First, Peter invokes Old Testament Scripture in which the Holy Spirit, speaking through David (Psalm 109:8), prophesied that the apostles would replace Judas (though the Scripture did not name him). Second, Peter stresses that Judas' replacement must be one who's been with the apostles, witnessed Jesus' earthly ministry, and most important, witnessed His resurrection (Acts 1:22).[14] This shows they understand the pivotal importance of the resurrection to their witness. It's not a matter of apostolic succession, as if it were some generic office to be occupied by others in the future. There could be no succession, as such.[15] The replacement must have been with them all along as a firsthand witness.

While Paul fails to meet all these criteria (he did later see the resurrected Christ), who can dispute that his direct commission from Christ supersedes these rules? That's probably one reason Luke mentions Paul's call three times in Acts, as when he relates that Christ told Ananias, "For he is a chosen instrument of mine to carry my name before the Gentiles and kings and the children of Israel" (9:15; see also 22:6–16; 26:12–18). Paul elsewhere refers to himself as an exceptionally called apostle, saying Christ appeared to him "as to one untimely born" (1 Cor. 15:8); and, as described earlier, he identifies himself as an apostle at the beginning of most of his epistles. Paul also relates that the other apostles accepted him as a fellow apostle (Gal. 2:1–2, 7–10). Adding further weight to Paul's apostolic authority is Peter's reference to his writings as wisdom God had given him (2 Peter 3:15) and as Scripture (2 Peter 3:16). They are inspired works.[16] Paul also affirms his writings as divine revelations (1 Cor. 2:6–16).

After the appointment of Judas' replacement, the apostles obediently await their empowerment by the Holy Spirit so they may begin to discharge Christ's command to spread the Gospel.

CHAPTER 2

The apostles and other believers gather together in Jerusalem on the day of Pentecost, anticipating God's promised Spirit. Pentecost, known as the Feast of Weeks (Lev. 23:15; Deut. 16:9), is one of the major annual Jewish feasts. Celebrating the end of the grain harvest, it usually lasts the entire fifty days—"pentecost" being the Greek word for "fifty"— between Passover and the Feast of Weeks.[17] During the intertestamental period, shortly before the New Testament period, the Jews also began to recognize Pentecost as the time when God gave them the Law at Mount Sinai, which occurred fifty days after the Exodus and was immediately preceded by the first Passover observance (Exodus 12:6–13).

Jesus was crucified and resurrected at the time of Passover, and He ascended forty days later. Now, just ten days later, on Pentecost, the Holy Spirit descends on the apostles from heaven "with a sound like a mighty rushing wind, it fills the entire house where they were sitting" (Acts 2:2), and what appear to be tongues of fire rest on each of them. Instantly filled with the Holy Spirit, they miraculously begin to speak in foreign languages they don't know. Many are amazed but confused. Others mock the speakers, accusing them of being drunk on wine. The arrival of the Holy Spirit at Pentecost is considered the birth of the Christian Church.[18] As such, it's interesting that Jesus was also conceived by the Holy Spirit (Luke 1:35).

Luke analogizes the Holy Spirit to the wind, which share a linguistic connection and a similarity of characteristics. The Hebrew term "ruah" in the Old Testament refers to "wind," "breath" or "spirit," including the Spirit of God.[19] While the Greek word for spirit—*pneuma*—generally does not refer to wind, the verbal form of the word *pneo* means "to blow," so there is still a strong linguistic association.[20] The wind and the Spirit share the attributes of invisibility, formidable force, mysteriousness, inscrutability, and uncontrollability. The effects of each can be found everywhere. Jesus compared the wind and the Spirit in His exchange with Nicodemus about His regeneration: "The wind blows where it wishes, and you hear its sound, but you do not know where it comes from or where it goes. So it is with everyone who is born of the Spirit" (John 3:8).

Peter, standing alongside the other eleven apostles, responds forcefully to the mockers who diminish the event's sacredness, telling them the speakers are not drunk, as it's only 9:00 a.m. Rather, they are experiencing what the Old Testament prophet Joel had described—the

pouring out of the Spirit on all flesh (Joel 2:28–32). Most scholars conclude that only part of Joel's prophesy was fulfilled at Pentecost and that
the remainder of it—the sun turning to darkness, the moon to blood,
and the coming of the great day of the Lord—will happen at the time of
Christ's second coming.[21]

After rebuking the mockers, Peter turns to the subject of Jesus Christ
and begins the first Christian sermon.[22] He talks of the mighty works
and miracles Christ has done in their presence, His crucifixion by lawless
men according to God's plan, and His resurrection and victory over
death. Jesus' executioners thought they were in charge of Jesus' fate;
Peter sets the record straight, affirming God's sovereignty in carrying
out this essential step of incomprehensible grace in His salvation plan.
Peter quotes Psalm 16, in which David rejoiced in the Lord for his secure
knowledge that God would not abandon his soul, just as He would not
allow His "holy one [to] see corruption" (Psalm 16:8–11). Though modern scholars disagree about whether this is a messianic prophecy,[23] Peter
clearly interprets it as such, as he cites David's statement that the Holy
One will not see corruption. (Christ's body did not decay, but David's
did.) Further, Peter cites the psalm in the context of his sermon about
the resurrected Christ.[24] Notably, Paul also regards this as a messianic
prophecy (Acts 13:35).[25]

Before the prophet David died and was buried, Peter observes, God
had assured David that He would place one of David's descendants on
his throne. And David "foresaw and spoke about the resurrection of the
Christ, that he was not abandoned to Hades, nor did his flesh see corruption. This Jesus God raised up, and of that we are all witnesses."
(Acts 2:31–32) Christ now occupies the highest position of authority,
having been exalted at God's right hand. He received from the Father
the promise of the Holy Spirit, which He has now given to them pursuant to that authority, as they are witnessing.

Peter proclaims that it was not David but his descendant—Jesus
Christ—who ascended into the heavens to share God's throne, as David
himself testified (Psalm 110:1): "The Lord says to my Lord, Sit at my
right hand, until I make your enemies your footstool." F. F. Bruce
observes, "This exaltation of Jesus in accordance with Psalm 110:1 is an
integral part of the primitive apostolic message, as it remains an integral

part of the historic Christian creeds."[26] Christ has ultimate authority over God's creation and will use it to conquer His enemies, which He has already begun to do with His triumph over death, and which He will complete in the future. To be sure, Christ, the Second Person of the Triune Godhead, is entirely capable of subduing His own enemies, but He is acting at the Father's direction; they are in complete harmony.[27]

Peter declares that all of Israel must "know for certain that God has made [Jesus] both Lord and Christ, this Jesus whom you crucified." This is a stark, convicting assertion. Not only was their craven act of crucifying the innocent and holy Jesus utterly futile, but they are also now wholly subject to His authority. When the audience hears these biting words, "they [are] cut to the heart" and ask Peter and the other apostles, "What shall we do?" Peter tells them to repent and be baptized in the name of Jesus Christ for the forgiveness of their sins, and they will receive the gift of the Holy Spirit. This promise is for them and their children, and for everyone whom the Lord calls. In response, some three thousand people are saved and baptized.

To repent means to change one's mind and heart, to change direction—to quit running away from God, to turn away from sin and self-centeredness, and turn toward Christ in obedience.[28] Baptism is a sign of obedience and appreciation for what Jesus has done for us. Those who practice infant baptism believe it may quicken the Spirit to accelerate one's faith walk, but most evangelical Christians do not believe it's necessary for salvation. There are numerous biblical passages affirming salvation by faith in Christ alone (John 3:16, 36; Romans 4:1–17; 11:6; Gal 3:8–9; Eph. 2:8–9; and others), including other passages in Acts in which Peter affirms the principle (5:31; 10:43; 13:38; 26:18). In this sermon, Peter is likely urging their baptism parenthetically, not as a condition to salvation.[29]

Theologian Wayne Grudem explains that if baptism is necessary for salvation, then we are not saved by faith alone. Recall that Jesus told the dying thief beside him on the cross, "Today you will be with me in paradise" (Luke 23:43). The thief couldn't have been baptized before dying, yet Jesus' promise is unambiguous. Additionally, our justification from sin (and salvation) occurs at the precise moment we have faith. Subsequent baptism cannot confer salvation that has already been given.

However, while it is not needed for salvation, baptism is still an important act of obedience to Christ.[30]

What follows the conversion of three thousand people is a remarkable display of Christian fellowship, love, sharing, learning, and worship
among the new believers. Hungry to learn about Christ and grow in the
faith, they steep themselves in the apostles' teaching. Filled with awe,
they witness many miracles performed by the apostles, further authen-
ticating the apostles' authority. They become an intimately close-knit
community of believers who freely share their personal assets with those
among them in need. They dine, worship, and pray together in the
Temple. As they eat together in their homes with joyous and grateful
spirits, they praise God. Consequently, God increases their numbers each
day through the salvation of new believers.

CHAPTER 3

After reporting that the apostles perform many signs, Luke describes
how outside the Temple Peter and John heal a man who has been lame
from birth. When the man asks them for money, the apostles direct him
to look at them, which he does, expecting to receive money. Instead,
Peter says, "In the name of Jesus Christ of Nazareth, rise up and walk!"
Peter takes his hand and raises him up, and his feet and ankles are immediately strengthened—the immediacy signifying a miracle. He leaps up,
begins to walk, and enters the Temple with them. The amazed people
recognize him as the lame man always begging at the Temple's Beautiful
Gate. Aware that he has been lame for forty years, they know this isn't
a staged event—the man is vigorously jumping around and praising God
ecstatically. While the man clings to Peter and John, the people, still in
awe, gather around them in Solomon's Colonnade.

Peter uses this healing and the gathered witnesses as an opportunity
to preach the Gospel. Some commentators suggest that the Jews present
would have taken special notice of this healing in light of the prophet
Isaiah's prediction that such things would occur: "Then shall the lame
leap like a deer, and the tongue of the mute sing for joy" (Isaiah 35:6).[31]
Peter asks them why they are staring at him and John as if they

performed this miracle on their own power. Then he draws them in, attributing the miracle to the very God they have always worshipped— "The God of Abraham, the God of Isaac, and the God of Jacob, the God of our fathers" (Acts 3:13). This same God—their God—also glorified Jesus Christ, whom they denied and gave over to Pilate to be crucified.

Then Peter openly calls Jesus "the Holy and Righteous One" and the "Author of Life"—unmistakable declarations of His deity and His activity in the creation. Notice the stark contrast: they "killed" the One who is the very Giver of life. Peter again declares they are all witnesses to Christ's resurrection, the lynchpin of the faith. For as Paul concedes, "If Christ has not been raised, your faith is futile and you are still in your sins. Then all those also who have fallen asleep in Christ have perished. If in Christ we have hope in this life only, we are of all people most to be pitied" (1 Cor. 15:17–19). This puts the lie to the lazy claim that Jesus was merely a great prophet but not the Son of God—an idea that is fundamentally irreconcilable with biblical Christianity. While Christianity would be pure myth without the resurrection, it is irresistible truth because of it. This is why Peter, Paul, and the other apostles forever highlight the resurrection.

Peter is careful to disclaim any credit for this healing. It was Jesus— and faith in His name—that restored the man's strength and health in their presence. Peter uses the power of the Holy Spirit to heal pursuant to the authority of Jesus Christ. Peter's derivative power is only possible because of His faith in Christ and His sacrificial work.[32]

Peter is determined that they understand that the man they crucified is the One the prophets pre-announced, whose suffering they foretold. Though shaming them for their actions, he acknowledges they and their rulers were acting in ignorance. Here Peter may be shrewdly hinting at the scriptural distinction between intentional and unintentional sins, the latter of which require a lesser sacrifice in atonement (Lev. 4:27–31; Num. 15:27–29). The apostle Paul would employ this same technique of tailoring his message to identify with particular audiences, sometimes by citing scriptures or extra-biblical ideas common to their culture— always meeting them on their own terms. As Paul tells the Corinthians, "For though I am free from all, I have made myself a servant to all, that I might win more of them. To the Jews I became as a Jew, in order to win Jews. To those under the law I became as one under the law (though not being myself under the law) that I might win those under the law. To those outside the law I became as one outside the law (not being outside the law of God but under the law of Christ) that I might win those outside the law. To the weak I became weak, that I might win the weak. I have become all things to all people, that by all means I might save some. I do it all for the sake of the gospel, that I may share with them in its blessings" (1 Cor. 9:19–23). This is a wise and timeless model for evangelism and one that premiere apologist Ravi Zacharias employs. Ravi trains his students to focus on the questioner as much as the question he is asking. To reach a skeptic, you must seek to understand the person behind the question and frame your responses accordingly.[33]

After extending them grace Peter goes further, offering them complete forgiveness through Jesus Christ provided they repent and turn away from sin and toward Christ. "Repent therefore, and turn back," says Peter, "that your sins may be blotted out, that times of refreshing may come from the presence of the Lord, and that he may send the Christ appointed for you, Jesus, whom heaven must receive until the time for restoring all the things about which God spoke by the mouth of his holy prophets long ago." (Acts 3:19–21) Peter urges them to repent and be redeemed, informing them Christ will remain in heaven until He returns in the future (at His Second Coming), as the prophets promised.

Winding up, Peter again emphasizes that the Gospel flows naturally from Old Testament Scripture, declaring they are the sons of the Old Testament prophets and of the covenant God made with their ancestor Abraham, whereby He promised Abraham that He would bless all the families of the earth through his offspring (the Abrahamic Covenant) (Gen. 12:3; 22:18). God's promise is now being fulfilled in Jesus Christ, a descendant of Abraham in the line of King David, whose finished work on the cross ensures salvation for all who place their faith in Him. Paul explicitly identifies God's promise of blessing to Abraham as the Gospel, saying, "Know then that it is those of faith who are the sons of Abraham. And the Scripture, foreseeing that God would justify the Gentiles by faith, preached the gospel beforehand to Abraham, saying, 'In you shall all the nations be blessed.' So, then, those who are of faith are blessed along with Abraham, the man of faith" (Gal. 3:7–9).

This is a stunning closing argument: the Gospel is not an affront to their Scriptures, but in fact, the completion of them. No, they are not condemned for their complicity in killing their own Messiah. No, their Scriptures are not invalidated by Christ's death. They merely need to open their hearts and allow the scales to fall from their eyes—to see Christ for who He is, turn from their sins, and embrace Him in saving faith. They can have their cake and eat it too—accepting Christ will not require them to reject their own Scriptures, but it will allow them to escape the penalty for their sins. Not a bad bargain!

CHAPTER 4

∞∞∞∞∞∞∞∞∞∞∞∞∞∞

While Peter and John are speaking to the crowd, religious leaders approach—the priests, the captain of the Temple guard, and the Sadducees, who are particularly annoyed at the duo's preaching on Jesus' resurrection, as the leaders don't believe in resurrection at all (Acts 23:8). It's bad enough to teach resurrection in the abstract, but to say it has already occurred is aggravated blasphemy to them. It isn't just a religious matter for the Sadducees, who are influential, though fewer in number than the Pharisees. This sect routinely panders to the Roman authorities, striving to maintain the peace at all costs in exchange for powerful political positions such as high priest.[34] They know that messianic ideas such as Peter and John are presenting have led to Jewish revolts in the past, and they must strenuously avoid that outcome here.[35]

The leaders arrest Peter and John and place them in custody until the next day—but by now, Peter's words have already created thousands of new converts. This brings to five thousand the total number of people who have been saved in Jerusalem—representing a substantial portion of the city's population, which scholars estimate was between twenty-five thousand and eighty-five thousand at the time.[36] Jewish historian Josephus estimates there were only six thousand Pharisees then in Judea.[37]

The next day, the rulers bring John and Peter before the Sanhedrin—the Jewish high council, which consists of seventy-one members, counting the high priest. They ask the pair by what power or name they performed their healing, implying they were presumptuous to have spoken authoritatively given their lack of credentials.[38] Peter, filled with the Holy Spirit, reiterates what he told the assembled crowds the previous day: they healed the lame man in "the name of Jesus Christ of Nazareth, whom you crucified, whom God raised from the dead." He continues, "This Jesus is the stone that was rejected by you, the builders, which has become the cornerstone. And there is salvation in no one else, for there is no other name under heaven given among men by which we must be saved." (Acts 4:10–12) This is an audacious move—to go beyond denying their own culpability to charging their accusers with the far worse crime of killing mankind's Savior.

The rulers are astonished at such defiance from uneducated and common men, whom they recognize as Jesus' disciples. But with the presence of the healed man and the many who witnessed the miracle, they can't rebut the charges. After conferring among themselves, they command Peter and John to speak to no one else in Jesus' name, hoping to prevent news of the healing from spreading further.

Undaunted, Peter and John reply that while the Sanhedrin is free to believe that its authority should supersede God's, they themselves are compelled to obey Him and proclaim what they have seen and heard. Seeing people praising God for the miracle, the Sanhedrin merely threatens the pair and lets them go. Jewish historian Joseph Klausner asserts that the Sanhedrin's arrest and release of the apostles "was the first mistake which the Jewish leaders made with regard to the new sect [Christianity]. And the mistake was fatal." He argues that arresting and then quickly releasing them made them martyrs while also signaling that it might not be so dangerous to be a disciple of Jesus after all.[39]

Perhaps, but the reality is that God is sovereign; the spread of the Gospel was not to be contained. If Peter and John hadn't been arrested, they would have continued to preach boldly, and if they had been punished, the Gospel would surely have proliferated just as explosively. There were too many witnesses of God's miracles and of the apostles' contagious message for this genie to be put back in the bottle.

Once released, Peter and John return to their friends and report what has happened. The people pray to God, quoting Psalm 2:1, 2: "Sovereign Lord, who made the heaven and the earth, and the sea and everything in them, who through the mouth of our father David, your servant, said by the Holy Spirit, 'Why did the Gentiles rage, and the peoples plot in vain? The kings of the earth set themselves, and the rulers were gathered together, against the Lord and his Anointed'—for truly in this city there were gathered together against your holy servant Jesus, whom you anointed, both Herod and Pontius Pilate, along with the Gentiles and the peoples of Israel, to do whatever your hand and your plan had predestined to take place. And now, Lord, look upon their threats and grant to your servants to continue to speak your word with all boldness, while you stretch out your hand to heal, and signs and wonders are performed through the name of your holy servant Jesus."

The new believers increasingly understand that God's salvation history had not begun with Jesus but was culminating in Him. In quoting the second psalm, the believers show they understand that Hebrew Scripture is still relevant and is being fulfilled in their day. The Romans are the Gentiles raging against God and His Anointed, Jesus, while the Jewish people and their rulers are those who plotted against Him. The psalmist's accurate prediction of the unfolding events, as described above, shows this has all been part of God's master plan for mankind.[40] Significantly, these believers consider both the Gentile authorities and the Jews as common foes of the Gospel in this case.[41] Many commentators believe this psalm was immediately fulfilled in the early Church and is also a prophecy of the end-times Tribulation.[42] "In the last days," Warren Wiersbe writes, "it will have its complete fulfillment as the 'kings of the earth' unite to fight against God" (see Rev. 1:5; 6:15; 16:12–16; 17:2, 18; 19:11–21).[43]

After praying together, the believers' meeting place shakes. They are all filled with the Holy Spirit and continue to speak God's word boldly. They come together as a finely tuned community "of one heart and soul," and again, they share all their belongings, sell their assets, and give the proceeds to the apostles for distribution to the poor. With great power, the apostles give their testimony to Christ's resurrection, and God brings grace to them all.

CHAPTER 5
◇◇◇◇◇◇◇◇◇◇◇◇◇◇◇◇◇◇◇◇◇◇◇◇◇◇◇

Not quite everyone practices this communal spirit of generosity. After Ananias and his wife Sapphira sell some property, Ananias, with

Sapphira's knowledge, retains some of the proceeds, giving only part of it to the apostles. Peter asks Ananias why Satan has filled his heart to lie to the Holy Spirit and keep part of the proceeds, clarifying that though it was his property to dispose of as he wished, and that the proceeds were his after he sold it, his sin was lying to God. Hearing this rebuke, Ananias immediately dies, striking great fear in all who hear of this. A group of young men wrap his body, carry him out, and bury him. Three hours later, Sapphira enters, unaware of what has happened. Peter asks her if they have given all the proceeds from the sale of their land to the apostles, and she says they have. Peter then asks why she and Ananias had agreed to test the Spirit of the Lord. She too instantly falls and dies, and the young men bury her beside her husband. Again, great fear comes upon the whole Church and everyone else who hears about these events.

Many commentators regard this as one of the most troubling passages in the New Testament. On first glance, it's difficult to reconcile it with our perception of God's grace in Jesus Christ. But some scholars' explanations strike me as either evasive or too harsh. Let me take a stab at presenting the issues.

First, most agree that the text, especially the original Greek, indicates the couple had agreed to sell the property and give all the proceeds to the Church, even though they weren't required to do so. If they hadn't agreed to this, such a severe penalty would not have been imposed because the infraction would have been different—selfishness or greed, rather than lying to God. The Greek translation reveals they virtually embezzled the money—meaning it was no longer theirs once they had pledged it to God and the Church.

The beginning chapters in Acts emphasize that the nascent Church was thoroughly community oriented and spirit-filled. Perhaps this is why Luke introduced the word "church" for the first time in the Book of Acts in the context of this story.[44] The two verses immediately preceding the Ananias and Sapphira story mention that Barnabas sold his field and delivered the proceeds to the apostles, presumably to draw a sharp contrast with the couple's attitude. We may safely assume God deemed that a high level of purity was needed to spur the rapid spread of the Gospel, which was for the benefit of all people. The couple damaged both the spirit-filled nature of the Church and the communal trust among its members—and if the "spirit" of the Church is compromised, so is its power. "The church can only thrive as the people of God if it lives within the total trust of all its members," writes John Polhill. "Where there is that unity of trust, that oneness of heart and mind, the church flourishes in the power of the Spirit. Where there is duplicity and distrust, its witness fails."[45]

If this corruptive taint were allowed to infect the Church at the beginning, it could severely inhibit its growth and the consequent spread of the Gospel in Jerusalem and beyond. So it may be that God regards the couple's actions and spirits as corrosive influences on the Church—a door for Satan to enter from the beginning. In response, He decides to eradicate the menace altogether and preserve the spirit-driven community.

It's not a great stretch to analogize this to those disturbing sections in the Old Testament in which God orders Israel to kill all the Canaanites in the Promised Land. One mitigating factor is that God's ultimate plan was to use His chosen people in the land to establish a nation from which would spring the Messiah, Who would offer salvation to all mankind. Allowing the depraved pagans to remain in the land would hinder His plan by promoting idolatry, so He demanded purity.

While I am not entirely comforted by these arguments, I am not one to contradict God, Who has the right to judge human beings He created. What gives me greater solace is that nothing in the story suggests that Ananias or Sapphira lost their salvation because of their sin. We don't know, and it isn't for us to know. All we know is that God took their earthly lives and preserved the spirit of the early Church. Perhaps Luke twice reports fear among the believers to elucidate that they understand how gravely God regards sin that taints the Church.[46]

The narrative picks back up with the apostles performing many miracles among the people gathered at Solomon's Colonnade. For unstated reasons—perhaps they are fearful of being judged[47]—some don't dare join the believers, though they highly respect them. But nonbelievers are being converted at an ever-increasing pace. The excitement repels some people and irresistibly attracts others. John Stott observes that this remains true today. "The presence of the living God, whether manifest through preaching or miracles or both, is alarming to some and appealing to others," he contends. "Some are frightened away, while others are drawn to faith."[48]

The people carry their sick into the streets and lay them on cots and mats, hoping that when Peter walks by, his passing shadow might heal them. Word of these healings spreads to surrounding towns, and people bring their sick and spirit-possessed into Jerusalem for healing. When they learn of the healings, the religious rulers are jealous and fearful for their authority. They again arrest the apostles and put them in the public prison. But during the night, an Angel of the Lord frees them and says, "Go and stand in the temple and speak to the people all the words of this Life." God will not be thwarted: He not only releases the apostles but commands them to preach the Gospel message of salvation and the spirit-filled life it entails, in all its fullness. An ironic twist is at play here: the Sadducees, who are behind the imprisonment, don't believe in angels (just as they don't believe in resurrection), yet it is an angel that foils their plan.[49] In obedience, the apostles enter the Temple at dawn and begin to teach.

The high priest convenes the Sanhedrin and orders the prisoners to be brought in. But the officers return and report that though the prison was securely locked with the guards at the doors, the apostles are gone. The unnoticed escape of the prisoners through locked gates and armed guards perplexes the authorities. When the rulers hear that the apostles are teaching in the Temple, they bring them back peaceably. They fear using force could provoke people to stone them, indicating the people's growing respect for the apostles. The authorities reprimand the apostles for disobeying their order not to preach in Christ's name, and for blaming them for Jesus' death. Curiously, the high priest does not inquire about their mysterious escape.

Just as in the first hearing, Peter and the apostles respond that they are compelled to obey God—Who has commanded them to preach in Jesus' name—rather than men, no matter how powerful. In this spirit, Peter continues with unpleasant truths, matter-of-factly rebuking the authorities for crucifying the Messiah sent by the God of their fathers— the same God they had always worshipped. Beyond defending himself, Peter is witnessing to the authorities, declaring that God has raised Jesus as Leader and Savior to give Israel repentance and forgiveness of sins.

As if to say, "I know you want us to shut up about this, but the truth is the truth," Peter testifies that, along with the Holy Spirit, Whom God has given to believers, they are eyewitnesses to these events. It is a striking illustration of the power of prayer, for they had prayed for the courage to preach Christ boldly in the power of the Holy Spirit. Whether the authorities fully comprehend the message, they are furious and want to kill Peter and the other apostles.

At that moment, the Pharisee Gamaliel—a well-respected teacher of the Law who had been Paul's instructor before his conversion—orders that the apostles be removed from the building temporarily. He urges his colleagues to be cautious, reminding them of past religious leaders who inspired rebellions. They should simply distance themselves from the apostles, he says, because unless it's truly inspired by God, their message will fail; but if God is behind it, it will succeed despite their resistance, and they would be opposing God.

It's unsurprising that an orthodox Jewish believer endorses God's sovereignty, but it's shocking that he allows for the possibility that the Gospel is authentic. Then again, Pharisees have far more in common theologically with Christians than do the powerful Sadducees. Unlike the Sadducees, Pharisees believe in angels, resurrection, the after-life, and a coming Messiah (Acts 23:8, Matt. 22:41). Perhaps Gamaliel is sensing that this new movement is inspired because of the miraculous healings, the apparent supernatural escape from jail, and the apostles' bold preaching in Christ's name based on their firm belief in His bodily resurrection.

It is ironic that this venerated rabbi, by intervening in the proceeding, has become God's instrument in advancing the Gospel. The authorities yield to his wisdom and call the apostles back in, beat them, and finally release them, after again ordering them not to preach in Jesus' name. After their release, the apostles rejoice that they have been persecuted in Christ's name, which they consider a high honor—the very type of reaction Peter would encourage in his first epistle: "But rejoice insofar as you share Christ's sufferings, that you may also rejoice and be glad when his glory is revealed. If you are insulted for the name of Christ, you are blessed, because the Spirit of glory and of God rests upon you" (1 Peter 4:13–14). Paul also promotes joy in suffering, as previously noted, because suffering produces endurance, then character, and then hope (Romans 5:3–5). Every day thereafter, the apostles, paradoxically empowered by their persecution for defending Christ, flagrantly ignore the Sanhedrin's commands and preach in Jesus' name in the Temple and in the people's homes.

CHAPTER 6

With the rapid expansion of the Church comes growing pains. The Hellenists (in this instance, converted Grecian Jews)[50] complain that their widows are not receiving their fair share of the daily food distribution. Assembling all the disciples, the apostles put seven upstanding men in charge of food distribution and free the rest to preach and teach the Word. The apostles lay their hands on the seven and pray for them. This problem solved, they continue to advance the Gospel, multiplying the number of believers, including many Jewish priests.

Stephen is one of the seven servants, full of grace and power, and is working great wonders and signs among the people. He stirs the ire of certain synagogue members when he begins to powerfully preach the Gospel, but they are powerless to refute Him and his Spirit-filled wisdom. This brings to mind Jesus' assurances to His followers: "for the Holy Spirit will teach you in that very hour what you ought to say," when challenged by authorities or faced with any adversity (Luke 12:11–12). Jesus also promised to give them wisdom that their adversaries could not withstand or contradict (Luke 21:15).

In frustration and anger, these Jews recruit men to frame Stephen for blasphemy against Moses and God. This stirs up people and the elders and scribes, who seize Stephen, bring him before the Sanhedrin, and produce false witnesses against him. They accuse him of blasphemy against Moses and the Temple, for he had allegedly quoted Jesus as saying He would destroy the Temple and change Jewish customs. Everyone in the council notices that despite these charges, Stephen's face has an angelic appearance—a reflection of God's glory—while he's poised to make an inspired defense of the Gospel.[51]

CHAPTER 7

◇◇◇◇◇◇◇◇◇◇◇◇◇◇◇◇◇◇◇◇◇◇◇

When the high priest asks him whether the charges are true, Stephen—though he's not an apostle—begins one of the most profound speeches recorded in Acts or elsewhere in the Bible. This has long been one of my favorite biblical speeches, for Stephen masterfully summarizes Old Testament history and demonstrates its continuity with the Gospel message. It's unfortunate that some Christians fail to appreciate, or even dispute, the relevance of the Old Testament. Stephen's speech is powerfully succinct, reviewing God's formation and superintendence of the Jewish nation. The following is a summary of his remarks with comments.

Stephen begins by telling of the "God of glory" calling Abram (Abraham) and commanding him to go to the land He would show him—Canaan. He gave Abraham and his descendants the land as an everlasting possession, though at the time of God's command, he had no descendants. Right off the bat, Stephen refers to God as the "God of glory," showing his reverence for the same God the Jews worship, Whom he would never blaspheme. His accusers must be perplexed at Stephen's endorsement of their God while being such an ardent follower of Christ—though, if they understood the Gospel, they would see there is no inconsistency.

God had told Abraham that his descendants would be enslaved (by the Egyptians) for four hundred years, and then God would judge Egypt, deliver His people from its clutches, and return them to the Promised Land, where they would worship Him. God gave Abraham the covenant of circumcision, which required all males to be circumcised as a sign of the covenant that God had made with him (Gen. 17:9–14). As God promised, Abraham became Isaac's father and circumcised him on the eighth day. Isaac became the father of Jacob, who became the father of the twelve patriarchs of Israel. These three men were God's chosen founding fathers of the nation of Israel—God referred to Himself as "the God of your fathers, the God of Abraham, of Isaac, and of Jacob" (Exodus 3:16). Throughout his speech, Stephen fully embraces the Old Testament narrative and recognizes God's special relationship with the Jewish people—something his accusers must have noticed.

Jealous of their brother Joseph, Stephen continues, the patriarchs sold him into Egypt, but God rescued him and gave him favor and wisdom before Pharaoh, who appointed him ruler of Egypt and of his household. When a famine fell upon Egypt and Canaan, Jacob sent his sons—the patriarchs—into Egypt to get grain. They didn't recognize Joseph, and he didn't reveal himself to them at that time. But on their second visit, Joseph disclosed his identity to his brothers and introduced them to Pharaoh. Joseph then sent for his father Jacob and his seventy-five relatives. After coming to Egypt, Jacob died and they buried him in Shechem in a tomb that Abraham had purchased.

As the promised four hundred year period of captivity was ending, the Israelites were multiplying and another king came to power who was unfamiliar with Joseph. He mistreated the Israelites, and even forced them to expose and abandon their infants so they would die. When Moses was born, he was exposed and meant to die, but Pharaoh's daughter adopted and saved him. He was instructed in Egyptian wisdom and became a great man of words and deeds.

When Moses was forty, he was moved to visit his fellow Jews. Though he killed an Egyptian who was persecuting one of them, the Jews did not understand Moses was trying to help them. The next day, when Moses tried to break up a quarrel between some other Jews, they rebuked him, asking who made him their ruler and judge. One asked if Moses wanted to kill him as he had the Egyptian, whereupon Moses fled to Midian, where he eventually fathered two sons.

Notably, Stephen accentuates the Jews' initial rejection of Moses, which could be a subtle reminder to his accusers that their fathers, not Stephen, were the ones who rejected Moses and thereby resisted God, Who was raising Moses up to be their leader. Stephen might be mentioning the initial failure of Joseph's brothers to recognize him as an example of the same kind of spiritual rebellion. John Polhill argues that Stephen could be comparing both events to the Jews' rejection of Christ. Polhill asks, "Would they now accept him when confronted by Christ through Stephen's preaching?"[52]

Stephen continues preaching. He tells how after forty more years had passed, an angel appeared to Moses in the wilderness of Mount Sinai, in a flame of fire in a bush. Amazed, Moses drew near and heard the voice of the Lord say, "I am the God of your fathers, the God of Abraham and of Isaac and of Jacob." Moses trembled and was afraid to look. Then God said to him, "Take off the sandals from your feet, for the place where you are standing is holy ground. I have surely seen the affliction of my people who are in Egypt, and have heard their groaning, and I have come down to deliver them. And now come, I will send you to Egypt." Stephen is highlighting God's trustworthiness and His steadfast protection of Israel. Polhill suggests that by including the account of God's directing the removal of Moses' sandals, Stephen is reminding his accusers that the Temple in Jerusalem is not the only place that is holy ground.[53]

Stephen then declares that this same Moses the Jews had mocked for trying to be their ruler and judge, God made a ruler and redeemer of his people. Moses led his people out of Egypt and performed miracles in Egypt, at the Red Sea, and in the wilderness for forty years. Stephen then pivots to Moses' announcement of God's promise of a prophet who would rise from His people, referring to Jesus Christ. Moses was in the congregation in the wilderness with the angel who spoke to him at Mount Sinai, and with the fathers. Moses was the one who received God's Law. The people disobeyed him and turned to Moses' brother Aaron, asking him to make Egyptian idols for them. They made a calf as an idol and offered sacrifices to it. So God turned away from them and gave them over to worship this idol, as the prophets had written.

Stephen is reminding his audience again that their fathers rejected Moses and God. Similarly, they are now rejecting Jesus Christ, whom Moses himself effectively embraced by predicting that God would raise him up. It is clear from Stephen's words that he is not only innocent of the charges being leveled against him, but that his accusers are culpable of those very misdeeds.

Stephen explains that the Israelites had a tabernacle in the wilderness, made according to God's instructions. They brought it with them into Canaan with Joshua when they drove the Canaanites from the land, using it as their temple until God allowed them to build the true Temple to worship Him. God denied King David permission to build the Temple but allowed Solomon to do it, though God does not actually dwell in houses made by human hands. Stephen quotes Psalm 11:4: "Heaven is my throne, and the earth is my footstool. What kind of house will you build for me, says the Lord, or what is the place of my rest? Did not my hand make all these things?"

After rehearsing this history, Stephen calls his accusers a "stiff-necked people, uncircumcised in heart and ears," who always resist the Holy Spirit, just as their fathers did. Their fathers also persecuted all the prophets and killed the ones who had prophesied the coming Messiah—the One whom his accusers had just betrayed and killed. Though the angels entrusted them with the Law, they did not keep it. In this final portion of his speech, Stephen connects the dots, pointedly indicting them while demonstrating his innocence. Their guilt is in failing to recognize the sins of their fathers unlike Stephen, who recognizes God's salvation plan and accepts His Son in faith. Repentance is theirs for the asking, but they are stiff-necked, hardhearted, and militantly resistant to God's offer of grace. In resisting the Holy Spirit as their fathers did, they are repeating their fathers' mistake, but with less excuse; after all, they have the Scriptures outlining their fathers' errors. "The pattern of rejection in the past," writes Polhill, "foreshadows the ultimate rejection of God's appointed Messiah in the present."[54]

Stephen is hardly the rebellious one among them. Rather, he is a mirror reflecting their guilt, which further enrages them against him. It is remarkable that they are blind to a corollary truth laced throughout Stephen's defense: God is a long-suffering God of grace and forgiveness, offering his people repeated chances at redemption—from Joseph's brothers, who had tried to murder Joseph, to His grace in the face of the Israelites' repeated rejections of Moses, to their idolatry in the wilderness, to their constant breaking of the covenant, and to His sending of His Son to die in their place and ours. Through it all, God watched over His people—He delivered Moses from the Egyptians so he could lead His people out of slavery, and He protected and kept His covenants with them despite their unending breaches.

This blistering indictment infuriates the authorities, who grind their teeth at Stephen. Full of the Holy Spirit, he gazes into heaven and tells his accusers what he sees: God's glory and Jesus standing at God's right hand. With this proclamation—even in the face of his own death—Stephen is committing blasphemy in their eyes all over again, and even more severely. His vision is a further affront to their authority since they, not Stephen, are supposed to have a direct line to God. How dare he say he has special access to Him! This is a far cry from a criminal defendant confessing his guilt or contritely begging the judge for mercy. They begin to yell and rush toward him before casting him out of the city and stoning him. During the stoning Stephen calls out, "Lord Jesus, receive my spirit," then falls to his knees and implores Jesus not to hold this sin against his murderers. Then Stephen dies.

It's impossible to miss that Stephen is imitating Christ in his final words—asking God to receive his spirit and making an intercessory prayer for his accusers. It's equally impossible to miss that during the stoning, the witnesses lay down their garments at the feet of a young man named Saul.

Believers in the nascent Church were persecuted from the outset. Hounded by Jewish leaders and Roman authorities, they were subject to arrests, trials, mob violence, and even murder. Yet the community persevered, enduring their suffering with dignity and grace. In fact, their tribulations clearly strengthened their resolve and created deep bonds among them. The authorities quickly found they could not lock up or otherwise eliminate believers as quickly as new believers were arising. However, that did not mean their persecutors would stop trying, as the apostles soon learned.

Indeed, the Church's greatest persecutor, Saul of Tarsus, will now enter the scene, determined to obliterate this blasphemous movement in its infancy. The Lord, however, has other plans. In His providence, He will re-channel Saul's animating passion into proclaiming and proliferating the Gospel instead of opposing it.

The world will never be the same.

CHAPTER THREE

ACTS 8–13

AN EQUAL OPPORTUNITY FAITH

*If you are feeling tired and therefore in need of
a spiritual tonic, go to the book of Acts.*

—MARTYN LLOYD-JONES[1]

CHAPTER 8

Perhaps to set the scene for Saul's dramatic conversion, Luke records Saul's support of Stephen's execution, which showcases his commitment to destroying the Gospel in its crib. He goes from house to house ravaging the Church and dragging men and women to prison. The Jewish authorities have shifted into full-blown persecution mode, ending any semblance of tolerance for this upstart religion. Stephen's death triggers a wave of persecution against the Church in Jerusalem, which results in the dispersion of most Christians into the regions of Judea and Samaria, though the apostles and some other believers remain in Jerusalem.[2] This faintly echoes Jesus' admonition, "When they persecute you in one town, flee to the next" (Matt. 10:23). God's sovereignty is on display again, however, as this persecution leads directly to the outworking of Christ's command to spread the Gospel to the ends of the earth (Acts 1:8), with Philip preaching the Gospel to receptive audiences in Samaria. This is not the Apostle Philip, but a Greek-speaking Jew—one of the seven selected to distribute food to the Church in Jerusalem.[3] Philip performs signs and exorcises and heals many, to the great joy of all who witness these events.

One recalcitrant Samaritan named Simon is a sorcerer who claims to have divine powers. Unable to resist Philip's Gospel message, Simon's followers become believers and are baptized. Simon himself, amazed by Philip's miracles and signs, becomes a believer and joins him. When reports of these conversions reach the apostles in Jerusalem, they send Peter and John to Samaria to pray for the people to receive the Holy Spirit.

Usually, the Holy Spirit indwells people at the moment of conversion, but this is apparently one of the few exceptions that occur at the very beginning of the Church era. Some commentators speculate that God delayed the delivery of the Spirit to the Samaritans until the apostles could preside over the event, to help unite the Samaritan and Jewish Churches, given the historical conflict between Jews and Samaritans.[4] The Jews loathed the Samaritans, whom they viewed as a mixed race who distort their Scriptures, and the Samaritans deeply resented the Jews' hostility to them.[5] Emblematic of the divide between the two peoples, the Samaritans had a separate holy site, Mount Gerizim, thus rejecting the Jews' Holy Place in Jerusalem.

Although there is no formal hierarchy in the Church at this time, and approval of every facet of local Church procedure isn't required, Church leaders still don't want ethnic conflict to impede the Gospel's advancement, so Peter and John personally handle this unique situation.[6] Exceptional circumstances warrant exceptional solutions.

When Peter and John lay their hands on the new Samaritan believers, they receive the Holy Spirit. Witnessing this, Simon offers them money to get the "power" to give the Holy Spirit to others, revealing that his purported faith was probably just a ruse to exploit people. Peter rebukes Simon and tells him to repent and be delivered from his "bitterness" and "bond of iniquity." Simon asks that they pray for him, but it's unclear whether he is sincerely repentant or merely terrified by their awesome power.[7] Their work completed, Peter and John return to Jerusalem, preaching the Gospel to many Samaritan villages along the way.

An angel of the Lord tells Philip to go southward to the road leading from Jerusalem to Gaza. On his way, Philip encounters an Ethiopian eunuch, a treasury official of Ethiopian Queen Candace. Returning from Jerusalem, where he was worshipping Israel's God as a God-fearing Gentile,[8] the eunuch is in his chariot reading the Prophet Isaiah. The Spirit tells Philip to join the Ethiopian, so Philip approaches him and asks if he understands what he's reading. Admitting that he doesn't, the eunuch invites Philip to sit with him and they read this passage: "Like a sheep he was led to the slaughter and like a lamb before its shearer is silent, so he opens not his mouth. In his humiliation justice was denied him. Who can describe his generation? For his life is taken away from the earth" (Isaiah 53:7, 8). The eunuch asks Philip whether Isaiah is talking about himself or someone else. Philip, beginning with that Scripture, explains the Gospel of Jesus Christ, reminiscent of Jesus opening the Scriptures for the disciples on the Emmaus Road, interpreting "to them in all the Scriptures the things concerning himself" (Luke 24:27). This eunuch is probably the first Gentile convert to Christianity.

I am particularly moved by this and similar passages that fully demonstrate the Christ-centered nature of the Old Testament, the unity of all Scripture, and the theme of God's salvation history coursing through the Bible from Genesis to Revelation. In my book *The Emmaus Code*, I detail the countless Old Testament prophecies, covenants, foreshadowings, types, portraits, offices, and appearances that point to Christ and are fulfilled in Him in the New Testament. Many Christians overlook the Christ-centered nature of the Old Testament and thereby miss an essential part of God's salvation history that enriches our understanding. A person recently asked me on Twitter, "What does the Old Testament have to do with Christianity?" Well, everything, that's what. God's sovereign preparation of this eunuch with a psalm predicting Christ's passion is a striking example.

Philip and the eunuch continue along the road. When they come to some water, Philip fulfills the eunuch's request to be baptized. After they emerge from the water, the Spirit of the Lord carries Philip away, and the eunuch goes on his way rejoicing. Philip ends up in Azotus (which is Ashdod, one of the ancient Philistine capitals located less than three miles inland from the Mediterranean, some twenty miles north of Gaza).[9] While passing through the area, he preaches the Gospel to all the towns until he arrives in Caesarea, a major port city of Herod the Great on the Mediterranean coast with a substantial Gentile population.[10]

CHAPTER 9

This chapter is a major turning point in the book, as it describes the conversion of Saul, who is transformed from a notorious persecutor of Christians to Christianity's foremost ambassador and God's chosen evangelist to the Gentiles. Saul, who God surely chose, in part, because of his unrivaled passion, is making murderous threats against members of the Way—followers of Christ. So intense is his antipathy for these blasphemers that he requests authority from the high priest to go on a six-day walking journey to Damascus to round them up from the synagogues and return them to Jerusalem. Widespread Christian worship services in the synagogues show that Christianity is closely connected to Judaism at this time.[11]

But why are the Jews so adamantly against the Christian movement? One reason is that they regard the Way not as a new religion but a perversion of Judaism. They must stop these heretics from coopting their faith. The Jews, with their zeal for the Law, are particularly offended by the Christians' attitude toward it.[12] Jesus said He came to fulfill the Law, and He preached a Gospel of grace based on faith in Him—not on the works of the Law. This is anathema to the Jews.

As Saul approaches Damascus, a light from heaven suddenly shines around him. He falls to the ground and hears a voice asking, "Saul, Saul, why are you persecuting me?" Saul replies, "Who are you, Lord?" The voice answers, "I am Jesus, whom you are persecuting. But rise and enter the city, and you will be told what you are to do." Jesus tells Saul that in persecuting Christians, he is really persecuting Him. The men with Saul are speechless, as they hear Jesus' voice but cannot see Him. Blinded, Saul is led by the hand into Damascus, where he remains without sight for three days and has nothing to eat or drink.

Saul, later known as Paul, goes on to record the event in his epistle to the Corinthians, asking, "Am I not free? Am I not an apostle? Have I not seen Jesus our Lord?" (1 Cor. 9:1). In recounting Jesus' resurrection appearances, He includes his own Damascus road experience, saying, "Last of all, as to one untimely born, he appeared also to me" (1 Cor. 15:8). Likewise, he writes to the Galatians, "But when he who had set me apart before I was born, and who called me by his grace, was pleased to reveal his Son to me, in order that I might preach him among the Gentiles…" (Gal. 1:15–16). In a later chapter of Acts, Luke supplies additional details of Paul's conversion, citing Paul's defense before Agrippa. At that trial, Paul relates that Jesus told him, "I have appeared to you for this purpose, to appoint you as a servant and witness to the things in which you have seen me and to those in which I will appear to you, delivering you from your people and from the Gentiles—to whom I am sending you, to open their eyes, so that they may turn from darkness to light and from the power of Satan to God, that they may receive forgiveness of sins and a place among those who are sanctified by faith in me'" (Acts 26:16–18). Jesus is clear here: He is sending Paul to the Gentiles so they may receive forgiveness of sins through their faith in Him.

While Saul is still blind in Damascus, he sees a vision of a man named Ananias coming to him and laying his hands on him to restore his sight. Meanwhile, Jesus appears in a vision to Ananias, a disciple in Damascus, and tells him to go to Judas' house on Straight Street to look for Saul of Tarsus. Ananias is apprehensive, having heard of Saul's evil deeds against Christians in Jerusalem and knowing of Saul's written authority from the chief priests to arrest Christians in Damascus. Jesus tells Ananias to assure Saul that he is His chosen instrument to spread the Gospel to the Gentiles and to the kings and the children of Israel, "for I will show him how much he must suffer for the sake of my name" (Acts 9:16). Formerly the Gentile believers' worst nightmare, Saul would now become their specially anointed witness of the Good News of salvation in Jesus Christ. He has inflicted much suffering on believers but now will suffer on their behalf and for all to whom he will spread the message.

Ananias goes to Saul, lays hands on him and, addressing him as "Brother Saul"—indicating He accepts Jesus' assurance that Saul is now a believer—tells him Jesus has sent him to help Saul regain his sight and be filled with the Holy Spirit. At once something like scales fall from Saul's eyes and he can see. He rises and is baptized, then eats and strengthens his body. Luke later adds an important detail about this event: Paul relates that Ananias also told him, "The God of our fathers appointed you to know his will, to see the Righteous One and to hear a voice from his mouth; for you will be a witness for him to everyone of what you have seen and heard" (Acts 22:14–15). Though Saul surely understands this already from his conversion experience, it couldn't have hurt to hear again that Jesus, Who has caused his conversion and is now enlisting him for service, is not some new God. "Jesus was one with 'the God of our fathers,' the only true God, the one who had revealed himself to Abraham, Isaac, and Jacob, and all the patriarchs of his chosen people," writes Werner Franzmann. "He had made his covenant of grace with them. It centered in the promise of a coming Messiah."[13]

After spending some days with the believers in Damascus, Saul begins proclaiming Jesus as the Son of God in various synagogues there. Those who hear him are shocked, as they are aware of his reputation for persecuting Christians. His conversion is one of the most remarkable events in Christian history, serving as a powerful apologetic in its own right. How could anyone so committed to destroying Christianity instantly reverse his position unless he truly encountered the living God? Saul now applies the same vigor promoting the Gospel as he did when suppressing it. While later admitting he is unworthy to be called an apostle because he persecuted the Church, he says he worked harder than any of the other apostles following his conversion, though he gives all the credit and glory to God working through him (1 Cor. 15:9–10). His conversion demonstrates God's boundless capacity for grace and forgiveness.

As he grows in strength, Saul confounds the Jews in Damascus by proving that Jesus is their long-awaited Messiah. It isn't long before he

receives some of his own medicine, going from persecutor to persecuted. After "many days had passed," Jews in Damascus plan to kill
Saul for his ostensible betrayal.[14] Saul learns of their plot—they are
watching the city gates day and night to catch him, so his disciples help
him escape the city by lowering him in a basket through an opening in
the wall. Paul corroborates this event in his second epistle to the Corinthians (11:32–33).

When Saul returns to Jerusalem he tries to join the disciples there,
but they are afraid and doubt he actually converted. Barnabas, however,
takes him to the apostles and describes his Damascus road conversion
and subsequent bold preaching of the Gospel. Saul begins preaching the
Gospel in Jerusalem, and in one instance, argues with the Hellenists (in
this case, Greek-speaking Jews), who want to kill him. When the Christians hear about this, they bring him to Caesarea and then send him to
Tarsus. Paul separately verifies these events, writing, "Then I went into
the regions of Syria and Cilicia" (Gal. 1:21). In the meantime, the Church
is growing and functioning in peace throughout Judea, Galilee, and
Samaria.

Before returning to the narrative and Peter's activities, let's look at
certain chronological issues concerning Saul's early travels that have long
interested scholars. In Luke's version in Acts, after regaining his sight
with Ananias, Saul spends "some days" with the disciples and proclaims
Jesus in the synagogues (9:19–20). A few verses later Luke writes, "When
many days had passed," the Jews in Damascus plot to kill Saul, but he
escapes the city (9:23–25). In the next verse, Saul is in Jerusalem to join
the disciples (9:26).

The wrinkle is that in his epistle to the Galatians, Paul says that
immediately after his conversion, he spent three years in Arabia and
returned to Damascus before going to Jerusalem to visit Peter for fifteen
days (1:17–18). Luke, however, mentions nothing about Saul's trip to
Arabia. Most commentators believe Saul went to Arabia after briefly
preaching in the Damascus synagogues, confounding the Jews there, and
regaining his strength (Acts 9:19–22). So Luke's phrase "when many
days had passed" (Acts 9:23) is interpreted as a vague reference to the
roughly three-year period Saul spends in Arabia and then back in Damascus.[15] It is unknown how much of this period is spent in Arabia and how

much in Damascus, but most commentators assume the lion's share is in Arabia.[16] Other scholars theorize that Saul's escape in a basket occurs during his first stay in Damascus, shortly after his conversion. He then goes to Arabia for three years before going to Jerusalem (9:26), and so the three years in Arabia happen between verses 9:25 and 9:26, instead of 9:23 ("when many days had passed").[17] Under either theory, at least three years pass between Saul's conversion and his trip to Jerusalem.[18]

Luke returns to the narrative focusing on Peter, who continues to evangelize throughout the area, including in Lydda—a town about nine miles east of Joppa, on the road from the seaport to Jerusalem[19]—where he encounters a paralyzed man named Aeneas who has been bedridden for eight years. Peter says, "Aeneas, Jesus Christ heals you; rise and make your bed." Immediately Aeneas rises, and as a result of his miraculous healing, all the residents of Lydda and Sharon—a segment of the coastal plain bordered on the west by the Mediterranean Sea and on the east by the Samarian mountains[20]—turn to the Lord.

In the ancient port city of Joppa, there is a disciple named Tabitha (also called Dorcas). A woman of good works and charity, she becomes ill and dies, and is washed and placed in an upper room. The disciples hear that Peter is in nearby Lydda and send two men to urge him to come to them immediately. When Peters arrives, they take him to the upper room where all the widows are weeping as they display tunics and other garments Dorcas made. Peter sends them outside, kneels down, prays, turns to the body, and says, "Tabitha, arise." She opens her eyes and sits up when she sees Peter, who gives her his hand and raises her up. He presents her alive to the saints and widows, and word of this resurrection spreads throughout Joppa, causing many to believe in Jesus.

Peter remains in Joppa for many days, staying with Simon, a tanner. Some scholars see symbolic significance in Luke's mentioning of the tanner because leatherworkers are deemed unclean under Jewish Law due to their contact with dead animals, and Luke is about to shift his focus to the Gentiles, who are considered unclean[21] and don't follow Jewish religious practices.[22] It is perhaps a foreshadowing of Peter's vision described in the next chapter.

With both healings, Peter is emulating Jesus' healing process. Just as Jesus told the paralytic to "get up, take up your bed, and walk" (John 5:8), Peter tells Aeneas, "rise and make your bed." And just as Jesus raised Jairus' daughter after sending people out of the room and commanding her to rise (Mark 5:40–41), Peter clears the room and commands Tabitha to rise (Acts 9:40). Furthermore, Peter works solely through Jesus' power and not his own—he tells Aeneas, "Jesus Christ heals you," and before healing Tabitha, he kneels and prays for healing power.[23]

CHAPTER 10

As we've seen, the Gentile barrier has already been broken, as Philip presented the Gospel message to the Ethiopian eunuch. But this was not the Apostle Philip, and in fact, no apostle has yet evangelized a Gentile. God is grooming Peter for that mission. Significantly, He prepares both the evangelist Peter and his subject Cornelius for this encounter by providing each with a visionary experience.

Cornelius, a centurion, lives in Caesarea, a beautiful spot on the Mediterranean Sea and the center of government for the Roman administration of Judea.[24] He and his family are worshippers of the Jewish God, though probably not full converts to Judaism. F. F. Bruce states that such God-fearers, as they are called, form the nucleus of the Christian community in many cities Saul visits on his missionary journeys.[25] So it's natural that the first Gentiles to accept Jesus—the Ethiopian eunuch and Cornelius—worship the God of Israel. They believe in the God of the universe, but probably aren't as steeped in the Law as the Jewish people, and thus are less resistant to the new Christian religion that dispenses with some of its provisions.

In the middle of the afternoon, Cornelius has a vision of an angel of God who declares, "Your prayers and your alms have ascended as a memorial before God. And now send men to Joppa and bring one Simon who is called Peter. He is lodging with one Simon, a tanner, whose house is by the sea." It appears that God intends to reward Cornelius for his faithfulness and charity. When the angel leaves, Cornelius sends two of his servants and a devout soldier to Joppa.

Around noon the next day, as Cornelius' men are approaching Joppa, Peter goes to the housetop to pray. Falling into a trance, he sees the heavens open and a great sheet being let down to earth by its four corners. The sheet contains all kinds of animals, reptiles, and birds, and a voice says to Peter, "Rise, Peter; kill and eat." Peter says he cannot do that because he has never eaten anything either common or unclean. The voice replies, "What God has made clean, do not call common." After this happens three times, the sheet is taken up to heaven. (Though Peter is already converted to Christianity, this vision shows he is still reluctant to violate Jewish dietary laws. That is understandable, seeing as the rules were implemented for sound health reasons, and no authority has yet commanded Peter to abandon them. The dream also brings to mind Jesus' admonition to the Pharisees and scribes: "It is not what goes into the mouth that defiles a person, but what comes out of the mouth; this defiles a person" [Matt. 15:11]).[26]

While Peter is pondering the meaning of the vision, Cornelius' men approach his gate and ask if Peter is lodging there. The Spirit then informs Peter that three men are looking for him, and he should go down to greet them at once. Peter goes down, identifies himself, and asks what the men want. They tell him an angel has directed Cornelius, a God-fearing man who is well respected by the Jewish people, to send for him to come to his house and hear what he has to say. The men surely include these details to entice Peter to return with them. Peter invites them in as his guests and the next day leaves with them to Caesarea along with some of his fellow believers from Joppa. Expecting them, Cornelius has gathered some of his close friends and relatives. When Peter enters, Cornelius falls at his feet and worships him. Peter quickly lifts Cornelius up and tells him that he is only a man—not someone to be worshipped. After all, idolatry is strictly forbidden in the Jewish religion, a principle enshrined in the Ten Commandments and demonstrated throughout the Old Testament in God's dealings with Israel.

With this gesture, Peter is affirming the Christian principle that all believers are equal before God.[27] He tells the many people gathered that although it's unlawful for a Jew like himself to associate with or visit anyone of another nation, God has shown him that he should not call any person common or unclean. From the Old Testament, Peter also knows that God "shows no partiality to princes, nor regards the rich more than the poor, for they are all the work of his hands" (Job 34:19). Christ's grace and peace is open to all, not just the elite. Paul endorses this principle in his epistle to the Romans: "But glory and honor and peace for everyone who does good, the Jew first and also the Greek. For God shows no partiality" (2:9). Similarly, James writes, "My brothers, show no partiality as you hold the faith in our Lord Jesus Christ, the Lord of glory" (James 2:1).

This is why, Peter explains, he came without objection. It has now become clear to him that, through the angelic vision, God was teaching him that no human beings are beyond cleanliness because their hearts can be cleansed by faith. The vision applies to the cleanliness of animals but can also be understood parabolically as applying to men—there is no longer any barrier between believing Jews and Gentiles or between God and people because of Christ's sacrifice (Romans 5:1).[28] Peter asks Cornelius why he has sent for him. Cornelius replies that when he was praying four days ago, an angel appeared to him in a vision and said that his prayer had been heard and his alms remembered before God, so he was to send for Peter. They are all now waiting before God, continues Cornelius, to hear what He has commanded Peter to do. Just as God has served up the Ethiopian eunuch on a platter, ripe for Philip's Gospel message, He has primed Cornelius to be fully receptive to the forthcoming Gospel message from Peter.

Peter reiterates that he now understands that God shows no partiality, and that anyone who fears Him and does what is right, regardless of his nationality, is acceptable to Him. Peter tells Cornelius that the God who delivered the Gospel message to Israel is the God of all people. He then briefly reviews the Gospel events and message, saying that after John the Baptist came, God anointed Jesus with the Holy Spirit and with power, and He did good works and healed those who were oppressed by the devil. Peter reports that he and his apostles are witnesses to all that Jesus did in Jerusalem and throughout Judea. Jesus was crucified, but God raised Him on the third day, and He appeared to him and the other people whom God had chosen as witnesses and who ate and drank with Him after He rose from the dead. Jesus commanded Peter and the apostles to preach to the people, testifying that Jesus was appointed by God to judge the living and the dead. Peter assures Cornelius and the others gathered that Jesus is the One Whom the prophets pre-announced, and that everyone who believes in Him receives forgiveness through His name (Isaiah 52:13–53:12; Ezek. 36:25–26).

While Peter is speaking, the Holy Spirit falls on all who hear His message. The Jewish believers who have come with Peter are amazed to see the Holy Spirit being given to the Gentiles, who are speaking in tongues and praising God—just like the converts at Pentecost. "Can anyone withhold water for baptizing these people, who have received the Holy Spirit just as we have?" declares Peter. He commands that they be baptized in Jesus' name.

Through the Spirit's power, God puts an exclamation point on this momentous occasion. He leaves no doubt among the Jewish believers that the conversion of these Gentiles is authentic and Spirit-filled. This is God's work, not the work of Peter or any other apostle or believer, who are merely His instruments. The glory goes to Jesus Christ.[29] This is a dramatic turning point in Christian history. Bruce Barton comments, "Peter's words marked a great change in the life of the church—the door of the gospel was swinging wide open to the Gentiles."[30]

Afterward, Cornelius asks Peter to remain for some days. We should not lightly skip over this seemingly inconsequential invitation. Cornelius is transformed and moved, glowing in the experience, and he doesn't want the moment to end suddenly. As a new believer, his world has been turned upside down—in a good way. He has discovered the true God and wants to drink in everything he can while Peter is there. This reminds us that we should always strive to grow in our Christian walk, seek God in prayer, and study His word to plum the unfathomable depths of His riches.

CHAPTER 11

This apostle-led conversion of Gentiles sends shockwaves throughout Judea. Peter gets an earful when he goes to Jerusalem, where Jewish

Christians demand to know why he broke bread with Gentiles and communicated the Gospel to them. How dare he? Why would he risk becoming ceremonially unclean? Instead of debating, Peter simply explains what has happened—from his vision in Joppa to the Spirit-led conversion of Cornelius and his group in Caesarea. In telling the story, Peter supplies a detail that was not in the Chapter 10 narrative: The angel had told Cornelius that Peter would proclaim a message by which Cornelius and his entire household would be saved.

Peter strongly emphasizes the role of the Holy Spirit in the conversion, saying the event reminds him of Jesus' words that John the Baptist baptized with water, but the apostles would be baptized with the Holy Spirit. And if God gave these Gentiles the gift of the Holy Spirit when they became believers, just as He had done for the Jewish converts at Pentecost, who was Peter to stand in His way? If Peter, an apostle, would not oppose God, his detractors better wise up and realize their opposition is not directed at him but at God. Peter doesn't need to defend himself personally; his actions were at God's direction, and he defends himself as God's agent. As God makes no distinction between Jews and Gentiles, who is Peter to do so?[31]

The Jewish Christians have to be shamed into realizing this isn't about them but something much bigger. The Holy Spirit descended on Cornelius and the other Gentiles just as He had the Jews. And why would it be any other way? This silences the critics, who come to their senses, realizing God initiated these conversions. They glorify God, saying, "Then to the Gentiles also God has granted repentance that leads to life." Notice the immediate effects of God working in these people. Their ethnic jealousy and opposition has turned to joy for the Gentiles' salvation. This won't settle the matter for all Jewish believers, as we shall soon see, but it's an important step in advancing God's plan to save the Gentiles.

Now the Gospel is about to spread north beyond Judea and Samaria, as Christ had commanded (Acts 1:8). The Jewish Christians who escaped Jerusalem after Stephen's execution have migrated as far as Phoenicia, Cyprus, and Antioch, and most of them evangelize only fellow Jews. Some, however, spread the Gospel in Antioch to Hellenists (in this instance, Greek-speaking Gentiles).[32] So the Gospel is spreading both geographically and culturally[33]—as Luke puts it, "The hand of the Lord was with them, and a great number who believed turned to the Lord." When the Christian Church in Jerusalem hears about this, it sends Barnabas to Antioch in Syria. Arriving joyfully, filled with the Holy Spirit and faith, he encourages the community to remain committed to their purpose.

As more people come to Christ, the job is apparently too big even for the enthusiastic Barnabas, so he goes to Tarsus to locate Paul. Barnabus knows him well, having been with him and vouched for him with the apostles in Jerusalem following his conversion (Acts 9:27–28). From his interactions with Paul, Barnabas is aware that Christ has commissioned him to evangelize to the Gentiles (Acts 9:15). By now, Paul has been whisked out of Jerusalem by his fellow believers and moved on to Tarsus by way of Caesarea because his former Jewish colleagues wanted to kill him for his betrayal (Acts 9:30). His exact whereabouts after that are unknown. But scholars, aware that Paul was a relentless missionary to the Gentiles, surmise that he was evangelizing in that region during this period.[34] (This assumption is based on Luke's later reference to Paul's building up churches in Syria and Cilicia [Acts 15:41], which Paul also mentions [Gal. 1:21].) Upon finding Paul, Barnabas brings him back to Antioch, where they meet with believers and teach many people for a full year. It is in Antioch that the disciples are first called Christians.

During this time, prophets come from Jerusalem to Syrian Antioch, which is about sixteen miles from the Mediterranean and about 300 miles north of Jerusalem. Today, it is a decaying town in Turkey called Antakia;[35] it was perhaps the third most important city in the Roman Empire, after Rome and Alexandria. When the prophet Agabus predicts a worldwide famine (Luke parenthetically notes that this famine occurred during the reign of Claudius, who ruled from 41 to 54 AD [Acts 11:28]),[36] the disciples determine, according to their respective means, to send relief to believers in Judea, to be delivered by Barnabas and Paul. Thus, from the very beginning, Christians have been charitable, taking to heart Christ's teachings and Paul's revelation that "God loves a cheerful giver" (2 Cor. 9:7).

CHAPTER 12
‹‹‹‹‹‹‹‹‹‹‹‹‹‹‹‹‹‹‹‹‹‹‹‹‹‹‹‹‹‹‹‹‹

Obediently following Christ's commission to spread the Gospel, the apostles have earned rich dividends, with thousands of conversions in Jerusalem as well as the conversions of the Samaritans, the Ethiopian eunuch, the Gentile centurion Cornelius and his group in Caesarea, and the various people in Antioch. However, in the midst of these successes, Luke details King Herod's escalated persecution of the Church. Charles Ryrie notes that this is the fifth time the young Church has been persecuted, including Peter and John's appearance before the Sanhedrin (Chapter 4); the Sadducees' arrest of the apostles for preaching the resurrection (Chapter 5); Stephen's trial and execution (Chapter 6); and Saul's vigorous persecutions (Chapter 8).[37]

King Herod Agrippa I, grandson of Herod the Great, reigns from 37 to 44 AD. After incurring debts in Rome, he fled to Palestine. Emperor Tiberius imprisoned him for making careless comments, but he was released following Tiberius' death.[38] Gaius Caligula, who succeeded Tiberius in 37 AD, delegated the former tetrarchies of Philip and Lysanias in Southern Syria to Herod (Luke 3:1) and made him king over those areas. When Caligula was murdered in 41 AD, Claudia became emperor—with Herod's help—and made Herod the ruler of Judea and Samaria. Because of his uncertain position with Rome, Herod seeks to ingratiate himself to the Jews by persecuting Christians.[39]

Herod orders the death by sword of the Apostle James, the brother of John (not to be confused with the brother of Jesus and author of the Book of James). James thus becomes the first apostle to be martyred (Stephen was martyred earlier, but he was not an apostle), having been accused by Herod of leading the city of Jerusalem to serve false gods.[40] As this pleases the Jews, Herod arrests Peter, the leader and chief spokesman of the apostles, during the Feast of Unleavened Bread—the week-long feast following Passover. He imprisons Peter and assigns four squads of soldiers to guard him, intending to put Peter on trial after the Passover feast has ended. While Peter is in prison, the Church earnestly prays to God for his deliverance.

Bound with two chains, Peter sleeps between two solders, with sentries standing guard at the door. His calm is a testament to his complete transformation from the coward who denied Jesus three times to a pillar of faith. Later, the Apostle Paul will show similar tranquility in Philippi when, instead of sleeping, he sings hymns to God (Philip. 16:25). Church father Chrysostom, in his commentary on this story, compares the two events. After explaining why God didn't rescue Paul from prison as he does Peter here—because God arranged for Paul to convert the jailer—he observes, "It is beautiful that Paul sings hymns, whilst here Peter sleeps."[41]

An angel of the Lord appears next to Peter and a light shines in the cell. Striking Peter on the side, the angel tells him to get up quickly. The chains fall from Peter's hands, and the angel instructs him to get dressed, put on his sandals, wrap himself with his cloak, and follow him. Peter complies, though he isn't sure whether this is real or he's having a vision. After passing the guards, they approach the iron gate to the city, which opens by itself. They go out along the street when the angel disappears. Realizing God has sent his angel to rescue him from Herod and the Jews, Peter goes to the home of Mary, the mother of John (sometimes called Mark), where many are gathered and praying. Some commentators surmise that this Mary contributes to the growth of the early Church by frequently opening her home for fellowship, which is probably why Peter goes there.[42]

When he knocks on the door, a servant girl named Rhoda recognizes his voice. She runs joyfully to report his presence instead of letting him in. The people tell her she's out of her mind, claiming it's Peter's angel, not Peter himself. When Peter continues knocking, they open the door and are amazed to see him. Signaling to them with his hand to be silent (a detail that lends authenticity to the account),[43] Peter describes how God has freed him from prison and tells them to relate these events to James (Jesus' brother, now leader of the church in Jerusalem) and the brothers, and then he departs. At sunrise, chaos ensues among the soldiers over Peter's absence. Unable to find him, Herod examines the guards, orders their execution, and then leaves Judea for Caesarea.

Some interpreters, probably predisposed against belief in the super-natural, suggest that a human messenger, working with sympathetic or bribed guards, facilitated Peter's escape from prison.[44] But why would guards risk their lives to conspire in Peter's escape? How do critics explain the flash of light that Luke describes in the cell when the "messenger" appears? How do they account for Luke's painstaking description of Herod's tightened security measures to ensure Paul won't escape? How about the automatic opening of the gate? Finally, what else could Peter mean when he explicitly instructs those at Mary's home to tell James and the brothers "how the Lord had brought him out of the prison"? It was no human being. God superintended Peter's escape.

Meanwhile, Herod is angry with the people of Tyre and Sidon, who come to him and ask for peace because they depend on his country for food. In his royal robes, Herod later delivers a speech to the people from his throne. The people respond as if he is a god, whereupon the angel of the Lord strikes him down—because he hasn't given glory to God—and he is eaten by worms. Thereafter the word of God multiplies, and Barnabas and Saul return from Jerusalem bringing John (also known as Mark) with them.

While some may regard Luke's description of Herod's death fantastical, Jewish historian Josephus independently confirms the event with strikingly similar details. Josephus relates that Herod had adorned himself with "a garment made wholly of silver, and of a contexture truly wonderful," and notes that "the silver of his garment [was] illuminated by the fresh reflection of the sun's rays upon it." It "was so resplendent as to spread a horror over those that looked intently upon him; and presently his flatterers cried out, one from one place, and another from another ... that he was a god; and they added, 'Be thou merciful to us; for although we have hitherto reverenced thee only as a man, yet shall we henceforth own thee as superior to mortal nature." Herod neither rebuked them nor rejected "their impious flattery," says Josephus, "but, as he presently afterwards looked up, he saw an owl sitting on a certain rope over his head, and immediately understood that this bird was the messenger of ill tidings, as it had once been the messenger of good tidings to him; and fell into the deepest sorrow. A severe pain also arose in his belly, and began in a most violent manner. . . . And, when he had been quite worn out by the pain in his belly for five days, departed this life."[45]

Apart from this interesting occurrence, we should not lose sight of Luke's summary statement capping the story: "But the word of God increased and multiplied." Rev. Werner Franzmann captures the essence of these events. "The persecuting, blasphemous Herod was struck down by the avenging hand of the Lord," writes Franzmann, "but he held his hand in blessing over the proclamation of his gospel-word, so that it kept on entering more and more dark, perishing souls and bringing to them the light of God's never-failing favor and the life which endures eternally."[46]

CHAPTER 13

This chapter marks a shift in the action, both geographically and biographically. Geographically, the Christian witness began in Jerusalem, then spread to Judea and Samaria in Chapter 8, to Antioch in Chapter 11, and now moves "to the end of the earth," all in accordance with Christ's command in Acts 1:8. Additionally, the first twelve chapters roughly focus on Peter, whereas now the action shifts to the missionary work of the Apostle Paul. This latter section of Acts features Paul's three missionary journeys in which he establishes himself as the greatest evangelist to the Gentiles. It also chronicles the Council at Jerusalem, where certain conflicts among the believers are resolved; Paul's captivity in Jerusalem; and his voyage to Rome, with his two periods of captivity there that sandwich an intervening period of freedom.

Saul, as he is still called at this time, launches his first missionary journey from Antioch in Syria to the island of Cyprus, then to the mainland cities of Perga, Antioch in Pisidia, Iconium, Lystra, and Derbe. When completing his work in Derbe, Saul returns to the cities he visited on the way, eventually arriving in Antioch. The term "journey" may be slightly misleading in that the trips involve far more than traveling. Saul's practice is to enter cities and plant stable churches there before moving on. Barnabas accompanies Saul on the first journey, and John Mark is with them for part of the mission.[47]

There are some key early Christian teachers, prophets, and other heavy-weights in the church at Antioch, including Saul and Barnabas, Simeon (called Niger), Lucius of Cyrene, and Manaen, a lifelong friend of Herod Antipas the tetrarch, who ruled Galilee and Peraea from 4 BC to 39 AD.[48] While the men are worshipping and fasting, the Holy Spirit tells them to set apart Barnabas and Saul for the work to which He has called them. The men fast and pray, then lay their hands on the two and send them off.

Paul's first missionary journey

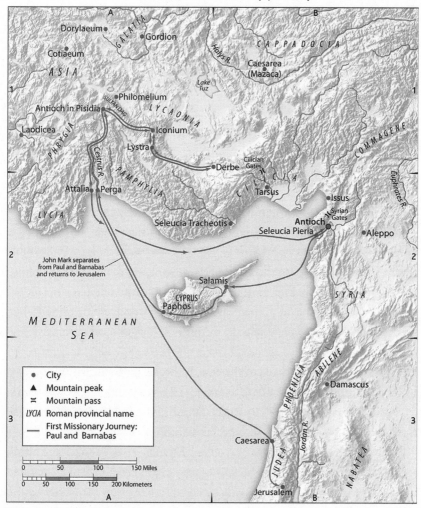

From The New Moody Atlas of the Bible by Barry J. Beitzel (©2009). Published by Moody Publishers. Used by permission.

Though Luke says the church members send Barnabas and Saul, he makes clear in the next verse that the Holy Spirit is the moving force. The pair travel from Antioch a short distance down to Seleucia, the port city, and from there they sail to the port city of Salamis on the east coast of the island of Cyprus, where they proclaim God's Word in the Jewish synagogues. Saul and Barnabas present the Gospel first in the Jewish synagogues of each city on their journey, conforming to the maxim Paul would announce in his epistle to the Romans: "For I am not ashamed of the gospel, for it is the power of God for salvation to everyone who believes, to the Jew first and also to the Greek" (1:16).[49] The Jews, as we've seen, have been scattered throughout the Roman empire, providentially setting the stage for the apostles' missionary work in the synagogues of these regions. John (John Mark) assists Saul and Barnabas on their journey.

After they've traveled about ninety miles to Paphos, the seat of the Roman government on Cyprus[50] on the western part of the island, they encounter a false Jewish prophet and magician named Bar-Jesus. With him is the Roman proconsul Sergius Paulus, an intelligent man who summons Barnabas and Saul because he wants to hear God's Word. But Luke has something more in mind than native intelligence in describing Sergius Paulus as intelligent. He recognizes him as wise—possessing a hunger for spiritual enlightenment. He seeks to know God, and the Bible teaches that "the fear of the Lord is the beginning of wisdom; all those who practice it have a good understanding" (Psalm 111:10).

We know God blesses those who seek His wisdom (James 1:5). When God asked him what He could do for him, Solomon didn't ask for "possessions, wealth, honor, or the life of those who hate you." He didn't even ask for a long life, but for wisdom and knowledge to govern wisely, and so God granted his request (2 Chron. 1:7–12). We should apply this lesson to our own lives, staying daily in the Word and prayer, seeking to know the heart and wisdom of God, and He will bless those efforts.

The magician Bar-Jesus, also called Elymas, tries to sabotage Saul's effort to evangelize. Saul, who Luke now begins to call Paul,[51] is filled with the Holy Spirit and responds forcefully. "You son of the devil, you enemy of all righteousness, full of all deceit and villainy, will you not stop making crooked the straight paths of the Lord?" Paul declares, "And now, behold, the hand of the Lord is upon you, and you will be blind and unable to see the sun for a time." Immediately, the sorcerer is blinded, and others lead him by the hand. How fitting that God uses a true miracle to punish Elymas, exposing the impotence of this charlatan's "magic."

Paul's choice of words is interesting. In accusing the sorcerer of making the Lord's straight paths crooked, he condemns him for doing the opposite of what John the Baptist instructed as he was preparing the nation for the coming Messiah. John said, "Prepare the way of the Lord, make his paths straight … and the crooked shall become straight" (Luke 3:4–5; see also Matt. 3:3; Mark 1:3). God wouldn't have sent John as a forerunner had it been unnecessary. He called people to repentance, insisting they reorient their minds and spirits toward Jesus, Who was about to begin His ministry. Elymas implements this process in reverse, attempting to poison Sergius Paulus against the Word, which earns Paul's special contempt. John Stott says Elymas "was guilty of causing 'perversion,' instead of 'conversion.'"[52] It is one thing for a person to be skeptical himself, but it is egregious for him to drag others down with him—to proselytize *against* God, for what could be worse than leading another to eternal damnation? As Paul repeatedly warns Christians, we should not be stumbling blocks to others (1 Cor. 8:12; Romans 14:13).

Despite Elymas' nefarious efforts, the proconsul becomes a believer, both because he sees what God has done and because of the sheer awesomeness of the message. In Luke's words, "He was astonished at the teaching of the Lord." This is the same pattern we observed before, with Jesus and the apostles using miracles to ready people for the Gospel message (Acts 3:11; 4:4). Notably, Luke describes Paul's message as "the teaching of the Lord," reminding us again that the message is from God and the apostles are His instruments, preaching in the power of the Holy Spirit (John 14:25–26). Sergius Paulus' conversion marks a turning point in the apostles' mission. Though he isn't the first Gentile convert, he is the first recorded one with no background in Judaism. Paul here begins to implement his plan to approach the Gentiles directly with the Gospel message.[53]

Paul and his group sail from Paphos north to Perga in Pamphylia, and John Mark leaves them and returns to Jerusalem. They go north from Perga to Pisidian Antioch, in the Roman province of Galatia (not to be confused with Antioch in Syria, where they began their journey—see map). On the Sabbath, they enter the synagogue and sit down. After the customary reading from the Law and the Prophets, the synagogue rulers invite them to speak "a word of encouragement for the people," as visiting rabbis or teachers would frequently be asked to address the congregation.[54] Paul stands up and addresses both the "men of Israel" and "you who fear God." He intends to include both the ethnic Jews and those who have converted to Judaism or believe in the God of the Jews.

Paul's speech, like Stephen's, masterfully interweaves important lessons from the Old Testament into the Gospel message. He discusses the roughly 450-year period starting with the sojourn in Egypt (400 years), through the wilderness wanderings (forty years), until the conquest of Canaan under Joshua and the distribution of the land (ten years). He affirms that God chose Israel and protected the Israelites when they were in Egyptian captivity, where they multiplied. Then He led them out of Egypt, and they wandered in the wilderness for forty years. During the wilderness years, God "put up with" Israel, meaning He patiently endured their disobedience and remained with them. To prepare the land He had promised them, God destroyed the seven nations in Canaan. These nations are identified in Deuteronomy 7:1: the Hittites, Girgashites, Amorites, Canaanites, Perizzites, Hivites, and Jebusites.[55] Throughout, Paul emphasizes God's sovereignty, identifying Him, not the people, as the Moving Force. God, not the Israelite army, defeated the Canaanites.[56]

This was followed by the period of the judges, until the prophet Samuel came onto the scene. The Israelites asked for a king and God gave them Saul, who reigned for forty years. Then God raised up David who was "a man after my heart, who will do all my will." Interestingly, Paul doesn't mention the third king of united Israel, David's son Solomon, because his purpose here is to trace Jesus' lineage back to David. So Paul declares that God brought to Israel from King David's offspring "a Savior, Jesus, as he promised." Paul is referring to the promise God made to David through His prophet Nathan, who said, "When your days are fulfilled and you lie down with your fathers, I will raise up your offspring after you, who shall come from your body, and I will establish his kingdom. He shall build a house for my name, and I will establish the throne of his kingdom forever. I will be to him a father, and he shall be to me a son. When he commits iniquity, I will discipline him with the rod of men, with the stripes of the sons of men, but my steadfast love will not depart from him, as I took it from Saul, whom I put away from before you. And your house and your kingdom shall be made sure forever before me. Your throne shall be established forever" (2 Samuel 7:12–16).

This promise was part of what theologians call the Davidic Covenant, in which God reaffirmed His promise to Abraham that his descendants will rule in Israel forever, and that He will establish a kingdom for Israel under kings in David's line (Gen. 17:6–16; 35:11). With the Davidic Covenant, God provided the means by which the Abrahamic blessing will be fulfilled[57]—the Messiah would come from David's line and God would establish His rule forever (cf. Isaiah 9:1–7, 11:1–5; Jer. 30:4–11; Ezek. 34:23–24, 37:24–25; Amos 9:11–15).

Other New Testament writers also identify Jesus as the eternal king who fulfills this promise. Matthew begins his Gospel describing Jesus Christ as "the son of David, the son of Abraham" (1:1), and other Gospel writers affirm it too. This theme is carried forward through the Book of Revelation, in which Christ is identified as "the Lion of the tribe of Judah, the Root of David ... [who] has conquered ..." (5:5). More important, Jesus identified Himself as such. In Revelation, He proclaimed, "I am the root and the descendant of David, the bright morning star" (Rev. 22:16). Moreover, during His earthly ministry, Jesus said He would sit on His glorious eternal throne (Matt. 19:28–29) and that He possesses an imperishable kingdom (Luke 22:29–30; John 18:36).[58]

Paul proclaims that John the Baptist, who called the people of Israel to repentance, preceded Jesus. John identified himself as a prophet, expressly denying he was the Messiah. Surely having their rapt attention, Paul identifies with his audience and reels them in, addressing them as "Brothers, sons of the family of Abraham, and those among you who fear God." He says that God has sent them—the Jews—the message of salvation, which is a distinct privilege. They missed it entirely, because they didn't recognize the Messiah or understand the words of their own prophets, which are read every Sabbath. But in condemning Jesus, they fulfilled those prophecies themselves. Though they found Jesus innocent, especially of any offense warranting the death penalty, they asked Pilate to execute Him. After Jesus died at their hands, as the prophets foretold, they took Him down from the tree and buried Him. But God raised Him from the dead, and He appeared for many days to those who had accompanied Him during His earthly ministry and who are now His witnesses to the people.

This is the heart of Paul's sermon, encapsulating the early Christian confession (or creed) that Paul includes in his first epistle to the Corinthians: "For I delivered to you as of first importance what I also received: that Christ died for our sins in accordance with the Scriptures, that he was buried, that he was raised on the third day in accordance with the Scriptures, and that he appeared to Cephas, then to the twelve." (15:3–5).[59] Throughout his sermon, Paul strives to connect with his audience, always demonstrating the continuity of God's story and that Jesus is the One the prophets promised.

In the middle of his speech, as noted, Paul identifies with his audience by addressing them as "Brothers, sons of the family of Abraham, and those among you who fear God, to us has been sent the message of this salvation." He is not just being polite. He wants them to know they are the targets of God's gift of salvation, and their eternal destiny depends on grasping this message. Now he invokes this message, saying, "And we bring you the good news that what God promised to the fathers, this he has fulfilled to us their children by raising Jesus, as also it is written in the second Psalm, 'You are my Son, today I have begotten you.'" Paul further quotes David (Psalm 16:10) predicting the resurrection: "You will not let your Holy One see corruption."

Paul here echoes Peter's words in his sermon at Pentecost, which we discussed earlier. David could not have been referring only to himself in this psalm because he, a mere mortal, did die, was buried, and his body decomposed.[60] As Paul explains, "David, after he had served the purpose of God in his own generation, fell asleep and was laid with his fathers and saw corruption, but he whom God raised up did not see corruption. Let it be known to you, therefore, brothers, that through this man forgiveness of sins is proclaimed to you, and by him everyone who believes is freed from everything from which you could not be freed from the law of Moses." Sin enslaves us, and the Law cannot liberate us from its stranglehold or bring salvation, which can only come through faith in Jesus Christ.

Paul discusses this theme further in his epistle to the Galatians: "So then, the law was our guardian until Christ came, in order that we might be justified by faith. But now that faith has come, we are no longer under a guardian, for in Christ Jesus you are all sons of God, through faith" (3:24–26). He further declares, "For freedom Christ has set us free; stand firm therefore, and do not submit again to a yoke of slavery" (5:1). Likewise, in his epistle to the Romans, Paul writes, "There is therefore now no condemnation for those who are in Christ Jesus. For the law of the Spirit of life has set you free in Christ Jesus from the law of sin and death. For God has done what the law, weakened by the flesh, could not do. By sending his own Son in the likeness of sinful flesh and for sin, he condemned sin in the flesh, in order that the righteous requirement of the law might be fulfilled in us, who walk not according to the flesh but according to the Spirit" (8:1–4).

Paul closes his speech with a stern warning: "Beware, therefore, lest what is said in the Prophets should come about: 'Look, you scoffers, be astounded and perish; for I am doing a work in your days, a work that you will not believe, even if one tells it to you.'" These Old Testament prophets warned the people that unless they returned to God, they would be judged. Accordingly, after many chances, God finally exiled them to Babylon. Paul is adapting that message to his audience's current predicament: God is offering them His grace, mercy, and forgiveness, but they must accept it or they will face His judgment and be spiritually exiled. Paul is plainly presenting them with the Gospel message: they must either believe or be judged.[61]

The people, deeply moved by the message, beg Paul to deliver the same message to them the next Sabbath. After the synagogue service is over, many Jews and Jewish converts follow Paul and Barnabas, who urge them to continue in God's grace. Word of Paul's sermon circulates among the people, and on the next Sabbath, almost the whole city gathers to hear God's word. But the Jews, seeing the crowds, jealously begin to contradict and revile Paul. Undeterred, Paul and Barnabas speak out boldly, declaring that the Gospel first had to be given to the Jews. Since they rejected it, however, they have judged themselves unworthy of eternal life, and so Paul and Barnabas are now turning to the Gentiles. Note that they control their own fate, as if they have the keys to their jail cell of damnation. Hearing this, the Gentiles rejoice and glorify God's Word, and many become believers.

The Gospel continues to spread throughout the entire region, but the recalcitrant Jews stir up hostility against Paul and Barnabas and drive them out of their district. Paul and Barnabas shake the dust from their feet against them and go on to Iconium. Paul is just doing what Jesus commanded of his disciples: "And if anyone will not receive you or listen to your words, shake off the dust from your feet when you leave that house or town" (Matt. 10:14; Luke 9:5; Mark 6:11). The disciples, beside themselves with gratitude, "were filled with joy and with the Holy Spirit."

The conversion of Gentiles marks a profound moment in the evolution of Christianity, immediately enabling the wider and faster spread of the Gospel. But this success comes at the price of stoking resistance among some early believers. The apostles work hard to navigate the resulting challenges, which will soon grow even more severe. Nevertheless, with Saul's conversion, the Church has gained a powerful new voice to settle disputes, establish the faith's doctrine, and spread the word of Jesus far and wide. Led and inspired by Paul's indefatigable evangelism, the apostles are well on their way to fulfilling Christ's Great Commission to spread the Gospel throughout the world.

CHAPTER FOUR

ACTS 14–20

SUFFERING AND SUCCESS WHILE SPREADING THE WORD

One who receives this Word, and by it salvation, receives along with it the duty of passing this Word on. . . . Where there is no mission, there is no Church, and where there is neither Church nor mission, there is no faith.

—EMIL BRUNNER[1]

CHAPTER 14

◇◇◇◇◇◇◇◇◇◇◇◇◇◇◇◇◇◇◇◇◇◇◇◇◇◇

Paul and Barnabas travel eastward to Iconium, where they continue to preach the Gospel in the synagogues and gain many converts, both Jews and Gentiles. Again, unbelieving Jews fiercely oppose the message and try to poison the Gentiles' minds against the Christians, but the apostles persist, boldly preaching and performing miracles. This divides the city between the apostles' supporters and opponents. When certain Jews and Gentiles conspire to stone the apostles, they flee south to the cities of Lystra and Derbe and the surrounding country, where they continue to preach the Gospel.

While preaching in Lystra, Paul notices a man who has been crippled from birth. Perceiving that he has sufficient faith to be healed, Paul tells him to stand. Just as the lame beggar in Jerusalem leapt to his feet at Peter's spirit-filled command, this man springs up and begins walking.

The crowds are moved and shout, "The gods have come down to us in the likeness of men," deifying Paul as Hermes and Barnabas as Zeus. This is similar to the crowd's reaction to Peter's healing of the lame beggar, which led Peter to rebuke them: "Men of Israel," he cried, "why do you wonder at this, or why do you stare at us, as though by our own power or piety we have made him walk?" (Acts 3:12). Similarly, Paul and Barnabas tell the crowds, "Men why are you doing these things? We also are men, of like nature with you. . . . You should turn from these vain things to a living God."

In the past, God allowed nations "to walk in their own ways," but even then, He showed Himself to them by providing rains, fruitful seasons, food, and gladness. But despite these disclaimers, the people still offer sacrifices to the apostles. Richard Longnecker comments that in referring to God's previous relaxed reign on nations, Paul and Barnabas imply that God is now assuming more direct control and leading mankind toward a divine climax of history culminating in Jesus Christ.[2] God had not been callously turning nations over to their own sinfulness. Rather, He was graciously and patiently giving them time to see the truth.[3] They had no special revelation then, and so were not held accountable; but now He has revealed Himself to them through Jesus Christ, and they will be accountable—which Paul will state more directly a few chapters later in his speech before the philosophers at the Areopagus in Athens (Acts 17:30).[4] Elsewhere, Paul writes, "For since, in the wisdom of God, the world did not know God through Wisdom, it pleased God through the folly of what we preach to save those who believe. For Jews demand signs and Greeks seek wisdom, but we preach Christ crucified, a stumbling block to Jews and folly to Gentiles, but to those who are called, both Jews and Greeks, Christ the power of God and the wisdom of God. For the foolishness of God is wiser than men, and the weakness of God is stronger than men" (1 Cor. 1:21–25).

Jews come from Pisidian Antioch and Iconium, inciting the crowds in Lystra to stone Paul and drag him out of the city. They assume they have killed him, but when the disciples gather around Paul, he rises and returns to Lystra. Paul is tough, but more important, he is absolutely committed to Christ. Imagine being stoned and left for dead, and then risking your life again by returning to town.

Paul and Barnabas travel to Derbe the next day and win many disciples there. They then circle back the way they came, going through Lystra, Iconium, and Pisidian Antioch, strengthening the souls of the believers and encouraging them to continue in the faith. They warn believers that as members of God's kingdom, they should expect to experience many tribulations. After Paul and his group appoint elders in every church, they commit them to the Lord with prayer and fasting.

Luke "does make it clear that the road his heroes were traveling was the way of the cross,"[5] writes British divinity professor C. K. Barrett. In his epistles, Paul articulates the same theme—that if we choose to share Christ's glory, we must be willing to suffer with Him (Romans 8:17; 2 Thess. 1:4; 2 Tim. 2:12). Indeed, Paul directly references these incidents and offers the same lesson: "My persecutions and sufferings that happened to me at Antioch, at Iconium, and at Lystra—which persecutions I endured; yet from all the Lord rescued me. Indeed, all who desire to live a godly life in Christ Jesus will be persecuted, while evil people and impostors will go on from bad to worse, deceiving and being deceived" (2 Tim. 3:11–13). While this seems unfair, Paul is assuring believers they will come under the Lord's eternal protection even though they will suffer persecution on earth. Peter affirms this as well: "Therefore let those who suffer according to God's will entrust their souls to a faithful Creator while doing good" (1 Peter 4:19).

Christians' suffering on Christ's behalf is "only for our good: it is purifying us, drawing us closer to our Lord, and making us more like Him in our lives," argues theologian Wayne Grudem. "In all of it we are not alone, but we can depend on the care of a faithful Creator; we can rejoice in the fellowship of a Savior who has also suffered; we can exult in the constant presence of a Spirit of glory who delights to rest upon us."[6]

Paul and company now leave Pisidian Antioch and return through Pamphylia and Perga and then down to the port city of Attalia before sailing back to Syrian Antioch, where the church gratefully welcomes them for their work. When they gather the church together, they describe all that God has done through them and how He has opened a door of faith to the Gentiles. They spend a considerable amount of time with the disciples.

It's encouraging that Gentiles with a background in Judaism have become believers, but it's especially gratifying that many who have no previous connection with Judaism are also coming to faith in Christ. This very phenomenon, however, is about to ignite a major controversy in the growing Church.[7]

CHAPTER 15

Some Jewish Christians from Jerusalem come to Syrian Antioch contending that circumcision under the Law of Moses is required for salvation. They are none too pleased that Gentiles have become Christians without being circumcised. These Judaizers, as they are called, made the same argument to Paul's recent converts in Galatia.[8] After Paul and Barnabas contentiously debate the issue with them, the pair take a group to Jerusalem to discuss it with the apostles and elders. On the way, they pass through Phoenicia and Samaria, bringing great joy to the believers with news that Gentiles are being converted. In Jerusalem, the church welcomes them, and they relate what God has done. Some Christians who were formerly Pharisees insist that the Law of Moses is still in force, so all believers must be circumcised. Having lived a life rigidly observing rules, they cannot wrap their minds around the "free grace" Christ offers. Christianity's future would depend on how this issue is resolved. Would it be a religion of grace and faith or of works?

As the apostles and elders are debating, Peter stands up and proclaims that in the early days of Christianity, God had arranged for him to preach the Gospel to the Gentiles. God's inclusion of the Gentiles was not a spontaneous decision but had been planned from the beginning, as witnessed by His prophets.[9] God, who knows everyone's heart, gave the Holy Spirit to believing Gentiles, cleansing and regenerating them through their faith, just as he had done with Peter and his fellow Jews. The only condition to salvation is authentic faith—not faith plus circumcision or any other kind of work.

Peter asks his opponents why they are testing God by placing a "yoke" on the disciples' necks that they and their ancestors couldn't bear. The yoke he refers to is the rigid set of laws and rules they have lived under and want to preserve. After all, their salvation is based on faith in Christ, not works of the Law. At this, the group becomes silent. Paul and Barnabas then share their miraculous work among the Gentiles on their just completed mission.

James—the half-brother of Jesus and leader of the Jerusalem church—tells the assembly that the Old Testament prophets foretold that God would visit the Gentiles, validating Peter's report to them. James quotes Amos 9:11–12, that someday God would rebuild David's "tent" and reestablish His united kingdom under the rule of David's Descendant (Christ). All the nations (Gentiles) called by God would become part of this kingdom. By raising up Jesus, the Son of David, God has, in effect, rebuilt David's fallen "tent." And before their eyes, the resurrected King is expanding His kingdom to include the Gentiles, as the prophets foretold.[10] This is a hard pill for some Jewish converts to swallow—that God is making the Gentiles His people too, a distinction formerly reserved exclusively for the Jewish people.

James expresses his "judgment" that they should not "trouble" Gentile converts by requiring them to be circumcised. They must impose no artificial barriers on Gentiles coming to faith. Instead, they should instruct them to "abstain from the things polluted by idols, and from sexual immorality, and from what has been strangled, and from blood"— practices that are particularly offensive to Jews. Gentiles need to be sensitive to Jewish believers but not burdened by unnecessary stumbling blocks.[11]

James concludes on a conciliatory note, observing that Moses is still being read every Sabbath in synagogues. Scholars differ on what he means. Some believe he is saying that as the Mosaic laws would continue to be taught in the synagogues, there would still be an opportunity for Gentile believers to learn them.[12] I doubt this, because it would imply that the Jerusalem Council's resolution—described below—is on shaky ground.[13] Others argue that James is admonishing Gentile Christians to be sensitive to Jewish believers and potential believers and to avoid disharmony in the Church.[14] Still others conclude that James is attempting to assuage the concerns of the Judaizers that abandoning Mosaic Law will inhibit the evangelism of Jews. We must understand that in those days, Jews in every city were teaching God's Word to the Gentiles—remember, only Jews had access to the Scriptures. As we've seen, the Gentiles who become believers in the Jewish God Yahweh are called God-fearers. If they stop teaching Jewish laws in the synagogues where Christian services occur, this might hinder the efforts of Jewish Christians to evangelize their unconverted Jewish friends.[15]

In any event, James imposes a compromise to promote harmony and peace in the Church: Gentiles can avoid circumcision and strict observance of the whole code of Jewish practices, but they should abstain from the practices James specified, by which they would demonstrate their respect for the consciences of the Jewish Christians.[16] It's a matter of priorities—keeping their eyes on what is important, which is spreading the Gospel and encouraging the Christian community. James' wisdom mirrors that of Paul, who, as we've seen, is always willing to compromise on the small stuff. He tailors his approach to accommodate the sensibilities of his various audiences, declaring, "I have become all things to all people, that by all means I might save some. I do it all for the sake of the gospel, that I may share with them in its blessings" (1 Cor. 9:22–23).

The church selects Barsabbas and Silas to accompany Paul and Barnabas to Antioch to deliver and personally vouch for the decision of the Jerusalem Council. They read the letter to the congregation, and the people are encouraged and rejoice. After spending time in Antioch, Barsabbas and Silas return to Jerusalem, but Paul and Barnabas remain to teach and preach the Word of God.

In the end, the Church averts a major schism by settling a doctrinal dispute, tempering it with a benign suggestion that the Church not unnecessarily alienate Jewish believers. However, this peaceful resolution will be short-lived; certain hardcore Judaizers are poised to oppose Paul and press demands that the requirements of the Law be imposed on Gentile converts.

After some time, Paul tells Barnabas they should return to every city in which they preached and check on the churches. But the two go their separate ways after disagreeing about John Mark (Mark)—Barnabas wants to take Mark along, but Paul strenuously objects, believing Mark shirked his duties when leaving them in Pamphylia. So Barnabas takes Mark to Cyprus while Paul takes Silas to strengthen the churches in Syria and Cilicia, thus beginning his second missionary journey. This dispute becomes a providential blessing, as it turns one fruitful mission into two. Thankfully, the conflict doesn't permanently destroy their friendship, as Paul subsequently speaks positively of Barnabas (1 Cor. 9:6; Col. 4:10).[17]

Paul's second missionary journey

From The New Moody Atlas of the Bible by Barry J. Beitzel (©2009). Published by Moody Publishers. Used by permission.

CHAPTER 16

Paul travels westward to Derbe and Lystra, both of which he visited on his first missionary journey. Having been beaten and left for dead in Lystra, he shows great courage to return, but such was his commitment to Christ and the churches he planted. His return is fortuitous, for he encounters a believer there named Timothy who will become one of his greatest companions and helpers in the faith. Timothy, whose mother is Jewish and father is Greek, becomes like a son to Paul (1 Cor. 4:17; 1

Tim. 1:2). He enjoys a good reputation among Christians at Lystra and Iconium.

Paul wants Timothy to join him and has him circumcised to appease the Jewish believers who know Timothy's father is a Gentile. Paul remains an ardent advocate of salvation by faith alone and still teaches that circumcision is irrelevant to salvation (Gal. 5:6; 1 Cor. 7:19), though he doesn't want to sabotage his efforts with Judaizers over these issues. "We endure anything," he writes, "rather than put an obstacle in the way of the Gospel of Christ" (1 Cor. 9:12). (Admittedly, Paul had refused to circumcise Titus [Gal. 2:3], but Titus was fully Gentile, and to circumcise him would have been surrendering to legalism.)[18] As they travel through the cities, they share the decision of the Jerusalem Council—which is also binding on churches outside Jerusalem[19]—that salvation is by faith alone. The churches are strengthened in their faith, and they grow daily.

They go through the region of Phrygia and Galatia because the Holy Spirit forbids them from evangelizing in Asia (a Roman province west of Phrygia and Galatia that comprises about one-third of the western part of Asia Minor. The region is part of modern Turkey.) When they reach Mysia, they want to enter Bithynia, a Roman province that runs along the northern edge of Turkey on the south shore of the Black Sea.[20] But the Spirit prevents them, so they continue to Troas, a port city in the province of Asia thirty miles south of ancient Troy, whose harbor is the main sea access to Macedonia.[21] During the night, Paul has a vision of a Macedonian man urging him to come to Macedonia to help them. Luke says that immediately "we sought to go into Macedonia, concluding that God had called us to preach the Gospel to them." This is the first time Luke uses "we" in Acts, and scholars conclude this means Luke was accompanying Paul.[22] The other verses in which he uses the collective pronoun in Acts are 16:10–17; 20:5–15; 21:1–18; 27:1–28:16.[23]

So they sail from Troas to Samothrace, the following day to Neapolis, and then to Philippi—a major Macedonian city and a Roman colony—where they remain for some days. Apparently there is no synagogue in which Paul can preach,[24] so on the Sabbath they go outside the city gate to the riverside hoping to find a place of prayer, and sit down to speak with women gathered there. One woman, Lydia, from the city of

Thyatira, sells purple goods and worships the Jewish God.[25] After the Lord opens her heart, she and her family become believers and are baptized. Luke denies Paul and himself any credit for this, acknowledging God's sovereign role in salvation. Note that Lydia's family members each personally trust Christ, as one cannot be saved through the faith of a family member. It is a personal matter between the individual and God. Afterward, Lydia invites them to stay in her home.

On the way to the place of prayer, Paul's group meets a slave girl who practices fortune telling, which profits her owners. She follows them and cries out, "These men are servants of the Most High God, who proclaim to you the way of salvation." After several days, Paul becomes annoyed and commands the spirit possessing her to come out in the name of Jesus Christ, which it does. Though the demon-possessed girl correctly identified God and proclaimed that He is the way of salvation, Paul probably didn't want the Gospel message to be tainted by being associated with such a person, so he exorcised her demon and eliminated any potential confusion.[26] This infuriates her owners, who seize Paul and Silas and drag them to the magistrates in the marketplace, telling them, "These men are Jews, and they are disturbing our city. They advocate customs that are not lawful for us as Romans to accept or practice." The crowds join in the attacks, and the magistrates tear off the men's clothes, have them beaten with rods, and imprison them. The jailer fastens their feet in stocks in the inner prison.

Around midnight, Paul and Silas pray and sing hymns to God as all the prisoners listen. An earthquake then shakes the foundations of the prison, opening all the doors and unfastening the prisoners' bonds. When the jailer wakes and sees the open doors, he decides to kill himself with his sword. Paul, however, tells him not to harm himself, because no prisoners have actually escaped. The jailer calls for lights, rushes into the cell, and trembling with fear, falls before Paul and Silas. He escorts them out of their cell and asks them what he must do to be saved. They reply, "Believe in the Lord Jesus, and you will be saved, you and your household." This is a clear expression of the doctrine of salvation by faith in Jesus Christ alone. Again, the jailer's household members would each have to trust in Christ individually to be saved. Paul continues to speak the Word of God to the jailer and his entire household. The jailer

washes their wounds, and they baptize him and his family. Bringing them
into his home, the jailor and his family rejoice at their conversion.

The next morning, the magistrates send the police to release Paul
and his group, telling them to go in peace. Paul says it won't be that
simple, for though they are Roman citizens, they've been publicly beaten
and imprisoned. The authorities can't just release them secretly, as if
nothing happened. "No! Let them come themselves and take us out,"
says Paul. When the police inform the magistrates that the prisoners are
Roman citizens entitled to due process under Roman law, the magistrates
fearfully apologize and release them, asking them to leave the city. Paul
and the others leave and head for Lydia's house, where they encourage
their Christian brothers and then depart.

To beat Roman citizens without a trial is an egregious violation of
their rights, which could result in the magistrates' dismissal and possibly
the revocation of Philippi's privileges as a Roman colony.[27] There are
only two instances recorded in Acts in which Gentiles threaten or harm
Paul. In both cases, it's because people believe Paul is damaging them
financially, and each time a Roman official comes to Paul's defense.[28]

CHAPTER 17

The believers continue to move westward through Amphipolis and
Apollonia until they reach Thessalonica—all three are cities on the
Egnatian Way, the main east-west Roman highway.[29] Paul visits the
synagogue on three Sabbath days, preaching the Gospel from the Scriptures and teaching that Jesus is the Messiah foretold in the Old Testament. Some are convinced, including certain devout Gentiles and several
leading women, who join Paul and Silas. But jealous Jews organize a
mob and riot. They attack the house of a man named Jason (likely a
meeting place for the local church),[30] looking for Paul and his group.
When they can't find them, they drag Jason and other believers before
the city officials and accuse them of receiving Paul and the others, "who
have turned the world upside down" and are violating Caesar's decrees
by proclaiming Jesus as another king. Tantamount to treason, this bogus
charge could result in the death penalty.[31] Though "turned the world

upside down" is hyperbole, it does indicate that the Gospel is spreading, and many find that disturbing. The city officials and the people are upset at these charges but release Jason on bond.

Fearful that the Jews might bring further charges against them, the Thessalonian Christians during the night send Paul and Silas to Berea, where they visit the Jewish synagogue. The Jews here are nobler than those in Thessalonica, and "they received the word with all eagerness, examining the Scriptures daily to see if these things were so." Luke is making an important point: the Bereans are hungry for God's Word and for the spiritual truths it contains. They want to soak up as much of it as they can, so they scour it meticulously, using it as a yardstick to measure the authenticity of Paul's teachings. Confirming through their diligence that the Old Testament Scriptures actually speak of Jesus, many of them become believers, including certain Greek women of high standing, just as in Thessalonica. When the Jews from Thessalonica get wind of this evangelism in Berea, they go there and again stir up the crowds. The Berean Christians whisk Paul out of the city and on to Athens, but Silas and Timothy remain with instructions to join him as soon as possible, which Timothy does later (1 Thess. 3:1–2, 6).

Paul is troubled by the rampant idolatry in Athens. It's as if there were an inverse relationship between its standing as an educational and cultural center and its spiritual health. (This is arguably the case today—a disproportionate percentage of academics are self-professed agnostics or atheists.)[32] He talks with the Jews and other God-fearers in the synagogue and with others in the marketplace, including some Epicurean and Stoic philosophers. Some accuse him of babbling, while others say he is promoting foreign divinities in preaching Jesus and the resurrection. They take him to the Areopagus—the high council in charge of religious and educational matters in Athens[33]—and ask him to explain his "new teaching," which brings "some strange things" to their ears. As people who often discuss the latest ideas, the Athenians are intrigued. This is not an official proceeding, but an informal session in which the local authorities and opinion makers question Paul to see whether his teaching threatens the state.[34]

This is a different kind of challenge for Paul, who is facing an intelligent and skeptical secular audience. He must tailor his presentation of the Gospel to reach them. I find Paul's response fascinating, as he employs the approach to evangelism he advocates in his epistles. He adroitly frames his remarks to relate to his audience, liberally marshaling Old Testament Scripture without identifying it to them as such. It is a consummate clinic in evangelism and apologetics. He begins by complimenting them as religious. He says he noticed one of their sacred altars with the inscription, "To the unknown god," and offers to reveal God's identity to them. Paul does not argue that all gods are the same, or that those worshipping other gods are unwittingly worshipping Christ. Rather, he finds a point of agreement with his hearers, using their professed ignorance of the identity of their own god as an opportunity to introduce them to the true God.[35] The Creator God, he explains, is Lord of heaven and earth, and does not inhabit manmade temples. We mustn't miss that Paul makes this claim with Athens' famous Parthenon—a temple to the goddess Athena—on the hill right above him. Here Paul is echoing Solomon's prayer when he dedicated his newly erected temple: "But will God indeed dwell on the earth? Behold, heaven and the highest heaven cannot contain you; how much less this house that I have built!" (1 Kings 8:27).

God needs nothing from human beings because He created them. He gives them life and breath and everything else (cf. Isaiah 42:5). Rather, God made every nation in the world from one man and in His sovereignty, established the periods during which they would rise and fall as well as their national boundaries. He intends for men to seek Him and "feel their way toward him and find him," for God is "not far from each one of us." Paul is on solid scriptural footing here, as the psalmist says, "The Lord is near to all who call on him, to all who call on him in truth" (Psalm 145:18; cf. Jer. 23:23). The Greeks' Stoic philosophy holds that God is near or accessible as well, except that the god of the Stoics is impersonal.[36]

Showing his learnedness, Paul next shrewdly borrows ideas from his listeners' familiar pagan literature and adapts them to Christian ideas. Probably quoting Epimenides of Crete, he says, "For 'In him we live and move and have our being.'" And, quoting from Aratus's poem "Phainomena," Paul declares, "For we are indeed his offspring." Without compromising the truth, he meets them on their own terms. "Paul does not mean that Zeus is the same as the Christian God, nor that we are children of

God in the way the poets view it," writes Chalmer Faw. "These quotations are points of contact from which he can proceed to preach the good news in Jesus."[37]

Building on this foundation, Paul teaches that as God's offspring, we should not believe that God is like a created image of gold, silver, or stone. Those are formed by the art and imagination of man; that is, human beings didn't create God—God created us. Here, Paul may be reflecting on words of the psalmist: "Why should the nations say, 'Where is their God?' Our God is in the heavens; he does all that he pleases. Their idols are silver and gold, the work of human hands. They have mouths, but do not speak; eyes, but do not see. They have ears, but do not hear; noses, but do not smell. They have hands, but do not feel; feet, but do not walk; and they do not make a sound in their throat. Those who make them become like them; so do all who trust in them" (Psalm 115:2–8; see also Deut. 4:28; 2 Kgs. 19:18; Isa. 37:19; Acts 19:26; See Isa. 44:10–20; Jer. 10:3–5).

Just as he explained to his opponents in Lystra, Paul says that in the past God overlooked man's ignorance, but now He is commanding all people of the world to repent because He will judge the world on a certain date. This judgment will be administered by a Man He has appointed, and Whom He has validated to human beings by resurrecting Him from the dead. Paul expresses a similar thought in his epistle to the Romans, writing that "in his divine forbearance, [God] had passed over former sins. It was to show his righteousness at the present time, so that he might be just and the justifier of the one who has faith in Jesus" (3:25–26). God will impose judgment, but the good news is that people can trust in the finished work of Christ on the cross instead of facing divine punishment. Paul intends to jolt them into recognizing that God's righteous judgment is imminent and inescapable. Upon hearing of the resurrection, some mock Paul, but others say they'd like to hear more. Some become believers, including Dionysius the Areopagite, a woman named Damaris, and others with them.

CHAPTER 18

From Athens, Paul goes to Corinth, an important city throughout the history of Greece, which at the time is a center of commerce and wealth as well as a hub of Roman paganism and sexual immorality.[38] Notably, he writes his stinging indictment of pagan sexual vices while in Corinth (Romans 1:18–32), probably on his third missionary journey, in 57 AD (Acts 20:2–3).[39] In his first letter to the Corinthians, he condemns sexual immorality and idolatry in the same sentence (6:9) because he knows they are correlated: where pronounced idol worship exists, sexual licentiousness is rampant.[40]

Paul encounters Aquila, a Jewish man who has recently come from Italy with his wife Priscilla because Emperor Claudius has banished Jews from Rome. Roman historian Suetonius corroborates this persecution— and also, probably, the historicity of Jesus Christ, writing, "Since the Jews constantly made disturbances at the instigation of Chrestus, [Claudius] expelled them from Rome."[41] (Many scholars believe "Chrestus" is a misspelling of "Christ.")[42] Paul visits the couple and works and stays with them because, like him, they are tentmakers. Every Sabbath he preaches to the Jews and Greeks in the synagogue.

Paul is still preaching Jesus to the Jews when Silas and Timothy arrive from Macedonia. When the Jews continue to oppose him, "he [shakes] out his garments" (similar to shaking the dust from his feet [Acts 13:51; Matt. 10:14]) and tells them he is innocent and that their blood is on their own heads. Just as he had told the mockers in Pisidian Antioch, they are condemning themselves. From now on, he will go to the Gentiles.

Paul next goes to the house of Titius Justus, a God-fearing Gentile. Crispus, the synagogue ruler, and his entire household become believers, and many other Corinthians believe and are baptized. Indeed, Paul leads a remarkable number of people to Christ, exemplifying the power of the Gospel and of Spirit-filled evangelism.

One night in a vision, the Lord reassures Paul, telling him to continue preaching fearlessly "for I am with you, and no one will attack you to harm you, for I have many in this city who are my people." Scripture is consoling in its sheer consistency, for Jesus Christ, Who is here assuring Paul He is with him, is the same One Who assured His disciples, "And behold, I am with you always, to the end of the age" (Matt. 28:20). This resembles God's assurance to the Israelites, through Moses, "Be strong and courageous. Do not fear or be in dread of them, for it is the Lord your God who goes with you. He will not leave or forsake you" (Deut. 31:6; cf. Exodus 3:12; Joshua 1:5, 9; Isaiah 41:10; 43:5; Jer. 1:8).[43]

As we've seen, God does not promise believers their faith will insulate them from hardship or persecution—quite the contrary. But He does promise to be with us, comfort us, and provide us strength. Similarly, Paul declares in Romans, "And we know that for those who love God all things work together for good, for those who are called according to his purpose" (8:28). The "good" that Paul promises is no guarantee of an earthly life free of hardship, but it's an assurance that we will be conformed to Christ's image (Romans 8:29), develop a closer fellowship with God, bear good fruit for the kingdom, and ultimately be glorified (Romans 8:30).[44]

Paul remains in Corinth a year and a half, teaching the Word of God. Other than his visits to Ephesus (20:31) and Rome (28:30), this is his longest stay anywhere.[45] In Corinth, the Jews bring Paul before the tribunal, accusing him of convincing people to worship God contrary to the Law. There is a legal basis for this claim if one assumes that Christianity is a radical departure from Judaism, an entirely new religion rather than an extension of it. Note that a Roman edict gave the Jewish religion formal legal standing.

The Jews are arguing that in representing Jesus as the Messiah, Paul is deviating fundamentally from the Jewish religion and thereby promoting a new religion unsanctioned by Roman law.[46] John Calvin highlights their chicanery, writing that they "did treacherously and wickedly slander the holy man [Paul], [and] endeavored to cover an evil cause with an honest excuse"[47]—meaning that they are cloaking their specious claim that Paul is twisting Mosaic Law with their insincere concern about the integrity of Roman law.[48] Had Paul been given the chance, he probably would have argued, as he often did, that Christianity is the logical and biblical extension of Judaism, and that Jesus Christ is the promised Messiah of the Old Testament Scriptures.[49]

Gallio, the provincial proconsul, tells the Jews he would accept their complaint if a wrongdoing or vicious crime were involved. Instead, this is an internal matter of Jewish law, so he dismisses the case. The crowd then seizes the synagogue's ruler Sosthenes and beats him in front of the tribunal while Gallio ignores the melee. (Interestingly, Sosthenes later becomes a believer in Christ [1 Cor. 1:1)]. Sir William Ramsay sees great significance in Gallio's ruling, arguing that it inspired Paul to appeal to the higher Roman tribunals instead of allowing his fate to be decided by "the petty outlying court of the procurator of Judea, who was always much under the influence of the ruling party in Jerusalem."[50]

Paul remains in Corinth many more days. After taking a vow and cutting his hair at Cenchreae, he leaves for Syria, taking Priscilla and Aquila. When they arrive in Ephesus, Paul goes alone to the synagogue and talks with the Jews. He declines their offer to stay longer, saying that if God is willing, he will return to them. He is clearly in a hurry to move on, but he will not pass up a chance to preach the Gospel: "For if I preach the gospel, that gives me no ground for boasting. For necessity is laid upon me. Woe to me if I do not preach the gospel!" (1 Cor. 9:16) He sets sail from Ephesus to Caesarea, and upon arriving "went up and greeted the church," meaning the church in Jerusalem. (Note that the phrase "up to Jerusalem" is used even when people are traveling south toward the city because it sits at a high elevation so that anyone approaching it, from any direction, is literally "going up to Jerusalem." Conversely, traveling from Jerusalem to any other location is generally expressed as "going down from Jerusalem.")[51] From Jerusalem, Paul heads to Antioch, completing his second missionary journey. He then begins what scholars now call his third missionary journey, going throughout the region of Galatia and Phrygia, lifting the Church and the disciples.

Apollos, a Jewish native of Alexandria, comes to Ephesus. He is well versed in the Scriptures and eloquent, teaching about Jesus to the extent of his limited knowledge. When Priscilla and Aquila hear his powerful speaking in the synagogue, they take him aside and instruct him more fully in the Gospel. Commentators differ on whether before this further instruction, Apollos was a Christian with insufficient knowledge or not yet fully Christian. Either way, he is inarguably a devoted and knowledgeable Christian not long after. When he prepares to go to the province of Achaia and its capital Corinth, the believers encourage him and write to the disciples there to welcome him. He greatly helps strengthen the faith of the believers there, as he compellingly outdebates the Jews in public, demonstrating through the Scriptures that Jesus is the Messiah.

Paul's third missionary journey

From The New Moody Atlas of the Bible by Barry J. Beitzel (©2009). Published by Moody Publishers. Used by permission.

CHAPTER 19

◇◇◇◇◇◇◇◇◇◇◇◇◇◇◇◇◇◇◇◇◇◇◇◇

When Apollos is in Corinth, Paul passes through the interior of the Roman province of Asia and reaches Ephesus on the Aegean coast (which he visited with Priscilla and Aquila during his second missionary journey). Finding about twelve disciples there, he says to them, "Did you receive the Holy Spirit when you believed?" They admit they haven't even heard of the Holy Spirit, so Paul asks them what they were baptized into. They reply, "Into John's baptism." Paul explains that John only baptized with the baptism of repentance, and he told people to believe in Jesus, Who was coming after him. Paul then baptizes all of them in the name of Jesus. When he lays his hands on them, the Holy Spirit comes on them, and they begin speaking in tongues and prophesying.

As we've noted earlier, the Holy Spirit indwells believers immediately on their conversion (John 7:37–39; 14:15–16, 17; Acts 11:16–17; Romans 5:5; 1 Cor. 2:12; 2 Cor. 5:5; 1 John 4:13; see also Acts 10:44).[52] Not to possess the Indwelling Spirit is the same as not belonging to Christ.[53] As Paul clearly affirms, "Anyone who does not have the Spirit of Christ does not belong to him" (Romans 8:9). But in this case, it appears the disciples don't receive the Spirit until after they are baptized and Paul lays hands on them. So how do we explain this anomaly?

Some scholars believe the disciples here are not yet Christians when Paul encounters them. John Stott suggests that when Paul first meets these disciples he assumes they are believers, but on closer inspection notices they bear no evidence of the indwelling of the Holy Spirit. Once he teaches them more about the Gospel, they place their faith in Jesus and are saved. The Spirit indwells them immediately when they place their trust in Him, but when Paul lays his hands on them, they begin to show outward signs of the Spirit having come on them, as the believers did at Pentecost.[54] It is not their baptism or the laying on of hands that saves them but their faith.[55]

But we should note there is one other example in Acts—involving the Samaritan converts in Acts 8:12–17—in which it appears that the Holy Spirit doesn't immediately indwell believers upon their conversion. As discussed in an earlier chapter, the Spirit didn't indwell the Samaritan believers until some of the apostles could be present with them. Once Peter and John baptized and laid hands on them, the Spirit entered them. Some theologians surmise this is an exceptional case in a very early phase of Church history, in which the Gospel is first moving beyond Jews to Samaritans. According to this theory, God makes a special case of empowering the new believers with the Holy Spirit only after the apostles can be present. The ESV Study Bible explains, "This would show that the Samaritans should be counted full members of the one true church, the new covenant community of God's people, founded and based at that time in Jerusalem. It would also guarantee that the Samaritans, who for many generations had been hostile toward the Jews, would not establish a separate Christian church or be excluded from the church by

Jewish believers. The Spirit was given only at the hands of the apostles, to show convincingly to Samaritan and other later, non-Jewish leaders of the church that both Jews and non-Jews who believed in Jesus now had full membership status among God's people."[56]

Paul boldly preaches the kingdom of God in the synagogue for three months. But when some congregants dismiss and insult the Christian movement, Paul takes the disciples to the hall of Tyrannus. He preaches there for two years "so that people throughout the province of Asia—both Jews and Greeks—heard the word of the Lord" (19:10 NLT). Other evangelists, of course, are also on the task, spreading the Gospel throughout the region. Churches in Colosse, Laodicea, Hierapolis, and doubtless many other places are established during this period.[57] It's likely that the seven churches of Asia—those John addresses in the Book of Revelation—are founded at this time.[58] Undeniably, the province is aggressively evangelized and becomes a Christian stronghold for centuries.[59]

Through Paul, God is performing spectacular miracles. When handkerchiefs or aprons touch Paul's skin and are taken to the sick, their illnesses and evil spirits leave them, not unlike those healed by touching Jesus' garment (Mark 5:27–34; 6:56) and by coming within Peter's shadow (Acts 5:15). Meanwhile, certain itinerant Jewish exorcists presume to do their work in Jesus' name. When seven sons of Jewish high priest Sceva attempt this, the evil spirit tells them, "Jesus I know, and Paul I recognize, but who are you?" Ironically, demons are among the first to recognize Jesus' identity during his earthly ministry (Matt. 8:28; Mark 5:7; Luke 4:34). James observes that the demons recognize Jesus, though they don't place their faith in Him (James 2:19). R. C. Sproul comments, "Jesus attached singular importance to the miracle of exorcising evil spirits as a sign and manifestation of the breakthrough of the supernatural kingdom."[60] As Jesus proclaimed, "But if it is by the finger of God that I cast out demons, then the kingdom of God has come upon you" (Luke 11:20).

The exorcism attempted by Sceva's sons ends poorly, as the possessed man jumps on them and overpowers them, chasing them out of the house naked and wounded. News of this circulates to all the residents of Ephesus, Jews and Gentiles. Fear comes over them all, and the name of Jesus is greatly honored. Many who have become believers come forth, admitting they have practiced the magic arts. They bring their books, with a value of fifty thousand pieces of silver, and burn them in front of everyone. For them to make such a substantial monetary sacrifice is a powerful testimony to the genuineness of their newfound faith. The Word of God increases and prevails mightily, no doubt in part due to this dramatic gesture by the reformed occultists.[61]

After all this has transpired, Paul, led by the Holy Spirit, resolves to travel to Macedonia and Achaia (southern Greece), then to Jerusalem, and finally to Rome. In his epistle to the Romans, Paul expresses his passion for going to Rome to help strengthen their faith, but explains that it's been difficult to get there (1:9–13). Paul stays in Ephesus a little longer while sending his friends Timothy and Erastus to Macedonia. We learn from his first epistle to the Corinthians why he remains: "But I will stay in Ephesus until Pentecost, for a wide door for effective work has opened to me, and there are many adversaries" (16:8–9).

At this point, there is a major controversy concerning the Way. A silversmith named Demetrius makes silver shrines of the Greek fertility goddess Artemis, which are profitable to many craftsmen. There is a large statue of Artemis in the great temple in Ephesus, one of the wonders of the ancient world. It has 127 supporting pillars six stories-high and is four times larger than the famous Athenian Parthenon.[62] Summoning the craftsmen and others in similar trades, Demetrius tells them that in Ephesus and throughout Asia, Paul has persuaded many people that gods made with hands are not really gods. He warns that the temple of Artemis—the goddess worshipped throughout Asia and the world—will be discredited and they will suffer financially because Christian converts will quit buying their goods. This enrages the crowd; they cry out, "Great is Artemis of the Ephesians!" The city is filled with confusion as the people rush into the theater, dragging with them Gaius and Aristarchus, Paul's Macedonian traveling companions. Paul wants to go inside, but his disciples and even some friendly high-ranking provincial officers urge him not to enter.

Chaos ensues. People don't even understand why they have gathered in the theater. Some Jews urge their fellow Jew Alexander to speak against Paul, because they don't want to be associated with Christians. The crowd, however, doesn't want to hear from a Jew; for two hours, they cry, "Great is Artemis of the Ephesians!" After the town clerk manages to quiet the mob, he tries to assuage their concerns. In his view, the God Paul is preaching is no threat to the great Artemis. "Men of Ephesus," he declares, "who is there who does not know that the city of the Ephesians is temple keeper of the great Artemis, and of the sacred stone that fell from the sky?" Scholars generally believe the referenced stone is a meteorite the locals interpret as an affirming sign of their god.[63] Stressing that everyone acknowledges Artemis, the clerk tells them to calm down, because the people they have brought into the theater are neither sacrilegious nor blasphemers of Artemis. They have proclaimed Jesus, but have not denounced Artemis. There is no harm in that in their pluralistic, pagan society. If Demetrius and the craftsmen want to make a complaint against anyone, they can do so before the proconsuls in the courts. Any other matters should be resolved in the regular assembly. Then he dismisses the crowd, warning that they all could be charged with inciting a riot.

CHAPTER 20

When things calm down, Paul sends for the disciples and after encouraging them, says goodbye and leaves for Macedonia. You will recall that before the riot in Ephesus, he sent Timothy and Erastus ahead of him into Macedonia and planned to join them later (Acts 19:21). He is now headed for Jerusalem (and then hopefully Rome), but wants to go first through Macedonia and Achaia (southern Greece, where Corinth is located) to collect offerings from the Gentile churches for the Jerusalem church. In Macedonia, Paul reassures the believers. "Nothing encourages and strengthens the people of God like the Word of God," observes John Stott.[64] We don't know how long Paul stays, but F. F. Bruce speculates—and Stott agrees[65]—that this may be the period when he travels as far west as Illyricum, the Roman province on the east coast of the Adriatic Sea, northwest of Macedonia, that contains modern Croatia, Bosnia-Herzegovina, and Montenegro.[66] Paul mentions this mission in Romans 15:19.

We really don't know if Paul goes to Illyricum then, as the record is incomplete. But after his journeys in the Macedonian region, presumably revisiting churches he established in Philippi, Thessalonica, and Berea,[67] (and possibly a side trip to Illyricum, as noted), Paul heads for Greece, where he spends three months. While there, he writes his epistle to the Romans—his main theological treatise and his manifesto on the Christian faith and life.[68] As he is preparing to sail from Greece to Syria, the Jews hatch another plot against him, so he decides to go back through Macedonia. Paul has surely infuriated the Jews on previous trips to Corinth when he proselytized two synagogue rulers, Crispus and Sosthenes, after starting a church adjacent to their synagogue (Acts 18:7–8; 17; 1 Cor. 1:1, 14), and thwarted their court case against him before proconsul Gallio.[69] He is accompanied on this trip by several friends, who go ahead of him to Troas. Paul and his group head from Philippi— after the Feast of Unleavened Bread (at the end of Passover)—to Troas, arriving there in five days and staying for a week.

On Sunday, the first day of the week, Paul preaches to local Christians until midnight in an upstairs room lit with flickering lamps. This is one of the earliest references to Christians meeting for worship services on Sunday. They may have still observed the Saturday Jewish Sabbath, but eventually Sunday—the day Jesus was resurrected—becomes the Christians' main day of worship.[70] As Paul speaks for a long while, a young man named Eutychus, sitting on the windowsill, falls asleep and plunges three stories below to his death. Paul goes down, bends over him, and takes him into his arms. "Don't worry," says Paul, "he's alive." Going back upstairs, they all share in the Lord's Supper and eat together, and Paul continues speaking to them until dawn, when he leaves. They take Eutychus away, and everyone is greatly relieved that he is indeed alive.

Paul's raising of Eutychus through the Holy Spirit is reminiscent of Jesus raising the dead widow's son at Nain (Luke 7:11–15), Jairus' daughter (Luke 8:49–56), and Lazarus (John 11:38–44), and also Peter's resurrection of Dorcas (Acts 9:36–41). This event also resembles the Old Testament resurrections by Elijah and Elisha, who stretched themselves over the dead person's body (1 Kings 17:21; 2 Kings 4:34), just as Paul does with Eutychus.[71] The abundance of such parallels throughout the Bible demonstrates its remarkable unity and validates its authenticity, which is one reason our faith is continually strengthened as we read the Bible and are reminded why we must stay in the Word.

John Polhill observes that all the New Testament resurrections are symbolic of Christ's resurrection, reinforcing that pivotal moment in the minds of Christians. Circumstances accompanying Eutychus' restoration to life are particularly suggestive of Jesus' resurrection: it's Easter time, the Passover has just ended, and it's Sunday, the day on which Jesus' resurrection occurred, as noted above.[72]

Luke and the others sail to Assos (an ancient city on the east coast of the Aegean Sea in the Roman province of Myasia in Anatolia),[73] while Paul travels by land and joins them there. Together they sail to Mitylene. The next day they sail past the island of Chios, and cross to the island of Samos the day after, arriving at Miletus a day later. Paul decides to sail past Ephesus to avoid spending further time in the province of Asia, as he is rushing to get to Jerusalem in hopes of making the Pentecost Festival. Some commentators speculate that Paul also may have skipped Ephesus out of fear for his life. He had recently written to the Corinthians "of the affliction we experienced in Asia. For we were so utterly burdened beyond our strength that we despaired of life itself. Indeed, we felt that we had received the sentence of death" (2 Cor. 1:8–9).[74] When they land at Miletus, Paul sends for the elders at Ephesus, inviting them to come and meet him, and he delivers his farewell address to them.

Paul reminds them of the many trials he endured in Asia doing God's work, humbly and with many tears, because of Jewish plots (referencing the adversity he encountered with nonbelievers, immature believers, and false teachers).[75] He never shies away from declaring the Gospel message: they must repent from their sin, turn to God, and have faith in Jesus Christ, for salvation is by faith alone, for both Jews and Gentiles. As he writes, "For by grace you have been saved through faith. And this is not your own doing; it is the gift of God, not a result of works, so that no one may boast" (Eph. 2:8–9; see also Gal. 2:21; Phil 3:9; Romans 1:16, 10:9–13).

This is not the only time Paul reminds his audience of his faithfulness in preaching the Gospel despite opposition. In his first epistle to the Thessalonians, he writes, "For you yourselves know, brothers, that our coming to you was not in vain. But though we had already suffered and been shamefully treated at Philippi, as you know, we had boldness in our God to declare to you the gospel of God in the midst of much conflict. . . . For we never came with words of flattery, as you know, nor with a pretext for greed—God is witness. Nor did we seek glory from people, whether from you or from others, though we could have made demands as apostles of Christ. . . . You are witnesses, and God also, how holy and righteous and blameless was our conduct toward you believers. For you know how, like a father with his children, we exhorted each one of you and encouraged you and charged you to walk in a manner worthy of God, who calls you into his own kingdom and glory" (2:1–2, 5–6, 10–12).

Paul explains that he is compelled by the Spirit to go to Jerusalem. He doesn't know the future, except that the Holy Spirit has warned him that jail and suffering lie ahead in city after city. Imagine Paul's predicament. He is duty bound to the Holy Spirit to go Jerusalem, though the Spirit has forewarned him of impending distress there. This probably explains why he requests prayer from the Roman church before his arrival in Jerusalem. He writes, "I appeal to you, brothers, by our Lord Jesus Christ and by the love of the Spirit, to strive together with me in your prayers to God on my behalf, that I may be delivered from the unbelievers in Judea, and that my service for Jerusalem may be acceptable to the saints [the believers], so that by God's will I may come to you with joy and be refreshed in your company" (Romans 15:30–32). Paul seeks God's protection for his works in Jerusalem, and for his planned trip to Rome to meet with those to whom is writing. Again, his predominant motives are always other-directed. To be sure, he asks for personal protection, but His ultimate aims are to preach the Gospel, strengthen and encourage believers, and glorify God.

Accordingly, Paul tells the Ephesian elders that his life means nothing to him unless he finishes the task of spreading the Gospel and the news of God's wonderful grace. He remarks that they will never see him again, but avers that he has been faithful in preaching the Word, so he is "innocent of the blood of all"—if anyone suffers eternal death, it will not be his fault, because he has faithfully declared to them "the whole counsel of God." Paul has never compromised the Gospel message, but has always preached God's complete revelation concerning Jesus Christ—both Old Testament and New Testament—through whom the believer is saved.[76]

As he won't be present to guide them, the Holy Spirit has made them overseers of the "flock," and they must remain vigilant and guard themselves and God's Church, which was purchased with Christ's blood. He is delivering them a daunting call. The Holy Spirit has appointed them as leaders. Paul is usually the human agent in making these appointments, but always under the guidance of the Holy Spirit. False teachers will approach the flock like vicious wolves. Even some of the brothers will distort the truth to draw followers to themselves. Having looked out for them and shed many tears on their behalf for three years, Paul says he is now entrusting them to God and His uplifting message of grace, which will save them and set them apart to Him. Invoking the familiar imagery of wolves and sheep employed by Christ (Matt. 7:15; John 10:12–13), Paul is warning them of inevitable attacks from both outside and inside the Church. The external foes, he adds, are easier to detect than false teachers inside the Church, whose attacks are insidiously disguised as faithful biblical teaching. They will say "twisted things" to lure believers away. The accuracy of Paul's predictions is confirmed in his epistles to Timothy and in the book of Revelation (1 Tim. 1:6–7, 9–20; 4:1–3; 2 Tim. 1:15; 2:17–18; 3:1–9; Rev. 2:1–7).[77]

This phenomenon continues today, as some pastors dilute or twist scriptural truth to cater to popular culture. We must never let our guard down or remove our spiritual armor, for we will always be plagued by spiritual warfare, which is occurring in the heavenly realms. Paul explains this in his epistle to the Ephesians: "For we do not wrestle against flesh and blood, but against the rulers, against the authorities, against the cosmic powers over this present darkness, against the spiritual forces of evil in the heavenly places. Therefore take up the whole armor of God, that you may be able to withstand in the evil day, and having done all, to stand firm" (6:12–13). The enemy will not be finally defeated before the end of time, and he will always be hunting for souls, so we have to remain ever vigilant.

Paul says he has never coveted other people's property, and that through his labor, he has provided for his own and other people's needs. His hard work should serve as an example of how to assist the needy. They must remember Jesus' words: "It is more blessed to give than to receive." They must order their priorities to reflect the superior importance of spiritual matters, avoid preoccupation with material things, and focus on advancing the Gospel.

After completing his speech, Paul kneels and prays with the elders. Saddened by Paul's prediction that he will never see them again, they cry as they embrace, kiss him, and escort him to the ship. This is a poignant scene, where Paul is parting with his companions for the final time. They have become foxhole friends, enduring together many hardships and obstacles to form an indelible bond of camaraderie and love. "How wonderful it must have been to be so thoroughly, completely, and healthily bound to others, not through the earthly cords of family or marriage, but with ties that are even closer—those of a shared Savior, a shared salvation, a shared solution to the deepest problems of the soul," writes Bruce Barton. "These believers possessed in Christ the kind of depth and integrity in relating to one another that the world longs for but so rarely finds."[78]

This shared love between Paul and his companions transcends ordinary human love among friends in the spirit of God's commandment that we love our neighbors as we love ourselves (Lev. 19:18). Jesus reiterated and endorsed this directive when one of the scribes asked Him to identify the most important commandment. He replied, "The most important is, 'Hear O Israel: The Lord our God, the Lord is one. And you shall love the Lord your God with all your heart and with all your soul and with all your mind and with all your strength.' The second is this: 'You shall love your neighbor as yourself.' There is no other commandment greater than these" (Mark 12:29–31). Our relationships with friends should be modeled on and reflect our love for God. In his epistle to the Galatians, Paul echoes this teaching, "For the whole law is fulfilled in one word: 'You shall love your neighbor as yourself'" (5:14).

In the next chapter, we'll see that the attacks on Paul continue in Jerusalem and even in his effort to stand before Caesar in Rome. Along the way, Paul encounters angry mobs, is protected by Roman soldiers, is thrown into prison, testifies boldly before two Roman governors, and is almost killed in a shipwreck. During this time, Luke records so many verifiable details that scholars can't help but admit it's eyewitness testimony. Let's join with Luke and Paul on their final trip.

CHAPTER FIVE

ACTS 21–28

ARREST OF AN APOSTLE

Once, when walking down a certain street in Chicago, D.L. Moody stepped up to a man, a perfect stranger to him, and said, "Sir, are you a Christian?" "You mind your own business," was the reply. Moody replied, "This is my business."

—D. L. MOODY[1]

CHAPTER 21

Paul and his group leave Miletus and sail down the coast of Asia Minor, then board a ship headed for Tyre to unload its cargo. They seek out the disciples in Tyre, who warn Paul through the Spirit not to go to Jerusalem. After staying in Tyre a week, the disciples accompany them outside the city to the beach, where they all pray together and say goodbye.

Continuing south along the coast and arriving at Ptolemais, they greet the believers and stay with them for a day. This city got its name during the intertestamental period when the Ptolemies of Egypt occupied the area after Alexander the Great's empire was divided following his death.[2] Still traveling south, they arrive the next day at Caesarea and go to the house of Philip the evangelist—one of the seven men the apostles had chosen to distribute food—whose four unmarried daughters have the gift of prophecy. Philip is called "the evangelist" because of his fruitful work in winning souls in Samaria (Acts 8:4–13) and along the Mediterranean coast (8:40), and possibly even founding the church in Caesarea.[3]

A few days later Agabus, a prophet from Judea, comes to Philip's house. He takes Paul's belt and binds his own feet and hands with it, saying, "Thus says the Holy Spirit, 'This is how the Jews at Jerusalem will bind the man who owns this belt and deliver him into the hands of the Gentiles." The phrase "handed over to the Gentiles" mirrors Christ's statement that He was going up to Jerusalem to be delivered over to the Gentiles (Luke 18:31–32). Agabus's use of visual signs is in the pattern of the Old Testament prophets Ezekiel, Isaiah, and Jeremiah, who repeatedly employed this technique to warn Israel of its coming exile if it did not repent (Ezek. 4:1–12, 12:3; Isaiah 20:2–3; Jer. 13:1; 27:2).[4] Old and New Testament prophets functioned differently in that the former were mainly engaged in revealing the coming Messiah, the impending exile, and other future events, whereas the latter, like Agabus, mostly predict events in the immediate future.[5]

Despite pleas from his group, Paul cannot be dissuaded. He asks, "Why all this weeping? You are breaking my heart! I am ready not only to be jailed at Jerusalem but even to die for the sake of the Lord Jesus." The men yield, saying, "The Lord's will be done."

These warnings from the Holy Spirit not to go to Jerusalem are curious in light of Paul's own promptings from the Holy Spirit to go there (Acts 19:21; 20:22). Why would the Holy Spirit send conflicting messages? As John Calvin asks, "Here ariseth a question, how the brethren can dissuade him by the Spirit from doing that which Paul did testify he doth by the secret motion of the same Spirit? Is the Spirit contrary to himself, that he doth now loose Paul whom he held bound inwardly?"[6] There is no inconsistency, however, because although the prophets are forewarning Paul of imminent danger, Paul knows his higher calling requires him to subordinate his own safety unless the danger will imperil his mission. Calvin suggests the prophets' admonitions were evidence of God's grace designed to prepare Paul for difficulties he would encounter as he pursued his Spirit-led mission. John Polhill comments, "The warnings along the way prepared Paul for the imprisonment and hardship that did indeed befall him there, fortified him for the experience, and convinced him that God was in it all."[7]

Thus, like Jesus, Paul is determined to go on to Jerusalem despite the danger (Luke 9:51). Moreover, Paul is no stranger to suffering for Christ's sake and never yields to it. "For the sake of Christ, then, I am content with weaknesses, insults, hardships, persecutions, and calamities," he writes. "For when I am weak, then I am strong" (2 Cor. 12:10). Furthermore, he declares,

> Whatever gain I had, I counted as loss for the sake of Christ. Indeed, I count everything as loss because of the surpassing worth of knowing Christ Jesus my Lord. For his sake I have suffered the loss of all things and count them as rubbish, in order that I may gain Christ and be found in him, not having a righteousness of my own that comes from the law, but that which comes through faith in Christ, the righteousness from God that depends on faith—that I may know him and the power of his resurrection, and may share his sufferings, becoming like him in his death, that by any means possible I may attain the resurrection from the dead (Phil. 3:7–11).

Finally, he exclaims, "We rejoice in our sufferings, knowing that suffering produces endurance, and endurance produces character, and character produces hope, and hope does not put us to shame, because God's love has been poured into our hearts through the Holy Spirit who has been given to us" (Romans 5:3–5). Without minimizing Paul's commendable spirit of sacrifice, it's noteworthy that he is fortified by the Christian fellowship he experiences in every town he visits. It's a biblical testament to the enduring importance of Christian community and the strength each of us receives from our Christian friendships. Paul writes from experience when he says, "Therefore encourage one another and build one another up, just as you are doing" (1 Thess. 5:11).

Significantly, Luke and the other believers finally capitulate—not based on Paul's power of persuasion, but because they know that despite the prophets' spirit-led warnings, God's will is that Paul complete his mission.

Soon they pack and leave for Jerusalem. Some believers from Caesarea go with them and take them to the home of Mnason of Cyprus, an early believer, where they are warmly welcomed. The next day they go to meet James (the brother of Jesus and leader of the Jerusalem church) and all the Jerusalem elders. Paul provides them a detailed account of what God has accomplished through him in his ministry to the Gentiles. Again, Paul's humility shines through, as he credits God rather than himself. Hearing this news, they praise God and inform Paul that thousands of Jews have also become believers while still earnestly following the Law of Moses. These Jewish Christians have heard that Paul is teaching the Jews who live among the Gentiles to abandon Mosaic Law and to refrain from circumcising their children or following other Jewish customs. They ask Paul, "What should we do? They will certainly hear that you have come." James and the elders support Paul's mission but are concerned that his attitude toward the Law is hindering their own mission to the Jews.[8]

They answer their own question, telling Paul he should go to the Temple with four men who have completed their vow, join them in the purification ceremony, and pay for them to have their heads ritually shaved. Then people will realize that Paul does in fact observe Jewish laws. Meanwhile, Gentile believers should continue following the rules decided at the Jerusalem Council, of which they were informed by letter: abstain from eating food offered to idols, from consuming the blood or meat of strangled animals, and from sexual immorality.

Paul complies and accompanies the men to the Temple the next day, probably caring more about restoring harmony to facilitate the advance of the Gospel than about vindicating himself. Paul is not withdrawing from the rules established by the Jerusalem Council, which dealt with whether Gentiles had to be circumcised to be saved. However, though observance of the Law does not contribute toward anyone's salvation, there is nothing wrong with Jews continuing to observe their customs as part of their national identity or as cultural expressions of piety.[9] Paul doesn't want to impose stumbling blocks for Jewish believers, and as long as these ritual observances cause no theological confusion (concerning salvation by faith alone) they should do no harm.

As the purification ritual has already begun, Paul publicly announces the date when the men's vows would end and sacrifices would be offered for each of them. When the seven days are almost completed, the Jews from Asia see Paul. They stir up the crowd and lay their hands on Paul, shouting out that Paul has been disrespecting the Law and the Temple. There is no small irony here in that two of these allegations were made against Stephen (Acts 6:13), in whose persecution and death Paul participated, as he freely admits. They accuse Paul of bringing Gentiles into the Temple and defiling it because they have previously seen the Ephesian Trophimus with him in the city and assume Paul has brought him into the Temple. Gentiles are not allowed to enter the Temple but only the outer courtyard, which is aptly called the court of the Gentiles.[10] These charges incite the crowd, which seizes Paul and drags him out of the Temple.

As they are trying to kill him, the commander of the Roman regiment learns of the uproar and leads his soldiers into the mob, saving Paul. The commander arrests him, has him bound with two chains, and asks the crowd who he is and what he's done. The people give varied answers, so the commander orders that Paul be taken to the barracks. When he comes to the steps, the soldiers carry him to protect him from the violent mob, which is following and shouting, "Away with him!"— the same words the mobs screamed at Jesus (Luke 23:18; John 19:15).[11]

As they are about to enter the barracks, Paul asks the commander for permission to speak. The commander asks him if he speaks Greek and whether he is the Egyptian who recently incited a riot and led four thousand assassins into the wilderness. Paul answers that he is a Jew from Tarsus and begs him for permission to speak to the people. After receiving permission, Paul stands on the steps and addresses them in Aramaic, the common language of Palestinian Jews.[12]

CHAPTER 22

Paul asks the people to listen to his defense, and when they hear him speaking in Aramaic they grow quiet. He says He is a Jew born in Tarsus but brought up in Jerusalem. He seeks rapport with his audience, emphasizing that he spent his formative years in Jerusalem, and instead of attending the prestigious colleges in his hometown of Tarsus, he studied under the renowned Jewish teacher Gamaliel, who taught him the strict manner of the Jewish Law. Gamaliel, you will recall from Acts 5:34–39, is the venerated rabbi who intervened at the Sanhedrin to prevent the Jews from killing Peter and the apostles, arguing that the matter would resolve itself—if God had not inspired their cause, it would naturally implode, but if He had, they would not be able to stop it.

Paul admits that in his zeal for God he persecuted and killed Christians and sent many men and women to prison, which the high priest and the Sanhedrin can confirm. Paul makes the same case in his epistle to the Galatians: "For you have heard of my former life in Judaism, how I persecuted the church of God violently and tried to destroy it. And I was advancing in Judaism beyond many of my own age among my people, so extremely zealous was I for the traditions of my fathers" (1:13–14). He says he obtained letters from the Jewish rulers to arrest Christians in Damascus and return them to Jerusalem to be punished. Then he recounts his conversion on the road to Damascus and tells how afterward Ananias, a devout and well-respected man among the Jews, restored Paul's sight and told Paul that "the God of our fathers" had appointed him to know His will, to see the Righteous One, and to hear His voice, and that he would be His witness for Him. The phrase "the God of our fathers" is meant to help Paul further identify with his listeners and to force them to deal squarely with the magnitude of their error in condemning him. For how dare they punish one whom God—the God of their fathers, Abraham, Isaac, and Jacob—specifically appointed as His messenger?

Paul says Ananias told him to rise and be baptized and have his sins washed away in the name of the Righteous One. Paul's baptism was important as the outward and visible sign of his spiritual rebirth in Christ and the inner cleansing power of His blood.[13] Paul continues, relating that when he returned to Jerusalem and was praying in the Temple, he fell into a trance and saw Christ, who told him to leave Jerusalem quickly because the Jews would not accept his testimony about Him. Paul told Christ that the people knew he had imprisoned and beaten people who believed in Him, and that he watched approvingly when Stephen was stoned. Christ told him to leave, as He was sending him far away to the Gentiles.

The crowd has listened to Paul to this point, but they suddenly shout that he isn't fit to live and throw off their garments. It's clear what agitates the crowd: Paul told them God had commanded him to bring salvation to the Gentiles—which confirms their assumption that he's a spiritual traitor and probably that he has, in fact, taken a Gentile into the inner courts of the Temple.[14]

The commander orders Paul be brought into the barracks and examined by flogging to determine why the crowd is so angry with him. As they are about to flog him, Paul asks whether it's legal for them to beat a Roman citizen who hasn't been convicted. Hearing this, the centurion asks the commander what he's doing. Then the commander asks Paul if he's a Roman citizen. Paul affirms he is; the commander says he himself paid a huge price for his own citizenship, and Paul responds that he is a citizen by birth. The interrogators withdraw immediately, and the commander fearfully realizes he has unlawfully bound Paul.[15]

The next day the commander unbinds Paul and orders the chief priests and the Sanhedrin to meet. He brings Paul to them, understanding the charges against Paul involve whether he violated Jewish Law and that such issues must be submitted to the Sanhedrin. If Paul were found innocent, the commander could release him, and if found guilty, he would go before the Roman governor.[16] Just as Pilate initially passed off the question of Jesus' fate to Herod, the commander, Claudius Lysias, wants to wash his hands of this matter. He will do so shortly.[17]

CHAPTER 23

Looking intently at the Sanhedrin, Paul declares he has lived his life before God with a clear conscience, whereupon the high priest Ananias commands those standing by Paul to strike him on the mouth. Paul is not trying to provoke them. He is merely telling them what he has told so many others—that he has a clear conscience. He is recorded as saying it more than twenty times (e.g. Acts 24:16; Romans 9:1; 1 Cor. 4:4, 2 Cor. 1:12, 1 Tim. 1:5; 3:9; 2 Tim. 1:3)[18] He is hardly claiming to be sinless—he says quite the opposite in his letters (cf. Romans 7:15, 19). But since his conversion, he has faithfully performed all the duties God has assigned him. What better way to stress his veracity than to look them straight in their eyes and speak forthrightly? After all, he has no one else speaking on his behalf. In this hearing, his accusers and his judges are the same people. While he desperately wants to be released to continue his mission, he is not about to compromise the truth to pander his way to liberty.

But Paul's declaration is particularly offensive to the Jewish authorities because he is not merely proclaiming his innocence; he is accusing them of wrongdoing. In essence, he is calling them liars, challenging their worldview and their entire reason for existence. They, the paragons of virtue and spiritual discernment, are unable to see that the Messiah their prophets had promised has already come. Couple that with what we learn about Ananias from Jewish historian Josephus—he is an insolent and ill-tempered Sadducee[19]—and it's no surprise Ananias reacts violently. Paul says to him, "God is going to strike you, you whitewashed wall! Are you sitting to judge me according to the law, and yet contrary to the law you order me to be struck?" This recalls Jesus' exclamation that the Pharisees were "like whitewashed tombs, which outwardly appear beautiful, but within are full of dead people's bones and all uncleanness. So you also outwardly appear righteous to others, but within you are full of hypocrisy and lawlessness" (Matt. 23:27–28).

Paul is hitting them squarely in their hearts—they are full of righteous appearances, but morally hollow inside. This infuriates Ananias. Those standing by Paul rebuke him for disrespecting the high priest, and Paul responds that he was unaware Ananias is the high priest, as he would not intentionally violate the biblical admonition against speaking evil of a ruler (Exodus 22:28).

Paul, realizing that some of the group before him are Sadducees and others Pharisees, shrewdly pits them against each other by claiming he is on trial because of his hope in the resurrection of the dead. To be sure, he is still denying his heresy from Pharisaic Judaism, which has now found its fulfillment in Christianity.[20] But in the process, he can hopefully divide the two groups and also evangelize—always his heart's foremost mission. He has squarely placed the centerpiece of Christianity—Christ's resurrection—at the forefront of the debate.

Immediately, a dispute arises between the two groups because the Sadducees don't believe in the resurrection, angels, or spirits, and the Pharisees do. A major uproar ensues, as some scribes among the Pharisees say they find nothing wrong with Paul, noting that it's possible a spirit or angel has spoken to him. Astonishingly, the Pharisees are so adamant about the resurrection and their theological differences with the Sadducees that they acknowledge Paul may be innocent. When the situation becomes violent the commander, fearing for Paul's safety, orders the soldiers to take him to the barracks. Appearing the following night, Christ stands by Paul and says, "Take courage, for as you have testified to the facts about me in Jerusalem, so you must testify also in Rome."

Paul must be profoundly reassured by Christ's reaffirmation that His hand of protection is on him. Christ will send him to Rome to preach the Gospel after all. Jesus isn't promising Paul freedom from suffering, but confirming that he will be allowed to complete his long-anticipated task of witnessing in the heart of the Gentile world.

Any calm in the action, however, is short-lived. Forty Jews bind themselves by oath not to eat or drink until they have killed Paul. They inform the chief priests and elders of their plan, telling them to join the Sanhedrin in notifying the commander to bring Paul before them. They pretend they will examine his case more thoroughly, but plan to kill Paul on his way there. Paul's nephew hears of the plot and tells Paul, who instructs one of the centurions to take his nephew to the commander to inform him. Upon learning of the scheme, the commander orders the nephew to tell no one else about it.

The commander—Claudius Lysias—orders two centurions to prepare two hundred soldiers, seventy horsemen, and two hundred spearmen to take Paul sixty miles to Caesarea at 9:00 that night to see governor Felix. Lysias writes a letter to Felix summarizing these events, reporting that he has rescued the Roman citizen Paul from a Jewish plot to kill him. He says the charges against Paul involve Jewish Law and do not warrant his death or imprisonment. Lysias tells Felix that when he learned of the plot he arranged to send Paul to him immediately, ordering Paul's accusers to bring their case before Felix.

The solders take Paul that night to Antipatris, some thirty-five miles from Jerusalem and a little over halfway to Caesarea, and send Paul with the horsemen the rest of the way. When they reach Caesarea and deliver the commander's letter to Felix, they also present Paul to him. Felix reads the letter and asks Paul what province he is from. Paul replies that he's from Cilicia, a Roman province united to the province of Syria, which is ruled by Felix's superior.[21] Accordingly, Felix says he will give Paul a full hearing when his accusers arrive, then commands that he be guarded in Herod's headquarters.

CHAPTER 24

Ananias and the elders come to Caesarea five days later with their lawyer Tertullus and present their case against Paul to Felix. After flattering Felix about his good governance, Tertullus describes Paul as a plague and a ringleader of the Nazarene sect who incites riots among Jews throughout the world and attempted to profane the Temple. Note that the Jews had previously accused Paul of profaning the Temple, but now they allege he merely attempted to do so.

F. F. Bruce argues that had the Jews found a way to produce any witnesses that Paul had taken a Gentile into the inner sections of the Temple, the Sanhedrin would have acquired jurisdiction over the case. But since no witnesses came forward, they now hoped to twist facts and convict Paul of the lesser offense of attempting to profane the Temple. This is still a gravely serious charge, because the Romans gave the Jews wide latitude on matters involving offenses against their Temple. Although the Jews have no general authority to impose capital punishment, the one exception to this is cases involving the sanctity of the Temple.[22] Indeed, Jewish historian Josephus reports that the Romans appeared to have authorized the Sanhedrin to execute perpetrators of blatant sacrilege.[23] At any rate, Paul's accusers charge that he was trying to take a Gentile into the Temple but was thwarted when the authorities arrested him. This is a lie; he was actually stopped by a riotous mob based on their false assumption that he'd profaned the Temple, as described above.[24]

At the hearing, Paul's opponents—just like Jesus' accusers at His trial—attempt to frame their theological dispute as a criminal and political matter, preposterously depicting Paul as a threat to the peace and security of Rome.[25] Nor, for that matter, is Paul a traitor to the Jews, as he would seek to clarify in his remarks. But it's fascinating that Jesus' Jewish enemies also charge Him with sedition and being a threat to the state, along with their bogus claims that He blasphemed and threatened to destroy the Temple.[26] And just like Jesus, who did not challenge Rome's political authority ("Therefore render to Caesar the things that are Caesar's, and to God the things that are God's" [Matt. 22:21; Mark 12:17; Luke 20:25]), Paul advocates submitting to governmental rulers: "Let every person be subject to the governing authorities" (Romans 13:1). The Gospel that Paul preaches, then, threatens neither Roman law nor Jewish Scriptures, but upholds them. Paul might challenge the Romans' misuse of their authority and the Jews' misinterpretation of their laws, but he does not dispute their authority or the integrity of the Law.[27]

Tertullus tells Felix he can confirm the charges by examining Paul. The Jews then level their charges, after which Felix permits Paul to respond. Paul tells Felix that, contrary to the Jews' claims, he was in Jerusalem for more than twelve days worshipping and neither got into arguments nor stirred up the crowds in the Temple, synagogue, or anywhere else in the city. He confidently asserts that his accusers cannot prove their charges against him.

Paul emphasizes his central theme: Christians worship the same God as his accusers—the God of Abraham, Isaac, and Jacob—and believe everything written in the Old Testament Scriptures, including that there will be a resurrection of both the just and the unjust. He is involved in no sect, but upholds the sanctity of the Jewish Scriptures. Paul tells Felix, just as he had told the Sanhedrin, that he strives to maintain a clear conscience toward both God and man. This is not merely Paul's proclamation of innocence, but constitutes further proof that he's in sync with the people of God—the Jews—who also seek to observe the Law and do good works.[28]

Paul aims to shame his accusers for bringing false charges against him. He says that after several years, he returned to bring alms to his people and to present offerings, and they found him purified in the Temple without causing any disturbances. He was observing and honoring the holiness of the Temple, not desecrating it. He notes that if the Asian Jews have anything against him, they should be there to argue their case. As they are not there, it falls upon the Jews who are there to make their own case against him—which they cannot do, other than to show that he confessed his hope in the resurrection of the dead. This is brilliant, because if Paul is guilty of believing in the resurrection, so are the many Pharisees who are members of the Sanhedrin.[29]

Admittedly, however, Christians differ from Pharisees on the resurrection as well. Christians believe in the resurrection not just as an abstract hope, but a reality that has already begun in Jesus Christ.[30] As Paul writes to the Corinthians, "For as by a man came death, by a man has come also the resurrection of the dead. For as in Adam all die, so also in Christ all shall be made alive. But each in his own order; Christ the firstfruits, then at his coming those who belong to Christ" (1 Cor. 15:21–23). Moreover, Christians believe their resurrection to eternal life depends not on their righteousness from following the Law but on their faith in Jesus Christ (Philipp. 3:9–11).

Here, Paul has artfully narrowed the relevant issue to one exclusively involving religion, not politics. Is Jesus the Messiah—the Way, the Truth, and the Life? For Paul and the other Christians say He is the only way, and the Jews say He is dead. You couldn't have more diametrically opposed positions, and these cannot be resolved by the Roman authorities, because not only have they ceded jurisdiction over such internal matters to the Jewish authorities, but they are wholly unequipped to pass on such decidedly sectarian issues.

Felix, who is well acquainted with "the Way," adjourns the proceedings and announces that he will make his decision when the commander Lysias arrives. Felix orders the centurion to keep Paul under guard but to give him some freedom and allow his friends to attend his needs. This is obviously a dodge, as Lysias has already stated in his written report to Felix that this is a matter of Jewish Law, and that he doesn't believe Paul is guilty of criminal wrongdoing warranting death or imprisonment. Moreover, as subsequent events prove, Felix has no intention of deciding the matter, especially not in the near future. There's a reason for that:

the Jews manifestly have not made their case against Paul, but Felix does not want to acquit Paul and alienate them. This could lead to more unrest and chaos, which Felix wants to avoid at all costs.[31]

A few days later Felix brings his Jewish wife Drusilla, and also sends for Paul, seeking to speak to them about Paul's faith in Jesus Christ. Paul's explanation of righteousness, self-control, and the coming judgment alarms Felix, who tells him to go away and that he will summon him later when it's convenient. Hoping Paul will offer him a bribe, Felix sends for him frequently. This is a fascinating turn of events. While Felix is seeking a bribe and wants to placate the Jews, he and his wife are also intrigued by the Gospel and want to learn more about it from one of its foremost authorities. They seem truly troubled by Paul's statements about righteousness and self-control (we know from Josephus that the couple had a marital history tainted by promiscuity)[32] and about the coming judgment. John Polhill likens this scene to a genuinely tragic plot. "A thorough skeptic," writes Polhill, "would have dismissed Paul's reference to the judgment as sheer fantasy, but not Felix. His fear was genuine. He was at the point of conviction. But he was never willing to go beyond that point and take the leap of faith. In the end his pride, his greed, his lust, and his desire to preserve his power carried the day."[33]

How many people have we met who fit that description? Who can deny the tragic nature of this all too frequent scenario? After two years, Porcius Festus succeeds Felix in office, but to placate the Jews, Felix leaves Paul in prison.

CHAPTER 25

Three days after Festus arrives in Caesarea, he travels to Jerusalem, where the chief priests and Jewish leaders present their case against Paul and urge him to summon Paul to Jerusalem. Still obsessed with the case after two years, they are jumping on the first opportunity to revive the matter once Festus is in office. But of course, their true motive, as Luke makes clear, is not to secure a change of venue from Caesarea to Jerusalem but to ambush and kill Paul while he is being transferred for trial. Festus replies that Paul will remain in Caesarea and that he himself will return there shortly, so if they want to bring charges against Paul they may go back with him.

A week and a half later, Festus goes to Caesarea, convenes the court, and orders Paul to appear before him. When Paul arrives, the Jerusalem Jews attempt to make their case against him. Their evidence has not strengthened after two years, but perhaps they are hoping a new judge will decide differently.

Paul defends himself with a simple denial of each charge, proclaiming his innocence of any offense against the Jewish Law, the Temple, or Caesar. Festus, seeking to appease the Jews, asks Paul if he wants to be tried before him in Jerusalem. Paul replies that he should be tried before Caesar's tribunal, which is the appropriate venue. He maintains he has done nothing wrong to the Jews, as Festus well knows. Paul adds that if he has committed any wrongdoing for which he deserves to die, he will not seek to escape the death penalty. On the other hand, if the Jews' charges against him are spurious, he must not be turned over to them. Paul declares, "I appeal to Caesar."

After conferring with his advisers, Festus replies, "To Caesar you have appealed; to Caesar shall you go." Roman citizens had long enjoyed the right to appeal a magistrate's decision to the people (perhaps since the founding of the republic in 509 BC),[34] and when Rome became an empire, the appeal began going to the emperor directly, replacing the former jury of peers[35]—although apparently, in some cases, there is no right of appeal. In any event, the right is limited to Roman citizens, and when there is a right of appeal, the magistrate is required to transfer the case to Rome.[36] By contrast, there is no such right to appeal for provincial subjects of the empire. Even as late as 112 AD under Pliny, Roman citizens convicted as Christians are sent to Rome for examination and judgment by the emperor, but non-citizens are summarily handled.[37]

It seems Paul really has no choice but to appeal to Caesar. The last thing a wrongly accused party wants is for politics to corrupt the legal process. It would be imprudent for Paul to consent either to be tried by the Jewish authorities or to have the Roman proceeding moved to Jerusalem, with all its attendant hatred and bias against him. Even if Festus were an honorable man, there would be immense pressure on him to find Paul guilty irrespective of the evidence, which is obvious from

Festus' newfound willingness to move the location of the trial. How could Paul reasonably expect fair treatment from the local authorities when he has been held in prison for two years, though completely innocent?

Some days later, King Agrippa and his sister Bernice, who are living together incestuously,[38] arrive in Caesarea and greet Festus. During their lengthy stay, Festus explains Paul's case to Agrippa, conceding that he didn't know how to investigate such issues, so he asked Paul whether he wanted to be tried in Jerusalem. This seems disingenuous, because Festus knew these religious charges were irrelevant in his tribunal, and he indicated he was going to remain the trier of fact even if he transferred the case to Jerusalem. He wasn't confused; he just didn't have the courage to declare Paul innocent, which was the only honorable option.[39] But since Paul requested to be tried by the Roman authorities, Festus kept him in custody until he could send him to Caesar. Agrippa then tells Festus he would like to hear from Paul, and Festus agrees to make that happen.

The next day, Agrippa and Bernice arrive with great pomp, entering the auditorium with their military officers and prominent city officials. At Festus' command, Paul is brought into the room. Paul is not physically imposing. One extra-biblical account describes him as "a man little of stature, thin-haired upon the head, crooked in the legs, of good state of body, with eyebrows joining, and nose somewhat hooked, full of grace: for sometimes he appeared like a man, and sometimes he had the face of an angel."[40] What Paul lacks in physicality, however, he more than compensates for with his grace and intelligence. Addressing Agrippa and others present, Festus reports that the entire Jewish community both in Jerusalem and in Caesarea has petitioned for Paul's death. Festus allows that he has found no conduct of Paul deserving of death, but has decided to send him to Rome because Paul appealed to Caesar. He explains that he has convened this assembly to ascertain facts that he can include in a letter to Rome specifying the charges against Paul. Knowing that Agrippa has deep knowledge of Jewish customs and laws,[41] Festus hopes Agrippa can give him wise counsel.

It's clear that this conference before Agrippa is not a trial. Festus was divested of authority to hear the case officially the moment Paul appealed to Caesar.[42] Yielding to pressure from the Jews, Festus has created a dilemma for himself—he wants to mollify the Jews without perverting Roman justice. He's looking for some way out of it, and is probably hoping that despite the lack of credible evidence against Paul, something might develop from this hearing to justify sending the case to Rome.[43]

CHAPTER 26

Agrippa grants Paul permission to speak in his own defense, and Paul begins by acknowledging his good fortune in appearing before Agrippa on these charges, as he is familiar with Jewish customs and controversies. After asking Agrippa to listen patiently, he articulates his defense. I notice that Paul repeatedly implores his audiences, whether Church congregants or judicial tribunals, to listen intently to his words. This is neither a clever device to mesmerize them nor the plea of one who protests too much; it is an expression of sincerity, emanating from a heart devoted to God. He has nothing to hide and appeals to his listeners to pay close attention because the truth will always vindicate him.

Paul rehearses his own relevant biographical background, from being a devoted Pharisee to his transition to preaching the Gospel and its core hope in the resurrection of the dead—a hope he claims is at the heart of his trial, which many of his Jewish accusers actually share. As in previous hearings, Paul is establishing his bona fides as a conservative Jew—an expert in the Law and Jewish customs and traditions, and therefore an authority on the issues under consideration. He didn't acquire his knowledge secondhand but through experience.[44] He is the real deal, capable of going toe-to-toe even with these zealots who crave his death.

Paul adroitly segues from the Old Testament to the Gospel, again demonstrating the unmistakable continuity between the two—a thread of redemption that anyone but the blind or dark-hearted can see. The Gospel is not a radical departure from the religion of Abraham, Isaac, and Jacob. It is act two in a two-part play, which has begun with Christ's coming in their lifetimes. Paul notes the irony in his being tried for perverting the true religion when in fact he is accurately expounding it. It is his accusers who fail to understand the complete picture of their religion. Paul is direct and explicit: "Now I stand here on trial because of my hope in the promise made by God to our fathers, to which our twelve tribes hope to attain, as they earnestly worship night and day. And for this hope I am accused by Jews, O king!" This promise on which Paul stands, of which he preaches, and for which he is on trial, is the same one God's Old Testament prophets made to their fathers and which the twelve tribes of Israel long to realize. He has not hijacked their sacred faith; he is its most faithful steward, and they would do well to open their eyes to God's progressive revelation through Jesus Christ and His apostles.

Before returning to his personal history of persecuting Christians, Paul raises a difficult question: "Why is it thought incredible by any of you that God raises from the dead?" As we've seen, the Pharisees, though not the Sadducees, believe in resurrection. Believing that, and having longed for the Messiah for thousands of years, why are they so incredulous now that the true Messiah has come? Why are stories of Jesus' resurrection so hard to believe? It's because they had always anticipated a different kind of Messiah, one who would conquer their political and military enemies, not one who would allow Himself to be hanged on a tree and thereby accursed (Deut. 21:22–23). Jesus came to sacrificially die for man's sins so that those who believe in Him can live with Him eternally, thereby fulfilling God's promise to bless all nations through Abraham (Gen. 22:18). Jesus is Whom they've been waiting for. They just can't see it. With this argument, Paul has strategically turned the tables and put them on defense, using his intimate knowledge of their faith to expose them. His work is cut out for him, however, for the Bible also foretold that the Jews would be resistant to the Gospel, and this prophecy is being fulfilled through his own agonizing experiences.

Paul then recites his background as a persecutor of the Way, culminating in his conversion on the road to Damascus, during which the Lord told him, "I am Jesus whom you are persecuting. But rise and stand upon your feet, for I have appeared to you for this purpose, to appoint you as a servant and witness to the things in which you have seen me and to those in which I will appear to you, delivering you from your people and from the Gentiles—to whom I am sending you to open their eyes, so that they may turn from darkness to light and from the power of Satan to

God, that they may receive forgiveness of sins and a place among those who are sanctified by faith in me."

Paul says he obeyed Christ and began preaching—first to those in Damascus, then in Jerusalem and throughout all of Judea, and finally to the Gentiles—that they should repent, turn to God and prove their repentance through their good works. Let's not miss the boldness of this statement. Paul is not boasting about his obedience. He is underscoring Christ's command itself: that he must preach the Gospel throughout the world. This order is not subject to interpretation, debate, or compromise; it's an inviolable directive from God—the God they worship. Paul had no choice. This may seem odd to Paul's accusers; it may contradict their expectations. But none of that matters. God is sovereign, and He has revealed Jesus as the Messiah, therefore He is. This is not just Paul's opinion; it is the truth grounded in Paul's firsthand experience. He encountered Christ Himself, Who called Him. He is not called to twist the Old Testament Scriptures to conform to some radical new ideas. It is to spread the Good News that the promises the Jews have always relied on are now being fulfilled.

Paul is not guilty of heresy; he is vindicating the God they worship. What's more, this Gospel Paul preaches is based on Christ's earthly ministry, His unjust crucifixion, His resurrection from the dead, and His multiple resurrection appearances to multitudes of people. The Way is not a cult based on some abstract, manmade philosophy. It is grounded in history and fact. Paul has preached only the truth, "saying nothing but what the prophets and Moses said would come to pass: that the Christ must suffer and that, by being the first to rise from the dead, he would proclaim light both to our people and to the Gentiles." Yet for obediently spreading this message with God's help every step of the way, the Jews seized him in the Temple and tried to kill him.

As he is speaking, Festus yells to Paul that he is out of his mind and that his great learning has driven him mad. Paul assures Festus he is sane and that he is speaking true and reasonable words. "For the king knows about these things, and to him I speak boldly. For I am persuaded that none of these things has escaped his notice, for this has not been done in a corner." Paul then confronts Agrippa directly, exclaiming, "Do you believe in the prophets? I know that you believe."

Paul has raised the stakes and made his message personal—boldly turning to Agrippa and telling him that he knows he's aware of Jesus' life, death, and resurrection. Agrippa can pretend otherwise, but he would have had to be in a cave to miss these things, for they were not done in a corner—a claim Paul would not have made and Luke would not have recorded unless it were true, because Agrippa could contradict him and make his life miserable if it were false.

He has put Agrippa on the spot. It would be awkward to ignore the question because people might draw the wrong inferences from his silence. He can either say he doesn't believe in the prophets and lose faith with the Jews, or he can say he believes, which could be tantamount to confessing he believes that Jesus is Who Paul claims He is, because Paul has just demonstrated that the Jewish prophets foretold of Jesus.[45] Even if he does believe, it's unlikely he will admit it in public and expose himself as a lunatic for believing such madness.[46]

Agrippa deflects the question, asking Paul whether he thinks he can persuade him to be a Christian so quickly. Whatever else we may say about Agrippa's response and the possible reasons for it, it's a classic case of human pride on display. John Calvin expresses this poignantly, writing, "The apostle prevailed thus far at least, that he wrung out of King Agrippa a confession, though it were not voluntary, as those use to yield who can no longer resist the truth, or at least, to show some token of assent. Agrippa's meaning is, that he will not willingly become a Christian; yea, that he will not be one at all; and yet that he is not able to gainsay, but that he is drawn after a sort against his will. Whereby it appeareth how great the pride of man's nature is until it be brought under to obey by the Spirit of God."[47]

In other words, deep down Agrippa knows—and is almost tacitly admitting— that he believes Paul's message, but his pride prevents him from openly admitting it and acting on it. The trappings of his worldly power are too great to risk. My friend, Christian apologist Frank Turek, often asks unbelievers, "If you discovered that Christianity is true, would you become a Christian?" Frank tells me that 90 percent of such people say no—because believing in God would preclude them from being gods of their own lives.

We have all encountered people whose infernal pride bars them from allowing the truth to seep into their souls. Toward such stubborn people, a different type of witnessing is required. As the psalmist writes, "In the pride of his face, the wicked does not seek him, all his thoughts are, 'There is no God'" (Psalm 10:4). Rev. Joseph Exell comments on this phenomenon and of Agrippa, "Paul made a favorable impression on Agrippa, but the spiritual testimony was disdainfully rejected. How often is this history repeated. There are those who come to acknowledge the reasonableness of Christianity, but still reject it as the spiritual rule of their lives. Persuasion has overpowered the intellect, but it has not overcome the pride of the heart."[48] This is why we say a person cannot be argued into the kingdom. You may break down every last one of his intellectual obstacles, but unless he is willing to accept Christ, he will be no more a believer than the demons who clearly recognize Christ for Who He is.

God does not look favorably on this resistance because every person, at some level, whether consciously or not, knows God exists, "For what can be known about God is plain to them, because God has shown it to them. For his invisible attributes, namely, his eternal power and divine nature, have been clearly perceived, ever since the creation of the world, in the things that have been made. So they are without excuse" (Romans 1:19–20).

Undeterred by Agrippa's skillful parrying of his question, Paul responds by ministering to him directly and in earnest, thereby showing that spreading the Word, in obedience to Christ's commands, is of greater importance to Paul even than protecting himself. Paul says, "Whether short or long, I would to God that not only you but also all who hear me this day might become such as I am—except for 'these chains.'" There you have it. Paul wants Agrippa and all who are listening to become what Paul is—a Christian—except without the chains binding him. He wants them to share what he has (his faith) but not his circumstances (his bondage). To lose one's liberty is horrific, but for Paul it would be more than that—incarceration would hinder his missionary activities.

"The Apostle was not thinking at the moment about his freedom," R. C. Sproul writes. "His heart was burdened by their chains, not by his."[49] We must note, however, that in Rome, as we'll see, Paul's evangelism flourished, even while under house arrest. After all, God is sovereign.

The king rises, and then the governor, Bernice, and those sitting with them follow suit. After they leave the room, they agree that Paul has done nothing to deserve death or imprisonment. Agrippa remarks to Festus that Paul could have been set free had he not appealed to Caesar.

CHAPTER 27

When it's time to sail for Italy, Paul and other prisoners are placed in the custody of the Roman officer Julius. They set sail from Adramyttium on the northwest coast of the province of Asia, with scheduled stops along the way. We know from the previous chapter they are headed for Rome, so why does Luke say they set sail for Italy without specifying the city? It's probably because visitors to Rome often traveled by sea to the southern part of Italy and then walked the rest of the way.[50] The next day when they arrive at Sidon, Julius graciously allows Paul to go ashore and visit friends who will attend to his needs. When they leave, they meet strong headwinds that threaten to blow them off course, so they sail north of Cyprus between the island and the mainland, passing along the coast of Cilicia and Pamphylia and landing at Myra, in the province of Lycia. There Julius finds an Egyptian ship from Alexandria bound for Italy. After several days of slow and difficult sailing, they near Cnidus— but as the wind is against them, they sail across to Crete and along the coast of the island, past the cape of Salmone. They continue with difficulty along the coast until they reach Fair Havens, near the town of Lasea.

Paul warns the ship's officers that it would be dangerous to proceed as winter approaches. But Julius defers to the ship's pilot and owner. As the harbor is not suitable for winter, they decide to sail on, hoping to reach Phoenix, a harbor of Crete, and spend the winter there.

When a gentle south wind begins to blow they start to sail along the shore of Crete, but soon a hurricane force wind called the Northeaster sweeps down from the island. As the ship cannot head into the wind, they let it drive the ship along. Running under the lee of a small island called Cauda, they struggle to secure the ship's lifeboat. After hoisting it aboard, they undergird the ship with supports. Then, fearing they will run aground on the sandbars of Syrtis, they lower the sea anchor and let the ship be driven along. They take such a battering from the storm that they throw cargo overboard the next day, and the day after they throw some of the ship's gear overboard as well.

The storm continues several more days. They haven't eaten for a long time and are beginning to lose hope. Paul says they should have heeded his warning not to leave Crete but should be encouraged; they will all survive, though the ship will be lost, he says. An angel of the God he belongs to and worships said to him, "Do not be afraid, Paul; you must stand before Caesar. And behold, God has granted you all those who sail with you." So Paul assures them, based on his faith in God, that they will arrive safely, though they will be shipwrecked on some island.

At about midnight on the storm's fourteenth day, as they are being pushed across the Adriatic Sea, the sailors suspect they are nearing land. They take soundings, and find the water is 120 feet deep, falling to ninety feet a little later. Fearing they will be driven against the rocks along the shore, they throw out four anchors from the back of the ship and pray for daylight. The sailors, planning to escape from the ship, lower the lifeboat into the sea while pretending they are going to lower some anchors. Paul warns the centurion and the soldiers that everyone will die unless those men remain aboard, so the soldiers cut the ropes and let the lifeboat drift away.

Close to dawn, Paul urges everyone to eat and gain strength, assuring them that although they have gone without food for fourteen days, none of them will die. He then breaks bread, gives thanks to God, and begins to eat. All 276 people aboard are encouraged and begin to eat. Afterward, they throw wheat overboard to lighten the ship's load. When day breaks, they notice a bay with a beach; they don't recognize the land, but decide to run the ship ashore there. The men cast off the anchors, leave them in the sea, and loosen the ropes that tie the rudders. Hoisting the foresail to the wind, they head for the shore but strike a sandbar, which causes the vessel to run aground. Then the bow becomes stuck, and the pounding surf breaks the stern to pieces. The soldiers are planning to kill the prisoners to prevent any from escaping, but the centurion stops them because he wants to save Paul. He orders those who can swim to jump overboard and head for land, and has the others float to shore on planks or pieces of the ship. All make it to land safely.

Paul's voyage to Rome

From The New Moody Atlas of the Bible by Barry J. Beitzel (©2009). Published by Moody Publishers. Used by permission.

John MacArthur sees this voyage as a striking example of biblical leadership from Paul. At the beginning of the journey, Paul is a prisoner with no special status or responsibilities. But when adversity strikes, Paul rises to the occasion and earns the respect and trust of passengers and crew, essentially becoming their leader.[51] By this time, Paul has already endured incredible hardship and persecution for his faith and answering Jesus' call. Violent storms are not going to defeat him; nothing else has. He writes, "We are afflicted in every way, but not crushed; perplexed, but not driven to despair; persecuted, but not forsaken; struck down, but not destroyed; always carrying in the body the death of Jesus, so that the life of Jesus may also be manifested in our bodies" (2 Cor. 4:8–10).

Paul also instructs that we are to rejoice in our sufferings because suffering produces endurance, character, and hope (Romans 5:2–4). Likewise, James writes, "Count it all joy, my brothers, when you meet trials of various kinds, for you know that the testing of your faith

produces steadfastness. And let steadfastness have its full effect, that you
may be perfect and complete, lacking in nothing" (James 1:2–4). Peter
adds, "In this you rejoice, though now for a little while, if necessary, you
have been grieved by various trials, so that the tested genuineness of your
faith—more precious than gold that perishes though it is tested by fire—
may be found to result in praise and glory and honor at the revelation of
Jesus Christ" (1 Peter 1:6–7).

The centurion Julius observes how Paul's character has been refined
by the trials he's endured. When Paul's unheeded warning came to fruition, Julius and the group obviously regretted that they had not listened,
and Paul's stature increased in their eyes. Indeed, when they encountered
difficulties, Paul told them they should have listened to him before. But
he did not hector them—rather, he sought to spare them from further
unnecessary troubles. Moreover, his overall message was encouraging,
telling them, based on direct assurances from an angel of God, that they
would all survive, though the ship would be damaged.

Perhaps Paul had an additional motive for telling them about the
angel's visit. Could he have been planting a missionary seed that they
would remember later when they arrived safely, as God had promised?
How could this fail to have a dramatic impact and possibly lead some
of them to faith, just as other miraculous deeds of Jesus, Paul, and Peter
had done for others? Luke is silent on this, but it's worth considering.
John Calvin writes, "Seeing angels coming down unto him from
heaven, they may easily gather that his cause is approved of God.
Therefore, there is in these words a secret commendation of the Gospel."[52] Similarly, Lutheran Pastor Richard Lenski asks, "Is God not
telling them that through Paul's mediation they, too, like him, are to
be this true, God's own, in order to serve him? They were to see and
to hear much more about God, and we may, indeed, conclude that
many of these men 'sailing with Paul' came also to be saved in the
higher sense."[53]

Throughout the rest of the journey, Paul demonstrates the same
leadership skills. He remains calm, unflappable, and in control for the
entire voyage, mainly, as John MacArthur observes, "because he had
absolute trust in God's promise (through the angel) to save all those on
the ship."[54] Even as they are struggling to land on the island, it is Julius'

acquired trust in Paul that spares all the prisoners, as Julius keeps his men from killing them out of concern for Paul.

F. F. Bruce remarks that Luke's narrative of this voyage and shipwreck is "a small classic in its own right, as graphic a piece of descriptive writing as anything in the Bible. It has long been acknowledged as "one of the most instructive documents for the knowledge of ancient seamanship."[55] Some commentators interpret this dangerous voyage allegorically, comparing it to the challenging storms of human life. Though Luke was reporting history, there are still valuable life lessons to be gleaned from this chapter. Its overarching message, though, concerns God's sovereignty and the outworking of His will. No matter what obstacles may arise, God is in control. It is His will that Paul preach the Gospel in Rome—the very epicenter of the Gentile world[56]—and He will not be thwarted by any obstacles, manmade or supernatural. He reigns over all.

CHAPTER 28

◇◇◇◇◇◇◇◇◇◇◇◇◇◇◇◇◇◇◇◇◇◇◇◇

Once they are on shore, they discover that the island, which is just south of Sicily, is called Malta.[57] The residents are unusually kind, building a fire and welcoming them when it's raining and cold. Paul places a pile of brushwood on the fire and a viper, escaping the heat, fastens on his hand. Talking among themselves, the islanders say that Paul must be a murderer who is receiving his due from the goddess Justice. But after Paul shakes off the snake and shows no symptoms from the poison, the people change their minds and conclude he is a god.

Publius, the chief official of the island, welcomes them to his home and shows them hospitality for three days. His father is bedridden with fever and dysentery, so Paul visits him, places his hands on him, prays for him, and he is healed. Thereafter, every sick person on the island comes to Paul for healing, and he cures them all. The islanders are kind to them for three months, providing them with all the supplies they need when they are ready to sail.

They leave on an Alexandrian ship with the figurehead of twin gods Castor and Pollux, patrons of navigation often worshipped by sailors.[58]

They first stop at Syracuse and stay three days before leaving for Rhegium. The following day, the south wind comes up, so the day after they sail up the coast to Puteoli, where they find some believers who invite them to stay for a week. Luke mentions this casually, but it's quite significant because it illustrates that the Gospel has already spread beyond Rome to this seaport.[59]

Continuing toward Rome, they encounter Christians who have traveled a long way to meet them at the Forum of Appius (a market community about forty-three miles from Rome) and the Three Taverns (thirty-three miles from Rome). This encourages Paul, and he thanks God. Imagine Paul's exuberance in meeting fellow believers after the hardships he has recently endured. When they arrive in Rome, Paul is placed in private lodging under a soldier's guard. Three days later, he calls together the local Jewish leaders and tells them he has done nothing against the Jews or the customs of the Jewish fathers, but that Jews delivered him to the Roman authorities. He tells of how, after examining him, the Roman authorities wanted to release him because he committed no offense warranting the death penalty. But because the Jews objected, he was forced to appeal to Caesar, though he has no intention of bringing charges against his own people.

Paul has asked to speak with them because the hope of Israel—the fulfillment of the Old Testament promises to Israel—is why he's in chains.[60] The people say they have received no letters from Judea about him and none of the Christians who have come from there have criticized him. But they tell Paul they want to hear his views because the Christian sect has been denounced everywhere.

Many people come to Paul's house, where he speaks to them all day on the kingdom of God, taking them through their Hebrew Scriptures (the Old Testament) to convince them of Jesus. Some believe and others don't. After they have argued among themselves and are about to leave, Paul says, "The Holy Spirit was right in saying to your fathers through Isaiah the prophet, 'Go to this people, and say, "You will indeed hear but never understand, and you will indeed see but never perceive." For this people's heart has grown dull, and with their ears they can barely hear, and their eyes they have closed; lest they should see with their eyes and hear with their ears and understand with their heart and turn, and

I would heal them.' Therefore let it be known to you that this salvation of God has been sent to the Gentiles; they will listen."

This is a familiar passage to them, and Paul uses it to make his point, even if it's lost on many of them. Paul has satisfied his duty to preach the Gospel to the Jews, and as the prophets foretold, they have largely rejected it. But Paul's conscience is clear because he has given it his all, and he will now turn almost exclusively to the Gentiles, who have been his special calling since his conversion.

Paul is confined to this private house in Rome for two full years. He lives at his own expense and welcomes everyone who comes to him, "proclaiming the kingdom of God and teaching about the Lord Jesus Christ with all boldness and without hindrance." Paul's evangelism thus makes enormous headway despite the restrictions on his mobility.

Acts abruptly ends at this point, leaving us to piece together Paul's subsequent fate from other sources. It's generally agreed that Paul was martyred in Rome, probably by sword, though the precise date is uncertain. Many scholars place his death around 62 AD, at the close of his two-year house arrest in Rome, while others say it could have been in 64 AD, and still others as late as 66 AD after a second arrest.[61]

Of course, Paul's influence did not end with his death, since he did more than anyone besides Jesus to expound and clarify the Gospel. Indeed, Paul's "true greatness is attested by the abiding power of his liberating messages," declares Pauline scholar F. F. Bruce. "Time and again, when the gospel has been in danger of being fettered and disabled in the bonds of legalism or outworn tradition, it has been the words of Paul that have broken the bonds and set the gospel free to exert its emancipating power once more in the life of mankind."[62] Additionally, Paul left behind untold numbers of Christian converts who followed his example and continued to implement Christ's command to spread the Gospel to the end of the Earth.

Finally, his epistles to local Christian churches, as enshrined in the New Testament, provide tremendous historical insights into the development and challenges of early Christianity. Let's now turn to these letters for a glimpse of the issues Paul faced and the controversies he addressed as fledgling churches gained their footing in Christ.

CHAPTER SIX

GALATIANS
FREEDOM IN CHRIST

Paul's letter to the Galatians is called the charter of Christian freedom. In it Paul proclaims the reality of believers' liberty in Christ—freedom from the law and the power of sin, and freedom to serve the living Lord.

—BRUCE BARTON[1]

THE PAULINE EPISTLES

The Apostle Paul writes thirteen epistles, which can be grouped into three categories: the Missionary Epistles, the Prison Epistles, and the Pastoral Epistles.[2] The Missionary Epistles, which he writes during his three missionary journeys, are: Galatians, 1 Thessalonians, 2 Thessalonians, 1 Corinthians, 2 Corinthians, and Romans. The Prison Epistles, which he pens from his house arrest in Rome (Acts 28),[3] are: Colossians, Ephesians, Philemon, and Philippians. The Pastoral Epistles, which he likely writes after the events described in the Book of Acts and are intended as counsel to two close friends on how to shepherd their congregations,[4] are: 1 Timothy, 2 Timothy, and Titus. In this book, we cover just the missionary epistles. We'll discuss them in the chronological order in which they are probably written, which differs from the order in which they appear in the Bible. We should note that the epistles are invaluable because they are written with the benefit of the entire Old Testament and the teachings of Jesus, and they instruct us on Christian doctrine and Christian living.

EPISTLE TO THE GALATIANS

At the time this epistle is written, "Galatia" has two meanings. A group of people called Galatians live in the northern part of Asia Minor (modern Turkey), where the Gauls had settled after migrating from western Europe. There is also a Roman province called Galatia that includes this northern territory, but also extends into the southern part of Asia Minor.[5] Scholars have long debated whether Paul writes this epistle to churches of the ethnic Galatians in northern Galatia or to those of the provincial Galatians in southern Galatia. The North Galatian theory holds that Paul writes to ethnic Galatians, not to provincial Galatians. The South Galatian theory is that Paul uses the term "Galatia" in a provincial sense— that is, he's referring to people who live in the Roman province of Galatia, in the cities he visits and evangelizes on his first missionary journey in southern Galatia: Pisidian Antioch, Iconium, Lystra, and Derbe (Acts 13–14).[6] Most scholars believe this would be around 48 AD.[7]

The North Galatian Theory is that Paul visits the northern part of Galatia during his second missionary journey after leaving the southern Galatian region and before he arrives in Troas (Acts 16:6–8). Some believe Acts 18:23 describes a second visit to this region.[8] According to the North Galatian theory, he could write this letter during his second missionary journey around 50–52 AD, on his third missionary journey between 54–55 AD, or even as late as 57 AD.[9]

It seems more likely that Paul is writing to the churches in southern Galatia. Scripture doesn't mention the establishment of churches in North Galatia, but it does those in South Galatia. Some other factors supporting the South Galatian theory are:

1. The main roads leading from Paul's hometown of Tarsus pass through the cities of South Galatia, not those of North Galatia;

2. There is a large Jewish element living in the southern cities;

3. When Paul gathers his offering for the poor in Jerusalem, representatives from South Galatia are with him but there are none from the north (Acts 20:4);

4. Barnabas is mentioned in Galatians, but he would not be known by those in the northern cities because he only travels with Paul on his first missionary journey.[10]

There is another important argument favoring the South Galatian theory: in this epistle, Paul is speaking to Gentiles who are being pressured to become circumcised. Yet in the letter, he doesn't refer to the Jerusalem Council (Acts 15)—which definitively decided this hotly contested issue—as authority to persuade the Gentiles. If the council already met, Paul could cite it to bolster his argument. That he doesn't strongly suggests he writes the epistle prior to the Council's convention.[11] I must mention, however, that the widely-respected John MacArthur, though he agrees the epistle was written to the churches in southern Galatia, thinks the letter was written after the Jerusalem Council, around 49 AD. That's because Paul refers to a visit to Jerusalem in Chapter 2 of Galatians, and MacArthur believes this was the Jerusalem visit during which Paul attends the Jerusalem Council.[12]

WHY PAUL WROTE TO THE GALATIANS

Paul, through the Holy Spirit, enthusiastically establishes the church in Galatia. But shortly after he leaves the church quickly falters, mainly because of false teachers (Judaizers) who insist new believers must be circumcised and keep the Law of Moses to be saved.[13] Perhaps these teachers are seeking their own glory, or maybe they're pandering to the Jewish authorities by showing they are converting Gentiles merely to a new form of Judaism, which would not be considered a threat to their religion. They could be leaders of the church without fear of Jewish persecution.

This doctrinal dispute is dividing the church, and Paul is compelled to address it; otherwise, its reverberations could dilute the Gospel far and wide. As such, Paul is quite critical in this epistle.[14] As Paul founded this church, his apostolic authority (and thus his Gospel message) is being directly challenged, so he affirms his credentials in the first two chapters. In the remainder of the letter he expounds on the doctrine of justification by faith alone and on the idea of Christian liberty.[15] What's the point of the Gospel, after all—why should Jesus have died for our sins—if we can earn our own salvation? This insidious heresy must be smothered immediately.

Yes, Paul is harsh, but not because he is ill-tempered or thin-skinned. He views this as a matter of life or death for the Gospel, and thus also of the eternal lives of countless people whose salvation depends upon their clear understanding of the Gospel message. His divine apostolic authority is essential to the Gospel's credibility. Moreover, Paul is not the only New Testament writer who is intolerant of false gospel messages. In addressing those who only partially embrace the faith[16] before leaving it as apostates, Peter writes, "What the true proverb says has happened to them: 'The dog returns to its own vomit, and the sow, after washing herself, returns to wallow in the mire'" (2 Peter 2:22). Likewise, Jude denounces false teachers as "hidden reefs at your love feasts, as they feast with you without fear, shepherds feeding themselves; waterless clouds, swept along by winds; fruitless trees in late autumn, twice dead, uprooted; wild waves of the sea, casting up the foam of their own shame; wandering stars, for whom the gloom of utter darkness has been reserved forever" (Jude 12–13).

Early Church father Marius Victorinus, who penned the first Latin commentary on Galatians, explains the problem confronting Paul:

> The Galatians are going astray because they are adding Judaism to the gospel of faith in Christ, observing in a material sense the sabbath and circumcision, together with the other works which they received in accordance with the law. Disturbed by these tendencies Paul writes this letter, wishing to put them right and call them back from Judaism, in order that they may preserve faith in Christ alone, and receive from Christ the hope of salvation and of his promises, because no one is saved by the works of the law. So, in order to show that

what they are adding is wrong, he wishes to confirm [the truth of] his gospel.[17]

CHAPTER 1

◇◇◇◇◇◇◇◇◇◇◇◇◇◇◇◇◇◇◇◇◇

Paul begins his letter to "the churches of Galatia" by identifying himself as an apostle whose authority is not derived from man, "but through Jesus Christ and God the Father, who raised him from the dead." He offers them grace and peace from God, saying Christ gave Himself for their sins, as God the Father had willed. He is astonished, however, that they are so quickly deserting him and turning to a different gospel—which is not really a gospel at all, because there is only one Gospel. They seek the approval of man rather than God. This should be a wake-up call to those today who succumb to the allures of pluralism and deny that salvation can only be found through faith in Jesus Christ. To appease the popular culture—which demands, under a twisted and self-defeating notion of "tolerance," that all ideas must be considered equally valid—they contradict the Gospel and disgrace the finished work of Christ on the cross.

Paul is charging his readers with ingratitude, as they were called in grace—they were freely given the gift of the Gospel and are allowing it to be corrupted. His dispute with them is not personal; anyone preaching a false gospel, even an apostle or an angel from heaven, shall be accursed. Besides, unlike them, he isn't seeking man's approval—only God's. Otherwise, he wouldn't be serving Christ. This is another way of saying that if one serves Christ, he will often displease men of the world.

Paul then defends his apostolic credentials. He derives his authority from God, not man, having received the Gospel through a direct revelation from Jesus Christ. He wouldn't have had time for anyone to teach him anyway, for immediately after his conversion he consulted with no one and did not go up to Jerusalem to meet the apostles. Instead, he left almost immediately for Arabia before returning to Damascus. From there, he went to Jerusalem to visit Peter for fifteen days. The only other apostle he saw there was James, the brother of Jesus. He next went to the regions of Syria and Cilicia, where he was

still unknown to the Christians except by reputation for having formerly persecuted the brothers.

CHAPTER 2

∞∞∞∞∞∞∞∞∞∞∞∞∞∞∞∞

After fourteen years, Paul says, because of a revelation he received,
he went with Barnabas and Titus up to Jerusalem again. He met with
influential Christians there and presented the Gospel he'd been proclaiming to the Gentiles. Some scholars believe this revelation was the prophecy of Agabus that there would be a famine (Acts 11:28–30), and that
the purpose of Paul's visit was to deliver aid he'd collected among the
churches.[18] Others believe Paul's language suggests he received a separate
revelation prompting him to go to Jerusalem.[19]

Paul did not require Titus, a Gentile, to be circumcised. Nevertheless,
false teachers tried to rob them of the freedom they had in Jesus and take
them back into slavery; but they wouldn't yield an inch, lest the purity of
the Gospel be compromised. Paul is introducing a central theme of this
letter: that the Gospel brings freedom in Jesus Christ. It liberates man from
his former slavery under the Law, whose stringent requirements cannot
be met by any man except Jesus, and which has no power to save. The
stalwarts of the faith in Jerusalem, including Apostles James and Peter,
perceived that Paul had received the Gospel by grace and welcomed him
as a colleague, vouching for his apostolic authority. Paul did not seek their
approval because he doubted his own authority, but because it promoted
apostolic harmony and their shared mission. Indeed, James, Peter, and
John confirmed Paul's authority without adding a single thing to his message, which we may safely infer they regarded as complete.

Paul is clear: he is equal in status to the other apostles. The apostles
recognized that Paul was set apart to preach the Gospel to the Gentiles,
while Peter was entrusted to preach to the Jews. Accordingly, the apostles
sent Paul and Barnabas to the Gentiles, requesting only that they remember the poor, which was music to Paul's ears. They reserved for themselves the task of preaching to the Jews.

Paul next describes an event that may have happened at a different
time but is relevant to his discussion of his apostolic authority and to the

subject of law and grace, central to this letter. Peter came to Antioch in Syria, the headquarters of the Gentile church and Paul's operating base for missions.[20] When he arrived, Peter readily ate with uncircumcised Gentile believers despite Jewish prohibitions against doing so. But when some friends of James arrived, Peter stopped eating with the Gentiles, fearing disapproval of the Jews who insisted that Jewish Christians be circumcised. This led other Jewish believers, including Barnabas, to refuse to eat with the Gentiles in Christ.

Unable to stand silent, Paul rebuked Peter immediately and forcefully, saying, "If you, though a Jew, live like a Gentile and not like a Jew, how can you force the Gentiles to live like Jews?" This was not a minor matter of etiquette that Paul could overlook—instead, it bore on the integrity of the Gospel.[21] The practice of excluding the Gentile Christians, writes Bruce Barton, was "nothing other than heresy."[22] How could Peter allow himself to be intimidated into treating the Gentile believers as second class Christians when Christ had taught him, in a special vision, that there is no longer any distinction between Jews and Gentiles in God's family?

This revelation led to Peter's successful evangelism of the Gentile Cornelius and his family, with whom Peter later dined in their home. When Peter related these events to the Jewish believers, they criticized him (Acts 11:3). But after Peter explained his vision, they dropped their objections and began praising God, rejoicing that He has also provided salvation for Gentiles who believe in Christ. Moreover, Peter had been justified by faith, and he stopped observing Jewish dietary laws.[23]

Paul states that a person is not justified by works of the Law but through faith in Jesus Christ. Even the Jews' salvation is based on their faith in Christ, not their works, which can justify no one. Paul poses a question: if he and other Jews accept Christ in faith and then abandon the Jewish Law, does that mean that Christ has led them into sin? "Certainly not!" he exclaims. "For if I rebuild what I tore down, I prove myself to be a transgressor. For through the law I died to the law, so that I might live to God. I have been crucified with Christ. It is no longer I who live, but Christ who lives in me. And the life I now live in the flesh I live by faith in the Son of God, who loved me and gave himself for me. I do not nullify the grace of God, for if righteousness were through the law, then Christ died for no purpose."

When he was a practicing Pharisaic Jew, Paul led an exemplary life under the Law. No one observed the Law more diligently than he did—"as to righteousness under the law" he was "blameless" (Philipp. 3:6). But his righteousness was only external, for no fallen human being—and we're all fallen—can measure up to the Law, which requires inward perfection as well: to love God will all our heart, soul, mind, and strength, and to love our neighbor as we love ourselves. Paul could not attain eternal life through the Law, and his failure to live up to it (coupled with Christ's revelation to Him) led him to see his wretchedness apart from Christ. As such, "he died to the law"—he finally gave it up and began to live in Christ.

Having died to the Law, he could not re-embrace legalism and its system of rituals and ordinances. In that case, he could not "live to God"—that is, God, not the Law, is Lord of the believer's life.[24] The Law has no power to save. The believer is not only saved by faith in Christ alone, but lives by faith in Christ, Who gave Himself for us. He cannot justify Himself by the onerous, unachievable yoke of the Law. Stated more succinctly, Paul lived strictly by the Law and thus was spiritually dead. This, along with Christ's special appearance to him, led him to set aside his pride, give up on the Law, and accept Christ's gift of grace.

Moreover, if after having been justified by faith in Christ, he would return to rigidly observing the Law (or forcing others to) and trying to perfect himself through his own unaided works, it would not be Christ's fault. Christ would not be aiding his sin. Rather, Paul would be the transgressor, for he would be rejecting Christ's grace, making His death meaningless, and dishonoring His sacrifice. If a Christian returns to the Law seeking a salvation he has already received through Christ, he is treating Christ as a liar. Christ's sacrifice is either sufficient to save us or it's not. Our faith in Him doesn't get us just halfway there, leaving the balance for us to earn on our own. We mustn't be seduced into believing we are responsible for any fraction of our salvation, which is a perversion of the Gospel.

This concept may seem counterintuitive, because we are so conditioned to believe we are not entitled to anything unless we earn it, and we especially don't deserve to be rewarded for being sinners. But we must accept that we are simply incapable of earning our salvation, so we better be grateful there is another way—through faith in Christ. No matter how much our own sense of justice resists this, we must let it go in order to accept His gift. Let's not allow our pride to masquerade as humility and pat ourselves on the back—it's just like Satan to disguise our sin as virtue. No, we must be still and listen to God instead of taking our own counsel (cf. Psalm 46:10), and God is telling us that we can't do anything to earn our own salvation. It's not our humility causing us to resist His gift, but our pride in clinging to the fantasy that we somehow must prove our own worth. One key to accepting the Gospel is to fully embrace God's Word that we are by nature fallen people and, apart from God, we are incapable of redemption. Finally coming to terms with that is immensely freeing and essential to our eternal destiny.

CHAPTER 3

Paul, seemingly frustrated and disappointed, asks the Galatians who has cast a spell on them. He began the letter addressing "the churches of Galatia," then called them "brothers" in verse 1:11. Now he is calling them "foolish"—they have the intelligence to understand the Gospel but are allowing false teachers to deceive them.[25] They were taught the Gospel of justification by grace, not works, and now they are already being duped into considering that their own works are also required. This doesn't just dilute the Gospel, it destroys it—because the suggestion that Christ needs our help to save us is ludicrous. "The Galatians, by yielding to this influence, had failed to understand that a Christ supplemented is a Christ supplanted," writes William Hendriksen.[26]

Why, when the Gospel was so clearly presented to them and they received the Holy Spirit through their belief, do they thoughtlessly insist on returning to the Law? They have the Spirit, Who helps them combat their sinful nature and impulses of the flesh, but are senselessly rejecting this Helper and starting all over again, trying to fight sin on their own power. Paul is clear that we are not only saved by faith—as opposed to our works—but we also grow in spiritual maturity through faith and dependence on the Holy Spirit.

Even in the case of Abraham, faith was at work—God counted him righteous because he trusted God (cf. Heb. 11:8–10). Paul invokes the great patriarch, for through God's grace he founded the Hebrew nation. Now, Abraham's proud descendants are rejecting the avenue of faith that he traveled. God's prophets foretold that God would bless all nations through Abraham, and Paul identifies the Gospel as that blessing because those who are saved through faith are blessed, along with and through Abraham.

Paul goes further, insisting that all those who rely on works of the Law are under a curse, quoting Old Testament scripture to seal the point (Deut. 27:26)—that is, if one follows the Law rather than trusts in Christ, he will fail and be accursed. That's because he cannot do it on his own power—indeed, no one can except for Jesus Christ. Rather, says Paul, quoting another Old Testament passage (Hab. 2:4), "The righteous shall live by faith." Note how at every turn, Paul cites Jewish scripture to the Judaizers, showing them that his Gospel of grace is nothing new, but was foretold and promised by their prophets.

Thankfully, Jesus Christ has redeemed us from the curse of the Law by becoming a curse for us under the Law: "Cursed is everyone who is hanged on a tree" (Deut. 21:23). We would all be hopelessly accursed but for Christ's substitutionary death on the cross for us, whereby He became accursed so that through faith in Him, the blessings of Abraham would benefit all nations and all peoples, who would receive the promised Holy Spirit through faith.

Paul continues to invoke the Old Testament to explain the Gospel. Indeed, the more I study Paul's writings, the more convinced I am that God chose him as much for his intimate knowledge of the Hebrew Scriptures as for his passion and intensity. Yes, the promise of blessing was made to Abraham and his offspring, but Paul says that God meant one offspring—Jesus Christ. God fulfilled every promise given in His covenant with Abraham through Jesus Christ and Him alone. God's promise to Abraham was made long ago but was not fulfilled until Christ came as Abraham's offspring. There is only one way a person can benefit from God's promised blessings to Abraham, and that is to become an heir with Christ through faith in Him.[27] So Christ is the only direct heir of Abraham, but God's blessings flow to all people who join in His inheritance through faith in Him. As Paul declares to the Romans, Abraham is "the father of all who believe" (4:11; cf. 4:16).

So why did God give the Law if it could not save? Salvation, even for the Jews, was never based on works, for God's promise to Abraham of salvation through faith was made some 430 years before He gave Moses the Law. As His promise (the Abrahamic Covenant) was unconditional and preceded His giving of the Law, the Law did not annul it—God does not break His promises. But He did have an important purpose for the Law, and it was consistent with his promise to bless all nations through Abraham. The Law facilitated it—that is, God added the Law to assist the Jews until the promised Messiah would come. The Law complemented God's unconditional and eternal promise of salvation to mankind by providing guidelines to the Israelites on how to live their lives and serve as the nation of priests and mediators through whom the Messiah would come to bless all nations.

"Now before faith came, we were held captive under the law, imprisoned until the coming faith would be revealed," writes Paul. "So then, the law was our guardian until Christ came, in order that we might be justified by faith." "The law served a limited purpose," Dale Leschert observes. "It was added as a temporary measure to check sin until the promised seed [Christ] arrived, but it was never intended to replace the promise as a means of imparting eternal life."[28] Before Christ, God used His Law to protect the Israelites from the evil, pagan nations encircling them.[29] It instructed them morally, gave them order, and helped them in their struggles with sin.

In a broader sense, the Law also makes us all aware of our utter depravity and our inability to live according to its rigid demands, so that we can readily see how desperately we need Christ. "The law whipped us to Christ and taught us that we could not be saved except by Christ," declares Charles Spurgeon. "The law acts as a pedagogue [teacher or master] by teaching us our obligations to God, by showing us our sinfulness, by sweeping away all our excuses."[30] He adds, "The spirit of the law condemns us. And this is its useful property; it humbles us, makes us know we are guilty, and so are we led to receive the Savior."[31]

Now that Christ has come, we are no longer under the guardianship of the Law, because in Christ we are all sons of God, through faith.

There are no distinctions among men—between Jew or Gentile, slave or free, male or female. We are all one in Jesus, and thus Abraham's spiritual offspring, by virtue of God's promise.

CHAPTER 4

Trying to get through to the straying Galatians, Paul analogizes man's position under the Law, prior to Christ's coming, to a minor's status under inheritance laws. Though a child stands to inherit from his parents in the future, his rights don't mature until they die. Being under his parents' care, he has little more freedom than a slave. Similarly, when man was under the Law he was hardly different from a slave. But when God's appointed time arrived, He sent His Son, born of a woman (Jesus Christ is fully human as well as fully God) and born under the Law as a Jew, and He was raised and lived under the Law. But God sent Him to redeem those who are enslaved by the Law, so that they might be adopted as God's sons and acquire full rights of spiritual inheritance—rights that have now matured because of their faith in Christ.

Having become God's children, the Galatians (and all believers) received the Holy Spirit, Who testifies to them that God is their "Abba! Father!" This means that as God's adoptive heirs, they are liberated from the Law and have gained an intimate relationship with Him. So why would they want to return to their slavery? Why would they want to go back to the weak and worthless "elementary principles of the world" and to observing "days and months and seasons and years"—the special days, feasts, rituals, rules, laws, and ordinances that they were required to fastidiously observe before they were liberated in Christ?

"What then has become of your blessedness?" Paul demands. They received Paul as an angel of God and accepted the Gospel eagerly but are now backsliding. The false teachers pretend to have their best interests at heart, but their sinister aim is to rip them right out of God's arms. The Galatians must learn to respect the truth and live the Gospel, whether or not Paul is there with them. But until they reach the point of spiritual maturity when Christ is formed in them, Paul will agonize over them. He wishes he could be with the brothers in person so he could relate to them more personally his genuine concerns.

Paul then allegorizes an Old Testament story. One of Abraham's sons, Ishmael, was born of the slave woman Hagar, and another son, Isaac, was born of the free woman Sarah. There was nothing abnormal about Ishmael's birth, but Isaac's birth was, in a sense, miraculous, for Sarah was too old for childbirth, yet God promised she would conceive (Gen. 17–16–19; 18:10). Paul likens these contrasting births to two of God's covenants. He compares Hagar to the Mosaic Covenant, whereby God gave His people the Law through Moses on Mount Sinai. She also corresponds to Jerusalem, which has been enslaved through strict adherence to laws and rules. By contrast, Sarah is like the heavenly Jerusalem (and the Abrahamic Covenant), which is free and glorious—she is the mother of those who are free under the grace of Jesus Christ.

Paul tells his Galatian brothers they are children of promise—they are the promised, adopted children of God who are free from the yoke of the Law because of their faith in Jesus Christ. Paul cautions them, however, that as Ishmael persecuted their spiritual ancestor Isaac, the false teachers now in slavery are trying to persecute them by luring them back into bondage. Therefore, they must figuratively "cast out the slave woman and her son"—they must rid themselves of the false teachers and the poison they're peddling and accept the freedom they have received through God's grace. They are not children of the slave woman and must quit acting like it. They are children of the free woman, heirs of God, and fellow heirs with Christ (Romans 8:17).[32] D. K. Campbell draws another valuable lesson from this allegory: like Isaac, who was supernaturally conceived, each believer in Christ is also supernaturally reborn (John 3:3) and is the recipient of the gift of salvation (Gal. 3:9, 22, 29).

CHAPTER 5

Now Paul comes to one of the central themes of his epistle: "For freedom Christ has set us free; stand firm therefore, and do not submit again to a yoke of slavery." He is adamant that the Galatians fully appreciate their freedom in Christ, especially compared with their former condition. This new life isn't about rules but is grounded in Christ's love and the good works that flow from it—as opposed to works performed out of fear of angering a disciplinarian Father. There is no intermediate position. If they return to the Law, they will reject Christ's grace. We are saved—declared righteous—by faith in Christ (justification). Also through faith—relying on the power of the Holy Spirit who indwells all believers—we become more Christ-like (sanctification). Further, believers eagerly anticipate their glorification upon Christ's return, when their righteousness will be perfected (Romans 8:18–25; Col. 1:5; 2 Tim. 4:8; 1 Peter 1:3–4; Heb. 9:24–28)[33] and their lowly bodies will be transformed into glorified bodies (Philip 3:21).

Paul praises the Galatians on their faith walk but observes that some people have enticed them off the path into false doctrine. He is confident they will ultimately come to their senses and reject the deceivers, who will be punished. Paul is not among those preaching that believers must be circumcised; otherwise he wouldn't be suffering persecution because "the offense of the cross [would then have] been removed." That is, if he were preaching that circumcision were still required, he would no longer be preaching the cross of Christ—because the two things are incompatible, and he would be free from persecution. As believers, the Galatian Christians were called to freedom, and they dared not squander their liberty by reverting to a works-based theology. Instead, they must be wise stewards of God's grace and serve one another through His love, which they can freely access through the Holy Spirit, as a result of their faith.

Christians have two conflicting natures, and the flesh will always battle with the Spirit and tempt them to sin (Romans 7:14–25). We don't become sin-free as believers but are empowered by the Holy Spirit to overcome sin daily. Consequently, Paul instructs believers to lean into the Spirit through faith, and He will empower them to resist the urge to sin. They must not return to a works-based system, which severs them from the Spirit and forces them to rely on their own human power to overcome sin, because that power will fail.

Paul provides a partial list of the sinful behavior they must strive to avoid through the power of the Holy Spirit: sexual immorality, impurity, sensuality, idolatry, sorcery, enmity, strife, jealousy, fits of anger, rivalries, dissensions, divisions, envy, drunkenness, orgies, and others. Those who engage in such things, Paul notes, will not inherit the kingdom of God. Paul does not mean that believers will lose their salvation through sin, or that believers won't sometimes engage in sinful conduct, but that if a person habitually engages in such behavior, He was probably never in Christ and does not have the Holy Spirit within (cf. 1 John 3:4–10).[34]

Paul closes the section on an uplifting note by identifying the fruit of the Spirit—that is, the good works the Spirit will produce in the heart of the believer who lives by faith, depending on the Spirit. These things are love, joy, peace, patience, kindness, goodness, faithfulness, gentleness, and self-control. Against these things there is no law—no one would prohibit such virtuous behavior. If we live by the Spirit, we must keep in step with the Spirit. Those who belong to Christ have crucified the flesh with its passions and desires.

This doesn't mean believers have permanently conquered their sinful nature (their flesh), but that they now have the means to overcome it daily by relying on the Holy Spirit, Which now indwells them as believers—and they must do so. As Jesus proclaimed, "If anyone would come after me, let him deny himself and take up his cross daily and follow me" (Luke 9:23). John Stott says that when we came to Christ as believers, we repented. We "crucified" all sinful behavior. We took our sinful nature and nailed it to the cross. But "we must renew every day this attitude towards sin of ruthless and uncompromising rejection. In the language of Jesus ... every Christian must 'take up his cross daily.'"[35]

When Paul says that we must live by the Spirit and keep step with it, he means that we should not only listen to the Spirit's promptings and follow Him, but also actively set our minds on the things of the Spirit. As Paul writes in his epistle to the Philippians, in one of my favorite verses, "Finally brothers, whatever is true, whatever is honorable, whatever is just, whatever is pure, whatever is lovely, whatever is commendable, if there is any excellence, if there is anything worthy of praise, think about these things" (4:8).[36] Please don't misunderstand—even here, we deserve no credit for our good works because they are done in the power of the Spirit. On the other hand, we should consciously exercise the spiritual disciplines—prayer, Bible study, fasting, etc.—to become closer to God, to walk with the Spirit, and to become more Christ-like. This is what we refer to as the process of sanctification, whereby we become holier and more Christ-like through the power of the Holy Spirit.

CHAPTER 6

Paul instructs those who are spiritual (mature Christians who are living and walking according to the Spirit)[37] to gently, through the power of the Spirit, restore anyone caught in any transgression. This means they should correct them without harshness. Paul is talking about fellow believers who are caught sinning, which is further proof that Paul is nowhere suggesting believers will become sin-free. Believers should constantly self-assess and not intentionally subject themselves to temptation. Likewise, Paul writes to the Corinthians, "Therefore, let anyone who thinks that he stands take heed lest he fall. No temptation has overtaken you that is not common to man. God is faithful, and he will not let you be tempted beyond your ability, but with the temptation he will also provide the way of escape, that you may be able to endure it" (1 Cor. 10:12–13). The constant theme is that in all cases, we must rely on God for the strength to overcome the relentless allures of the flesh, to protect us against a temptation beyond our ability, and to provide a means of escape from any such temptation. Faith in Christ is the way to salvation, but also of living in the Spirit and growing spiritually.

Paul admonishes the Galatians to bear one another's burdens and thereby fulfill the Law of Christ. If they insist on following some law, instead of resubmitting themselves to the bondage of the Jewish Law, let them follow the "law" of Christ and carry one another's burdens in the Spirit of Christ.[38] The Law of Christ is not a set of rules but involves selfless, sacrificial service for others and bearing their burdens. Remember, Christ did not come to abolish the Law but to fulfill it (Matt. 5:17). The moral law was always perfect, and He did not invalidate it. But it was never a means to salvation, and the civil and ceremonial aspects of the Law under Moses were made obsolete by Christ's coming. Indeed, as noted earlier, Jesus affirmed the moral law of God when He summarized it with the first two commandments: loving God and loving our neighbors (Matt. 22:36–40; John 13:34; 15:12; 1 John 3:23).[39] It's just that we can't obey the law on our own power, and must live under the power of the Holy Spirit. The Law of Christ is not works-based; it is following Christ's example in love through a spirit-empowered life of faith.

Paul cautions them not to be conceited and not to judge their conduct by comparing it to that of others. Rather, it should be a matter between a person and God: "Let the one who boasts, boast in the Lord" (1 Cor. 1:31). He then encourages them to share all good things with (financially support) teachers of the Word, which is not only the right thing to do but also facilitates the spread of the Word and the Church's spiritual enrichment. Paul warns that God shall not be mocked—each person will reap what he sows. They must "sow to the Spirit" and reap eternal life from the Spirit; they must not sow to their own flesh, which will only breed corruption. They must not revert to their old sin nature but consciously live in the Spirit. They must never tire of doing good and must, as the opportunity arises, do good to everyone, especially believers.

In keeping with the rest of the epistle, Paul closes his letter in a serious vein,[40] warning the brothers again about those who seek to draw them off the spiritual path to curry favor with other men and to avoid the persecution that is almost guaranteed to believers who reject the road back to circumcision. The false teachers advocating circumcision can't keep the Law themselves, but they want to boast about having enticed others off the pathway of truth and back into their lair. The only boasting should be in the cross of Christ. To boast in oneself is sinful pride, but to boast in Christ is to show humble gratitude for what He has done for us.

Paul says that by the cross, the world has been crucified to him, and he to the world. He has rejected the old way, the way that led him to wrongly persecute believers. He has accepted Christ in faith, put off his sin nature, and become a new creature in Christ. Jesus said, "If anyone is in Christ, he is a new creation. The old has passed away; behold, the new has come" (2 Cor. 5:17; cf. Romans 6:4). He is in the world, but no longer of the world (John 17:16). Paul says that no one, including the Judaizers, should criticize him—not because he is virtuous, but because he has given himself to Christ, has figuratively taken up his own cross and followed Him (Luke 9:23). He bears on his body the marks of Jesus. He has been persecuted in every conceivable way for following and preaching Christ, so he needs no lectures from false teachers.

Despite frustration with the Galatian brothers, Paul has genuine love for them in Christ, and he has a heartfelt passion that they remain on course and in God's love. Paul, even in his firmness, is ever full of grace and affection. That comes through even more in the next epistles to the Thessalonian church, another congregation Paul established, which seems to occupy a special place in his heart.

CHAPTER SEVEN

1 THESSALONIANS & 2 THESSALONIANS
CHRIST'S RETURN AND THE DAY OF THE LORD

*I and II Thessalonians may be regarded therefore as
an important source for the subsequent formulation
of doctrine, as an indispensable guide for the study of
the man Paul, and as an important chapter in a handbook for missionaries. . . . It is above all a part of
God's infallible special revelation, which comes to every
believer with absolute, divine authority, and shows
him what he should believe and how he should live.*

—WILLIAM HENDRIKSEN[1]

1 THESSALONIANS

Paul twice identifies himself as the author of this epistle (1:1; 2:18), though Silvanus (Silas) and Timothy are included in the opening salutation because they work closely with Paul.[2] As you will recall from Acts, Paul completes three missionary journeys before his voyage to Rome. During his second journey, he and his group take the Gospel into Macedonia (north of Greece), establishing churches along the way. They are well received in Thessalonica but encounter fierce opposition from Jewish groups, including a violent mob, causing them to leave for nearby Berea during the night. From Berea, they travel south into Athens and then on to Corinth.

Concerned for the new believers in Thessalonica and for the progress of the church there following his precipitous departure, Paul sends Timothy back to check on them. Timothy's favorable report leads Paul to write this letter from Corinth to the church in Thessalonica toward the end of his second missionary journey around 50–51 AD, within two decades of Christ's death and Resurrection. We know from this letter, from his second letter to the Thessalonians, and to a lesser extent from his letters to the Philippians, the Corinthians, and the Romans that Paul is pleased with the churches he founded in Thessalonica and elsewhere in Macedonia (2 Cor. 8:1–5; 11:9; Romans 15:26) and with their steadfast faith and generous giving, including to the church in Jerusalem.[3]

Despite the overall progress of the church, however, there are issues he needs to address. Some congregants have died since Paul founded the church, and the believers are anxious about their status upon Christ's return (1 Thess. 4:13). Would they not witness Christ's second coming? In the letter, Paul answers their questions and instructs them on other matters, including the practice of wealthier brothers supporting some church members. Additionally, Paul evidently feels compelled to explain to the Thessalonians why he has not yet returned.

CHAPTER 1

In his initial address, Paul describes the church in Thessalonica as being "in God the Father and the Lord Jesus Christ." Australian New Testament scholar Leon Morris says this phrase, which is unique to the two epistles to this church, is significant because it includes the Father and the Son in one breath. No one besides the Son could be linked with the Father like this, notes Morris, as it shows their relationship could not be any closer. "And all this in a letter written only about twenty years after the crucifixion," writes Morris. "From very early times Jesus was seen to have the highest place."[4] This helps to debunk the modern notion that Jesus' deity was an afterthought superimposed on Christianity in the second century or later. In fact, He was accepted as fully God (and fully man) from the very beginning, as this statement—and so many other New Testament passages—elucidates.

Paul begins the letter effusively praising the Thessalonians, assuring them he constantly prays for them and thanking God for their "work of faith and labor of love and steadfastness of hope in our Lord Jesus Christ." This is a different tone from the one adopted in his letter to the Galatians, which is more critical than complimentary—but Galatians is one of a few exceptions, for Paul writes approvingly in most of his epistles.[5] He constantly asks for God's beneficent superintendence of these newly formed churches, which is an encouraging reminder to us of the timeless value of prayer, and that we should cultivate it as our constant practice. Interestingly, John Stott proposes that we pray and work for better memories because when we remember people—their faces, names, and needs—we are moved to thank God and to pray for them.[6]

Paul's emphasis on "faith, hope, and love" is vitally important, as these three interrelated qualities are central to one's Christian character (1 Cor. 13:13)[7] and often appear together in Paul's letters (Romans 5:1–5; 1 Cor. 13:13; Gal. 5:5–6; Eph. 1:15–18; 4:2–5; Col 1:4–5; 1 Thess. 5:8) and in other New Testament writings (Heb. 10:22–24; 1 Peter 1:3–8, 21–22). Paul observes that because of their conversion, the Thessalonians are exhibiting these winsome attributes.[8] As in Galatians, Paul underscores that their good works flow from their faith, not from their efforts (cf. Gal 2:16), and from their love, which is tied to their faith—for faith works through love (Gal. 5:6).

There are several Greek words translated as "love" in English, such as *eros*, *phileo*, and *agape*. *Eros*, meaning sexual love, is not used in the New Testament.[9] *Agape* is used much more than *phileo*. Some scholars say that *phileo* means "spontaneous natural affection" and includes the concepts of brotherly love and friendship.[10] Others say it's difficult to distinguish between the usage of *agape* and *phileo* in the New Testament.[11] In a quick Bible word study, I could only find two instances of Paul using *phileo* (1 Cor. 16:22 and Titus 3:15, although it may be used in other variations) as opposed to more than a hundred uses of *agape*.

Agape was apparently not used much before Christians started invoking it, and that's because the Christian idea of love is more profound than any previous notions of love. Just imagine the revolutionary notion that love fulfills and summarizes the entire Law (Matt. 5:17, 22:36–40), as

Jesus plainly taught. Similarly, Paul writes, "For the whole law is fulfilled in one word: 'You shall love your neighbor as yourself'" (Gal. 5:14). Paul also talks of Christian love as the law of Christ: "Bear one another's burdens, and so fulfill the law of Christ" (Gal. 6:2).

Selflessness and other-directedness are central to this idea. Consider *eros*, which often describes a love based on merit (love that is deserved) and on a desire to possess. *Agape*, in its Christian sense, denotes the opposite: to love the undeserving despite disappointment and rejection.[12] In His earthly ministry, and especially in His death, Christ showed his love for undeserving sinners (John 3:16; Romans 5:8; 1 John 4:10.). As He said, "Greater love has no one than this, that someone lay down his life for his friends" (John 15:13). Christ's love emanates not from a desire to possess in the human sense, but to give.[13] We noted that faith and love are interconnected. "For in Christ Jesus," writes Paul, "neither circumcision nor uncircumcision counts for anything, but only faith working through love" (Gal. 5:6).

Love, as we are describing it, is God's gift to the believer through the Holy Spirit. Christ, through the Holy Spirit, now lives in the believer (Gal. 2:20), and it is His love that should characterize that of the believer. Paul sets out the Christian ideal for love in a famous passage in 1 Cor. 13.[14] Elsewhere he explains that the Christian's love reflects "God's love [that] has been poured into our hearts through the Holy Spirit who has been given to us" (Romans 5:5), and is both directed toward Christ (1 Cor. 16:22; Eph. 6:24) and our fellow human beings.[15]

We noted that Paul thanks God for the Thessalonians' faith, hope, and love, and we've briefly discussed faith and love. The meaning of "hope," as used in the New Testament, differs slightly from the modern term. It is not simply a longing for a future event to materialize. It is a confident expectation that it will occur—a firm confidence that God's promises will be fulfilled. Nothing is more fundamental to Christianity than the Christian's confident assurance that he will be resurrected to eternal life because of his faith in Jesus Christ, Who was first resurrected. Indeed, as Paul writes, "And if Christ has not been raised, your faith is futile and you are still in your sins. Then those who have fallen asleep in Christ have perished. If in Christ we have hope in this life only, we are of all people most to be pitied" (1 Cor. 15:17–19).[16]

Note how certain is the Christian's hope in his eternal life in Christ, as described by Peter: "Blessed be the God and Father of our Lord Jesus Christ! According to his great mercy, he has caused us to be born again to a living hope through the resurrection of Jesus Christ from the dead, to an inheritance that is imperishable, undefiled, and unfading, kept in heaven for you, who by God's power are being guarded through faith for a salvation ready to be revealed in the last time" (1 Peter 1:3–5). In the context of this epistle, however, Paul uses "hope" to describe another of God's promises—that Christ will return in His Second Coming.[17] This is a particular concern the Thessalonian Christians convey to Timothy, which Paul addresses in this letter.

Paul repeatedly uses the terms "brother" and "brothers" in his two letters to the Thessalonians as well as in his other writings. We've reviewed the conflict in the early Church arising from Jewish believers clinging to their former rules and insisting that Gentile believers adopt these rituals. But in Christ, there is no distinction between Jew and Gentile (Romans 2:10–11), so not only are the ceremonial laws no longer applicable, but Jewish believers can now dine with Gentile believers. It's remarkable that these distinctions have already been obliterated to the point that Paul can now address his Gentile converts as "brothers," with all the acceptance, equality, and intimacy it implies.

St. Augustine observes that the Jews thought the Gentiles were weak, sinful, servants of demons, and idol worshippers, though their Scriptures taught that all men are sinners (Psalm 14:3). But in Christ, "they have laid down their pride, and have not envied the salvation of the Gentiles, because they have known their own and their weakness to be alike: and in the Corner Stone being united, they have together worshipped the Lord."[18] Similarly, Leon Morris argues, "The tie that bound the proud Pharisee to despised Gentiles was a close one. Barriers insurmountable to men were done away in Christ."[19] Of course, we have seen through history that this is a two-way street, and Jews have suffered mightily at the hands of Gentiles.

In Romans, Paul further explicates the concept of brotherly love in Christ: "Why do you pass judgment on your brother? Or you, why do you despise your brother? For we will all stand before the judgment seat of God" (14:10). Furthermore, "May the God of endurance and encouragement grant you to live in such harmony with one another, in accord with Christ Jesus, that together you may with one voice glorify the God and Father of our Lord Jesus Christ. Therefore, welcome one another as Christ has welcomed you, for the glory of God" (15:5–7). Finally, he adds, "For I tell you that Christ became a servant to the circumcised to show God's truthfulness, in order to confirm the promises given to the patriarchs, and in order that the Gentiles might glorify God for his mercy" (15:8–9). Paul's teachings support Jesus' admonition: "By this all people will know that you are my disciples, if you have love for one another" (John 13:35; cf 1 John 3:14). Let us take this lesson to heart. "Then let the Jews not condemn the Gentiles as 'sinners,' writes Allen Verhey, "and let the Gentiles not despise the Jews into whose promises they enter."[20]

Paul assures the Thessalonians he knows their faith is authentic because he and the apostles communicated the Gospel to them with conviction, both in word and in the power of the Holy Spirit. Paul isn't boasting about the quality of his evangelism, but is confidently asserting that God is speaking through him and the other apostles.[21] For Paul, the glory always belongs to Christ. The content of the Gospel is expressed in words, but it is more—it's the living Word of God, full of His Spirit and power. It transforms lives. The Thessalonians don't merely respond with comprehension and assent but with a Spirit-led conversion, and they demonstrate their conversion by their fruit.

With the Gospel radically altering their lives, the congregants become imitators of the apostles and of Christ as they embrace Him joyously, despite enormous opposition and persecution. In following the apostles' Christ-like example, they model such behavior to believers throughout Macedonia and Achaia (the southern portion of Greece), and their example reverberates beyond those areas as news of their transformation circulates widely.[22] In turn, new believers in these places imitate them, to the extent that Paul and the apostles don't need to evangelize there. "The imitators became the imitated!"[23]

Here, the Gospel is not spreading through some mystical, euphoric trance, but through the power of the Holy Spirit and the evidence of His presence in the Thessalonian believers, who are world-class witnesses for God's glory. These believers have reported to Paul how well received he and his group were in Thessalonica, and how the Thessalonians had turned from worshipping pagan idols to serving the true and living God and waiting for His Son to return. Let's understand the import of Paul's words: there is one and only one God. Those who argue that other religions worship the same God are preaching a false Gospel, knowingly or not.

CHAPTER 2

◇◇◇◇◇◇◇◇◇◇◇◇◇◇◇◇◇◇◇◇◇◇◇

Paul assures the brothers that his mission to them was not in vain because their acceptance of Christ was worth any hardship the apostles endured. The apostles deemed the mission so important that they risked their personal safety to bring the Good News to them on the heels of being assaulted at Philippi. It is their duty to share God's Word with the world, a message that is perfect and true because it emanates from God, and God superintends their evangelism. Their motivation is not to please man but God, as they have demonstrated repeatedly. If personal glory were their goal, they could have used their standing as apostles to demand special treatment. Instead, they treat the new believers with gentle care. Paul goes to great lengths to reiterate his credentials and the integrity of his Gospel message, probably because false teachers are trying to discredit them and their message and turn the Thessalonians to a false gospel.[24]

While Paul and his group obediently preached the Gospel to the Thessalonians—working day and night to support themselves so as not to burden them—they developed a deep bond of Christian love with them. Paul explains they are witnesses to how well Paul's group treated them—as a father treats his children—exhorting them, encouraging them, and challenging them to walk the Christian walk.

Paul thanks God constantly that the brothers accepted the Gospel not as if it were merely a message from men, but as God's Word. As a result, the Word is now at work in them as believers. They have become imitators of the churches in Judea in suffering persecution from their own countrymen (both Thessalonian Gentiles and Jews),[25] just as the Judean churches were abused by their Jewish opponents—the ones who killed Jesus Christ and the prophets, drove out Paul and the apostles, and displease God and oppose all mankind by hindering the spread of the Gospel to the Gentiles for their salvation. But wrath has finally come upon them. Paul's words here are particularly harsh toward his fellow Jews. Douglas Moo—and many other commentators—notes that Paul is expressing frustration with those who are threatening the Gentile mission. Moreover, it's crucial to note that Paul is not generalizing about all Jews, but only referring to those who committed these specific acts.[26]

Paul laments that he was forced out of Thessalonica and that Satan has obstructed his earnest desire to return. The brothers are his glory and joy. To prove he has faithfully executed his apostolic duties, he looks forward to presenting them as his converts to Jesus at His second coming.[27]

CHAPTER 3

Though Paul doesn't want to lose Timothy's company and assistance in Athens, he is so anxious to follow up with the Thessalonians that he sends him back to check on them and to support them in their faith, as they are being attacked and tested. Paul elsewhere calls Timothy his "fellow worker" (Romans 16:21) and frequently uses the term to describe others as well (Romans 16:3; 9; 2 Cor. 8:23, etc.), but here he calls Timothy God's coworker in the Gospel of Christ, which implies that in addition to helping Paul, he has his own ministry.[28] Paul might be emphasizing Timothy's credentials to mitigate any possible resentment the Thessalonians may feel—he doesn't want them to think he is short-changing them by sending Timothy instead of coming himself.[29]

Commentators relate that English doesn't quite capture the Greek term describing what Paul means by allowing himself to be "left behind" in Athens. The Greek word *kataleipo* conveys a sense of desolation, like one would experience in leaving his parents when he marries (Eph. 5:31) or when someone dies (Mark 12:19). Paul reinforces this sentiment with the word "alone"—he is being left behind alone in Athens.[30] Paul has deep, conflicting feelings—he does not want to lose his strongest ally in Timothy and fend off the Athenian scoffers by himself, but he does not want to abandon the Thessalonians either. In the end, as usual, he opts for the selfless route. Paul is following his own advice to the Philippians to model Christ's example of sacrificial love: "Let each of you look not only to his own interests, but also to the interests of others" (Philip 2:4). He warned them they would continue to be persecuted; that is their destiny as Christians.

Paul also confesses that part of his motive in sending Timothy to them is his concern that Satan might have lured them away from the faith. This is the second time in the epistle that Paul mentions Satan, the first being verse 2:18, when Paul tells them Satan has repeatedly prevented him from returning to them personally. Paul is quite anxious about his burgeoning church in Thessalonica, and he can hardly stand to be in the dark about its spiritual condition, even in the midst of his own suffering. This is a testament to his love for them—a love that resembles the concern of a parent for the proper development of his child.

Paul is comforted by Timothy's good report about their faith and love. He is invigorated—as if he has a new lease on life[31]—by the news that they are standing firm in the Lord. Paul's heart is on fire for Jesus Christ, and he is overflowing with loving affection for his Thessalonian brothers.[32] He can't thank God enough for the happiness He brings him and his fellow missionaries for safeguarding the Thessalonians in their faith. Every day and night he prays that the missionaries can return to them and supply any further instruction they need to shore up their faith.

This seems completely natural to me. New believers, no matter how well instructed or how diligently they read the Bible and pray, often have questions and need spiritual mentorship to reassure them and nurture their spiritual growth. Paul is concerned that deficiencies in their knowledge might render them vulnerable to Satan, but Timothy's positive report has assured him their faith can fend off the enemy. But he is still determined to return to "see them face to face and supply what is lacking in [their] faith," and he prays to God the Father and Jesus Christ to enable this trip. He asks God to infuse the brothers with an ever-growing love for one another and for others, so they will be made holy before God the Father when Jesus returns.

CHAPTER 4

∞∞∞∞∞∞∞∞∞∞∞∞∞∞∞∞∞

Having reviewed his personal relationship with the brothers and other matters, Paul imparts practical instructions on living their lives to please God. Earlier, he mentored them on their Christian walk. They are proving to be faithful and must continue on this path, walking ever closer to God because God wills they continue in the process of sanctification (becoming more holy and Christ-like). Specifically, they should abstain from sexual immorality and control their bodies in holiness and honor, eschewing the passion and lustfulness practiced by godless pagans. They mustn't lure others into sexual sin or harm them through their own sexual misconduct, for God will hold them to account.

Paul often repeats and reinforces themes to ensure his readers understand and remember them. While believers in the early Church are familiar with essential Christian doctrine through passed-down creedal formulas,[33] they don't yet have the New Testament, though this letter would later become a part of it. As Christians, they have the Holy Spirit and are called to holiness. To disobey that charge is to dishonor God, Who gave them the Spirit. Paul's instructions, then, are not informal guidelines from the apostles but commands from God Himself, through the apostles as messengers.[34]

Even with the Holy Spirit, however, new believers are not insulated against the temptations of the flesh (Gal. 5:17). Therefore, they must be taught and encouraged to walk with the Spirit (Gal. 5:16) and remain vigilant because their adversary, the devil, prowls around like a roaring lion seeking someone to devour (1 Peter 5:8). Paul acknowledges that the believers are filled with brotherly love, but exhorts them to love one another even more. They must be financially independent and not rely on the generosity of fellow believers, which apparently, some have been doing. No explanation is given for their idleness, but because they believed Christ could return soon, they might have decided to just sit and wait.[35] We'll find that this problem later intensifies, forcing Paul to address it more aggressively in 2 Thessalonians 3:6–15.[36]

Paul next addresses their nagging concern about their Christian brothers who have already died. Most translations use the term "sleep" instead of death, but it's just a euphemism. It does not mean, as some cults contend, that when believers die they enter into a form of unconscious soul sleep as they await their resurrection (cf. Luke 23:43; 1 Thess. 4:17; Philip. 1:21–23).[37] "The Bible teaches that between death and resurrection, the human soul/spirit survives consciously apart from its body," Dr. Norman Geisler observes. "This is neither a state of annihilation nor a state of unconscious 'sleep'; this is an eternal state of conscious bliss for the saved and conscious anguish for the lost."[38]

Christians shouldn't grieve like nonbelievers who have no hope. They may grieve (cf. Acts 8:2), but their grief should not be hopeless.[39] Their faith in Christ's resurrection assures them that God, through Christ, will bring with Him those believers who have already died before His return. Those still alive when Christ returns will see Him, but not before those who have died earlier. Jesus will descend from Heaven with a commanding cry, the voice of an archangel, and the sound of God's trumpet. Then the deceased believers will rise first, when their new, imperishable resurrected bodies will be reunited with their souls (cf. 1 Cor. 15:51–53),[40] followed by living believers. They will all be caught up together in the clouds to meet Christ in the air,[41] and they will always be with Him.

This passage (1 Thess. 4:13–18) together with John 14:1–3 and 1 Corinthians 15:51–52 constitute the biblical basis for the Rapture of the Church.[42] Paul is teaching the Rapture as a revelation of previously hidden truth or mystery (1 Cor. 15:51).[43] Scholars differ on when the Rapture will occur, but I believe it's immediately prior to the seven-year period referred to as the Great Tribulation—Christ will remove believers during the Rapture, sparing them from this agonizing period when the Antichrist will reign down his evil schemes on the earth. (There are other legitimate views on this, which I briefly discuss in the footnotes.)[44]

We must distinguish between "the Rapture," the "Day of the Lord," and Christ's "Second Coming." Christ does return at the Rapture, as Paul discusses in this chapter, but this is not what scholars mean by His Second Coming. At the Rapture, He draws believers—those who have already died and those still living at the time—up from the earth into the clouds to be with Him. In Chapter 5, Paul goes on to discuss the Day of the Lord. This has several meanings, one of which includes the Second

Coming, as we discuss below. "Apparently, the Thessalonians were informed fully about the Day of the Lord judgment (cf. 5:1, 2), but not the preceding event—the rapture of the church," writes John MacArthur. "The Rapture was kept secret prior to Paul disclosing it as God's revelation to him—the only prior mention is Jesus' teaching in John 14:1–3."[45]

CHAPTER 5

Paul now discusses the Day of the Lord. He tells the brothers that the precise date of Christ's return should not be their concern, echoing Jesus' admonition to the apostles before Pentecost that "it is not for you to know the times or seasons that the Father has fixed by his own authority" (Acts 1:7). They well know that the Day of the Lord "will come like a thief in the night," meaning it will happen unexpectedly.[46] People will believe they have peace and security, and suddenly, inescapable destruction will descend on them like labor pains upon a pregnant woman.

The Thessalonian brothers, however, being children of light and not of darkness, will not be caught by surprise, for they are already in Christ and will already be with Him.[47] The present world is sometimes described as a place of darkness (Eph. 6:12). But God "has qualified [the believer] to share in the inheritance of the saints in light. He has delivered us from the domain of darkness and transferred us to the kingdom of his beloved Son" (Col 1:12–13). He brings light to the hearts of those in darkness (cf. Luke 1:78–79; Acts 26:18)[48] and has "made His light shine in our hearts to give us the light of the knowledge of God's glory displayed in the face of Christ" (2 Cor. 4:6 NIV).

The phrase "the Day of the Lord" is used some nineteen times in the Old Testament (e.g., Amos 5:18; Isaiah 13:6; Jer. 46:10) and four times in the New Testament, (Acts. 2:20; 1 Thess. 5:2; 2 Thess. 2:2; 2 Peter 3:10). It can be confusing because the term has multiple meanings. Old Testament prophets used the phrase variously to describe either judgments that would come in the near future, such as the fall of Babylon to the Assyrians as prophesied by Isaiah,[49] or judgments that would come in the distant future (end times).[50] These are God's judgments for man's sinfulness and sometimes His blessings for his obedience.

Paul is referring in this epistle to the Day of the Lord that will occur in the end times, so let's narrow our discussion to that context. Some scholars believe this future Day of the Lord has two distinct components, both involving horrifying judgments from God for the consummate sinfulness of the world.[51] The first is Christ's Second Coming, which these scholars believe will occur at the end of the seven-year tribulation period that immediately follows the Rapture (cf. Rev. 19:11–21), and the second, approximately a thousand years later, is God's judgment that will occur at the end of Christ's thousand-year millennial reign on the earth (cf. 2 Peter 3:10; Rev. 20:7–15).[52] Scripture teaches that in both instances—Christ's coming in judgment at the end of the seven-year tribulation, and the judgment at the end of Christ's millennial reign—the Day of the Lord "will come like a thief in the night." The phrase, as noted above, is never used in connection with the Rapture of the Church.[53]

Other scholars believe the Day of the Lord is a more general term to describe a continuous thousand-year period that begins with Christ's Second Coming and ends with His millennial reign.[54] The main difference between the views seems to be that one considers the Day of the Lord and the Second Coming to be two separate events that begin and end Christ's millennial reign, while the other believes it includes the whole period. The important thing for our limited purposes here is to understand that the future Day of the Lord includes Christ's Second Coming to the earth and is distinct from the Rapture, in which Christ does return but draws believers up to meet Him in the clouds rather than coming down to the earth to begin His millennial reign. (For a brief outline of major end time events, see the footnotes.)[55]

Regardless of the timeline and order of events, the brothers must remain sober-minded, vigilant, and aware, ever shielded by their breastplate of faith and love and their hope of salvation, which is their helmet; for they are destined for salvation through faith in Jesus Christ, not for God's wrath. As such, they can rest assured of their eternal life in Him, whether they are awake (alive) or asleep (physically dead) when He returns. Therefore, they must continue to uplift one another.

Paul implores the brothers to respect their fellow Christians and spiritual leaders in love because of their work. They must remain in peace. Further, they should admonish idle and unruly people (and correct their behavior), encourage those struggling in their faith, aid the weak and fainthearted, and be patient toward them all. Patience is included in Paul's list of characteristics of the Spirit-filled person (fruit of the Spirit—Gal. 5:22) and is an oft-touted Christian virtue (1 Cor. 13:4; 2 Cor. 6:6; 1 Thess. 5:14; Eph. 4:2; Col. 1:11; James 5:7, 8; Rev. 2:2). Those who are further along in their faith walk must not be puffed up and disrespectful toward less advanced believers. They must be gracious, patient, and supportive of them. As taught by Jesus (Matt. 5:44) and the Old Testament (Prov. 25:21), they must not respond to evil with their own evil (cf. Romans 12:17). They should strive to treat everyone well, believers and non-believers alike (Gal 6:10). This is consistent with Paul's earlier prayer for the growth of the Church and for their increasing love for one another (1 Thess. 3:12).

The brothers must constantly rejoice and continually pray, thanking God for everything because this is His will for them in Christ. They should not be condescending and judgmental toward others and taint the Church's positive spirit. Rather, Christian assemblies should be infused with God's love, and His spirit of goodwill should contagiously infect the congregation (cf. 1 Cor. 14:15–17; Eph. 5:19–20; Col. 3:16–17)[56]—which is not to say that preachers should avoid tough issues of sinning.

For Paul, joy is essential to a healthy Christian life.[57] Further, thankfulness—giving thanks to God—is not just the Christian's duty, but should be his privilege. Even in difficult times, we must be grateful for our unearned salvation. Ingratitude is characteristic of the rebellious, unrighteous, and hard-hearted (cf. Romans 1:21; 2 Tim. 3:2).

The brothers dare not "quench" (suppress) the Holy Spirit, which is God's gift to believers to empower them to overcome sin and to escape its bondage. Elsewhere, Paul admonishes Christians not to "grieve the Holy Spirit" (Eph. 4:30), meaning we should not resist Him or sadden Him through our sinning.[58] Some scholars reject the notion that people's actions can affect God's emotions, and I concede it is paradoxical that an omniscient being would react emotionally to events he foresees. Nevertheless, I believe it marvelously demonstrates that we worship a personal and interactive God. To grasp this concept, we can refer to the prophet Isaiah's description of the Israelites rebelling and grieving the

Holy Spirit in their wilderness wonderings (Isaiah 63:9; cf. Judges 10:15–16). "God was afflicted and saddened," Gary Smith notes, "when his people sinned and did not trust him to give them the land."[59]

Specifically, the Thessalonians must not disrespect the Spirit's gift of prophecy, though they must test prophecies against the truth. Prophecy doesn't just include predictive utterances, but any authoritative messages from God. These are usually from Scripture but sometimes from His prophets' spoken revelations.[60] The Bible repeatedly addresses the testing of prophets and teachers. Moses says, "And if you say in your heart, 'How may we know the word that the Lord has not spoken?'—when a prophet speaks in the name of the Lord, if the word does not come to pass or come true, this is a word that the Lord has not spoken; the prophet has spoken it presumptuously" (Deut. 18:21–22). Jesus warns us to beware of false prophets who come to us in sheep's clothing but are like ravenous wolves. We will recognize them by their fruits (Matt. 7:15–16). John counsels that true prophets confess that Jesus Christ has come in the flesh and "every spirit that does not confess Jesus is not from God" (1 John 4:1–3). And Peter writes that false prophets "will secretly bring in destructive heresies, even denying the Master who brought them, bringing upon themselves swift destruction (2 Peter 2:1). Scripture is consistent: we must use our Spirit-led discernment and weigh the prophet's words against the inviolable truth of Holy Scripture to determine whether he is speaking truthfully.

Paul further instructs the believers to abstain from evil in all its forms—another admonition from Old Testament prophets (cf. Isaiah 1:16–17) that Paul stresses in his other letters (cf. Romans 12:9).

In closing, Paul prays they continue their process of sanctification so they will be blameless when Christ returns—which He will, because the God who called them is faithful and will fulfill His promise to send Him. Paul asks for their prayers and instructs them, under oath before God, to read this letter to all their fellow believers.

2 THESSALONIANS

Certain critics have disputed Paul's authorship of this epistle, but he mentions his own name twice in the body of the letter (1:1; 3:17), and the early Church fathers attribute it to Paul.[61] As with 1 Thessalonians, Paul includes Silvanus (Silas) and Timothy in the salutation because they are his close coworkers. Scholars believe Paul writes this letter from Corinth shortly after he wrote his first letter to this church (around 50 AD). Having evidently received a report that conditions at the church had deteriorated (3:11), he writes this letter to correct the believers' misapprehension that the Day of the Lord has already come, to reassure them in view of their ongoing persecution, and to address their reported idleness.[62] The church members, believing they were to be exempted from God's judgment, fear their persecution indicates that the Day of the Lord has already come.[63]

Paul sometimes writes with a more direct, authoritative voice than in the first letter, but he still shows warmth and affection.[64] For example, he refers to the letter's recipients as "brothers" about as often as he did in the longer first letter. Paul's bluntness probably stems from his urgency to address the congregation's unresolved problems. In his first letter, he strongly encouraged them to live in the Spirit, to be joyful and thankful, and not to grieve the Holy Spirit. Yet they are anxious and gloomy, and don't seem to be exercising the Spirit-filled characteristic of self-control. This letter is a wake-up call to correct their errors and reorient them to the path of Christian living.[65]

CHAPTER 1

Paul begins this epistle by saying, "We ought always to give thanks to God for you, brothers." Some question Paul's sincerity here,[66] but I do not, seeing as Paul quickly compliments the congregants on their abundantly growing faith and their increasing love for one another. Though their theology is confused, they are growing in the Lord, which Paul specifically prayed for in his first letter to them (1 Thess. 3:12; 4:1). He praises them for remaining steadfast in their faith even under persecution, and notes that he boasts about them to other churches.

Their perseverance through suffering is evidence of God's righteous judgment and their worthiness of the kingdom of God. They are Christ-centered, honoring Jesus' command to "seek first the kingdom of God and his righteousness" (Matt. 6:33), which has enabled them to cope with their persecution.[67] The great evangelist John Wesley was convinced that suffering is a gift from God that authenticates one's Christian walk. He told an anecdote illustrating this point: one day, as Wesley was traveling, he became alarmed when he realized he had gone three days without suffering. He fell to his knees and asked God to show him where he had gone astray. A cantankerous man across the hedge recognized Wesley and said to himself, "I'll fix that Methodist preacher." He threw a rock at him, which missed but fell beside Wesley, who leapt to his feet and exclaimed, "Thank God, it's all right. I still have his presence."[68]

Of course, it's not their persecution alone that proves believers' worthiness. John Stott argues that it's both their suffering for Christ and their faith, love, and endurance during trials that prove God's judgment is righteous.[69] Leon Morris concurs, writing, "We should not understand the evidence to be the sufferings. It is not the persecutions but the attitude of the Thessalonians in their troubles that is the decisive thing. Such constancy and faith could come only from the action of God within them."[70]

Paul assures the Thessalonians their suffering is not the final chapter in this story. God will eventually vindicate them, bring their tormentors to judgment, and provide relief to the afflicted brothers and others who have endured persecution for His sake. This will occur when Christ is revealed from heaven with His mighty angels in flaming fire, inflicting vengeance on those who do not know God or obey the Gospel. Paul is not describing the Rapture but Christ's Second Coming (or the Day of the Lord) as he's discussing Christ's judgment, and no judgment accompanies the Rapture.[71] The brothers can rest assured that Christ has not yet returned, because when He does, there will be no mistaking it—He will come with great fanfare and judgment and with power and great glory (Matt. 24:30). Ever since Christ's ascension there have been false Messiahs, just as Christ predicted (Matt. 24:24), but none of them has or could remotely simulate the glorious supernatural nature of His return.[72]

Paul declares that those who do not know God will be subject to eternal destruction, away from God's presence and glory. As difficult as some may find this language, it is clear. Paul is not describing the permanent annihilation of the godless (Matt. 25:46; Rev. 14:9–11),[73] but their unending punishment in which they remain in a conscious state, aware of their predicament and their separation from God's presence (Rev. 20:14, 15). Like it or not, Jesus taught precisely the same thing (Matt. 5:29–30; 8:12; 12:32; 18:8–9; 22:13; 25:30, 41; 46; Luke 16:23–26). This has been the predominant view among believers, Church fathers, and theologians throughout Christian history, including Tertullian, Augustine, Anselm, and Jonathan Edwards.[74]

When Christ comes on that day, He will be glorified in his believers who will marvel at Him, because they have believed in Him. Don't miss the significance here. Believers, in the process of sanctification through the power of the indwelling Spirit, manifest the fruit of the Spirit (Gal. 5:22–23), as they are progressively transformed into Christ's likeness (cf. Eph. 4:23–24; Col. 3:10).[75] They "are being transformed into the same image from one degree of glory to another" (2 Cor. 3:18), but when they meet Christ they will be glorified with Him (Romans 8:17) and will reflect His light and attributes immeasurably more than during their earthly Christian walk. At this point, their sanctification will be complete. "Every vestige of sin will have been banished from their soul," notes William Hendriksen. "They will mirror forth his image and walk in the light of his countenance (Ps. 89:15–17)."[76] Christ will rejoice in His reflection in the believers and in their joy (cf. Zeph. 3:17).[77] This description would surely reassure the believers, which is one of Paul's primary aims in writing this letter.

In anticipation of these events, Paul and his companions always pray for the brothers, that God may make them worthy of His calling, give them the power to live holy lives, and accomplish good works through their faith in Him. Then the Lord Jesus' name will be glorified in them and they will be glorified in Him, which is made possible by the grace of God the Father and His Son Jesus Christ.

CHAPTER 2

In his first epistle to the Thessalonians, Paul assured the brothers that, contrary to their fears, believers who had already died would not miss the resurrection. In this epistle, he addresses a different fear—that they have missed the Rapture because they understand it will occur prior to the Day of the Lord, which they assume has already occurred because they are suffering persecution.

Paul tells them that in reference to Christ coming and gathering all believers to Himself (the Rapture), they don't need to be alarmed if they learn from a spirit, the spoken word, or even a letter purportedly from him, that the Day of the Lord (Christ's Second Coming) has already occurred.[78] When Paul told them about the Rapture, he had assured them that they, as believers, would be spared the Day of the Lord, and he meant it. They must not allow anyone to deceive them, for certain events, which have not yet transpired, must precede the Day of the Lord. (Here he's referring not to the Rapture, but probably to Christ's coming in judgment at the end of the seven-year tribulation.)[79] These events include 1) the rebellion and 2) the revealing of the man of lawlessness (the Antichrist, or the one who brings destruction).

The New Testament frequently warns of this great rebellion or "apostasy" that will occur prior to Christ's Second Coming.[80] Jesus taught that many will fall away and betray and hate one another. False prophets will lead people astray, lawlessness will spread, and the love of many will grow cold. But those who endure will be saved, and His Gospel will be proclaimed throughout the whole world before the end will come (Matt. 24:10–14). Paul issues similar warnings in his other letters (1 Tim. 4:1; 2 Tim. 3:1–5; 4:3–4), as do James (5:1–8), Peter (2 Peter 2; 3:3–6), Jude (1:18–19), and John (Rev. 3:10).

Many scholars contend that this rebellion will feature people inside the Church turning away from God and worshipping the Antichrist.[81] F. F. Bruce emphasizes this will involve more than just an internal Church issue. It will likely be a "general abandonment of the basis of civil order … a large-scale revolt against public order"—a rebellion against "the whole concept of divine authority over the world."[82] There was a period of apostasy that preceded Christ's first coming, but it was nothing compared to that which will precede His Second Coming. The next one will be vastly worse because Christ's death on the cross will have already occurred, whereby God demonstrated His infinite love by sacrificing His only Son so that sinners may live.[83] To affirmatively rebel against such love and to incite others to do the same is beyond description.

The Antichrist will exalt himself and defy everything that people call god and every object of worship. He will even sit in the temple of God, claiming that he himself is God. Paul asks the brothers to remember what he said about all this when he was with them. Specifically, the lawlessness of the Antichrist has already begun in secret, and it will remain secret until what is restraining him now steps out of the way, at which time the Antichrist will be revealed—but the Lord Jesus will kill him with the breath of his mouth and destroy him by the splendor of His coming. Paul doesn't specify what is holding back the Antichrist and his lawlessness, and commentators offer various possibilities ranging from the government and law, to Satan, to the Holy Spirit. It seems likely that it is, in fact, the Holy Spirit, because only He has sufficient supernatural power to accomplish it.[84]

This Antichrist will come to do Satan's work, using false signs and wonders to deceive those who are perishing because they refuse to love truth and be saved by faith. Because of the unbelievers' hard-heartedness, their rejection of the truth, and their delighting in unrighteousness, God will send them a strong delusion, so they will believe what is false and be condemned. Satan's main goal is to ensnare people in his pit, and this "father of lies" uses all sorts of trickery to do it.

Satan empowers the Antichrist to act as his agent to lure away as many people as he can from eternal life with God. Yes, Jesus also empowers His apostles to perform miracles, but this is completely different because the apostles' actions are compassionate and beneficent, designed to bring glory to God. The Antichrist's signs and wonders will serve evil and be designed to promote himself, not God.[85] The Antichrist's powers and activities are further described in the Book of Revelation, which speaks of a second beast, apparently empowered by the Antichrist, that "performs great signs, even making fire come down from heaven to earth in front of people" (13:13). Charles Ryrie observes that Satan, the Antichrist, and this second beast form an evil trinity.[86]

Some may wonder why God will send unbelievers a strong delusion to make them believe in the lie. Well, it won't begin that way. Only after men repeatedly reject the Gospel and become increasingly rebellious will God give them over to their wicked ways. Relevant examples abound in the Bible. Pharaoh hardens his own heart (Exodus 7:13–14: 8:15, 19, 32; 9:7) before

God hardens it (Exodus 9:12); and only after King Ahab rejects God's true prophets does God commission a demonic spirit to inspire other false prophets to deceive him (2 Chronicles 18:18–27). When unrighteous men grow increasingly rebellious and reject God in favor of idols, serving the creature rather than the Creator, God gives them up in the lusts of their hearts to impurity (Romans 1:18–32).[87]

God is pure love. He does not gratuitously harden people, but after a point, He will accept their choice to harden their own hearts. Scripture assures us God wants no one to perish and all to come to repentance (2 Peter 3:9). But, being omniscient, God knows in advance who will repent. My sense is that in some cases, after they repeatedly reject Him, He will give them over to the sinful behavior they chose as a form of imposing His judgment on them.[88] "God righteously sends delusion," writes G. K. Beale, "because it is a beginning part of his just judgment. As is clear elsewhere in Scripture, God punishes sin *by* sin (Deut. 29:4; Isaiah 6:9–10) … God causes these people to be deluded because they refused to love the truth and so be saved and because they have not believed the truth but have delighted in wickedness."[89] This is why we should all pray for discernment, for the humility to fear God, for His wisdom, for His gracious revelation to us of truth, and for the Spirit to intercede for us according to the will of God (Romans 8:27).

Paul next repeats his earlier expression, "We ought always to give thanks to God for you," because God chose the brothers as the firstfruits to be saved—they were among the first to be saved through the sanctifying work of the Spirit and through belief in the truth. Paul is speaking of salvation from both the divine side (our regeneration through the Holy Spirit) and the human side (our belief in the truth and our faith in Jesus Christ).[90] He is reassuring them that despite all the difficulties they've encountered in standing firm for Christ, they have been sealed by the Holy Spirit through their faith in Christ and are destined to be in His presence throughout eternity.

Paul explains that God called them to salvation when he and his companions presented the Gospel to them, and now they can share in Christ's glory. They needn't fear being swept up in God's judgment of condemnation, but must stand firm and hold to the truths Paul taught them either verbally or through his letters. They must guard themselves against backsliding under the daily pressures and influences of the world, and the temptations of the flesh and the devil.[91] Paul prays that Jesus Christ and God the Father will comfort their hearts and strengthen them in every good deed and word.

CHAPTER 3

∞∞∞∞∞∞∞∞∞∞∞∞∞∞∞∞∞

Paul requests the Thessalonians' prayers that God's Word be spread rapidly and honored, as happened with them, and that he and his missionaries be protected from evil men. I am fascinated that Paul, by now a veteran and learned Christian, solicits prayers from the newly minted believers. It shows that all Christians, no matter how established in the faith or how close to God, need prayers—note that Jesus Himself never ceased praying. It also demonstrates that we are all equal in Christ, and that no Christian is beneath God's radar. God loves all of us; no one is too insignificant to pray. This is not a polite, perfunctory request, but Paul's earnest entreaty for prayer warriors to lift the work of the Gospel by interceding for those who have dedicated their lives to sharing it.

Paul commonly requests prayers from congregations and shares his prayers for them (1 Thess. 5:25; Romans 15:30–32; 2 Cor. 1:11; Col. 4:2–4; Phil 1:19; Philem. 22). He strongly believes in the Christian brotherhood, which is united by a common love for Christ and for one another, and for the Word of God they are jointly committed to sharing in the face of intense worldly opposition. Not all people have faith, and many are inclined to resist the Gospel. But the Lord is faithful, and will strengthen and protect them against the evil one (Satan). Paul's prayer for himself and his fellow missionaries certainly involves their own safety, but primarily reflects his earnest desire that their work in spreading the Gospel proceed unhindered.

Expressing confidence in the Lord that they will follow his instructions, Paul asks God to direct the Thessalonians' hearts to the love of God and to the steadfastness of Christ. Paul's perspective is fundamentally Christ-centered, recognizing that the believers' power doesn't come from themselves but from their faith in God. He understands the proper relationships—it is God Who will build them up in faith, empower them to accomplish their own missionary tasks, and enable them to live their lives in loving obedience to Christ. It might seem odd for Paul to ask Christ—who is God—to direct them to the love of God, but we should take this to heart ourselves, for our appreciation of God's love for us is enormously reassuring and reinforces our faith. As John Stott comments, God's love for us arouses our love for him. Paul could also be asking that the Lord lead the Thessalonians into a love resembling God's love and a steadfastness (or an ability to persevere)[92] like Christ's.[93] When Christians meditate on God's love and marvel at Christ's patient endurance, they are inspired to obey His Word and stand firm through adversity.[94]

Paul warns against idleness in the Church, commanding the believers, under Christ's authority, to avoid members who aren't carrying their own load. John MacArthur comments on the Christian value of work. "There is no such thing as a secular job for a Christian," writes MacArthur, "all work is a spiritual duty to be done as an opportunity to give glory to God (1 Cor. 10:31)."[95] God exalts work by commanding it in the Fourth Commandment. (The flipside of keeping the Sabbath on the seventh day is working on the other six [Exodus 20:9]). Through His own work in creating and sustaining the universe—and in our redemption—God set an example for us to follow. Work is not just to enable us to procure life's necessities, but a gift from God that provides value and fulfillment in our lives. It gives us a sense of self-worth.[96]

Paul commands the brothers to imitate the work ethic he and his missionaries exhibited among them. While ministering to the brothers, they supported themselves, so as not to be a burden. Though they were entitled to compensation, they forwent it to model sacrificial behavior in the Christian spirit. "If anyone is not willing to work," says Paul, "let him not eat. For we hear that some among you walk in idleness, not busy at work, but busybodies. Now such persons we command and encourage in the Lord Jesus Christ to do their work quietly and to earn their own living."

This doesn't violate the axiom that Christians should care for the poor. Paul is not reflecting an ungracious spirit toward the slothful, but is cautioning the brothers against cultivating an attitude of entitlement, as if the Church or anyone else owes them a living.[97] It is the opposite of Christ-like to expect others to sacrifice for you while you remain idle, though able-bodied. That attitude is selfish, not selfless, and must be rejected. Paul is also concerned about "busybodies" flitting about and bothering those who are working, possibly because they are anxious about their misunderstanding that Christ has already come.[98] They must mind their own business and get back to work, earning their own livelihood and not interfering with the livelihoods of others.

Paul says they must not tire of doing good. We should not lightly brush over this exhortation. As parents, we tell our children to be good, to do the right thing, to behave and treat others well. But it's especially encouraging that we follow a Savior, whose apostles and whose Word repeatedly remind us to avoid evil and keep our hearts and minds focused on what is good, true, and right, and to shun evil (Philip 4:8; see also 2 Cor. 13:7; Gal. 6:9).

Paul tells the brothers to have nothing to do with those who disobey the instructions in this letter. They should not treat such people as enemies, but approach them in the spirit of brotherly love and lead them to repentance and corrective behavior, which will benefit them and the whole church.

Paul closes with a prayer that the Lord of peace be with the Thessalonians and give them peace always and in every way. He notes that He is writing this letter in his own hand to prove he is the author, as is often his practice (1 Cor. 16:21; Col. 4:18; Philem. 19).

Paul's affection for the Thessalonians permeates these epistles, especially the first. It's clear that in the midst of Paul's persecution and hardships, he finds true joy in seeing congregations he founded grow wiser and more pious. They're not perfect—they struggle to understand some theological questions and are prone to idleness, among other problems. Yet they seek Paul's help to grow in Christ, and Paul is happy to oblige. Despite their challenges, the Thessalonians seem to be functioning as a close-knit, mutually supportive community. That is markedly different from the factionalism and sexual immorality plaguing the Corinthians, which we will turn to next.

CHAPTER EIGHT

1 CORINTHIANS 1–8
A CALL FOR UNITY
IN THE CHURCH

The letters to the Corinthians reveal to us more of the personal
character of the apostle [Paul] than any of his other letters. . . .
They reveal his wisdom, his zeal, his forbearance, his liberality
of principle and practice in all matters not affecting salvation, his
strictness in all matters of right and wrong, his humility, and per-
haps above all, his unwearied activity and wonderful endurance.

—CHARLES HODGE[1]

BACKGROUND AND PURPOSE

Paul identifies himself as the author of this epistle and is generally accepted as such. He planted the church in Corinth (scholars estimate in 51 AD),[2] to which this epistle is written, during his second missionary journey (Acts 18:1–11). He writes the letter from Ephesus (1 Cor. 16:5–9, 19) between 54 and 55 AD, during his third missionary journey, close to the end of his three-year ministry in that city.[3]

Corinth is an extremely important city at the time of Paul's writing. The capital of the Roman province of Achaia, it is situated on the isthmus connecting the Greek mainland with the Peloponnesian peninsula,[4] forming a strategically located bridge between the east and west. There is widespread worship of pagan gods in Corinth, especially Aphrodite, the goddess of love, and this pagan culture permeates governmental

affairs, civic festivals, trade guilds, social clubs, and life in general.[5] As
noted previously, Corinth is notorious for its sexual immorality and vice,
which are connected to the worship of Aphrodite. The temple dedicated
to her is located on the Acrocorinth, the great hill of Corinth said to
house some one thousand prostitutes who aid in Aphrodite's cult.[6] Cultural preoccupation with sex contributes to the problems of the early
church in Corinth. Notably, Paul writes his letter to the Romans from
there, inveighing against man's depravity.

We know from Acts 18:1–17 that on his second missionary journey,
Paul comes to Corinth from Athens, where he stays with fellow tentmakers Aquila and Priscilla and preaches in the synagogue. When the Jews
oppose him, he resolves to focus on the Gentiles. One night, Jesus
appears to Paul in a vision and tells him to continue preaching without
fear because He is with him and He has many people in the city who
will protect him. Jesus' promise comes to pass, as many people are converted during Paul's eighteen-month stay there.

Paul previously wrote a letter to the Corinthian church (which has
been lost) about Christians engaging in sexual immorality (1 Cor. 5:9).
He writes 1 Corinthians, his second letter to the Corinthian believers,
in response to reports from the household of a Corinthian woman named
Chloe about problems facing the church. Various factions are following
different teachers—Paul, Peter (Cephas), Apollos, and Christ Himself
(1:12–13). Members are quarreling when they meet for the Lord's Supper,
some are suing others, and there is even a disturbing report of incest in
the church.[7] Paul also addresses questions from individuals named
Stephanas, Fortunatus, and Achaicus on Christian marriage, food sacrificed to idols, spiritual gifts, and fundraising for the Jerusalem church.
While Paul's letter to the Romans is a systematic theological treatise, this
letter deals primarily with various ethical and practical issues down-
stream of theology that have arisen among the Corinthian congregants.[8]

The letter follows a fairly simple structure, with the first six chapters
addressing issues raised by Chloe's household and the last ten covering
questions raised by certain Corinthians in a letter to Paul.[9] It gives us a
view of the problems of one first-century church, which aren't much
different than those facing churches today. Secular influences in the
culture are challenging Christians, who are struggling with their

sanctification. The spirit of the world seems to be prevailing over the Spirit of God, and Paul is determined to help them correct that.[10] "The Church was in the world, as it had to be," Leon Morris writes, "but the world was in the Church, as it ought not to be."[11] Paul strongly exhorts the members to live together in harmony as a Christian community united in mind and thought. They must rely on the Holy Spirit to live spiritual lives, grow in Christ, and resist the sordid lifestyle of the secular culture surrounding them. They should build up one another in Christ, especially encouraging the weak, and work together to advance the Gospel.

As we study this epistle, we should consider its relevance to problems of the modern Church and to issues facing Christians today in our predominantly secular culture. "It is in this epistle we get the clearest view of the actual difficulties encountered by Christianity in a heathen community," argues Scottish minister and biblical scholar Marcus Dods. "We here see the religion of Christ confronted by the culture, and the vices, and the various social arrangements of paganism; we see the ferment and turmoil in its introduction ... we see the principles on which we ourselves must proceed in solving the social and ecclesiastic difficulties that embarrass ourselves."[12]

CHAPTER 1

Paul identifies himself as an apostle and mentions his colleague Sosthenes, a former leader of the Corinthian synagogue who became a Christian (Acts 18:12–17) and is probably acting as Paul's secretary or scrivener. They address the letter to the Corinthian church and to all others who call upon the name of the Lord—the only opening greeting in any of Paul's epistles that addresses all believers.[13] He thanks God for the grace He provided to the Corinthians in Christ and through which they learned about the Gospel. He is grateful these gifts will sustain them until Christ returns, when they will be without guilt because of their justification through faith in Him.

Chloe's people have reported to Paul that church members are quarreling over which leaders to follow and have split into factions. He beseeches them in Jesus' name to unify in Christ—the One who died for their sins and in Whose name they were baptized. Paul baptized a few of them, but Christ did not commission him primarily to baptize—he was meant to preach the Gospel and "not with words of eloquent wisdom, lest the cross of Christ be emptied of its power."

Paul is not diminishing the importance of baptism (see Romans 6:3–7),[14] but simply saying his own gifts are preaching and teaching. Since Paul's overwhelming focus is on bringing the Gospel and salvation to people, it's fair to say he's implying that water baptism is unnecessary for salvation. That teaching is clear throughout his letters, as he always emphasizes that salvation is by faith in Christ alone. Neither is he criticizing elegant speech. He knows the Greeks greatly admire rhetoric and philosophy and are attracted by clever arguments, but Paul is arguing that content is more important. The Gospel message must not be overshadowed by fancy wordsmithing, lest the message of Christ crucified be robbed of its saving power. Philosophical speculations about God are moot because we have God's special revelation in Jesus Christ. As Solomon proclaimed, "A fool multiplies words, though no man knows what is to be, and who can tell him what will be after him?" (Eccles. 10:14) Christians, then, must savor God's revelation.

Paul then expands on his countercultural argument.[15] The message of Christ's crucifixion is "folly to those who are perishing," but is the "power of God" to those who are saved by it. This "message of the Cross," explains David K. Lowery, "cuts to the heart of self-centeredness. Paul saw it as central to salvation which he understood to be a process begun by *justification*, advanced by *sanctification*, and climaxed in *glorification*."[16]

Justification is God's declaration of a sinner's righteousness when he is saved through faith in Jesus Christ and Christ's righteousness is imputed to him.[17] It does not mean the believer becomes righteous, but that he is acquitted before God as righteous because he has placed his faith in Jesus Christ and His finished work on the cross.[18] Once a sinner is justified, which occurs at the instant he places his faith in Christ, he is freed from the *penalty* of sin—death. He is regenerated, or given a new birth in Christ (John 3:3–15). At the point of justification, or conversion, the believer is freed also from the *power* of sin as the process of sanctification begins. The Christian is no longer a slave to sin (Romans

6:6), but is empowered by the indwelling Holy Spirit to resist it, though it will be a daily struggle.

Sanctification, then, is the process whereby the believer becomes holier and more Christ-like through the power of the Holy Spirit.[19] Sanctification is a life-long process that is never completed this side of eternity; but when the believer meets Christ face to face, he will be glorified (Romans 8:29–30; cf. Eph. 1:13–14) and freed from the *presence* of sin.[20] "In glorification," writes Millard Erickson, "the individual will also be perfected, morally and spiritually" (Col. 1:22).[21]

In saying that the cross is folly to those who are perishing but the power of God to those being saved, Paul is echoing the Old Testament teaching that God will destroy the wisdom of the wise and thwart the discernment of the discerning (cf. Isa. 29:14; Job 5:12, 13; Jer. 8:9; Matt. 11:25). "Where is the one who is wise?" asks Paul. "… Where is the debater of this age? Has not God made foolish the wisdom of the world?" The world did not know God through its own "wisdom," but pleased God to save those who believe in the "foolishness" of the Gospel. There is a distinct difference between worldly wisdom, detached from God's revelation, and Spirit-infused wisdom. Man, with all his worldly wisdom, didn't find God on his own.

The Jews demand signs and Gentiles seek wisdom (on their own power), continues Paul, but the apostles preach Christ crucified, which is a stumbling block to the Jews and folly to the Gentiles. As we've discussed, the Jews can't accept that God would bring salvation through a man who was nailed to a cross—a fate the Roman authorities usually reserved for criminal slaves. How could such a man be the Lord and Savior of mankind?[22] This idea was a stumbling block to Jews because they expected a conquering Messiah, not One who would die on a cross, for their Scripture taught that those who hang on a tree are cursed (Deut. 21:22–23; cf. Matt. 16:22; Gal. 3:13). The Gentiles coveted honor, esteem, and success, so the idea of salvation through belief in a Man who appeared to suffer a humiliating defeat on the cross struck them as pure foolishness.[23] But to those who God calls and who are saved through faith in His Son Jesus Christ, the Gospel message is the fulsome power and wisdom of God. "For the foolishness of God is wiser than men, and the weakness of God is stronger than men."

So much in the Bible strikes the scoffer as sheer silliness. But if the Bible is just nonsense written by ancient fools, how does it so accurately capture human nature across the ages? Puffed up with pride, skeptics are blind to God's truth and wisdom. This theme is evident throughout Scripture: "The fool says in his heart, 'There is no God'" (Psalm 14:1; 53:1); "The discerning sets his face toward wisdom, but the eyes of a fool are on the ends of the earth" (Prov. 17:24); and "Whoever trusts in his own mind is a fool, but he who walks in wisdom will be delivered" (Prov. 28:26).

God chose to save people the world considers foolish—not powerful or noble people, but seemingly insignificant ones. He did this, says Paul, to shame those who are wise in their own eyes and according to worldly standards. Again, the wisdom of Proverbs is illuminating: "The way of a fool is right in his own eyes, but a wise man listens to advice" (12:15); "Do you see a man who is wise in his own eyes? There is more hope for a fool than for him" (26:12).

God chose the weak and lowly to shame the strong and proud so that no one would boast in the presence of God. But He revealed Himself through Jesus Christ, Who became wisdom, righteousness, sanctification, and redemption for those who have faith in Him. Thus any boasting must be done in the Lord (cf. Jer. 9:24). Wisdom comes from God, and it inheres in Jesus Christ, through Whom believers become wise. United to Christ through the indwelling of the Holy Spirit, we acquire spiritual wisdom to know God.[24] Through Christ, our hearts are enlightened that we may know the hope to which He has called us (Eph. 1:18).

Paul is saying God calls to salvation people the world considers insignificant, to remove any basis for human pride.[25] God's saving work in Christ directly contradicts human notions of wisdom and power, achieving what human wisdom and power cannot.[26] It shows man's impotence and hopelessness without God, and the necessity of relying on Him through trust in Christ. God's election of ordinary, humble people excludes boasting in one's ancestry or achievement.[27]

Paul is simply following the teachings of Jesus, Who often turned conventional wisdom on its head. He shamed the strong by valuing things the world considers weak. He exposed men's distorted values, such as when He dined with sinners (Matt. 9:11) and when He regarded the small offering of the poor widow to be more valuable than the offering of a rich man (Luke 21:1–4). Another example is found in the parable of the great banquet (Luke 14:16–24), in which Jesus treated the poor, the crippled, the blind, and the lame rather than the privileged as the invited guests. "So the last will be first," said Jesus, "and the first last" (Matt. 20:16).[28] This paradoxical elevation of the poor and reversal of human status is also foretold in the Old Testament (1 Sam. 2:1–8: Isaiah 61:1–1).[29] The overarching theme is that God's choice of individuals for his kingdom reflects the message of the cross. Both preclude human boasting and confound human wisdom.[30] People do nothing to deserve their own salvation, so believers may only boast in the Lord, not in their own achievements.

CHAPTER 2

Now that Paul has established the superiority of God's wisdom over man's, he shows how he applied that principle to his own ministry. When he came to the Corinthians, he didn't attempt to dazzle them with lofty speech or wisdom, but preached only Jesus Christ and Him crucified. Paul came to them when he was weak, after being mocked, beaten, and imprisoned. Through that weakness, he relates to his audience and is empowered by God's grace. His personal bearing mirrors his message, which is targeted to the weak.[31] Paul uses the same approach everywhere he presents the message (cf. 1 Thess. 2:1–10; Gal. 1:10).

Paul is denouncing sophism—rhetoric that elevates form over substance. He doesn't employ polemical arguments to win praise for his eloquence. He is by no means anti-intellectual, as is clear from his logically sophisticated writings. "Paul constantly strove for wise argument," observes English theologian Anthony Thiselton. "His respect for reason precludes any anti-intellectualism as such. His aim here is to expose the true basis and nature of Christian proclamation in contrast to the 'self-presentation' of the visiting sophist. Christian proclamation does not allow for high-sounding rhetoric or a display of cleverness which could impede the gospel by putting first what pleases the audience and the personal 'style" of the speaker."[32]

Indeed, Paul realizes it's an affront to the Gospel and to his own message if in delivering the Good News he draws attention to himself and away from his teachings. "The gospel always points beyond humans to God and Christ," says Professor David Garland, "and becomes garbled whenever humans exploit it instead to headline themselves as stars."[33] Paul's goal is to focus his audience on the message of the Gospel, which speaks for itself because it's infused with God's power and wisdom. It is not man's persuasive skills that change hearts, but the living Word of God as revealed by the Spirit. Faith must be grounded in God's power, not in man's wisdom. The Gospel is God's wisdom, and it's the implicit answer to Job's question, "But where shall wisdom be found? And where is the place of understanding? Man does not know its worth, and it is not found in the land of the living" (Job 28:12).[34] Job cannot grasp God's ways, but wisdom is ultimately found in Christ (1 Cor. 1:30; Col. 2:3).[35]

Though Paul presents a message that doesn't sound wise to the world, mature and discerning believers recognize it as wisdom. This wisdom—the salvation of man through faith in Jesus Christ—has been God's secret plan from the beginning (Eph. 1:4), which he has now chosen to reveal. This wisdom is lost on the world's rulers; otherwise they wouldn't have crucified Christ. Paul is not suggesting this mystery is beyond human comprehension, but that man can only grasp spiritual truths with the benefit of God's revelation, and that revelation has now been given.[36]

Indeed, the Spirit searches the depths of God's wisdom and reveals this mystery to those charged with spreading the Gospel message. Their revelations come from the Spirit, not from men or human wisdom, and they can interpret and impart spiritual truths to others who are also spiritual. The psalmist beseeches God, "Open my eyes, that I may behold wondrous things out of your law" (Psalm 119:18; cf. Deut. 29:29; John 5:37–40). Those who are not of the Spirit and lack spiritual discernment cannot comprehend these truths, so they reject them as foolishness. Nonbelievers cannot discern the value of these teachings; only those who have the mind of Christ can grasp them. So even the believer doesn't comprehend these spiritual truths on his own; it is through the clarifying power of the Spirit that he acquires the mind of Christ and thereby can comprehend them.

The Old Testament provides insight on these issues. In the Book of Job, Zophar asks, "Can you find out the deep things of God? Can you find out the limit of the Almighty? It is higher than heaven—what can you do? Deeper than Sheol—what can you know?" (11:7–8). Paul essentially answers these questions by quoting the prophet Isaiah: "For who has understood the mind of the Lord so as to instruct him?" (Isaiah 40:13). "But," writes Paul, "we have the mind of Christ."[37] The New Living Transition is a little clearer here: "But we understand these things, for we have the mind of Christ" (1 Cor. 2:16).

What does Paul mean by "the mind of Christ?" While Job and Isaiah are obviously correct that no one can fathom the depths of God's mind, we do have the mind of Christ in the sense that Christians have the Holy Spirit, Who clarifies spiritual truths to us. Those united to Christ in faith have God's wisdom, embodied in Christ's crucifixion. Believers understand the meaning of the cross and its necessity for mankind's salvation.[38] "The expression, mind of Christ," writes Wendell Willis, "signifies the believer's knowing Christ through the working of the Spirit and the appropriation of the Gospel message."[39] Possessing the mind of Christ means that believers will have their outlook shaped by an awareness of Him.[40] Willis argues that a passage from Paul's epistle to the Philippians further clarifies what Paul means by the "mind of Christ." Here Paul is describing what I would consider Christ's mindset (His attitude of humility, obedience, and selfless service) rather than His mind, but Willis makes a valid point. Paul writes:

> So if there is any encouragement in Christ, any comfort from love, any participation in the Spirit, any affection and sympathy, complete my joy by being of the same mind, having the same love, being in full accord and of one mind. Do nothing from selfish ambition or conceit, but in humility count others more significant than yourselves. Let each of you look not only to his own interests, but also to the interests of others. Have this mind among yourselves, which is yours in Christ Jesus, who, though he was in the form of God, did not count equality with God a thing to be grasped, but emptied himself, by taking the form of a servant, being born in the likeness of

men. And being found in human form, he humbled himself by becoming obedient to the point of death, even death on a cross. Therefore God has highly exalted him and bestowed on him the name that is above every name, so that at the name of Jesus every knee should bow, in heaven and on earth and under the earth, and every tongue confess that Jesus Christ is Lord, to the glory of God the Father (Philip. 2:1–11).

When Paul tells the Corinthians they have "the mind of Christ," he means they share Christ's comprehension of the meaning of the resurrection. But it seems reasonable to infer that he's also encouraging them to adopt Christ's attitude of humble selflessness in their interactions with one another, to avoid the destructive divisions plaguing their church.[41]

CHAPTER 3

Paul tells the brothers he couldn't address them as spiritual people at first because they were new believers—merely "infants in Christ." As Christians, they had the Holy Spirit, but they were not acting like it. Some today consider such people "carnal Christians"—those immature in their faith. Others believe that term is an oxymoron and deny such people are authentically Christian at all. Paul himself, however, clearly views these congregants as fellow Christian "brothers."[42] "The carnal Christian is regenerated but is carnal and spiritually imperfect, retarded in his development," explains A. W. Tozer. "They have never developed into a mature, functioning Christian. They are where they were when they were saved."[43]

Tozer admits he knows of no single experience that would instantly transform a carnal Christian into a spiritual Christian. But he would advise such a person to let the Spirit teach him, discipline him, mature him, grow big within him, and walk within him. He "must learn by trial and error and prayer and repentance and fears and trials of heart." He must believe in the power of God to fill him with His spirit and lead him away from self-centeredness and into love for God and the entire world. He must pray for God to transform him into a mature Christian, and grow in grace and the knowledge and character of Jesus Christ.[44] Carnal Christians must practice the spiritual disciplines and earnestly seek to be filled with the Spirit.

Paul feeds these immature Christians "milk" rather than "solid food," which they are not yet ready to ingest. Mildly rebuking them, he says they're still not ready for solid food because they're embroiled in conflict, jealousy, and strife—things of the flesh. Pointing to certain biblical passages (Heb. 5:11–14; cf.1 Peter 2:2), some commentators believe Paul's metaphor describes the difference between elementary and advanced teaching.[45] Others disagree, arguing that the Corinthians' immaturity is not due to a lack of knowledge since Paul correctly taught them the Gospel. The true contrast, they say, is not between elementary and advanced Christian doctrine but between the "the true food of the Gospel ... (whether milk or meat) and the synthetic substitutes which the Corinthians have preferred."[46] Gordon Fee agrees that Paul's point is not that they should progress into deeper teaching "but that they abandon their present 'childish' behavior altogether so that they may appreciate the 'milk' for what it is, 'solid food.' ... Thus the Corinthians do not need a change in diet but a change in perspective."[47]

Paul next frames his teachings around three metaphors for the Church: the Church as God's field (3:5–9), as God's building (3:10–15), and as God's temple (3:16–17). In these passages, he is not addressing the spiritual lives of individual believers but the corporate church community as a whole.[48] This makes sense, because Paul's letter mostly deals with problems in the church community. This entire section is a powerful statement on the fundamental importance of local churches in the body of Christ.

The brothers, says Paul, must not proudly claim to be followers of some human leader such as Apollos or Paul himself. As important as the apostles are as God's messengers, they are just messengers. This is not about them but about God's church and the Gospel message. They should not put leaders on a pedestal and proudly identify with them as heads of competing factions. Such misguided rivalry can undermine the unity of the church and God's plan for spreading the Gospel.[49] Yes, Paul planted the seed in their hearts and Apollos watered it, but God made it grow—they would have been powerless to do any of this without God, so all the credit goes to Him. As the psalmist writes, "Unless the Lord builds the house, those who build it labor in vain" (Psalm 127:1). Paul, Apollos, and other workers for Christ will be rewarded for their efforts.

Shifting metaphors from farming to construction, Paul says that he and Apollos are God's fellow workers (not coworkers with God, but fellow workers under God's authority),[50] and that church members are God's field—His building. Through God's grace, Paul laid a foundation like a skilled master builder and now someone else is building upon it. But other builders must be careful, for Jesus Christ (and His crucifixion) is the only foundation. That is, through the power of the Holy Spirit, Paul established the church on a solid foundation of Jesus Christ, and now the work has been taken over by other builders (ministers) who must continue to preach salvation through faith in Christ, not false gospels.

Those builders (preachers, teachers, and other Church leaders) may add different types of materials—gold, silver, precious stones, wood, hay, and straw—but eventually, the value of their work will be revealed. Those who made lasting additions to the building will be rewarded. If anyone's work is burned up, however, he will suffer, but he'll still be saved—though just barely. The ministers and other teachers who use the valuable materials (gold, silver, and precious stones) are obediently teaching sound doctrine that will endure and survive,[51] but those who contribute the worthless materials—wood, hay, and straw—are introducing false teachings or other improper influences. Their work will not strengthen the church and won't endure. The fire of God's judgment will expose the poor quality of their workmanship and their inferior materials.[52]

In discussing rewards and punishments, Paul is not teaching works-based salvation but is saying that God will reward people for their commendable work (cf. Matt. 5:12; 1 Cor. 9:15–18, 23, 27; Romans 2:6–10; Philip. 2:16). Even the incompetent workers in this analogy, however, do not lose their salvation. They will be saved, but it will be like a burning stick snatched from the fire (cf. Amos 4:11).[53] They will not receive the same reward as those who perform faithfully and competently.[54] "This should inspire all Christians to take more thorough care how we are building," contends David Prior. "Yet, whatever the extent of loss we shall suffer, nothing in the eternal justice of that fire can tear us away from the love of God or from his salvation. . . . No amount of wood, hay, straw and other such rubbish can put us back on the downward spiral to eternal destruction."[55]

Paul now turns to a third metaphor—God's temple. This does not refer to the Temple building itself but to the community of God's people.[56] Rather than a hierarchical institution, Paul depicts the Church as a tight-knit community of people in a particular town or city.[57] The Corinthian church, like all local churches, is God's temple. God's Spirit dwells in it, so if anyone destroys it, God will destroy him—for God's temple is holy. Those who harm God's people are offending God,[58] just as surely as Christ told Paul on the Damascus Road that in persecuting the Church Paul was actually persecuting Him. Although later in this letter Paul teaches that the Spirit dwells in the individual Christian (6:19; cf. John 2:21), here he is talking about the Spirit dwelling in the gathered community of God's people—the local church, which he calls the temple.[59] This is a remarkable statement, considering Paul's background as a Pharisaic Jew who had such abiding reverence for the singular Temple in Jerusalem. But Paul is now a converted Christian who teaches that God's temple is the local church (and the bodies of individual believers) in which the Holy Spirit dwells. "In order to grasp the full audacity of this claim," writes Richard Hays, "we must remember that when Paul wrote to the Corinthians the Temple in Jerusalem was still standing and active. . . . The Spirit of God no longer can be localized in a sacred building: it is to be found in the gathered community of God's elect people in Christ."[60]

The driving thread throughout this section is that the local church—the Christian community—is indispensable. Christian relationships are vital. We are made in God's image, and God is a Triune God Who is relational by nature. Some say they don't need church because their relationship with God is personal, and they can study and worship on their own. While it's true that our relationship with God is one-on-one, the Bible teaches us to worship together, build up one another, help one another to learn, and hold one another to account. For Christians, there is strength in numbers (cf. Matt. 18:20; 1 Cor. 5:4). Being a Christian is not only about our individual relationship with God but being a part of the body of Christ.[61]

Paul says those who consider themselves wise are deluded, and they should become fools for Christ. That's because they're only concerned with worldly wisdom—but apart from God, worldly wisdom is foolishness. This sentiment is found throughout the Bible: God "catches the wise in their own craftiness" (Job 5:13), and "the Lord knows the thoughts of the wise, that they are futile" (Psalm 94:11). No one, therefore, should boast about following certain spiritual leaders. "For all things are yours," writes Paul, "whether Paul or Apollos or Cephas or the world or life or death or the present or the future—all are yours, and you are Christ's and Christ is God's." Gordon Fee clarifies, "These five items, 'the world, life, death, the present, and the future,' are the ultimate tyrannies of human existence, to which people are in lifelong bondage as slaves."[62]

Yet all these things belong to believers because Christ has liberated them from their bondage, and they are no longer slaves, but possessors.[63] "For those in Christ Jesus," says Fee, "what things were formerly tyrannies are now their new birthright. This is the glorious freedom of the children of God. They are free lords of all things, not bound to the whims of chance or the exigencies of life and death. The future is no cause for panic; it is already theirs."[64] So Paul urges them to expand their perspective—they don't belong to this leader or that; they are no longer subject to eternal death, but through Christ they are free and, in a sense, in possession of all these things.

CHAPTER 4

◇◇◇◇◇◇◇◇◇◇◇◇◇◇◇◇◇◇◇◇◇◇◇◇◇

Paul and his colleagues are Christ's servants who have been entrusted with explaining God's mysteries. Such stewards must be faithful and careful with their sacred calling, as they are presenting God's life-giving Gospel to the people. Bible teachers are held to a higher standard, as their knowledge makes them responsible both for what they teach and how they live (cf. James 3:1).[65]

As a teacher and steward of the Gospel, Paul isn't concerned with the judgment of other people. Unaware of any shortcomings in his own stewardship, he has a clear conscience, but God will be his judge. Paul isn't suggesting he's superior to others; he is setting forth a general principle: people should not be quick to judge others because God knows our hearts and secret motives.[66] He will be our judge, and will praise those entitled to it. The Bible consistently teaches that through our faith, obedience, and service, we should seek God's praise rather than man's (John 8:29; 2 Cor. 5:9; Gal. 6:8; Eph. 5:10; Col. 1:9–10; 1 Thess. 2:4, 4:1; Heb. 11:6).[67]

Christ's teachings confirm that we will not be judged based on our actions alone but also on our hearts (Matt. 10: 26–33; Mark 4: 22; Luke 8: 17; 12:2–3; Romans 2:16). Again, Paul is not teaching salvation by works, but reiterating that God will reward believers who obediently do His will, as shown by the parable of the talents in which Jesus commends the good and faithful servant (Matt. 25:21, 23).[68]

Paul has used himself and Apollos as examples to illustrate that the Corinthians must not disregard scriptural admonitions against elevating any of their leaders above the others, because they all derive their power and authority from God. Paul has richly earned credibility in advising them to honor Scripture, as he has repeatedly invoked Scripture to support his teachings (cf. Isaiah 29:14 [1 Cor. 1:19]; Jeremiah 9:22–23 [1 Cor. 1:31]; Isaiah 64:4 [1 Cor. 2:9]; Job 5:13 [1 Cor. 3:19]; and Psalm 94:11 [1 Cor. 3:20]).[69] Indeed, scripture must always be our truth north, and we must rely on it for God's wisdom and guidance.

If Paul and Apollos have no special authority, gifts, or abilities apart from God, the Corinthian brothers certainly don't either. Any gift they possess they received from God, so they must not boast about it. Sadly, however, the Corinthians are behaving as though they are self-sufficient, spiritually rich, and no longer in need of Paul's advice. Paul tells them, sarcastically, that he wishes he had their gifts and could operate at their level of spiritual maturity.

God has put Paul and his missionaries on display like men sentenced to death; they have become a spectacle to the world—to angels and to people—which is the price they must pay for preaching the Gospel. Unlike the self-satisfied Corinthians who appear wise and strong in Christ and are esteemed by the world, they have been fools for Christ's sake (having allowed themselves to look foolish to the pagan world) and held in disrepute. While the Corinthian brothers enjoy counterfeit esteem,

Paul and company are hungry and thirsty, poorly dressed, brutally mis-treated, and homeless. They support themselves by working with their hands. When they are cursed, they bless; when persecuted, they endure; when slandered, they respond with kindness. They are treated like trash. Paul is hardly complaining at his plight, however. He is honored to suf-fer for Christ's sake, so that his boasting can be in Christ. He willingly endures persecution to share God's Word, which leads to eternal life (John 20:31; 1 John 5:13).

Paul seeks not to shame the brothers but to lovingly warn them as his children (cf. 2 Cor. 6:13; Gal 4:19; 1 Thess. 2:11; 3 John 4). While many people try to teach them in Christ, they don't have many fathers. But Paul is their spiritual father who established their church and taught them the Gospel. As such, they should imitate him, and so he sent Timothy to remind them of how Paul follows Jesus and models Christ in every church he establishes. Paul is not boasting of his own spiritual maturity, stressing his humility throughout his letter and elsewhere admitting his sinfulness (1 Tim. 1:12–16). But he's been bold for Christ, and he's urging them to do the same instead of growing complacent in their smug self-satisfaction. He delivers the same message to every church. All must preach Christ and Christ alone—the cross, the Resur-rection, and salvation by faith alone. It must never be about the leaders, preachers, and teachers, but always about Jesus Christ, His sacrificial death, and His supreme and perfect love.

Some of the brothers are arrogant, thinking Paul will never visit them again and hold them to account so they can continue as masters of their own universe. To the contrary, Lord willing, he will soon visit them and determine whether they are all talk or acting in God's power. Is God reigning in the life of the church? Is His power working through the leaders as it should be? The kingdom of God consists not in talk but in God's power. Christ warned, "Not everyone who says to me, 'Lord, Lord,' will enter the kingdom of heaven, but the one who does the will of my Father who is in heaven. On that day many will say to me, 'Lord, Lord, did we not prophesy in your name, and cast out demons in your name, and do mighty works in your name?' And then will I declare to them, 'I never knew you; depart from me, you workers of lawlessness'" (Matt. 7:21–23).[70] The Corinthians must choose whether Paul should come with a punishing rod or with love in a spirit of gentleness.

CHAPTER 5

Paul has heard reports of sexual immorality among the congregants even worse than among the pagans, such as a man having relations with his stepmother. Jewish laws prohibit such behavior (Lev. 18:8; 20:11) as does Roman law, according to Cicero.[71] Instead of being arrogant, Paul warns, they should be sorrowful and expel the offender from the church. Though Paul is not physically with them, he is there in spirit and has already pronounced judgment on the man. He instructs them to assemble, expel the person, and deliver him to Satan for destruction of the flesh so that his spirit may be saved when Jesus returns. Here we are reminded of the Apostle John's words, "We know that we are from God, and the whole world lies in the power of the evil one" (1 John 5:19).

Paul's recommendation may seem harsh, but it's designed to restore order in the church and to encourage the offender to come to repentance and salvation. Paul's grace is always present, as shown in his instructions to the Galatians: "Brothers, if anyone is caught in any transgression, you who are spiritual should restore him in a spirit of gentleness. . . . Bear one another's burdens, and so fulfill the law of Christ" (Gal. 6:1, 2). Paul's main purpose in turning this sinner over to Satan, argues Craig Blomberg, "clearly remains remedial."[72]

The Corinthians' boasting is wrong; they should understand that a little leaven spreads through the whole lump. They tolerate the sinner's behavior at their own peril, for this type of unchecked behavior can infect the entire church. They must cleanse the old leaven—remove the offender—and purify the body. Scripture teaches that God purifies what is unholy and preserves the holiness of the Church. He ordered the Israelites to remove the depraved Canaanites completely from the land, He limited access to Holy sections of the Temple, and He insisted in the purity of the sacrifices, foreshadowing Christ and the Passover lamb. Now Jesus Christ—the Passover lamb—has been sacrificed so they could celebrate the festival, not with the old leaven of malice and evil but with the unleavened bread of sincerity and truth. Once they remove the sinner, the church will consist of God's people—a new lump—who have been made holy through faith in Jesus Christ. Just as the blood of the Passover lamb protected the Israelites from God's destruction (Exodus 12:23), Jesus takes away the sins of the world (John 1:29) and protects believers from destruction.[73]

In a previous letter, Paul had commanded the Corinthians not to associate with fellow Christians who engage in sexual sins, greed, idolatry, drunkenness, abusiveness, or cheating. They mustn't even eat with such people. Paul is not interested in them judging the unbelievers, but they must judge the church members and purge evil people from their ranks.

Paul is making careful distinctions. He is not forbidding Christians to engage with unbelievers, for to do that they "would need to go out of the world." Instead, he is commanding them to purge habitual sinners (cf. 2 Thess. 3:15) from the church.[74] His consistent theme in this letter is the spiritual vitality of the church, which must exhibit holiness. He is not saying that only sinless people can remain in the church, for we are all sinners.[75] He has in mind self-professed Christians who sin persistently and intentionally (1 John 3:9; 5:18). It's one thing for a church to accommodate believers who struggle with sins and repent. It's another for it to allow an openly defiant sinner to remain and corrupt the church from within. Believers must pledge obedience to Christ, and the church must discipline those who rebel and live in disobedience.[76] To tolerate this behavior is good for neither the persistent sinner nor the church community.

CHAPTER 6

Paul counsels that the Corinthians shouldn't settle disputes with fellow believers in secular courts. Since the saints will judge the world, shouldn't they be equipped to resolve these trivial disputes among themselves? Paul is not contradicting his statement in Chapter 5 that the church shouldn't judge nonbelievers, but is saying when God imposes His judgment in the future, His people will be part of that process (Dan. 7:22;

Matt. 19:28; Luke 22:30; Rev. 3:21; 20:4).[77] Paul's admonition here should probably not be interpreted too broadly. It surely applies only to civil and not criminal litigation, and most likely concerns disputes among members of the same local church. Regardless, the stated principle is always the preferred path: believers should always try to settle disputes among themselves and turn to litigation only as a last resort.[78]

The church is in its beginning phase, Paul says. How would it look for petty, quarreling believers to air their dirty laundry before unbelievers and ask them to decide their disputes? Would that attract non-Christians to the church? Since believers are to judge angels, shouldn't we be even more equipped to resolve disputes between fellow human beings? With that last, cryptic question, Paul probably means that believers will judge angels when believers join with Christ in the future judgment, for Scripture teaches that angels will be judged (2 Peter 2:4; Jude 1:6; Rev. 19:19–20; 20:10). After all, Satan is a fallen angel (see Ezek. 28:12–18; Isaiah 14:12–14; Rev. 12:4; Matt. 25:41; Rev. 12:9).[79]

If believers will possess such authority, why would they submit their disputes to unbelievers? They should be ashamed if they can find no believer wise enough to decide their disputes. They are already failing if they sue one another. It would be better to suffer an injustice than to besmirch the church with this poor example. Instead, they are defrauding and committing other wrongs against fellow believers.[80]

The unrighteous will not inherit the kingdom of God, nor will the sexually immoral, idolaters, adulterers, practitioners of homosexuality, thieves, the greedy, drunkards, abusers, or swindlers. Though some of the brothers were once guilty of these things, they have now been washed, sanctified, and justified in the name of Jesus Christ by the Spirit of God. Again, Paul is contrasting believers with unbelievers. The latter will not inherit the kingdom of God. Those who habitually, intentionally, and remorselessly sin are probably not believers. "Paul's purpose here is not to give a list of sins that will indicate one has lost his salvation," argues John MacArthur. "There are no such sins. He is rather giving a catalog of sinners who are typical of the unsaved."[81] Accordingly, believers shouldn't live like non-Christians who continue to sin in disobedience. They mustn't succumb to the temptations of the flesh, allow their sin nature to dominate, or take on the appearance of the unbeliever.[82]

Paul cites a statement the Corinthians invoke to justify living licen-
tiously: "All things are lawful for me." It could be that the believers
misinterpret the teaching that our sins are forgiven to mean they can sin
without consequence. Though Paul addresses this more directly in
Romans 6:1–14, for now he simply says that regardless of what things
are allowed, not all things are helpful, and no one should become a slave
to these things.

Paul cites another statement the brothers have adopted: "Food is
meant for the stomach and the stomach for food." Perhaps they believe
that because eating is merely physical and will not affect one's spiritual
life, the same would apply to sexual immorality. Paul squarely dis-
abuses them of this error. He acknowledges that eating is temporal but
disputes that everything involving the body is only of temporal importance.[83] The body is not meant for sexual immorality but for the Lord,
and the Lord is meant for the body. God raised the Lord, and He will
also raise us.

Are the brothers unaware that their bodies are members of Christ?
Why, then, would they unite them with a prostitute? Never! They must
understand that one who is joined to a prostitute becomes one body with
her—as the Scriptures say that the two will become one flesh. But the
person who is joined to Christ becomes one spirit with Him. Since Christians are members of Christ, a Christian's sexual intercourse with a
prostitute effectively unites the members of Christ with that prostitute.[84]
They must disavow sexual immorality. Every other sin is outside the
body, but sexually immoral acts are sins against one's own body.

But how can Paul say that other sins such as gluttony, drunkenness,
self-mutilation, and suicide are not against the body? He means that
sexually immoral sin "strikes at the very roots of our being," says Leon
Morris. "He does not say that it is the most serious of all sins, but that
its relation to the body is unique. This sin involves the body in a far more
intimate way. Other sins may have effects on the body, but this sin, and
this sin only, means that a man takes that body that is 'a member of
Christ' and puts it into a union which 'blasts his own body.' ... The
sexual sinner sins against his own body."[85] This sin (fornication), says
Alan Johnson, "is done inwardly, in the body, not outside it like other
sins."[86] The body is a temple of the Holy Spirit, Whom they have from

God. Their bodies do not belong to them because they were purchased with a price, so they must be used to glorify God.

CHAPTER 7

◇◇◇◇◇◇◇◇◇◇◇◇◇◇◇◇◇◇◇◇

Paul now turns to the issues the Corinthians wrote him about, beginning with sexual relations. We've already noted that Corinth is a hotbed of sexual immorality and prostitution. This is probably why the church needs special instruction on marriage and sexual relations. Apparently, some are advocating complete abstinence even among married couples, believing that all sexual relations are wrong. Others are counseling divorce and separation to avoid sexual temptation.[87]

Some commentators claim Paul advocates celibacy for Christians—as certain Corinthian congregants evidently believe—but most scholars disagree.[88] In verse 6:16, he approvingly quotes Genesis 2:24, stipulating that man and woman should become one flesh, and he disapprovingly cites the deceitful spirits' and demons' opposition to marriage in 1 Timothy 4:3. In the next verse in 1 Timothy, Paul affirms that everything God created is good, and he has already acknowledged that God created marriage (Gen. 2:24). Further, God instituted marriage when He declared, "It is not good that the man should be alone; I will make him a helper fit for him" (Gen. 2:18). God also commanded Adam and Eve to be fruitful and multiply (Gen. 1:28), and marriage was instituted, in part, for procreation.[89]

Paul acknowledges the Corinthians' statement that it's good for a man to remain single and not to have sexual relations with a woman. Because we are tempted, however, men and women should be married and have relations exclusively with each other. Paul is probably saying that singleness is good and honorable for those who choose it, but it's not more noble or spiritual than marriage.[90]

While abstinence is good for single people, it's not for married people, who mustn't deprive their spouses of sexual pleasure, lest they be tempted to infidelity. "The underlying assumption," says D. F. Wright, "is that by divine appointment marriage and sexual relations go together, as do singleness and abstinence from sex."[91]

Marriage is good for the reasons already stated, but it's also important in helping people avoid sexual immorality. "The implication is clear," says Wright, "the satisfying of sexual desires is not wrong, and marriage is its appointed setting. . . . Moreover, sex is not a dispensable dimension of marriage; like responsible love and respect, it is one of the mutual obligations of husband to wife and wife to husband."[92]

Paul teaches that the husband has authority over his wife's body, and the wife has authority over her husband's. They must not deprive each other of sexual relations other than for limited times as mutually agreed for prayer—otherwise Satan will tempt them because of their lack of self-control. In marriage, the two are one flesh, and their respective rights over each other's body inheres in the relationship. They belong to each other and have mutual responsibilities.[93] Each spouse has a duty to satisfy the other's sexual desires and to abstain from sexual relations with anyone else. I think Gordon Fee's interpretation accurately describes the spouses' reciprocal duties: "Paul's emphasis, it must be noted, is not on 'You owe me,' but on 'I owe you.'"[94] Having authority over the spouse's body does not mean "possessing" the other's body, but that a spouse does not have total authority over his or her own body exclusive of the other spouse. A spouse doesn't have a right to sexually control the other, but he does have a duty not to deprive her.[95]

Paul wishes that all were single like he is, but recognizes that each has his own gift from God, probably meaning that some have the gift of celibacy and others of marriage.[96] He says it would be good for single people and widows to remain single, unless they can't exercise self-control—in which case, they should marry rather than to burn with temptation. God says that wives should not separate from their husbands, but if they do, they should remain unmarried unless they reconcile with their husbands. Likewise, husbands should not divorce their wives.

In Paul's opinion (and this is not a command from God), if any believers are married to unbelievers and the unbelievers agree to live with them, they should not divorce them. The believing spouse makes the unbelieving spouse holy as well as their children. This doesn't mean that an unbelieving spouse will automatically become a believer if married to one, or that the children automatically become Christians. As the adage goes, God has no grandchildren—being a Christian is a choice for each individual to make for himself by trusting in Christ as his or her Savior. It means that a believer in the home sets the home apart and infuses it with a Christian influence.[97] As Christian parents, we mustn't underestimate the importance of Bible reading and prayer in the home, and of striving to model Christ-like behavior for our kids.

If, however, the unbelieving spouse separates, the believer is liberated from the other because God has called him or her to live in peace. But if the unbelieving spouse stays with the believer, the latter should remain as well, because the believer's influence might eventually lead to the belief (and salvation) of the other. The apostle Peter's words are instructive here: "Likewise, wives, be subject to your own husbands, so that even if some do not obey the word, they may be won without a word by the conduct of their wives, when they see your respectful and pure conduct" (1 Peter 3:1–2).

The church should let each person remain in whatever situation God has placed him, continues Paul, because He has called them. This is Paul's rule for all churches. Was anyone, he asks, already circumcised at the time he was called? If so, he shouldn't try to remove the marks of circumcision. Was anyone uncircumcised when called? If so, he should not become circumcised. For neither circumcision nor uncircumcision counts for anything. What is important is that they keep God's commandments. Each should remain in the condition he was in when called to faith.

Were they a slave at the time? If they were, and they can gain their liberty, they should do so; but if not, they must keep the eternal view in perspective. "Unfortunately, they might have to keep living as slaves," writes Bruce Barton, "but they should serve Christ wholeheartedly in their position."[98] While slavery was common throughout the Roman Empire, converted slaves could at least gain solace that their Christian faith had freed them from the power of sin in their lives.[99] Those who were free when they became believers are slaves of Christ. They were bought with a price and should not become slaves of the flesh and of worldly values. They should not try to please man, but keep their focus on Christ. Jesus is the great equalizer. Our social status isn't what is important. Whether a person is enslaved or free, married or unmarried,

Jew or Gentile at the time of his conversion, all are under the authority of Christ.[100]

Paul has no command from God concerning women who are not yet married, but as one who is trustworthy based on God's grace to him, he advises people to remain as they are—either unmarried or married. This is consistent with his previous advice that they should remain in whatever condition they were in when God called them to faith. While it's not a sin for single people to marry, they should be aware that they will have worldly troubles. As time is short, those who have wives should live as if they didn't. Paul doesn't mean they should ignore their spouses, but that their animating focus should be on Jesus Christ. Those who mourn, rejoice, buy things, or otherwise deal with the world should not be preoccupied with those things because the world is passing away. Paul wants the brothers to be free from worries. Unmarried men and women are anxious to please the Lord. But married people worry about how to please their spouses, and so their interests are divided. Paul is concerned with facilitating their undivided devotion to Christ.

Some infer that Paul is counseling singleness over marriage if possible but realizing that for many, it is not. To the contrary, as an obedient servant of God and an ardent adherent of Scripture, he endorses the institution of marriage but laments that marriage can cause anxiety and thus distract us from our primary purpose in life, which is to love God. Apparently operating under the assumption that Christ will return soon, he doesn't seem to be as concerned about the procreation of humanity at this point. He urges people to center their lives on Christ. This means they should marry if by remaining single, their passions will lead them to sin and distract them from Christ. They should remain single if they have the gift of celibacy, because that is the optimum condition in which to focus on Christ. As a rule, they should remain in whatever state they are in—married, single, free, slave, circumcised, uncircumcised, etc.—because that will reduce stress and promote peace in their lives, both of which are conducive to Christ-directedness.

Again, we should not infer that Paul is endorsing slavery, but emphasizing freedom in Christ. In fact, Paul's teachings often undermined slavery. For example, he encouraged Philemon to treat his slave Onesimus as "a beloved brother" (Philem. 16), thereby endorsing the intrinsic equality and dignity of all human beings.[101] "There is no good reason to doubt that Paul supported the various means for emancipation of individual slaves that were available in the Greco-Roman world," writes Walter Kaiser. "And yet, Paul's emphasis in the entire chapter, as in the present passage, is his conviction that the most critical issue in human life and relations and institutions is the transformation of persons' lives by God's calling. External circumstances can neither take away from, nor add to, this reality."[102]

Finally, Paul tells the Corinthians that if a person who is engaged is tempted to have sexual relations outside marriage, he should marry if he wants to, and it will be no sin. But if a person can remain unmarried and keep his passions under control, he will be even better off. Furthermore, a wife is bound to her husband as long as he lives, but if he dies she is free to remarry another believer. Paul confesses that he thinks she would be happier to remain unmarried—and he is saying this as someone who has the Holy Spirit.

For more New Testament teachings on marriage, the following Scriptures are instructive: John 2:1–11; Ephesians 5:21–33; 1 Timothy 5:14; Hebrews 13:4; 1 Peter 3:1–7.[103]

CHAPTER 8
◇◇◇◇◇◇◇◇◇◇◇◇◇◇◇◇◇◇◇◇◇◇

Paul next turns to the Corinthians' question concerning food offered to idols. Should they eat or purchase at the market the remainders of animals that were offered in sacrifice to pagan gods? Pagan temples that offered these animals for sacrifice sometimes functioned as butcher shops or banquet halls and sold or served the remainders.[104] Pagan neighbors and friends would also sometimes offer such food to Christians at a dinner.

Paul begins with the quote, "all of us possess knowledge," remarking that this knowledge puffs people up, whereas love builds them up. This may be language from the Corinthians' letter to Paul. Regardless, Paul uses it as a jumping off point to discuss the pitfalls of being proud of one's knowledge. When a person is proud of his knowledge, he doesn't know as much as he thinks. But if anyone loves God, God knows him.

Self-indulgently showing off one's knowledge can harm that person (because pride is an obstacle to a true relationship with God) and can be off-putting to others. People must be less focused on self and more on loving God, and this will lead to a greater love for their neighbors. We must not consider ourselves superior to those less knowledgeable. "In our salutary emphasis on truth and knowledge," writes D. A. Carson, "we must never succumb to an intellectual arrogance that assigns a small importance to self-denying love for those who do not know as much."[105]

There is only one God, and idols are not real. There may be so-called gods in heaven or on earth, but for us there is one God, the Father, from Whom are all things and for Whom we exist. And there is one Lord, Jesus Christ, through Whom are all things and through Whom we exist. But not everyone knows these things. Some believe idols are really gods, so when they eat food that was offered to idols, they believe they are worshipping real gods, and this bothers their consciences. But food itself is irrelevant to our relationship with God. Paul is not approving Christians' participation in feasts dedicated to false, pagan gods while they claim to worship the true God (see Chapter 10)—that is forbidden. One must not eat food in a ceremony that inherently signifies the worship of a false god.[106] In this chapter he is addressing a different matter—the propriety of eating the remainders of animals that have been offered to idols.

It doesn't matter whether Christians eat food that's been sacrificed to an idol, since they know the idol is nonexistent. But it might bother new Christian converts who worshipped idols in the past. If more mature Christians exercise their freedom to eat in an idol's temple, a weaker Christian may follow their example and feel guilty for having eaten defiled food. The lesson is that we always must be sensitive to others and that believers should not impose an unnecessary obstacle to converts' Christian faith. Paul explained it this way in his letter to the Romans: "Those who have doubts are condemned if they eat, because they do not act from faith" (14:23).

A Christian should never induce another Christian to sin. He must never use his superior knowledge to destroy another person for whom Christ died, for that is sinning against Christ. Accordingly, Paul says he will never eat food that will cause another Christian to stumble. Note that Paul isn't saying that he or other strong Christians must give up their liberties. To the contrary, he's saying that he is exercising his liberties in a manner that will best serve Christ. His voluntary choice is to make small sacrifices for a far greater cause. In the next chapter, Paul indicates he will go even further—he will actually give up his liberties to bring people to the Lord.

We're halfway through Paul's first epistle to the church at Corinth. He's saved some of the most important chapters in the entire Bible for the second half, to which we now turn.

1 CORINTHIANS 9–16

THE PRIMACY OF LOVE, AND A SPIRITUAL GIFT FOR EVERY BELIEVER

*I found that I believed in the action of the Holy Spirit, but
in a limited sphere; in me the Spirit could not call forth
from the organ all the melody he wished; some of the
pipes did not function, because they had not been used.*

—LEON JOSEPH SUENENS[1]

CHAPTER 9

P aul reiterates his right to compensation for his apostolic ministry. He is humble to a fault but won't ignore attacks on his apostolic authority, which could undermine his Gospel message. He asks the Corinthians, "Am I not free? Am I not an apostle? Have I not seen Jesus our Lord? Are not you my workmanship in the Lord?" At the very least, he is an apostle to the Corinthians, because they are the seal of his apostleship in the Lord—they came to Christ through his preaching, which validates his ministry. One of the essential criteria for apostleship is having been an eyewitness to Christ's resurrection, and on that score Paul qualifies based on his Damascus Road experience (Acts 9:1–43).

Paul asks whether he and his missionary team have the right to eat, drink, and get married to believers as do other brothers and apostles, including Peter. Are he and Barnabas the only ones who must support themselves? Do soldiers work for free? Can farmers not eat the fruit they plant? Are shepherds not allowed to drink some milk produced by their flock? They should not mistake his refusal to be paid for his work (or to have his basic needs supplied)[2] as an admission that he doesn't deserve it. Though he deserves compensation, he's forgoing it to avoid burdening the church, and so people won't assume he's only promoting the Gospel for money (1 Thess. 2:5–10; 2 Thess. 3:7–9). Instead, he supports himself through his tent making. As an apostle, he also has the right, at the financial expense of the churches, to take a believing spouse along with him to lighten his load and provide companionship—but he'd rather sacrifice for Christ.[3] Paul is not contradicting his earlier statements concerning his voluntary choice to remain single (7:7), but merely listing some of the apostolic privileges he is foregoing for the cause of the Gospel.

Paul isn't speaking on his own authority but is relying on Scripture, which says, "You shall not muzzle an ox when it treads out the grain." God surely had human beings in mind rather than oxen, Paul says, because the plowman should plow and the thresher should thresh in hope of sharing in the crop. Since Paul and his team have sown spiritual things among the Corinthians, don't they have an even greater right to receive payment than others? Those who work in the Temple receive food from the Temple, and those who serve at the altar share in the sacrificial offerings, so the Lord commands that those who proclaim the Gospel should be compensated for doing so. Note that Paul is continuing to apply the Old Testament to his teachings, underscoring its enduring relevance.

Paul is not writing to request compensation. He would rather endure hardship than obstruct the spread of the Gospel. Bishop of Constantinople and early Church father John Chrysostom writes that Paul declined compensation to avoid causing "so much as the slightest suspense and delay to the course of the Word."[4] He would rather die than forfeit his right to boast in the Lord. If he preaches the Gospel voluntarily, he will be rewarded, but if he does it against his will, he will still have responsibility as a steward. Paul is not saying he doesn't want to preach the Gospel; rather, he is acknowledging that he is under divine compulsion to do so, and is therefore entitled to no reward. If he had a genuine choice in the matter—which could only happen if he weren't painstakingly obedient to God—and still chose to preach the Gospel, he might be entitled to a reward.[5] But he considers it a privilege to preach the Gospel free of charge, and that is sufficient reward.

Why would receiving just compensation hinder the Gospel? Paul might believe it would create a patron-client relationship with the Corinthians—in line with the patronage system of ancient Roman society—thereby creating a conflict of interest. This could diminish his freedom to be all things to all people (as he is about to explain) and otherwise limit his autonomy, even if only in their perception. He must maintain his freedom to correct them, if necessary. Accepting compensation for his services might create the impression that he's beholden to his financial supporters rather than representing God's interests or those of all people to whom he ministers.[6]

Though he is a free man, Paul chooses to be a servant to win more converts to Christ. He becomes as a Jew to win Jews, and as one under the Law to win those under Jewish Law—even though he is not under that Law. To the weak he becomes weak, and to those outside the Law he becomes as one outside the Law (though he is not outside the Law of God, for he is under the Law of Christ). He has become all things to all people, that by all means, he might save some. He does it all for the sake of the Gospel, that he may share with them in its blessings.

Paul has not readopted Jewish practices, but on morally insignificant issues he would obey Jewish ceremonial laws—as long as the Gospel is not compromised—while ministering to Jews. Paul applies the same principle when evangelizing Gentiles.[7] By living outside the Law, Paul is not implying he behaves as a libertine with no restraints. He would never adopt pagan practices to convert pagans, nor would he impose Jewish ceremonial laws on his Gentile mission field. Indeed, he adamantly opposed these things, along with Peter and James, at the Jerusalem Council (Acts 15).

While he is free in Christ, he is under the Law of Christ. This Law doesn't entail many rules, but is a life of willful obedience grounded in Christ's abundant, sacrificial, and selfless love. By becoming weak to win the weak, Paul probably means setting aside his liberties, such as the freedom to eat the remains of foods that have been offered to idols in order to help convert those of weak conscience troubled by those practices.[8] His willingness to become all things to all people is not hypocritical, for he only adapts his behavior in minor matters to advance the Gospel without compromising the message, never to win personal acclaim.

All runners participate in a race, continues Paul, but only one receives the prize. So all should run as if competing for the prize. All athletes exercise self-control in all things to receive a perishable wreath, but believers do so to receive an imperishable one. Paul says he does not run aimlessly or shadow box, but acts with purpose. He disciplines his body, keeping it under control so he doesn't disqualify himself after preaching to others. By invoking the athletic analogy of disqualification, Paul is not suggesting that he (or other believers) would lose his salvation for insufficient effort, but is more likely noting that he would lose his rewards from Christ (cf. 3:15).[9] "Paul's fear was not that he might lose his salvation," declares Leon Morris, "but that he might suffer loss through failing to satisfy his Lord."[10]

Paul is not advocating fierce competition among evangelists and believers. Instead, he's exhorting all to serve Christ with the zeal, self-control, and discipline of a competitive athlete. Christians must be individually obedient but also must work together as members of a loving, united community. They do not compete against one another but against all obstacles to spreading the Gospel, whether external or from within. Their goal is an imperishable crown of righteousness (2 Tim. 4:8).[11] They act to win souls for Christ, and rewards are promised for His good and faithful servants.

CHAPTER 10

Paul draws lessons from numerous Old Testament stories involving God's dealings with Israel and applies them to current Christian experiences. Their Jewish fathers were all under the cloud in the wilderness and walked through the sea on dry ground. Here, he's alluding to God's leading the Israelites during their wilderness wanderings in a pillar of cloud in the daytime and a pillar of fire at night (Exodus 13:21), and His miraculous opening of the sea to permit their escape from the Egyptians (Exodus 14:22). They were baptized into Moses (united with God's servant and their spiritual leader),[12] and all ingested the same spiritual food (manna from heaven [Exodus 16:4–35]) and drink. They drank from the spiritual Rock that followed them: Jesus Christ (Exodus 17:1–7; Num. 20:2–13). Still, despite God's special provision for them in the wilderness, they persisted in disobedience. God was displeased with most of them and scattered their bodies in the wilderness.

Christians must apply these lessons to navigate through life's difficulties. They must not desire evil or worship idols as the Israelites did with the golden calf (cf. Exodus 32:4–6). And they must not dishonor God by participating in idol festivals in the pagan city of Corinth.[13] As we noted previously, there is a difference between eating sacrificed animals as part of a pagan festival dedicated to worshipping false gods, and eating the remainders of animals that were previously sacrificed to idols at a non-religious event.[14]

Christians, Paul continues, must not engage in sexual immorality as some of the Israelites did, which resulted in 23,000 of them dying in a single day. Paul could be referring to an incident in which the Israelites "began to whore with the daughters of Moab" (Num. 25:1) and worshipped the false god Baal of Peor, which resulted in Israelites being struck by the plague (Num. 25:1–9).

They mustn't put Christ to the test, as some Israelites did after God had delivered them from Egypt. With ingratitude, they complained to God and Moses, "Why have you brought us up out of Egypt to die in the wilderness? For there is no food and no water, and we loathe this worthless food" (Num. 21:5). God then sent fiery serpents that killed many of them (Num. 21:6). Instead of testing God, Christians must strive to be obedient and grateful for all He has done for them. Again, Christians shouldn't indulge in sin simply because they've been liberated from its yoke; they live under the love-driven law of Christ.

The Corinthians mustn't grumble, says Paul, as some of the Israelites did before being destroyed by the Destroyer—the angel of death. Not all commentators agree, but this could refer to the Israelites' bitter complaint against Moses and Aaron—and God—recorded in Numbers 14:1–4. Alternatively, it could allude to complaints about the punishment

of Korah and other Israelites who rebelled against Moses and were swallowed by a hole that opened in the earth (Num. 16:32–33).[15] Regardless,
the principle accords with the lesson Paul is teaching throughout this
chapter: people of God must be grateful and obedient.

Paul reiterates that these events occurred as examples, and were
written down for the instruction of Christians as the end of the ages
draws near. If the Corinthians think they are not vulnerable to these
pitfalls, they will risk falling prey to them. All the temptations they are
experiencing are common to man. But God is faithful, for He will not
let them be tempted beyond their ability to resist, and He will provide a
means of escape. Countless Christians have been greatly relieved and
assured by this passage, trusting God's promises that He will not allow
us to be tempted beyond our capacity to resist and that He will also
provide a means to escape it—provided we rely on Him for such strength.

God's Word is reliable—it does not paint a Pollyannaish picture of
the world but soberly reports the genuine human condition. While the
Bible doesn't deceive us about reality, it does reveal a personal God with
Whom we can have a relationship and in Whom we can trust in difficult
times. We gain comfort knowing we are not alone—others endure the
same types of temptations, and no human being has endured more suffering than Jesus Christ, which enables us to enjoy a deep personal
relationship with Him. "For we do not have a high priest who is unable
to sympathize with our weaknesses, but one who in every respect has
been tempted as we are, yet without sin," the writer of Hebrews assures
us. "Let us then with confidence draw near to the throne of grace, that
we may receive mercy and find grace to help in time of need" (4:15–16).
Thanks to the Bible and our assurance that it's God's Word, we know
how the story of humankind will end and who will win the spiritual war
that rages beyond our field of vision. Jesus Christ has triumphed over
Satan, sin, and death, and He will deliver His final victory when He
returns to reign forever.

Paul next issues a stern warning with an intimate introduction:
"Therefore, my beloved, flee from idolatry." Our status as believers
doesn't immunize us from evil, as Paul's discussion of temptation makes
clear. We must never be smug and underestimate the devil. Rather, we
should aggressively avoid evil, especially idolatry. Satan is the father of

lies and false gods, and even false doctrine has a way of seducing the unsuspecting believer. Corrupt theology can infect the Church and dilute the Gospel. Paul is specifically warning the Corinthians here, but his injunction to flee from idols applies to all Christians. In studying the Old Testament, I have discovered that few sins incur God's wrath like the worship of false gods—indeed, the first two of the Ten Commandments directly forbid it (Exodus 20:4–6; Deut. 5:8–10). In his first epistle, John also affirms the principle (1 John 5:21).

Paul introduces the next topic, the Lord's Supper, by saying that as reasonable people, the brothers will recognize he's speaking truthfully. When Christians drink from the cup and eat from one loaf of bread at the Lord's Supper they are sharing in the blood and body of Christ. Because they all eat from one loaf, though they are many, they are of one body—just as the Israelites were united in eating the sacrifices at the altar. Notwithstanding disagreements among Christians today as to the precise meaning of communion, Paul teaches that Christians are united with Christ in a special and profound way when they take communion. He stresses that it's wrong for Christians to participate in any similar ceremony dedicated to idols instead of the true God.

According to Paul, food offered to idols in pagan sacrifices is actually offered to demons, not God. No, he's not saying that food offered to idols is being offered to deities—these idols are connected to a dangerous spiritual reality.[16] They are created at the behest of demons masquerading as real gods, so anyone who worships them is worshipping demons. These demons "don't literally live in a statue," writes Craig Blomberg, "but they can work through the abuse of those wooden or stone statues."[17] Therefore, Paul forbids the brothers from participating in ceremonies that involve demons. They cannot share the Lord's cup and eat at the Lord's Table while also drinking the cup of demons and eating at their table. We must not provoke the Lord to jealousy. Do you think we are stronger than He is, asks Paul? Do we dare provoke Him through blasphemous, idolatrous acts?

Paul then summarizes the subject he's been discussing since Chapter 8: when a Christian can eat meat sacrificed to idols. All things that are lawful are not necessarily helpful. Christians must not seek their own good but the good of their neighbor. They should eat whatever is sold in the market without raising questions on the ground of conscience, because the earth and everything in it is the Lord's. If an unbeliever invites you to dinner and you want to go, eat whatever he serves without raising any questions of conscience. But if he tells you it was offered in sacrifice, then do not eat it, for the sake of the one who tells you and for the sake of his conscience. Our liberty shouldn't be governed by someone else's conscience.

Paul means that freedom involves choice, and the way to preserve it is to use it wisely. A Christian doesn't forfeit his liberty by choosing to refrain from eating food that doesn't bother his own conscience. He is exercising his liberty in a loving way to be sensitive to others. If we eat the food with thankfulness, says Paul, why should we be denounced because of that for which we give thanks? So eat, drink, and do everything else to the glory of God.

Believers must not offend Jews or Gentiles or God's Church, just as Paul seeks to please everyone not for his own sake but to help save as many as he can. Christians, then, must not participate in pagan ceremonial meals, but in all other ways, when possible, they must conduct themselves so as to promote rather than imperil the salvation and spiritual health of others.[18] When dining with friends at home, they are free to eat meat—even remainders of animals offered to idols—unless by doing so they will trouble the consciences of weaker Christians and cause them to stumble.[19] We must exercise our Christian liberty prudently, always keeping in mind how our behavior might impact others.

CHAPTER 11

Paul instructs the brothers to imitate him as he imitates Christ. (This first verse of Chapter 11 logically belongs at the end of Chapter 10.) He then commends them for remembering him in everything and maintaining the traditions he delivered them.

Next, Paul discusses the nature of the relationships between husband and wife and their relationship to Christ. Jesus is the head of every man, and a husband is the head of his wife, and God is the head of Christ. Christ is, in essence, equal to the Father, but He submitted to the Father's will (with which He agreed) to sacrifice Himself for the salvation of mankind. If he hadn't subordinated Himself, mankind's redemption would have been impossible.[20] In like fashion, human beings must submit themselves to Christ in appropriating His gracious offer of salvation through faith. In turn, Paul seems to be saying, women should submit to men for the sake of order in the family and society. God has structured the world on the pattern of His relationship with human beings, and issues of authority and subordination are part of this structure.[21]

This message seems offensive to some Christians today, but we should consider certain mitigating factors. First, as noted, men and women are equal in dignity and essence as created in God's image. The subordinate role does not mean they are inferior to men, any more than Christ's subordinate role in certain functions means He is inferior to the Father. Second, being in a position of headship could be considered more a responsibility than a privilege. Elsewhere, Paul commands husbands to love their wives as Christ loved the Church and gave Himself up for her. Additionally, they should love their wives as their own bodies (Eph. 5:25–28). Christ is the head of man, but He suffered immeasurably for mankind, making the ultimate sacrifice.[22]

Paul then addresses the subject of head coverings during worship services—perhaps because someone has questioned him about it. Every man who prays or prophesies with his head covered dishonors his head, but every wife who prays or prophesies with her head uncovered dishonors her head, because that is the same as if her head were shaven. If a wife will not cover her head, she should cut her hair short (because short hair is culturally appropriate for men, at least, to show respect to God).[23] But since it's disgraceful for a wife to cut off her hair or shave her head, she should cover her head. A man should not cover his head, since he is the image and glory of God. But woman is the glory of man, for man was not made from woman, but woman from man. Neither was man created for woman, but woman for man.

As noted, Paul firmly believes that both man and woman are created in God's image (Gen. 1:26–28). So why does Paul say that man is both the image and glory of God, but woman is the glory of man, leaving out the word "image?" New Testament scholar Simon Kistemaker says it's because he is discussing man's headship and is not focused on Eve being created in

God's image.[24] Another possibility is that homosexuality was rampant in first-century Greece, and Paul might have been saying that a woman, not another man, is the appropriate partner for man and his glory.

A more likely interpretation is that Paul is echoing the creation narrative in which God creates woman from Adam's rib and so woman is made for man. Later in Genesis, we read, "Then the Lord God said, 'It is not good that the man should be alone; I will make a helper fit for him" (Gen. 2:18). Thus, woman is for man's glory.[25] That is why a wife ought to have a symbol of authority on her head—"and because the angels are watching" (NLT). While women should wear head coverings to acknowledge their submission to God's authority, they are equal to men before God, are similarly free in Christ (Gal. 3:27–28), and are permitted to pray and prophesy in worship services provided their heads are covered. Gordon Fee says this verse is "clear evidence" that women participated in ministering and worship in Christian communities.[26] Also recall that in Acts, Priscilla joined with Aquila in teaching Apollos the Gospel message more accurately (18:24–26).

Nevertheless, in the Lord, woman is not independent of man, nor man of woman—because a woman is made from man, and man is born of a woman. All things are from God. Mutually interdependent and complementary, men and women both bring glory to God. The brothers must judge for themselves whether it's proper for a wife to pray to God with her head uncovered. Nature teaches that it's disgraceful for a man to wear long hair, but that long hair for a woman is to her glory. That's because her hair is given to her for a covering. But if anyone is prone to argue about this, says Paul, we have no other practice, nor do the churches of God.

In other words, don't get too worked up over this issue. Every other Christian congregation follows these guidelines, so the Corinthian church should not cause a stir over them. Paul's basic argument seems to be that men and women, though equal before God, are different from each other, and those differences are expressed in various cultural practices. Men and women, while recognizing their equality, should cherish the differences between masculinity and femininity.[27]

Paul now strongly rebukes the Corinthians for their conduct at the Lord's Supper. When they come together, they do more harm than good.

He has heard there are divisions among them, which he tends to believe. Admittedly, some differences are permissible to show which of them have God's approval. That is, Christians cannot allow false teachers to gain prominence in the Church, so a degree of divisiveness may be needed to purge such elements. This provides a lesson for the modern Church: while Church harmony is essential, it should not come at the expense of sound doctrine.

But when the brothers come together for the Lord's Supper, they defeat its purpose; some people hurry to eat, leaving no food for others, while others get drunk. At the least, they should confine such behavior to their own homes and not dishonor the Church and humiliate the poor in this way. Paul reminds the brothers that what God has revealed to Paul, Paul has revealed to them—that on the night Jesus was betrayed, He took bread, gave thanks to God, and broke it, saying, "This is my body, which is for you. Do this in remembrance of me." Similarly, after supper, He took the cup and said, "This cup is the new covenant of my blood. Do this, as often as you drink it, in remembrance of me."

Thus, every time they celebrate the Lord's Supper together until Christ returns, they must commemorate the Lord's death. Anyone who eats and drinks unworthily will be sinning against the body and blood of the Lord. They must each examine themselves before participating in the Lord's Supper, because if they take part without honoring the body of Christ, they will bring judgment on themselves. This is why so many of them are weak and sick, and why some even have died.

But if they will examine themselves beforehand—and reflect on the gravity of what they're doing—they won't be judged. When they are judged, they are being disciplined so they will not be condemned along with the world. Therefore, when they gather to eat, they must wait for one another. If they are too hungry to wait, they must first eat at home to avoid dishonoring the Lord and bringing judgment upon themselves when they gather together. Paul says he will give directions about "the other things" when he comes to them.

Paul's concerns about the Corinthians' conduct at the Lord's Supper are real, and we must take them to heart because of the profound importance of this sacrament. Further, he believes this conduct reflects their wider failure to fully comprehend their part in the body of Christ generally and their casual lack of appreciation for the significance and magnitude of Christ's sacrifice. To profane this sacred occasion—to treat it as nothing more than an ordinary meal—is a sign of gross disrespect and spiritual immaturity. When we prepare to participate in Holy Communion, our attitude and conduct must fit the message and solemnity of the occasion.[28] We must pause and reflect on what it represents, enter the meal with humble gratitude, and fix our minds on Christ's loving sacrifice for us. As you partake of the Lord's Supper, Christian theologian James Montgomery Boice counsels, you should say to the world, "I am not my own. I am Christ's. I am in fellowship with him."[29] Let's remember that Christ Himself instituted this meal, declaring it to be his body (Luke 22:19). We should also note that, from the beginning of Christianity, Christians worshipped Jesus as God, which explains the controversy over the Lord's supper in this early letter. Christ's deity was a central part of the birth of Christianity.

CHAPTER 12

Paul turns now to spiritual gifts. A spiritual gift is any ability that is empowered by the Holy Spirit and used in a church ministry. This includes both gifts involving natural abilities, such as teaching, wisdom, and faith, and those that are more miraculous, such as prophecy, healing, and speaking in tongues.[30] Paul says that when they were pagans they were led astray to mute idols. No one who speaks in the Spirit of God says, "Jesus is accursed," and unless people have the Holy Spirit, they cannot say, "Jesus is Lord." This is one acid test to determine whether a person is speaking by the Holy Spirit: if he curses Jesus, he is not; if he proclaims that Jesus is Lord, he is, because only through the power of the Spirit can one acknowledge Christ's lordship.[31]

Paul affirms the important role of each person of the Trinity in relation to spiritual gifts. There are many gifts, but they are all from the same Spirit; there are varieties of service, but they are from the same Lord; and there are varieties of activities, but there is only one God who empowers all of them. Every believer is given a spiritual gift—not for his own benefit, but for the common good. Some of these gifts are speaking wisely, knowledge, faith, healing, the working of miracles, prophecy (which means speaking a special message from God, whether predictive or not),[32] the ability to distinguish between spirits, speaking in tongues, and interpreting tongues. The Holy Spirit allocates these gifts and empowers believers with them as He wills.

"For just as the body is one and has many members," says Paul, "and all the members of the body, though many, are one body, so it is with Christ." It is significant that Paul ends this sentence with "Christ" instead of "church." "It is important not so to identify Christ with his church," writes David Prior, "that we lose sight of his pre-eminence and transcendence. Nevertheless, Paul is clearly referring here to the way Christ today manifests himself by the Spirit to the world through his church."[33] During His earthly ministry, Jesus had a human body that He used to accomplish His work. Today, He has a body of human beings who carry out His work through the power of the Holy Spirit. Christians are united in the body of Christ through the Spirit.[34]

For in one Spirit, says Paul, we were all baptized into one body—Jews, Gentiles, slaves, and free men—and all were made to drink of one Spirit. The Spirit Who gives us our diversity also gives us our unity. Each member, just like each body part (ears, feet, eyes), is necessary for the proper functioning of the whole—the Church, the body of Christ. The more honored members of the body of Christ must not act superior to other Church members, because just like all body parts, all members are indispensable. All must show mutual respect and concern. If one member suffers, all suffer together; if one member is honored, all rejoice together.

Each member is an individual but also a vital part of the unified body of Christ. God has appointed Church members to various offices, and has given each certain gifts. First, there are the apostles; second, the prophets; and third, the teachers. Paul mentions these positions because they serve to clarify and teach God's Word. He then lists various spiritual gifts that are important to the Church: miracles, gifts of healing, helping, administrating, and various kinds of tongues. Not all are apostles, prophets, or teachers. Not all work miracles, perform healings, or speak or interpret tongues. Some positions are more important than others, and people should earnestly desire some of these higher gifts, but all are important, and everyone contributes to the whole. Thus, all members should appreciate all others, as they complement one another. As essential as the spiritual gifts are, however, they would be nothing without love, as Paul explains in the next chapter.

CHAPTER 13
<><><><><><><><><><><><><><><><><><><>

If one speaks in the tongues of men and angels but doesn't have love, declares Paul, he is but a noisy gong or a clanging symbol. If he has prophetic powers, understands all mysteries and knowledge, and has enough faith to remove mountains, he is nothing if he has no love. If he donates everything he has and even sacrifices his entire body but has no love, he gains nothing. What better way to express the primacy of love than to compare it to other qualities and gifts that God approves as good and beneficial? Christian love is far superior to any of the spiritual gifts, explains Jonathan Edwards. It is "the sum of all that is essential, distinguishing and saving in Christianity, and was...the very life and soul of all religion, without which all extraordinary gifts, such as prophecy and the gift of tongues, and knowledge, and miracles, and all morality and religion, even to such great things as giving all one's goods to feed the poor, and the body to be burned were nothing."[35]

We've explored the self-sacrificial nature of Christian love (*agape*). Emanating from the Holy Spirit, it is directed toward Christ and our fellow man. "This special word agape, which through Christ takes on a unique meaning in the history of ideas, matches the uniqueness of his Incarnation and Atonement," declares Paul Barnett. "The word 'love' perfectly fits the person, Christ. Just as the word 'radar' was coined to name a new reality, so the writers of the New Testament began to use the word agape to describe the new and radical kind of 'love' manifested in Jesus."[36]

To love God and one's neighbor is the sum of the commandments. Christ said, "A new commandment I give to you, that you love one another: just as I have loved you, you also are to love one another. By this, all people will know that you are my disciples, if you have love for one another" (John 13:34–35). It's important we grasp the distinguishing characteristics of Christ's love, for Christ's new commandment does more than just summarize the Ten Commandments; it deepens and transforms them. The command to love God and love our neighbor is not new, but the nature of that love is.[37] Christ commanded us even to love our enemies (Matt. 5:44; Luke 6:27; Luke 6:35). More important, we are to love one another just as Christ loved His disciples. Christ gave His life for His disciples (and for us) so there is no mistaking the quality—not to mention the quantity—of the selfless love He describes and Paul here endorses. Christ says, "Greater love has no one than this, that someone lay down his life for his friends" (John 15:13).

"What a great thing is love!" writes Augustine. "It is the soul of Scripture, the force behind prophecy, the salvation inherent in the sacraments, the power that makes knowledge solid, the fruit of faith, the riches of the poor, the life of the dying. What is as generous as dying on behalf of those who are ungodly (Romans 5:8)? What is as kind as loving one's enemies (Matt. 5:44)?"[38]

But as eloquent as are Edwards and Augustine, no one—besides Jesus—more poignantly describes love than Paul, whose words in this chapter speak for themselves:

> Love is patient and kind; love does not envy or boast; it is not arrogant or rude. It does not insist on its own way; it is not irritable or resentful; it does not rejoice at wrongdoing, but rejoices with the truth. Love bears all things, believes all things, hopes all things, endures all things. Love never ends. As for prophecies, they will pass away; as for tongues, they will cease; as for knowledge, it will pass away. For we know in part and we prophesy in part, but when the perfect comes, the partial will pass away. When I was a child, I spoke like a child, I thought like a child, I reasoned like a child. When I became a man, I gave up childish ways. For now we see in a mirror dimly, but then face to face. Now I know in part; then I shall know fully, even as I have been fully known. So now faith, hope, and love abide, these three; but the greatest of these is love.

CHAPTER 14

◇◇◇◇◇◇◇◇◇◇◇◇◇◇◇◇◇◇◇◇◇◇◇◇◇◇

Paul now returns to the subject of spiritual gifts, exhorting the brothers to pursue love and earnestly desire spiritual gifts, especially prophecy. He wants all to speak in tongues, but even more to prophesy, because the former involves speaking to God, not to men. Speaking in tongues (*glossolalia*) here does not mean speaking in earthly languages, though most Pentecostals and scholars apparently believe the "other tongues" spoken at Pentecost (Acts 2:4) involved known foreign languages.[39] But the spoken tongues described in this section, argues Wayne Grudem, refer to prayers or praises directed to God and spoken in an ecstatic or heavenly language that comes from a person's spirit. It is usually not understood by listeners or even the speaker himself, unless someone interprets it for them.[40]

The speaker of prophecies, by contrast, communicates with other people to encourage and console them. He lifts the church. Speaking in tongues only builds up the speaker, usually by drawing him closer to God through the power of the Holy Spirit, even if the speaker doesn't understand his own words. Considering the importance of church harmony, the speaker of prophecy is greater than the speaker of tongues unless the latter provides some revelation, knowledge, prophecy, or teaching that someone interprets to build up the church.

Paul invokes the analogy of musical instruments to illustrate the limitations of speaking in tongues. Unless musical instruments, such as the flute or harp, play distinct notes, no one will know what's being played. If the bugle gives an indistinct sound, no one will get ready for battle. Similarly, if people speak an unintelligible language, no one will understand them. Moreover, tongues, like cacophonous musical sounds, can be off-putting to those who don't understand them. So tongues, while serving a constructive purpose, can be unhelpful and even destructive to the congregation. Whether Grudem is correct that Paul is referring to tongues as some private prayer language solely between the speaker and God—as opposed to a foreign language unknown to the hearers— the point is that unless someone interprets the communication to the hearers, they can be disruptive to the church body. There are many different languages in the world, all of which have meaning, but if those communicating don't speak the same language, they will not understand one another. People eager to acquire gifts of the Spirit should seek those that build up the church.

One who speaks in tongues should pray he is able interpret his own speech, so he can explain it to the congregation and build up the church.[41] Some scholars believe that Paul is saying the speaker should pray that another person is present who can interpret the otherwise unintelligible speech.[42]

Either way, if one prays in a tongue, and neither he nor anyone else present understands what he's praying, his spirit prays but his mind is unfruitful. One must pray with his spirit but also with his mind, just as one must sing praise with his spirit and his mind. Otherwise, if you give thanks with your spirit, how will outsiders be able to say "Amen" to your thanksgiving? They won't understand what you are giving thanks for, and they will not be built up.

Speaking in unintelligible tongues, then, involves the activity of the Spirit but the disengagement of the mind. Ralph Martin says this "implies that the human intellect in this kind of ecstatic praying lies dormant, contributing nothing to the process of articulating thought into words. . . . It suggests an enraptured fellowship with God when the human spirit is in such deep, hidden communion with the divine Spirit that 'words'—at best broken utterances of our secret selves—are formed by a spiritual upsurge requiring no mental effort."[43] Acknowledging that the mind is disengaged while speaking in tongues, Paul prays that his mind will also be engaged.[44] "Those who pray or sing in tongues," he says, "should simultaneously pray and sing with their mind so that they are benefited with understanding as well as a good feeling."[45]

Paul admits he is grateful to God that he speaks in tongues more than others, but he would rather speak just five instructive words with his mind than ten thousand words in a tongue. Paul is not opposed to speaking in tongues (remember his wish that all could speak in tongues [14:5]), but his priority is building up the church.

The Corinthians must not think like children; they should be infants in evil but mature in their thinking. They shouldn't behave like selfish children and speak tongues to the congregation when it's inappropriate.[46]

The Scripture says, "By people of strange tongues and by the lips of foreigners will I speak to this people, and even then they will not listen to me, says the Lord" (14:21). Paul says that tongues are a sign for unbelievers, while prophecy is a sign for believers. If an unbeliever or outsider witnesses the entire church speaking in tongues, he will think the church members are out of their minds. But if they all prophesy and an unbeliever or outsider enters, he will be convicted by all, called to account by all, the secrets of his heart will be disclosed, and he will fall on his face and worship God, declaring that God is among them.

This section is confusing, because in verse 22, Paul says that tongues are a sign for unbelievers and not believers, whereas prophecy is a sign for believers and not for unbelievers. Then in verse 23, he says that if unbelievers come into church when people are speaking in tongues, they will think the people are crazy. In verses 24 and 25, he says that if an unbeliever enters during the speaking of a prophecy, he might come to faith. How can speaking in tongues be a sign for unbelievers when unbelievers might be repelled by it? And why isn't prophecy a sign for unbelievers as well as believers if it can lead unbelievers to faith?

Commentators differ, but a plausible explanation is that Paul is using the term "sign" negatively in relation to tongues (as a sign of judgment, in the sense that unintelligible tongues leave a believer in his unbelief, in fulfillment of the Old Testament Scripture, cited in verse 21 above). But he's using the term positively regarding prophecy, which can lead to Christian conversions and thus signals God's presence and grace among believers.[47] Therefore, it's understandable that Paul says prophecy is a sign for believers—because it encourages them to see God working in people's hearts and bringing them to Christ through prophecy.[48]

But why doesn't Paul say that prophecy is a positive sign for unbelievers as well as believers if it can lead to their conversion? He may just be emphasizing the effect on the believing Church, or he might be saying that prophecy "makes believers out of unbelievers."[49] In other words, it is technically a sign for unbelievers, but these particular unbelievers, for all practical purposes, are now believers. Unlike those who are confirmed in their unbelief through tongues, they are converted to belief through prophecy.

Paul continues to promote harmony and order in the church to encourage believers, saying that when the brothers meet in church, each one has a hymn, a lesson, a revelation, a tongue, or an interpretation, all of which should be used for encouragement. Accordingly, no more than two or three people should speak in tongues together, one at a time, and someone should interpret them. If no one can interpret, then they should only speak in tongues directly to God. Can you imagine the confusion if multiple people were speaking in tongues at once?

Similarly, only two or three prophets should speak, and others should comment. If someone is prophesying and another person receives a divine revelation, the one speaking must stop. People should prophesy in turn, so all may be encouraged. In charge of their own spirits, the prophets should control themselves because God is not a God of confusion but of peace. "Those who received and proclaimed the truth were to have clear minds," writes John MacArthur. "There was nothing bizarre, ecstatic, trance-like, or wild about receiving and preaching God's Word, as with demonic experiences."[50]

Paul next says, controversially, that women should keep silent in churches and be in submission as the Law says. If they are curious about something in church, they may ask their husbands at home, but it's shameful for them to speak in church. How can these words be reconciled with Paul's earlier indication that women often prayed and prophesied in public worship (11:4–6)? How can they be squared with Paul's comments in Chapters 12–14 that women are given spiritual gifts and are encouraged to use them to build up the church?

Some commentators are so hostile to this passage that they argue Paul didn't write it and that certain Christians added it later.[51] Others say Paul isn't addressing this issue globally but speaking to the Corinthian church specifically, and counseling that women disengage from chattering and disruptive speech.[52] Bruce Barton lends credence to this, suggesting that Paul was addressing women's disruptive speech at Corinth along with other practices that were dividing the church. His words were corrective and local, advising the women not to flaunt their Christian freedom during worship. "The purpose of Paul's words," writes Barton, "was to promote unity, not to teach about the role of women in the church."[53]

Paul Barnett adds that Paul was troubled that wives in the Corinthian church were disrupting the service by shouting out questions to

their husbands across the room.[54] Ben Witherington agrees, noting that
at the time, some women who saw themselves as prophetesses might
have weighed in with questions and disrupted the service. Paul prohibited
this practice because he didn't want Christian worship to be turned into
a question-and-answer session. "In light of... pagan prophecy," writes
Witherington, "it is very believable that these women assumed that
Christian prophets or prophetesses functioned much like the oracle at
Delphi, who only prophesied in response to questions, including questions about purely personal matters. Paul argues that Christian prophecy
is different: Prophets and prophetesses speak in response to the prompting of the Holy Spirit, without any human priming of the pump."[55] This
view eliminates any conflict between these passages and Paul's earlier
acknowledgment of women praying and prophesying in church.

Another view is that the prohibition applies only to married women
whose husbands can instruct them at home.[56] David Garland argues that
we must consider Paul's instructions in view of the social realities of his
age and his interest in preventing any breaches in decorum. If wives
publicly interrupted or contradicted their husbands, it could bruise male
egos and deter unbelievers. Paul might have feared that outsiders witnessing this would mistakenly assume that the church was like the pagan
cults that undermined public order and decency when women exercised
a greater role.[57]

Still another view held by many esteemed interpreters is that Paul
meant precisely what the text indicates—that women should be silent in
church in accordance with the order that God established in His creation.
In his first letter to Timothy, Paul issues a similar instruction (1 Tim.
2:11–15). Women are not inferior, but they must submit in love as part
of God's design. "God has ordained order in His creation," writes John
MacArthur, "an order that reflects His own nature and that therefore
should be reflected in His church. When any part of His order is ignored
or rejected, His church is weakened and He is dishonored."[58]

I confess discomfort with this passage, especially because I believe
in the inerrancy of Scripture, if not the inerrancy of the transcription
process. I'm not sure how to interpret it. I doubt it means women should
stay silent in churches, but if that's what it means, several mitigating
factors are worth mentioning. One is that God clearly gives women the

gift of prophecy—as noted earlier, Luke reports that Priscilla joined with Aquila in teaching Apollos the Gospel message more accurately (Acts 18:24–26). Even the Old Testament affirms women's prophecy (Joel 2:28). Additionally, if women were expected to be silent, that did not mean they were inferior in any way. Rather, their silence was designed to bring order to the service, reflecting the order in God's creation—just as Christ, who is God, voluntarily assumes subordinate functions in deference to the Father.

Warren Wiersbe, who was anything but a theological liberal, urges us to read this passage in light of other scriptures bearing on the subject. He observes that Paul is not saying that women have no spiritual gifts or that they should be slaves to men; to the contrary, Paul continually teaches that both men and women should build up and not tear down, and the thrust of his message is to admonish women not to abuse their gifts or use them out of place.[59] "Ultimately, Paul's goal in the passage is to reestablish order in worship," writes John Barry, "not to demean the honor of women or devalue their worship of God."[60]

Paul asks the Corinthians whether they think they are the only ones who have received God's word—gently chiding them for their arrogance. If they truly have spiritual discernment, they will recognize Paul as writing authoritatively and sharing commands from God. If they don't realize this, they are discrediting themselves. They must earnestly desire to prophesy and not forbid speaking in tongues. But all these things must be done appropriately and in order—a point he's been emphasizing throughout the epistle.

CHAPTER 15

This chapter is one of my favorites in the Bible because it deals with the resurrection of Jesus Christ, the lynchpin of Christianity.[61] Paul reminds the Corinthians of the Gospel he preached to them and they received, which they now profess and by which they are being saved. They must hold fast to the Gospel message unless they believed in vain, meaning they never truly embraced the Gospel in the first place. From the very inception of Christianity, the survival and growth of the faith depended on the hard-core truths of the Gospel. The Gospel is the life-blood of the Church—its reason for existence. Without it, the Church is an empty shell.

Paul adamantly instructs that the church is imperiled by distortion and dilution of the Gospel message due to internal or external pressures. They mustn't be misled by false teachers who deceitfully preach that there are other avenues to God. Paul is crystal clear: there is no other Gospel, and there is no other Savior. The Gospel is the message that has life-saving power and that has saved these Corinthian brothers. To ensure the vibrancy of the church and the spread of the Gospel, they have a solemn duty to hold fast to these truths and to resolve any petty internal disputes. "Therefore we must pay much closer attention to what we have heard, lest we drift away from it," says the writer of Hebrews. "For since the message declared by the angels proved to be reliable, and every transgression or disobedience received a just retribution, how shall we escape if we neglect such a great salvation?" (2:1–3)

In this chapter, Paul reviews the fundamentals of the faith, especially the bodily resurrection of Jesus Christ, which Christ communicated to him directly. "The doctrine of the resurrection of the body," evangelical theologian William G. T. Shedd observes, "was from the beginning a cardinal and striking tenet of the Christian Church."[62] Dr. Norman Geisler adds, "Historically, the bodily resurrection has been taken to mean a physical, material body."[63]

N. T. Wright, who has written extensively on the resurrection, notes that we should not assume this topic was an afterthought just because it's addressed toward the end of the epistle. Rather, "the regular references to resurrection and cognate ideas throughout the letter strongly suggest that Paul regarded this topic as one of the keys to everything else he wanted to say, and had deliberately been saving it for the end...because it was the unifying theme of this particular letter."[64]

Paul writes, "For I delivered to you as of first importance what I also received: that Christ died for our sins as foretold in the Scriptures, that he was buried, that he was raised on the third day in accordance with the Scriptures, and that he appeared to Cephas, then to the twelve. Then he appeared to more than five hundred brothers at one time, most of whom are still alive, though some have fallen asleep. Then he appeared to James, then to all the apostles. Last of all, as to one untimely born, he appeared also to me." Paul's statement here is an early oral creed that he memorialized in writing in this letter. Even skeptical New Testament scholars concede that this creed is very early, perhaps within two years of the Resurrection.[65]

Paul, of course, affirms Christ's physical death, His burial, and His resurrection. The burial is a crucial event to demonstrate the genuineness and reality of His death and resurrection.[66] Paul then recites a non-exhaustive list of Jesus' resurrection appearances, identifying the names of many witnesses.[67] This is the specificity of a historical account, not a mythical tale.[68] Geisler maintains that Paul's statement that Jesus appeared to more than five hundred brothers simultaneously, most of whom are still alive, "is a powerful testimony to the bodily resurrection of Christ." It has the ring of truth, and it's sobering that Paul is writing in 55 or 56 AD, only 22–23 years after the resurrection. Most of the eyewitnesses Paul mentions could be interviewed—it's as if Paul is inviting skeptics to do just that. Jesus' appearances to different people at different times over forty days—including some appearances not listed here—stand as powerful evidence of the resurrection and of Christianity's truth claims. On all twelve occasions Jesus was seen and probably heard. With several of them he offered Himself to be touched and was touched on two of those occasions. He ate food in four of these appearances.[69]

Paul caps his list by briefly mentioning His own encounter with Christ on the Damascus Road. He describes himself as one untimely born because he wasn't with Christ and the other apostles during His earthy ministry. As such, and because he was a notorious persecutor of the early Church (Acts 22:4; 1 Tim. 1:15–16), he calls himself the least of the apostles. But God's grace toward him was not in vain, as he worked harder than any of the other apostles to establish and grow the early Church, despite enormous persecution and personal hardship.[70] Paul acknowledges that it was not actually him but God's grace working in him. What matters is that he and the other apostles presented the Gospel to the people, and they believed.

Apparently, some Corinthian brothers are denying the resurrection. Perhaps they are so enraptured by their charismatic experiences through the Spirit that they believe they've tasted all that Christianity has to offer, thinking it's only about living life in the Spirit while losing sight of the event that makes any of this possible. Alternatively, they might be falling prey to the Greek pagan teaching that only the soul is immortal, and that there will be no bodily resurrection—recall from Acts that some Athenians mocked Paul's teachings about the resurrection (17:32).[71] Based on this pernicious skepticism, Paul lays out the case for the resurrection, showing how utterly meaningless Christianity is without this crucial historical event.

As Christ has been proclaimed as resurrected from the dead, declares Paul, how can some say there is no resurrection? For if there is no resurrection, even Christ has not been resurrected. And if Christ has not been raised, then the apostles' preaching and the believers' faith are in vain. If Christ has not been raised, then the apostles are misrepresenting God by claiming that God raised Christ. If Christ has not been raised, their faith is futile, they are still in their sins, and those who have died in Christ have perished. If their faith in Christ is for this life only, and there is no resurrection, then Christians should be the most pitied of all people.

It's hard to imagine a more logical, interdependent set of propositions. There is no excuse for imposing any corrupting ambiguity into this sequence, and Paul will have none of it. The Gospel wholly depends on the resurrection; it is a nullity without it. Christ's death without the resurrection would have accomplished nothing. If He remains in the grave, then so do we—we are dead in our sins. Don't the brothers realize how pointless their lives are if there is nothing beyond their earthly existence, no matter how euphoric their current experiences in the Spirit? Are they so deluded as to believe it doesn't matter if Christ was raised?[72] If so, they are truly to be pitied. They are faced with only two options: either embrace the fact of the resurrection or be counterfeit Christians.

Christ has been raised from the dead, Paul insists, the firstfruits of those who have died. The term "firstfruits" is enormously significant. There's no point in someone being first if others don't follow. Firstfruits was a Jewish feast held at the beginning of the grain harvest to thank God for His provision, and no grain could be harvested until the firstfruits offering was made (Lev. 23:9–14).[73] It was an assurance that the rest of the harvest was coming. Applying this term to Christ, Jesus' resurrection guarantees the resurrection of those who have faith in Him.[74] "For as by a man came death," says Paul, "by a man has come also the resurrection of the dead. For as in Adam all die, so also in Christ shall all be made alive." The man, Adam, through his sin, brought death to the human race. Jesus Christ, the God-man, brings man's resurrection and eternal life.

Paul specifies the order in which people will be raised: Christ first, then at His coming, all who belong to Him. Then the end will come, when Christ will deliver the kingdom to God the Father after destroying every earthly and spiritual authority and power (cf. Col. 1:16), for Christ must reign until He has put all His enemies under His feet. Death will be the final enemy to be destroyed, as God has put all things in subjection under Christ except God Himself, Who is the source of Christ's authority. Once all things are subjected to Christ, God's Son, then He will surrender all things to God's authority, and He will reign supreme. "In these words, Paul was not attempting to take the three persons of the Trinity and decide their relative importance," observes Bruce Barton. "Their essential nature is always one and the same; however, the authority rests through the work each has accomplished. God sent the Son; the Son will finish the work and then will turn redeemed humanity back over to God [the Father]."[75]

The resurrection sequence, which Paul provides in more detail in 1 Thessalonians 4, is that Christ will be first, then all who belong in Christ (believers who have already died, followed by those alive when Christ comes to gather His people at the Rapture). Subsequently, Christ will return in judgment and destroy all enemy forces and authorities, including spiritual ones, and subject everyone and everything to His power for a thousand years in His millennial reign (Rev. 20:4–6). At the end of the thousand-year period, Satan will be released and Christ will finally and permanently destroy him and death itself. After putting all things under His control, He will deliver His people to God the Father.

Paul asks pointed questions, forcing the brothers to deal with the logical consequences of people's disbelief in the resurrection. What is the purpose of being baptized on behalf of the dead if there is no resurrection? Would evangelists risk their lives promoting a religion that has no hope in the afterlife? Paul faces death daily because of what Christ has done, but what has he gained by fighting beasts at Ephesus (opponents of the Gospel) if the dead are not raised? Don't be fooled by those who say we should eat and drink, for tomorrow we die—bad company corrupts good character. There is more to life than the satisfaction of our physical appetites. Presumably to relate to his readers, Paul quotes a saying from Menander's Greek comedy *Thais* that bad company ruins good morals. This illustrates that false teachers who deny the resurrection corrupt the Gospel and the Church.[76] They must wake from their drunken stupor and quit sinning. It is shameful for those who have no real understanding of God to lead others away from Christ.

The Corinthians have apparently asked about the nature of the resurrection body, not quite understanding how our dying human bodies could survive into eternity. Paul says their current bodies are but a glimpse of the superior resurrection body God has chosen for them. Just as various creatures have different kinds of bodies, there are heavenly and earthly bodies, each having a different kind of glory. There are different kinds of glories for the sun, the moon, and the stars.

The same principle applies to the resurrection of the dead. The earthly body is perishable but the resurrection body is imperishable. The earthly body is weak and material, while the resurrection body is powerful and spiritual. The Scripture says, "The first man Adam became a living being;" the last Adam became a life-giving spirit. The natural is first, and then the spiritual. Adam, the first man, was from the earth, a man of dust. Christ, the second man, is from heaven. Earthly men are like the first man Adam, but resurrected men are like the man from heaven. Just as we have borne Adam's image on earth, we shall bear the image of the man of heaven.

In using the term "spiritual body," Paul is not saying that it will be an immaterial body but one that is superior, imperishable, glorified, and fit for eternity.[77] Our earthly bodies are like Adam's, natural and good but perishable and imperfect. Christ's resurrection body is the prototype for our heavenly bodies.[78] Paul seems to be saying, as many commentators surmise, that our heavenly bodies will be spiritual but also physical[79]—remember that in His resurrection appearances, Christ ate and could be touched, but His resurrection body was not bound by the laws of nature (Luke 24:31; 24:36–37).[80] "We will bear the image of His body fit for heaven (Acts 1:11; Phil. 3:20, 21; 1 John 3:1–3) as we have borne the image of Adam's on earth," writes John MacArthur.[81]

Our natural bodies have natural limitations, but our resurrection bodies are spiritual in that they will have all the capacity of God's spirit.[82] "Who can imagine a body without weakness? or infection? or tiredness? Or sickness? Or death?" asks George Eldon Ladd. "This is a body, utterly unknown to earthly, historical existence ... [It will be] a body transformed by the life-giving Spirit of God adapted for existence in the new redeemed order of the Age to Come. . . . Such existence [is not] unreal or non-existent; [but] it is an order of existence in which the 'laws of nature' and normal historical causality no longer obtain. In fact, when one puts his mind to it, it is quite unimaginable."[83]

Flesh and blood cannot inherit the kingdom of God, nor can the perishable inherit the imperishable. Paul is revealing a mystery to them—that they will not die but will be changed in a moment at the last trumpet, when the dead will be raised imperishable and we will be changed. We will then put on our imperishable bodies, and our mortal bodies will become immortal.

There is a profound contrast between the imperfect, dying human body and the perfect, interminable spiritual body, comparable to the difference between a seed and the plant into which it grows. Jesus used a related analogy to express that His death would result in an abundant harvest (the salvation of many), but He had to die before this could happen. "Truly, truly, I say to you, unless a grain of wheat falls into the earth and dies, it remains alone; but if it does, it bears much fruit" (John 12:24). Through dying, God transforms our dying body into a new and better body. The body "is sown" in death into a spiritual body.[84] This makes perfect sense, for how could a perishable body function in eternity? Our transformed body, however, will be indestructible.

When the perishable body becomes imperishable, the events described in the following Scriptures will come to pass: "Death is swallowed up in victory" (Isaiah 25:8); "O death, where is your victory? O death, where is your sting?" (Hosea 13:14)

"The sting of death is sin, and the power of sin is the law," declares Paul. "But thanks be to God who gives us the victory through our Lord Jesus Christ." Therefore, the Corinthian brothers must be steadfast, immovable, always abounding in the work of the Lord, knowing that in the Lord their labor is not in vain.

Christ's final and glorious triumph over death has eternal consequences for the beneficiaries of His grace. Death entered our existence through human sin (Romans 5:12), and man's sin was his rebellion against God's Law. As Gordon Fee puts it, "Sin is the deadly poison that had led to death"[85]—and the law is what gives sin its power.[86] "The sting of death—of the law that produces death," writes Craig Blomberg, "is sin."[87] We don't want to miss the significance of sin in this mortal equation. But for sin, man would have lived eternally, as originally created. The body wasn't initially designed to decay naturally. But sin infected the body and made it terminal.[88]

The ultimate pain of death is to die in our sins—to die unforgiven[89] and thus separated from God. But this is not the end of the story, for as the prophets Isaiah and Hosea predicted, death will be swallowed up in victory and shorn of its sting. Therefore, Paul tells his "beloved brothers," they must remain steadfast and firm in their faith and work energetically on Christ's behalf, knowing their labor is not in vain, for through their faith in Jesus Christ they are the inheritors of eternal life in Him.

CHAPTER 16

We must not be complacent about the gift of life we have received, but should respond in obedient gratitude to advance the kingdom. Accordingly, Paul instructs the brothers about the collection for the Jerusalem church, just as he instructed the Galatian churches. They should each put aside money on the first day of every week, saving it so they won't have to collect it when he comes. At that time, he will send the representatives they choose to take their gift to Jerusalem and, if it seems appropriate for Paul to go along, they can go together. He will visit them after passing through Macedonia and possibly stay with them—or even spend the winter there—so that they might help him on his journey, wherever he might go. He doesn't want to just pass through but hopes to spend more time with them, God willing. But he will stay in Ephesus until Pentecost because a wide door for effective work has been opened to him there, and there are many opponents. He asks the brothers to comfort his dear friend Timothy when he comes, for he too is doing the Lord's work. They must let no one despise him, but help him on his way in peace so he may safely return to Paul along with the other brothers.

Paul strongly urged Apollos to visit the brothers. He declined, but said he will come when he has a chance. They must be watchful, stand firm in the faith, act like men, and be strong. They must do everything in love. He reminds them that people of the household of Stephanas were the first converts in Achaia, and they have devoted themselves to serving the church. The brothers must serve people like them.

Paul rejoices that Stephanas, Fortunatas, and Achaicus are coming. They have made up for his inability to see the Corinthians by refreshing his spirit, just as they had for the Corinthians. They must give recognition to such people. Christians doing servant work should not seek recognition, but other brothers should nevertheless encourage and praise them. In this case, the brothers should also follow their guidance. Paul has written this epistle to address problems in the church and to rehabilitate himself against attacks by some in the church. Since he cannot be there personally, he commends these leaders, who are loyal to him and support his message, to lead and mentor this struggling congregation.[90]

Finally, Paul sends greetings from the churches of Asia and from Aquila and Priscilla and the church in their house. He writes this greeting with his own hand. If anyone doesn't love the Lord, let him be accursed. In closing, Paul calls for Jesus to return and sends them his love and the grace of Christ.

Some frustration with the Corinthians is occasionally noticeable in this epistle, but Paul's love and concern for the congregation is evident throughout the letter. Paul both preaches and practices the virtue of patience, explaining the Corinthians' mistakes and guiding them toward the proper path of righteous living and Christian worship. Paul's forbearance, however, will be tested more severely when his authority is directly challenged by Corinthian congregants, leading him to draft another epistle defending himself against harsh accusations from fellow believers. Let's turn to this second epistle now.

CHAPTER TEN

2 CORINTHIANS
STRENGTH IN WEAKNESS

No letter in the [New Testament] reveals the true character
of the Christian ministry as does this one. No letter says so
much about Christian giving, suffering, or spiritual triumph.

—WARREN W. WIERSBE[1]

BACKGROUND AND PURPOSE

P aul identifies himself as the author of this epistle (1:1; 10:1), and his authorship is not seriously disputed.[2] He wrote it from Macedonia around 56 AD, about one year after writing 1 Corinthians. His main purpose in writing this letter is to prepare the Corinthian church for his upcoming visit and to instruct its members on how to handle the problems they are confronting.[3] Many scholars believe this is Paul's fourth letter to the Corinthian church. The first was a lost letter Paul mentions in 1 Corinthians 5:9; the second was 1 Corinthians; and the third was a severe and sorrowful letter he mentions in 2 Corinthians 2:3–4.[4] Events that occurred between Paul's writing of 1 and 2 Corinthians shed light on this epistle.

In 2 Corinthians, Paul does not mention certain problems in the church he addressed in 1 Corinthians, such as issues concerning the

Lord's Supper and lawsuits among congregants. Some scholars infer from Paul's silence that the church has now corrected these problems. Nevertheless, other problems persist, including worldliness and false teachings. These troubles largely stem from conflicts instigated by Paul's opponents from Palestine, causing Paul to make another trip (a "painful visit") to Corinth. During or after this visit, one of Paul's opponents publicly insults Paul, accusing him of vacillating (1:17), being domineering (1:24), ministering without proper qualifications (3:1), weakness (10:1, 10), being insufficiently humble (10:13–17), and walking according to the flesh (10:2).[5] In response, Paul sends Titus from Ephesus to the Corinthian church to deliver a severe letter—so severe Paul later admits he has some regrets about it—that recommends the main accuser be punished. Paul also instructs Titus to organize the collection for the Jerusalem church.[6]

After visiting the Corinthians, Titus is supposed to meet Paul in Troas with their response to his letter and a report on their subsequent behavior.[7] As the Lord has opened a door for him, Paul intends to preach the Gospel in Troas. But he becomes restless in spirit because Titus is not there, so he proceeds to Macedonia to attend the churches and organize a collection (2 Cor. 2:12–13; Acts 20:1, 2).

Titus comes to Macedonia reporting that the Corinthians responded favorably to Paul's "severe letter" (2 Cor. 7:5–16).[8] Paul is relieved and joyful to learn they have taken his letter to heart and dealt with the main culprit. As it turns out, most congregants are loyal to Paul, and Titus has grown fond of the church. This might well account for Paul's thanksgiving to God for the improvements at the church in the first seven chapters of 2 Corinthians. But there are still problems in the congregation due to a restless minority being stirred by Paul's opponents to reject him and his Gospel.

Paul writes this epistle from Macedonia, addressing the church's improvements as well as lingering problems among certain congregants.[9] Because of the abrupt change in tone in Chapter 10, some commentators contend that Paul wrote the first nine chapters while doing pastoral work in various areas, including Macedonia along the Egnatian Road and possibly in Illyricum (Romans 15:19–21). They argue that he wrote the last four chapters after returning to Macedonia and learning of new problems in the church.[10] (We'll address this argument later in this chapter.) Subsequently, Paul mainly visits Corinth in Greece for three months (Acts 20:2, 3), where he most likely writes his Epistle to the Romans.[11]

2 Corinthians is a spirited defense of his apostolic credentials and his ministry. You can sense the depth of Paul's anguish and incredulity at having to spend so much time and energy defending his authority. Uncomfortable "boasting" of his credentials, he stresses that he doesn't seek self-aggrandizement but to rehabilitate the integrity of the Gospel message that he presented to the Corinthians and continues to clarify for them. Far from being prideful, Paul exhibits remarkable humility and selfless concern for the brothers throughout the epistle.[12] Indeed, in this epistle, we see the personal toll Paul has suffered from his refusal to compromise the truth of the Gospel and from his struggle to communicate the truth, in love, to those resistant and hostile to the message. "No preacher in the history of the church has faced such intense persecution as did Paul," writes John MacArthur, "and in this letter, he models how to handle suffering in the ministry (2 Cor. 1:4–10; 4:7–12; 6:4–10; 11:23–33).[13]

CHAPTER 1

∞∞∞∞∞∞∞∞∞∞∞∞∞∞

Paul introduces himself as an apostle of Christ and as the letter's author, also mentioning Timothy, his beloved brother in Christ. He praises God the Father Who comforts us all in our affliction, which enables us to comfort others who are afflicted. This foreshadows a subsequent portion of this epistle that describes Paul's personal suffering in preaching the Gospel. Here he exhibits his Christ-like attitude: we should not dwell on our suffering but instead use our experiences to help others, just as God comforts us.

Paul extends the principle further, demonstrating the paradoxical relationship between suffering and comfort. He connects our suffering with Christ's ("as we share abundantly in Christ's sufferings") and ties our shared suffering with our shared comfort in Christ. But for Christ's sufferings, we would be lost in our sins; His sufferings bring our comfort. Christians might endure their own suffering while obediently honoring the Great Commission, but Christ will comfort all who receive the message. Their converts repeat the process as they evangelize, as do those to whom they preach, creating a chain reaction.[14]

Moreover, when Christians suffer afflictions, they are comforted through their identification with Christ and are gratified because they're delivering a life-giving message. This strengthens them to persevere when they're attacked for their faith. When their suffering persists, they can turn to Christ for comfort. This entire process is immensely sanctifying for believers because it produces endurance, character, and hope (Romans 5:3–5). Though reassuring, this message doesn't mean God will spare Christians from hardship if they have enough faith, as some prosperity Gospel preachers seem to suggest. We will face adversity—in some cases, we will face it precisely because we live out our faith. But God will console us when we turn to Him, and He'll give us the means and guidance to withstand it.[15]

Paul describes "the affliction" he and his missionaries experienced in Asia: "For we were so utterly burdened beyond our strength that we despaired of life itself. Indeed, we felt that we had received the sentence of death." Paul may be referring to the conflict described in Acts 19:23–20:1, when the silversmiths rioted after hearing rumors that Paul was denigrating their goddess Artemis. He could be speaking about some other incident—there's no scholarly consensus—but it matters little, for the point is that the experience was clearly severe, even life threatening. Constructively applying principles he has just articulated, Paul says the hardship forced them not to rely on themselves for deliverance but on God, "who raises the dead." If God can cause the dead to rise and live again, He can certainly assist His missionaries with their gravest human struggles—and He did. They are confident He will deliver them again as they continue to evangelize. In the meantime, Paul requests the brothers' prayer, which will help them and inspire gratitude among the praying Christians who see their prayers being answered.

I find this an encouraging verse because it shows Paul's firm belief in prayer's benefits. God's chosen disciple to the Gentiles, who is operating under God's direction and superintendence, is actively praying for God's intercession. Jesus Himself prayed profusely, and commanded us to pray ceaselessly (Luke 18:1, 7; 1 Thess. 5:17). Paul constantly puts this principle into practice, realizing that prayer will help heal divisions in the church, embolden the brothers, and advance God's will in countless ways.

Paul discusses the concept of boasting more in this letter than in all his others combined,[16] mainly to defend himself against false charges from his opponents who are boasting in their own work. Paul's "boasting," by contrast, is not about himself but about Christ. He never takes personal credit for God's powers working through him. This is a somewhat nuanced point because Paul testifies that he and his companions have behaved with simplicity and sincerity, which some could misconstrue as bragging. However, he isn't seeking to rehabilitate his image for personal acclaim—rather, he seeks to ensure that false teachers don't undermine the Gospel message by discrediting him and his fellow messengers. Paul defends himself for the benefit of the Corinthian brothers who have been teetering back and forth between the truth and false teaching.

They must understand his letter as he intends it, Paul says, resisting any misinterpretations the false teachers may concoct. He has inserted no hidden meanings in his letters.[17] Paul prays that the Corinthians will come to fully understand his message so that when Christ returns and validates the message, they may boast in each other. Paul will rejoice in them on that day because their faith will prove he has honored his direct commission from Christ to preach the Word to the Gentiles. In turn, they will rejoice in him for witnessing to them and bringing them the message that inspires their life-giving faith.

Because of his affection for the Corinthians, Paul originally planned to visit them twice—first on his way to Macedonia, and again on his way back.[18] His opponents claim his failure to come the first time proved he is undependable. His failure to visit Corinth, however, was not due to personal reasons but because he was following God's schedule, not his own. Contrary to his opponents' propaganda, he is a man of his word; he has not vacillated. His words to them are certain and reliable because God is certain and reliable, and he is doing God's work. All of God's promises find their Yes in Christ. God promised that He would provide a Savior for mankind and Jesus answered the call with His Yes. Therefore, Christians say Amen to God, and they join Jesus in saying

"Yes" to God.[19] God joins them together in Christ, and has anointed them, put His seal on them, and given them His Spirit as a guarantee of His promises to them of what is to come.

Paul delayed visiting the Corinthians to spare them. He does not want to exert undue control over the brothers just because he brought them to Christ, but instead strives to work hand in hand with them to bring them joy and security in their faith.

CHAPTER 2

Paul explains that he refrained from visiting them again to avoid causing them pain, which would in turn cause him pain. Instead he wrote them, so that when he visited he wouldn't feel pain but joy—which would make them joyful as well. He wrote them—with great sorrow—not to hurt them but to express his abundant love for them. Paul is referring to "the severe letter" he wrote shortly after his "painful visit."[20] This letter was lost, but it presumably directed them to discipline their disruptive members.

Paul wanted to correct them without unduly impairing their joy, so he offered his remedial advice constructively. As we've seen, Paul tailors his message to meet people where he finds them, and while he doesn't spare them uncomfortable truths, he also doesn't gratuitously distress them. He opted to give them more time to work through their problems before returning to them. His decision wasn't selfish, as it probably anguished him to wait patiently while they struggled to resolve their problems. Indeed, we can see throughout Paul's epistles his immense love for the churches he planted and his desire to be with each of them. As this is physically impossible, he strives to carefully communicate the Gospel to them when he's with them, and to impart clear and instructive messages in his letters when he's not there. In God's providence, these circumstances result in Paul's divinely inspired epistles, which have benefitted billions of people throughout the years.

Paul notes that if anyone has caused pain, it hurt the brothers, not him. But the majority of church members have sufficiently punished the offender, so the whole church should now forgive and comfort the man, to spare him overwhelming sorrow. The brothers must reaffirm their love for him. While Paul's driving concern is the doctrinal health and harmony of the church, he never loses sight of individuals, even rebellious ones, for whom he also has great love.

Churches, in the first century and still today, must strike a balance when addressing disciplinary problems. "Both truth and grace," writes Simon Kistemaker, "should be applied in keeping a sound and balanced approach to offense and offender in the church."[21] Disciplining members is sometimes necessary, but it should never be excessive. Disproportionate discipline defeats the purpose of helping the individual and spreads negativity that can crowd out the church's love. On the other hand, excessive permissiveness in the name of love and tolerance can also corrupt the church.[22] Paul's reference to the majority decision suggests there were dissenters, but we don't know whether they wanted less or more punishment for the offender.[23] Regardless, Paul's statement shows that he respects the church and its informed decision.

Now is the time for healing, for the offending member and the church. Paul had written them earlier to test their obedience, and they passed the test, as Titus' report shows (2 Cor. 7:13–16).[24] Further demonstrating his sincere esteem for the church, Paul says, "Anyone whom you forgive, I also forgive." Paul forgives the offender for their sake in the presence of Christ, Whom he mentions because, writes John Calvin, "there is nothing that ought to incline us more to the exercise of mercy."[25] Christians must forgive others because they have been forgiven themselves (Matt. 6:14–15; 18:35; Col. 3:13).[26]

A spirit of forgiveness prevents Satan from exploiting negativity and injuring individuals, or gaining a foothold in the church. A spiritual battle is already raging in the church between God and Satan over the soul of the rebellious member and over the church itself. "For it very frequently happens, that, under color of zeal for discipline," notes Calvin, "a Pharisaical rigor creeps in, which hurries on the miserable offender to ruin, instead of curing him. . . . If Paul had not [cautioned mercy and forgiveness] Satan would have prevailed by kindling strife among them."[27]

As noted above, when he came to Troas to evangelize, Paul was too anxious in spirit to pursue the opportunity because his brother Titus was absent, so he continued to Macedonia. This is less a statement about Paul's anxiety—it is more so about his heartfelt concern for the Corinthians and his eagerness to hear from Titus about their welfare. His suffering is personal, but it springs from his concern for others.

Paul gives thanks to God for the marvels of the Gospel and for the privilege and opportunity of preaching it. Here, writes William Baker, Paul provides "the most in-depth reflections on the true nature of ministry anywhere in the New Testament."[28] Paul compares the advance of the Gospel over fierce opposition to the triumphal procession of the Roman armies. He likens the knowledge of Christ to a fragrance disseminated throughout the world by the preaching of the Gospel. The apostles and missionaries presenting the message "are the aroma of Christ to God among those who are being saved and among those who are perishing, to one a fragrance from death to death, to the other a fragrance from life to life."

Paul is likely invoking the Old Testament description of burnt offerings as "an aroma pleasing to the Lord" (Lev. 23:18). But it's not the smell of animal sacrifices that pleases God; it's the sacrificial work of Christians spreading His Word, for Christians present themselves as a living sacrifice, holy and acceptable to God (Romans 12:1; cf. Hebrews 13:15–16). Paul reiterates that this "aroma"—the Gospel—is foolishness and death to those who reject it, but eternal life for those who receive it. He notes that he and his team, unlike the false teachers, are sincere spokesmen of the Gospel, which they deliver with Christ's authority and with God watching.

CHAPTER 3

Paul claims he doesn't need a letter of commendation to validate his apostolic authority. He has already proved himself by bringing the Gospel to the Corinthians and through the changed lives of the church members. *They* are his letter—a letter from Christ written not on tablets of stone, but on human hearts to be known and read by all. They are a living testament to Paul's credentials, and he is their spiritual father. The phrase "written on human hearts" conjures language of the New

Covenant promised by the prophet Jeremiah: "I will put my law within them, and I will write it on their hearts" (Jer. 31:33; Heb. 8:10).

The New Covenant replaced the Old Covenant and is superior, providing salvation of sinners through faith in Jesus Christ. With the Old Covenant, God made Israel His treasured possession—a kingdom of priests—from whom would come the Messiah. But there was nothing in the Old Covenant, neither its sacrifices nor laws, that could save (Gal. 3:21). The Law under the Old Covenant brings death because it cannot save, but the Spirit under the New Covenant gives life. That's why the writer of Hebrews calls the Old Covenant "obsolete" and notes that it "is ready to vanish away" (8:13). Paul fully credits God for authorizing and equipping him for the ministry of this New Covenant.

Paul says that "if the ministry of death, carved in letters on stone, came with such glory that the Israelites could not gaze at Moses' face because of its glory, which being brought to an end, will not the ministry of the Spirit have even more glory? For if there was glory in the ministry of condemnation, the ministry of righteousness must far exceed its glory. Indeed, in this case, what once had glory has come to have no glory at all, because of the glory that surpasses it."

Paul is metaphorically referring to the radiance of God's glory reflecting on Moses' face when he came down the mountain carrying the stone tablets on which God had written the Ten Commandments (Exodus 34:29–30). If such glory emanates from the Old Covenant, which was coming to an end, how much more glorious is the ministry of the Spirit under the New Covenant, which is permanent?

Christians are bold in their hope—the certainty of their salvation in Christ—unlike Moses, who veiled his face so the Israelites wouldn't see that its radiance was diminishing. Moses didn't veil his face when he was meeting with God, but would cover his face after he came out and relayed to the people what God had commanded (Exodus 34:35). The Old Testament doesn't explicitly state that the radiance on Moses' face was fading, but Paul takes liberties to use Moses' restoration of the veil as a symbol of the diminishing significance and ultimate passing away of the Old Covenant.[29] The Israelites' minds were hardened and they didn't realize the impotence of the Old Covenant to save. This same veil remains in place today, Paul says, and only Christ can remove it. That is, the unbelieving Jewish people in Paul's day are still clinging to the Old Covenant, impervious to the Gospel message.

Where the Spirit of the Lord is, argues Paul, there is freedom. Through our faith in Christ, we have the Holy Spirit and are liberated from the penalty and power of sin. All believers, with unveiled faces, behold the glory of the Lord and are being transformed by the Spirit into His image in one degree of glory to another. This is a beautifully crafted description of the process of sanctification, whereby in reliance on the power of the Holy Spirit, the Christian increasingly becomes more Christ-like and reflects His glory.

This journey toward holiness is a process (Romans 8:29; Gal. 4:19; 1 John 3:2) whereby we are being transformed (Romans 12:2). Some are farther along than others, but no one will complete the journey until he is joined with Christ upon His return or upon His death, when He will be glorified. "But our citizenship is in heaven," Paul tells the Philippians, "and from it we await a Savior, the Lord Jesus Christ, who will transform our lowly body to be like his glorious body, by the power that enables him even to subject all things to himself" (Philip. 3:20–21). John adds, "Beloved, we are God's children now, and what we will be has not yet appeared; but we know that when he appears we shall be like him, because we shall see him as he is" (1 John 3:2).

CHAPTER 4

The beginning of this chapter offers valuable insight into Paul's perspective. Notice he considers it a privilege to minister the Gospel. God, in His mercy, has commissioned him for this task, and he will not lose heart. His mission is wholly different from that of itinerant preachers who mislead people with false gospels and sometimes profit from their disgraceful conduct. He will not tamper with God's Word. He has a sacred trust to deliver the Gospel message entirely as God gave it to him, for it isn't just mostly correct; it is entirely true.

Paul communicates the message, undiluted, in God's sight, and invites everyone to evaluate its trustworthiness through the filter of his own conscience. If the message seems obscure to anyone, it's only because

Satan (the god of this world) has blinded their minds and hardened their hearts to the truth of God's glorious offer of salvation in Jesus Christ. "They are darkened in their understanding, alienated from the life of God because of the ignorance that is in them, due to their hardness of heart" (Eph. 4:18).

Paul's preaching is not self-serving—he is not in a personal contest for glory against the false preachers and teachers. He is acting solely as Christ's servant. Referring to the creation story in Genesis 1:3, he writes, "For God who said, 'Let light shine out of darkness,' has shone in our hearts to give the light of the knowledge of the glory of God in the face of Jesus Christ." Paul may also be remembering that when Christ called him to be an apostle, He did so with a blinding light, instantly transforming Paul's dark ignorance into a light of understanding. Christ then commanded him to go to the Gentiles "to open their eyes, so that they may turn darkness to light and from the power of Satan to God, that they may receive forgiveness of sins and a place among those who are sanctified by faith in me" (Acts 26:17–18).[30]

As believers, this light shines in our hearts; we carry this treasure in jars of clay, in our imperfect lives, to show that this amazing power does not emanate from us but from God. Paul's metaphor highlights God's graciousness in sharing the light of Christ with us—His imperfect vessels—just as God sent Him to be sin for us. But through their imperfect and flawed lives, Paul and his missionaries struggle through hardship to present the Gospel message, thereby sharing in Jesus' death. In their suffering, they reflect Christ's light in their actions so that His life will be manifested in their mortal flesh. They are afflicted in every way, but not crushed; perplexed, but not driven to despair; persecuted, but not forsaken; struck down, but not destroyed—and they persevere. By risking death itself to preach the Word to others, they bring spiritual life to others through the "death" that is at work in them.

Through his suffering, Paul affirms his undying faith in God, identifying with the psalmist who, in his suffering, prayed to God for deliverance: "I believed and so I spoke" (Psalm 116:10). Likewise, says Paul, "We also believe, and so we also speak, knowing that he who raised the Lord Jesus will raise us also with Jesus and bring us with you into his presence." Similarly, Paul and his team, despite their travails, preach the

Gospel because they are confident that God, Who raised Jesus from the dead, will also raise them to eternal life with Him. Their missionary work is for the brothers' sake, so that they may share in the same spiritual blessings and in eternal life. The more Paul suffers, the more God's grace extends to others, enabling their salvation. All of this increases their thanksgiving and redounds to God's glory.

Though their physical bodies are decaying, their inner spirits are renewed daily, so they do not lose heart. The temporal afflictions believers endure in this life are dwarfed by the "eternal weight of glory" that awaits them as they focus on those eternal things ("the things that are unseen") instead of temporal things ("the things that are seen"). Elsewhere Paul assures the Romans, "Now hope that is seen is not hope. For who hopes for what he sees? But if we hope for what we do not see, we wait for it with patience" (Romans 8:24–25). The writer of Hebrews concurs: "Now faith is the assurance of things hoped for, the conviction of things not seen" (11:1). And Jesus says, "Do not lay up for yourselves treasures on earth, where moth and rust destroy and where thieves break in and steal, but lay up for yourselves treasures in heaven, where neither moth nor rust destroys and where thieves do not break in and steal. For where your treasure is, there your heart will be also" (Matt. 6:19–21).

CHAPTER 5

If our earthly bodies are destroyed, Paul writes, we will receive an eternal, imperishable body free of disease, decay, and death.[31] In this life we groan, longing for our eternal dwelling—our new, glorified body. It's not that we don't appreciate our mortal bodies—rather, we anxiously await our eternal ones. Aware that Greeks believed the soul would be liberated from the body on death, Paul emphasizes that we will receive perfect bodies in exchange for the imperfect ones. God has given us the Holy Spirit as a guarantee of our eternity. "In him you also, when you heard the word of truth, the gospel of your salvation, and believed in him, were sealed with the promised Holy Spirit, who is the guarantee of our inheritance until we acquire possession of it, to the praise of his glory" (Eph. 1:13–14). The Spirit within us gives us assurance that we are in Christ: "For you did not receive the spirit of slavery to fall back into fear, but you have received the Spirit of adoption as sons, by whom we cry, 'Abba! Father!' The Spirit himself bears witness with our spirit that we are children of God" (Romans 8:15–16). Douglas Moo observes, "The Holy Spirit is not only instrumental in making us God's children; he also makes us *aware* that we are God's children."[32]

In our human bodies, we are away from the Lord and would prefer to be at home with Christ; but we walk by faith and not by sight, and so we remain courageous. Being away from the Lord does not mean that we are not *in Christ*. We are away from His physical presence—we can't see Him.[33] In any event, we strive to please him, "for we must all appear before the judgment seat of Christ"—we will be accountable to Him for our actions in this life.

This does not mean the salvation of believers is in doubt. Our faith guarantees our salvation but, as previously mentioned, Christ will evaluate believers' lives to determine whether they will receive rewards.[34] "The judgment seat of Christ has to do with our service for the Lord," writes William McDonald. "It will not be a matter of whether we are saved or not; that is already an assured fact. But it is a matter of reward and loss at that time."[35] Indeed, "believers do not face condemnation at Christ's tribunal (see Romans 5:17, 18; 8:1)," observes Paul Barnett, "but rather *evaluation* with a view to the Master's commendation given or withheld (1 Cor. 3:10–15; 4:5; cf. Luke 12:42–48)."[36]

Knowing they will sit before Christ in judgment, and given their deep reverence for God, Paul and his team dedicate themselves to serving Him and evangelizing others to bring them to knowledge of Him. God knows their hearts and sees their actions, and Paul hopes the Corinthians will understand them, too. They can discern Paul's motives by comparing his work to that of the false teachers who boast of their external qualities—eloquent but empty speech and arguments—but aren't spiritually true. Paul writes, "If we are beside ourselves, it is for God; if we are in our right mind, it is for you."

Paul realizes his evangelizing might have seemed overzealous, but it was only because of his passionate devotion to God[37] and his love for the lost, as he hoped to bring as many as possible to Christ. He and his team are driven by Christ's love because they know He died for all who have died so they may live for Christ. Not only is our salvation possible because of Christ's substitutionary death, but once saved, through faith in Him, we begin to live *for* Him—committing our daily lives to walking the Christian walk and becoming more Christ-like through the power of the Holy Spirit working within us.

Before he was saved, Paul saw Jesus as a mere human being—in fact, he saw him as a charlatan and blasphemer.[38] But he now understands that He is the Savior of mankind, God in the flesh. Many people today still think of Jesus just as a great prophet or moral teacher instead of as God, but believers know better. Additionally, Christians should no longer look at people in solely human terms. They must see their fellow Christians through a different prism—according to their standing with Christ. Once a person is saved he is a new creation, as the old has passed away and the new has come. When a sinner is saved, he is reborn—regenerated—and becomes a new creature in Christ (John 3:3; Titus 3:5; 1 Peter 1:23; 1 John 2:29; 3:9; 5:4). He doesn't just turn over a new leaf but begins a new life under a new Master. He is not simply reformed, rehabilitated, or reeducated, but recreated and "living in vital union with Christ (Col. 2:6–7)."[39]

God reconciled us to Himself through Christ, and in return we have a duty, as Christ's ambassadors, to call others to be reconciled to God. What an honor to be entrusted as God's representatives to communicate His offer of salvation to others! Lest we get puffed up about this, we must also recognize the magnitude of responsibility this delegation confers. Paul implores the Corinthians, on behalf of Christ, to be reconciled to God. As they are already believers, He is not evangelizing them, but calling them to align themselves more closely with God—to reject all false teachings and accept God's Word and the sound doctrine Paul has imparted. Even as Christians, we still commit sin, and we must repent of it to be reconciled to God—again, not for salvation, which we have already received, but to conform to Christ's image, to walk in His footsteps, and to live as His servants.[40]

Why should we be reconciled to God? Because for our sake God made Christ, Who was without sin (Heb. 4:15; 1 John 3:5), to be sin for us—to take on the sins of the world (John 1:29; 1 Peter 2:24; 1 John 2:2) so that we could acquire His righteousness (Romans 5:17). "Jesus took our sin," comments David Guzik, "but gave us His righteousness. It is a tremendous exchange, all prompted by the love of God for us!"[41]

CHAPTER 6

◇◇◇◇◇◇◇◇◇◇◇◇◇◇◇◇◇◇◇◇◇◇

Paul appeals to the Corinthians not to receive God's grace in vain. Commentators interpret this in various ways. He could be urging Christians confused by legalistic teaching about their spiritual growth to mature in their faith (cf. Matt. 13:18–23), or he could be appealing to those who haven't received the real Gospel because they have accepted the message of false teachers who teach salvation by works (cf. 2 Cor. 13:5; Gal 5.4). John MacArthur believes Paul is addressing both groups.[42] N. T. Wright seems to prefer the first view, saying that Paul is appealing to the Christians not to squander the grace they've received. "Don't let it go for nothing! Make the most of it! The new creation is already here."[43]

David Garland insists Paul is talking to Christians because unbelievers wouldn't have already received God's grace in the sense Paul describes it. He says Paul could be exhorting all Christians to allow God's grace to produce fruit in their lives, but he believes he has a more specific concern for the Corinthian believers based on what follows in verses 6:14–7:1—that they not be led astray by associating with idols.[44] Paul tells the Corinthians that now is the day of salvation—the time of the New Covenant in which Christ has died for our sins and offers salvation through faith in Him. They must not turn back to a works-based legalism, follow idols, or otherwise squander God's gracious gift of salvation.

Paul and his team have imposed no obstacles to their belief. They have conducted themselves in an exemplary way and meticulously avoided unchristian-like behavior that would deter people from the message. Though they have endured hardship and persecution as a result, they have remained pure, patient, and kind, through genuine love, truthful speech, and God's power. They have marshaled righteousness as a weapon and served God regardless of whether people honor or dishonor them, slander them or praise them. They are treated as imposters, yet they are true; they are disrespected as unknown, yet they are well known;

they are described as sorrowful and poor, yet they are always rejoicing; and, though having nothing, they possess everything. They live lives of self-denial and material abstinence, yet are spiritually rich and fulfilled beyond measure.

You can't help but feel Paul's flood of emotions in these words. He has spoken to them freely with an open heart, but they have rebuffed him with cold-heartedness, so he urges them to open their hearts to him and his missionaries.

After this earnest appeal, Paul counsels the brothers not to be unequally yoked with unbelievers. This doesn't mean Christians shouldn't associate with nonbelievers. After all, he elsewhere instructs Christians to remain with their unbelieving spouses. Indeed, we are to take the Gospel message to unbelievers and model Christ-like behavior for them, which we couldn't do if we shunned them.

Paul likely means we shouldn't unite with non-Christians in any spiritual enterprise or relationship that would be harmful to our Christian testimony.[45] Nor should we engage in any activity or learning that could compromise our faith or that of anyone else. Despite our duty to be Christ-like and loving toward all, we shouldn't betray the truth itself by indulging the misguided beliefs of false religions as if they are true, just for the sake of pleasing man. Sometimes Christian doctrine is compromised today, even in our churches, when conflated with false teachings of other religions or worldviews. This isn't just a matter of academic purity. The Gospel, rightly taught, is the power of the living God to save lives. If we permit the truth to be distorted, we are accomplices in leading people astray from the path of salvation. That's why Paul warned his disciple Timothy, "Keep a close watch on yourself and on the teaching. Persist in this, for by so doing you will save both yourself and your hearers" (1 Tim. 4:16).

Idols have no place in the temple of God. Idols are entirely false gods, not partially true and partially false. Worshipping them is antithetical to the Christian faith and a grave insult to Christ's sacrifice. Paul quotes Old Testament scripture to emphasize that just as God dwelt with Israel, Christians are now the temple of the living God, Who indwells us. Just as Israelites were God's people, so too are Christians God's people. Just as Israel was to separate itself from the nations and their idolatry, so must

Christians be separate from false teachings and all forms of idolatry. Christians are commanded to be Christ-like and holy—to be separate and apart in their faith. By setting themselves apart to God, Christians will enjoy the richness of their adoption as God's children in Christ (Romans 8:15–16, 23; Gal. 4:5; Eph. 1:5). Recall that Jesus affirmed that His followers are His family: "For whoever does the will of God, he is my brother and sister and mother" (Mark 3:33:34).

CHAPTER 7

◇◇◇◇◇◇◇◇◇◇◇◇◇◇◇◇◇◇◇◇◇◇

Since God has promised to dwell with believers and be their Father, they must cleanse themselves from bodily and spiritual defilements and become holier out of their great respect for Him. They must avoid sexual immorality and false teachings from counterfeit teachers and the pagan world. Thus separating themselves from worldly impurities, they should strive to grow more Christ-like through the power of the Holy Spirit. The brothers must not be suspicious or distrustful of Paul and his team but should open their hearts to them, for they have wronged no one, corrupted no one, and have never used their influential positions to exploit anyone. It appears that Paul is responding here to relentless criticism from his opponents.[46]

He assures them he is not condemning them, as he has a strong, intimate bond with them that unites them in death and life. In mentioning death first, perhaps he is referring to the Christian fellowship that derives from their shared faith in Christ's sacrificial death and their new life in Him. Paul has great pride in them but speaks to them frankly, delivering his message in Christian love. Despite the afflictions he has endured, he is filled with comfort and joy in their spiritual development and expresses his great confidence in Christ's work in them.

So great is his love for them that he couldn't relax as he awaited Titus' report on their progress, and through it all he continued to face hardships from all directions. But God comforted him and his missionaries through the arrival of Titus, who reported that the Corinthians had welcomed and encouraged him, and that they longed for Paul, which pleased him all the more.

Paul is an open book, confessing that even if he grieved them with his letter, he does not regret sending it. Yet he also betrays ambivalence, admitting that he does regret hurting their feelings but is thankful it was only for a little while. On balance, their Godly grief is beneficial because it leads to their repentance. Godly grief produces the kind of repentance that leads to salvation, whereas worldly grief produces death. Worldly grief is what happens when the sinner's pride and self-absorption makes him sorry for what he has done and for having been caught; Godly grief is what happens when the sinner recognizes his sin hasn't just harmed himself or other people but is also an offense to God. It motivates the sinner to make things right with God by showing true sorrow and regret for his behavior and earnestly seeking His forgiveness. Godly repentance occurs when people are initially saved—they consciously turn away from their sins and toward God. They must also feel genuine sorrow over their actions and vow not to repeat them. This regretful mindset is the mark of a Spirit-filled person, while worldly repentance is the mark of one who doesn't have the Spirit.

Paul praises the Corinthians for the earnestness their Godly grief has produced in them. They are anxious to please God in every way by turning away from their misconduct, atoning, and accepting the consequences of their sin. Paul's previous letter was not meant to shame them but to help them see for themselves, in God's sight, how loyal they are to Paul and his team. His primary aim is to help them return to a Godly path. By showing their loyalty to Paul, they are proving they're trying to align themselves with God's will, for Paul has taught them His truths. Their demonstration of loyalty, and thus their Christ-centeredness, is greatly encouraging to Paul. Even more uplifting is the joy they gave Titus, which vindicates Paul's pride in them. Titus' affection for them has grown even stronger as he has recalled their obedience, respectfulness, and gratefulness. Based on Titus' encouraging report, Paul is completely confident in them.

CHAPTER 8

Paul happily reports that through God's grace and despite severe affliction and extreme poverty, the churches of Macedonia—Philippi, Thessalonica, and Berea[47]— have given generously and with great joy to the Jerusalem church. This foundational church of Christianity desperately needed assistance for food shortages and accommodations for countless visitors to the holy city.[48] D. A. Carson observes that while material prosperity can conceal spiritual poverty, material poverty can conceal spiritual wealth.[49] It's an observable fact that some people, despite their material disadvantages, are joyful in the Lord; this is convicting to those who are more materially blessed and inspiring to everyone.

The Macedonian churches freely contributed beyond their means, considering it a privilege to help the relief effort for the Jerusalem saints (believers). They far exceeded Paul's expectations as they sought to honor God, not to receive praise for their generosity. This is reminiscent of Mark's description of people putting money into the offering box, with the rich contributing large sums and the poor widow offering two small copper coins. Jesus told His disciples, "Truly, I say to you, this poor widow has put in more than all those who are contributing to the offering box. For they all contributed out of their abundance, but she out of her poverty has put in everything she had, all she had to live on" (Mark 12:41–44).

Having shared the story of the Macedonians' charity, Paul explains that he urged Titus to complete his task of collecting contributions from the Corinthians for this same relief effort. They excel in so many ways—in their faith, speech, knowledge, and earnestness, and in the love Paul and his team kindled in them—so it's important that they also excel in charitable giving. He's not commanding them to contribute but is appealing that they prove their love is Christ-like; Christ was rich but became poor for our sake, so that we might become rich.

Despite living in complete bliss and Trinitarian love with the Father and the Holy Spirit in eternity past, Christ decided, before the foundation of the world, to become a human being and die for our sins. He would endure all the indignities of human existence and undergo indescribable suffering to become sin for us—receiving God's wrath in our place for all our past, present, and future sins—and experience excruciating separation from God so that we could live. Paul encourages them to imitate Christ, as he had the Philippians: "Let each of you look not only to his own interests, but also to the interests of others.

Have this mind among yourselves, which is yours in Christ Jesus, who, though he was in the form of God, did not count equality with God a thing to be grasped, but emptied himself, by taking the form of a servant being born in the likeness of men. And being found in human form, he humbled himself by becoming obedient to the point of death, even death on a cross" (Philipp. 2:4–8).

What is important is their attitude in giving, not the amount they can give. They don't have to suffer to ease the burdens of others, but in fairness, in their abundance they should help those in need. "This is not, however, a scheme of Paul's to redistribute wealth within the church," writes John MacArthur, "but rather to meet basic needs."[50] As an illustration, Paul notes that God provided manna from heaven to the Israelites in the wilderness, and He sovereignly arranged that every person would have just as much as he needed. "Whoever gathered much had nothing left over, and whoever gathered little had no lack" (Exodus 16:18).

Paul is grateful to God for inspiring Titus to love the Corinthians just as he does. Titus has not only agreed to revisit them but is genuinely happy to do so. Paul will send another brother along with Titus who is known among the churches for his preaching and who will help oversee the collection efforts to ensure the monies are properly collected and delivered to their intended recipients in Jerusalem. They will all travel together to protect themselves against any criticism of their handling of the fund. Of course, they want to do what is right before God, but it's also important that Christians be honorable stewards.

They will also send another brother who has often proved his commitment to the cause and who has great confidence in the Corinthians. Titus is Paul's trusted partner and co-worker for their benefit, and the other brothers are messengers of the other churches and are an honor to Christ. Paul urges the Corinthians to demonstrate their love to all these men and to vindicate Paul's boasting about them.

CHAPTER 9

Paul needn't have persuaded the Corinthians to contribute to the saints, for they showed their readiness a year ago, and he brags about that to the Macedonians. Their zeal for this charity has inspired most of the Macedonian churches to give as well. But he is sending the brothers to them to follow through with the collection, just to be sure they complete the task in an orderly manner. After all, it would be humiliating to Paul and the Corinthians if the Macedonians came with them and witnessed that they were not ready. Thus, he sent the brothers ahead of him to help organize the collections so that the giving would be done in the proper spirit, not like coercively collecting a debt.

Whoever sows sparingly will reap sparingly, and whoever sows bountifully will reap bountifully. The NLT rendering is helpful: "a farmer who plants only a few seeds will get a small crop. But the one who plants generously will get a generous crop." This is consistent with the Old Testament teaching, "Whoever has a bountiful eye will be blessed, for he shares his bread with the poor" (Prov. 22:9).

Each person must follow his heart in giving, and not do it under compulsion. God loves a cheerful giver. It's one thing to give out of a sense of duty or Godly obedience—certainly many who tithe fall into this category. I don't think God disapproves an obedient giver, for the Scripture doesn't say that. (Indeed, Paul says a few verses later that their generosity proves their obedience to the Gospel [9:13].) But it is clear He loves the one who enjoys giving because he has a charitable spirit, not because he expects to receive anything in return, including accolades from others.

A proper attitude toward giving derives from the giver's conviction that everything he owns is a result of God's graceful provision. One reason God provides for us is so we will provide for others. "Precisely because of the grace of God given to them," writes Mark Seifrid, "they will be empowered and enriched to give to others."[51] Paul notes that God is able to graciously provide for our needs in all things at all times so that we may be equipped for every good work, citing this passage: "He has distributed freely, he has given to the poor; his righteousness endures forever" (Psalm 112:9).

The farmer must scatter his seed freely on the ground to produce an abundant harvest, and Christians should be charitable toward the poor to reap God's blessing.[52] God blesses the charitable giver, materially or otherwise, in this life and in eternity. When we give charitably, we are doing God's bidding; it is His good work operating through us. "The charitable acts of Christians, then, are all 'part of that larger righteousness of God by which they themselves live and in which they will remain forever,'" writes David Garland. "Their righteous acts are 'taken as the acts of God.'"[53] Dr. Bob Tuttle, a seminary professor, author, and enthusiastic evangelist, says that Christians are instruments of God's grace. It strikes me that his description is perfectly germane to this discussion—when we distribute freely to the needy, we function as instruments of God's grace, which is a humbling but exhilarating thought.

Paul writes, "He who supplies seed to the sower and bread for food will supply and multiply your seed for sowing and increase the harvest of your righteousness." He is paraphrasing an Old Testament passage: "For as the rain and the snow come down from heaven and do not return there but water the earth, making it bring forth and sprout, giving seed to the sower and bread to the eater..." (Isaiah 55:10). That is, God provides the rain and snow as His instruments to germinate the grain that is sown.

God does all the work—providing even the seed to be sown—so that farmers are dependent on him throughout the entire process. Without seed, there will be no crop. Just as seeds and harvests come from God, all our material and spiritual blessings come from Him and are sustained and increased by Him.[54] God abundantly blesses our cheerfully given charitable contributions to the poor. He will increase the harvest of our righteousness (Hosea 10:12). "He will increase the blessings of multiplied human joy, and of lessened human sorrow," writes George Clark. "God will increase the means and the blessed results of doing good. Both temporal and spiritual blessings are included."[55]

God will enrich Christians in various ways so they can continue to be generous—and this wonderful cycle will continue. The recipients of this charity will give thanks to God. So not only will their material needs be met (such as the poor in the Jerusalem church), but they will benefit spiritually, offering their thanksgiving to God and giving Him glory. Through their generosity, the Corinthians will show their obedience to the Gospel. The recipients of their largesse will pray for them because of God's abundant grace flowing through them. Paul says, "Thanks be to God for his inexpressible gift!" His thanksgiving could easily apply to this entire process of the saints organizing and distributing material gifts to the needy in Jerusalem and all the spiritual blessings that flow from it, but most commentators believe that Paul has God's extraordinary gift of salvation in mind when he uses the term "inexpressible gift."[56]

CHAPTER 10

Paul begins this section saying he was gentle, meek, and humble in their presence but bold and direct in his letters. He hopes he doesn't have to show the same boldness to them as he intends to show his critics who accuse him of walking according to the flesh.

Some detect biting sarcasm here, and I agree. It is as if Paul is saying, "Sure, I'm weak and cowardly, just like the Savior of mankind." They shouldn't mistake his gentleness for weakness, otherwise he'll have to be as forceful with them as he'll be with those who are trying to slander him. Meekness does not mean weakness or fearfulness, but "a moral quality of humility and gentleness, usually exhibited during suffering or difficulty and accompanied by faith in God."[57] It is part of the fruit of Christ-like character produced only by the Spirit (Gal. 5:23).[58] Paul has already shown himself willing to confront people face to face, such as with Peter in Antioch after he refused to eat with the Gentiles (Gal. 2:11). He is prepared to be firm with his opponents and other members of the church if necessary, but that doesn't mean he must be overbearing and flaunt his authority.

Paul's opponents suggested he walked in the flesh and displayed worldly standards instead of Godly ones. He admits he walks in the flesh—in the sense that he is human—but adds, "We are not waging war according to the flesh. For the weapons of our warfare are not of the flesh but have divine power to destroy strongholds." Paul would use the same metaphor in his epistle to the Ephesians: "Put on the whole armor of God, that you may be able to stand against the schemes of the devil. For we do not wrestle against flesh and blood, but against the rulers, against the authorities, against the cosmic powers over this present darkness, against the spiritual forces of evil in the heavenly places" (6:11–12).

Christians are engaged in a spiritual war against spiritual forces opposed to Christ. Human weapons are impotent in this conflict.

Christians must rely on God's power to combat these enemies. They must "put on the whole armor of God"—weapons that have the divine power to destroy strongholds, such as the divine attributes of truth, honesty, integrity, justice, holiness, righteousness, and faithfulness.[59] The Holy Spirit empowers Christians to engage in this battle and supplies the necessary weapons (Eph. 6:10–20).

Satan's war against the Church is grounded in lies—a counterfeit Gospel—designed to steer people away from the path to salvation. The way to fight it is with God's truth: presenting the Gospel in clear terms, not watered down to please the itching ears of those who prefer a message that better suits their worldly ideas and sensibilities. Spiritual warfare largely takes place at the level of people's minds, which is the doorway to the spirit. "It is primarily about bringing truth to bear on people's minds," writes J. Philip Arthur.[60]

Arthur says that because of the way spiritual warfare is depicted in Christian literature, we tend to think of it exclusively as an exotic, cosmic battle between angels and demons, or as involving exorcisms. While it certainly includes these things, it's also waged on a more mundane level. The enemy seeks to undermine our value system, our worldview, and our normal patterns of thought. He seeks to twist God's truth and distort Christian doctrine. Through his mostly unwitting agents in the culture, he stands the truth on its head, pulverizing the very notion of truth. He disguises good as evil and evil as good, and shatters our moral compass such that we teeter on the brink of moral and intellectual chaos. Arthur readily concedes that cosmic forces are locked in battle beyond our range of vision, but says that by unduly focusing on that, "we often miss the true theater of operations. . . . Think of it this way," he says, "Far more souls have been lost through Satan's manipulation of the intellectual and theological fashions of the age than through his recruitment of a handful of witches, or luring people into dabbling with the occult. The mind is the seat of man's rebellion against God; it is where he asserts his desire for autonomy, his longing to answer to nothing and no one outside of himself."[61]

Paul regards the Gospel as the antidote to the demonic assault on truth and everything we hold dear. It reorients us to think as God thinks. In Paul's words, "We destroy arguments and every lofty opinion raised against the knowledge of God, and take every thought captive to obey Christ, being ready to punish every disobedience, when your obedience is complete."

This means the Corinthians must return to their senses and recognize that Paul is God's authorized representative. They cannot be led astray by the flashy, charismatic frauds challenging Paul's authority. Once they correct themselves, he's prepared to visit them again and punish the instigators of this war on the church. Paul is also issuing a battle cry to refute any arguments and prideful assumptions that contradict the teachings of Christianity, lest people be led astray from the truth and thereby reject Christ.

The false teachers can claim they are of Christ, just as Paul does, and just as anyone else could. But their claims are empty if they don't exhibit evidence of it. Paul is truly of Christ, who directly called Him to be His main evangelist to the Gentiles. He prefers not to boast of his authority, but he will not hesitate to invoke it to encourage believers.

Paul disputes the charge that he is weak in body and speech but oddly bold in his letters. His message is consistent whether delivered personally or in writing. The false prophets belittle Paul's appearance and bearing, wholly ignoring his enduring qualities and his teaching. Their accusations reveal their pettiness, jealousy, pride, and lust for power. These frauds measure themselves by crass human standards, which do not apply. For his part, Paul will use God's standards and let Christ's appointment speak for itself. He and his team are following Christ's commands, which include presenting the Gospel to the Corinthians. Unlike the false teachers, they do not boast of work done by others. He fervently hopes the Corinthians' faith will mature enough that he may expand his mission to places such as Spain and Rome.

Paul then returns to his oft-repeated theme— "Let the one who boasts, boast in the Lord." That is, let's not brag about our accomplishments for Christ as if we did them on our own, but humbly acknowledge we are working through His power. He is paraphrasing the prophet Jeremiah, who writes, "Thus says the Lord: 'Let not the wise man boast in his wisdom, let not the mighty man boast in his might, let not the rich man boast in his riches, *but let him who boasts boast in this, that he understands and knows me*, that I am the Lord who practices steadfast

love, justice, and righteousness in the earth. For in these things I delight,'
declares the Lord" (Jer. 9:23–24). People don't prove themselves as
Christ's apostles or authorized missionaries simply by their empty self-
assertions of authority. The true test is whether Christ has commended
them.

CHAPTER 11

Paul asks his readers to indulge him "in a little foolishness" as he
defends himself against these false charges. He is divinely jealous of them
(jealous on Christ's behalf) because he promised them to Christ, as if He
would be their husband and they would be faithful to Him. But he's
concerned that just as the serpent came to Eve in the Garden, false teachers are deceiving them with a false gospel, leading them astray from their
pure devotion to Christ. There is no other Jesus, no other Spirit, and no
other Gospel than those they have received.

Paul declares he is not inferior to these self-described "super-apostles." Even if he lacks eloquence, he makes up for it in knowledge, as he
has repeatedly shown. Or do the brothers believe he sinned in humbling
himself by preaching the Gospel to them free of charge? He was so committed to them that he "robbed" other churches, allowing them to sub-
sidize his missionary work with the Corinthians. Instead of seeking
payment from them, he received it from the visiting Macedonian Christians, and he will continue to forgo support from the Corinthians.

Though he will not boast in a human sense, it's important that he
set the record straight on the false charges against him because they
could undermine his credibility and his Gospel message. Out of his deep
love for the brothers, and not for egotistical reasons, he defends himself.
They must open their eyes and recognize the false apostles masquerading
as Christ's apostles, just as Satan masquerades as an angel of light.
Satan's servants—the false apostles—will get what's coming to them.

Paul says no one should think of him as foolish, but he'll indulge the
fiction to counter his critics. Sardonically, he proclaims that he might as
well get on the level of the false preachers, for the wise Corinthians have
suffered fools gladly. They have willingly received the twisted teachings

presented to them, while Paul and his team are too weak to employ those tactics. He then ticks off his apostolic credentials to highlight the absurdity of the brothers' listening to the false teachers instead of him. He is a Hebrew, an Israelite, an offspring of Abraham, and a servant of Christ, a better one "with far greater labors, far more imprisonments, with countless beatings, and often near death. Five times I received at the hands of the Jews the forty lashes less one." (It was against Jewish Law to administer more than forty lashes, so they made a practice of stopping at thirty-nine [Deut. 25:1–3].)[62] Paul continues,

> Three times I was beaten with rods. Once I was stoned. Three times I was shipwrecked; a night and a day I was adrift at sea; on frequent journeys, in danger from rivers, danger from robbers, danger from my own people, danger from Gentiles, danger in the city, danger in the wilderness, danger at sea, danger from false brothers; in toil and hardship, through many a sleepless night, in hunger and thirst, often without food, in cold and exposure. And apart from other things, there is the daily pressure on me of my anxiety for all the churches. Who is weak, and I am not weak? Who is made to fall, and I am not indignant? If I must boast, I will boast of the things that show my weakness.

Paul is admitting he is weak in the human sense of the term, thereby identifying with the weak, who are persecuted for their faith.[63] He is drained from caring for his brothers, but it's his duty to endure such hardships on behalf of Christ, and he gladly does so. He stands before God and proclaims that he is not lying to them. He then reiterates that when he was in Damascus, ready to begin his missionary life, he had to escape the Jews by being let down in a basket through a window in the city wall.

CHAPTER 12

Paul says he will continue to boast (in the sense he's describing) and will tell of visions and revelations he received from the Lord. He knows a Christian who was caught up to the third heaven fourteen years ago. The levels of heaven Paul is describing are these: the atmosphere where birds fly (the first heaven); the cosmos, where the sun, moon, and stars are (the second heaven); and the unseen realm where God dwells (the third heaven), which Paul equates with paradise.[64] In the Old Testament, paradise refers to the Garden of Eden (Gen. 2:8–10; 13:10; Isaiah 51:3; Ezek. 28:13; 31:8–9). In the New Testament, it is a place of blessedness where God dwells (Luke 23:43; Rev. 2:7).[65]

This Christian heard things that cannot be told, that man may not utter. Paul isn't sure whether the man had a vision or was actually transported to heaven, but in any event, he learned divine secrets that are not supposed to be communicated to people.[66] Paul says he will boast on the man's behalf, but not on his own, although he could. He doesn't want to boast about himself to the Corinthians but impress them only through his ministry.[67] To ensure that Paul wouldn't become conceited by the wonderful revelations he himself received, God gave him a "thorn in the flesh"—a messenger from Satan to torment him and keep him from becoming proud. He begged the Lord three times to remove the thorn, but He replied, "My grace is sufficient for you, my power is made perfect in weakness." Consequently, Paul will boast all the more in his weaknesses, so the power of Christ will come upon him even more. For Christ's sake, he is content with his weaknesses and the insults, hardships, persecutions, and calamities he endures. "For when I am weak," says Paul, "I am strong," which is a theme he expresses in more detail to the Romans (Romans 5:3–5).

Through the years, commentators have speculated about the nature of Paul's thorn in the flesh. Some believe it describes those who persecuted Paul for his faith and for spreading the Gospel. Others imagine it could be some physical ailment ranging from headaches, to epilepsy, to eye problems, to malaria. There is no way to know, but it's crucial that we understand it causes Paul great anguish.[68] But ultimately, it appears to have been a positive force, as it increased Christ's power working through Paul, which explains his paradoxical axiom, "For when I am weak, then I am strong." Stated another way, "Weakness in the flesh is accompanied by strength in the Spirit."[69] Linda Velleville comments,

"Human strength is like the flower of the field that has its day in the sun but then shrivels up and dies. Enduring strength lies in God alone."[70]

Having completed his "boasting," Paul laments that he needed to resort to this "foolish" speech, but insists the brothers forced him to do it by falling for the slander against him. Though he is nothing—because every gift he has he received is from God—he is not inferior to the "super apostles." In addition to bringing the congregants the miraculous gift of salvation, he performed the signs, wonders, and mighty works of a true apostle among them. (According to numerous biblical accounts, signs and wonders authenticate the apostles' authority [Acts 2:22, 43; 4:30; 5:12; 14:3; Romans 15:18, 19; Heb. 2:3, 4]).[71] Note that Paul is clearly claiming to have performed miracles in the presence of the Corinthians—the very people he's trying to re-convince that he's an apostle. Unless Paul really did these things, he would have completely discredited himself and his entire message in this letter. Paul says he did not shortchange the Corinthians in any respect—except, he quips facetiously, by refusing their support, for which he asks their forgiveness.

He is now ready to visit them a third time, promising not to be a burden because he doesn't want anything from them—except that they embrace the Gospel, be saved, adhere to true doctrine, and live as Christians. Using a family analogy, he likens them to his children, and says it's not the responsibility of children to support their parents, but parents to support their children. Though he expends his own resources, time, effort, and energy for the salvation of their souls, will they love him less as he loves them more? Paul is obviously mystified that his selfless love for them is met with such aloofness and opposition. Perhaps he is intentionally revealing his perplexity, hoping they will embrace him anew when he returns.[72]

Next, Paul refers to an apparent claim that he exploited the congregants. Some commentators speculate that the brothers may have thought he would skim profits from the funds collected for the Jerusalem church. Others suggest Paul is preemptively refuting the accusation so no one will make it.[73] Regardless, Paul adamantly denies that he or anyone with him, including Titus, took advantage of them. They all acted in the same spirit—working on behalf of the Corinthians and not themselves.

He reiterates that he has taken great pains to answer these false charges, not to defend himself personally, but to strengthen them in Christ. He fears that when he visits they might still oppose his message and be bogged down in quarrels, jealousy, anger, hostility, slander, gossip, conceit, and disorder—the fruit of paganism.[74] If that happens, he may have to administer God's judgment rather than wait any longer for their repentance,[75] which would cause him to mourn over any who had not repented from their sinful practices.

CHAPTER 13

As noted, Paul is about to visit the Corinthians for the third time. The first was when he presented the Gospel to them, and the second was when he found they were in opposition to him and his teaching. He implies he's concerned they're still engaging in sinful practices, for he says that every charge against them must be demonstrated by two or three witnesses, adopting the forensic rules of the Old Testament (Deut. 19:15). He reminds them that he previously warned the sinners and all others that if he found it necessary to return, he would not spare them from disciplinary measures. This would show them, contrary to their claims, that Christ is speaking in Him, and that he is powerful in dealing with them. Just as Christ was crucified in weakness but lives in the power of God, Paul and his team are also weak in Him—but in dealing with the Corinthians, they will be living with Him and by God's power, and thus be strong.

In anticipation of his visit, they should contemplate whether they are in the faith. If they are, Jesus Christ is in them; if not, they will fail the test. Paul prays they pass the test, but if they don't, it won't indicate that he has failed in his mission, for he presented them with the truth of the Gospel. He hopes his apostolic services are not needed for them and prays for their restoration to spiritual strength in Christ. He doesn't want to use his authority severely when he comes, for Christ appointed him to build up, not tear down.

He urges them to rejoice and comfort one another and live in peace and harmony, assuring them that the God of love and peace will be with them. He wishes that they all enjoy the grace of Christ, the love of God, and the fellowship of the Holy Spirit—a genuine prayer that all three persons of the Godhead unite to bring them to full restoration and peace.

IS 2 CORINTHIANS ONE LETTER OR TWO?

Many commentators have struggled with the dramatic change in tone in this epistle beginning with chapter 10. In the first part of the letter, Paul expresses his elation at the Corinthians' positive response to the "severe letter" he'd sent. One theory is that after he wrote (but hadn't yet sent) the first part of the epistle, he learned of major backsliding by some members of the church. He then completed the letter and sent it.[76]

Another view is that Chapters 10–13 constituted the severe letter itself, which was later tacked on to this epistle.[77] But then how would we explain that Chapters 10–13 contain strong rebukes of the false teachers, while Chapters 1–9—which would have been written later, under this theory—are totally silent about them? Additionally, Paul refers to the severe letter in verse 2:4, which he says he wrote out of much affliction and anguish of heart. When you read Chapters 10–13, however, they have a more sarcastic than anguished tone.[78]

Others believe he might well have intended to compartmentalize problems and address them separately, as he did throughout 1 Corinthians. The argument here is that he saved a major problem to address at the end of 2 Corinthians—possibly for greater impact, since he was preparing to visit them soon—hoping to avoid a dramatic encounter over a disciplinary issue by fixing their attention on the problem in this letter.[79]

Most conservative commentators believe in the letter's integrity and reject the notion that it comprises two separate letters. They note:

1. All the contents relate to a single, unified purpose: to prepare the Corinthians for Paul's third visit to Corinth;
2. Throughout the letter, Paul defends himself against false charges leveled against him;
3. Numerous expressions in the second section seem to relate to statements in the first section;

4. There could have been a lapse of time between the writing of the first and second sections, as noted, during which Paul learned of worsening conditions in the Corinthian church;

5. If they are two separate letters, it would be difficult to explain the absence of an ending to the first one and the lack of a beginning to the second one;

6. There is no evidence from the writings of the early Church fathers to suggest there were two letters; and

7. No manuscript evidence exists to support the multiple letter theory.[80] On this point, R. C. H. Lenski summarizes, "One fact in regard to Second Corinthians must be strongly emphasized at the very beginning: all, literally all textual evidence proves this letter a unit. No abbreviated text has ever been discovered that might raise a question on this score, and no text that showed an omission or omissions has ever been found. This fact alone stands as a bulwark against the hypotheses of our day."[81]

John MacArthur, who argues strongly for the unity of the letter, says Paul's change in tone between the two sections is perfectly understandable. Chapters 1–9 are addressed to the majority (cf. 2:6) who repented after receiving the severe letter, while 10–13 primarily respond to the unrepentant minority who still follow the false apostles and who believe Paul walks "according to the flesh" (10:2).

I firmly believe this is one unified letter, and that hypercritical reviewers will always find a way to discredit the integrity of God's Word. As the epistle makes clear, Paul's critics were already active in his own lifetime, seeking to discredit his qualifications, his theological teachings, and his humility. Paul rebuts these allegations directly and convincingly, denouncing the false teachers and "super-apostles" attacking him. His passionate response springs from his deep concern for the Corinthian church, which he himself established and is now being urged to rebel against his authority. Despite his harsh words, his abiding affection for the Corinthian brothers permeates the letter. This is characteristic of Paul's teachings—uncompromisingly defending the Gospel's integrity while expressing love and respect for his Christian brothers, even when they are in error. True to his word, after writing this epistle Paul does make a third visit to Corinth to assist the believers there. And it is most likely during this trip that he writes what many believe to be his most important letter, the epistle to the Romans, which we turn to next.[82]

CHAPTER ELEVEN

ROMANS 1–7
RIGHTEOUSNESS THROUGH FAITH

[Romans] is the profoundest piece of writing in existence.
—SAMUEL TAYLOR COLERIDGE[1]

BACKGROUND AND PURPOSE

Paul asserts his authorship of this epistle (1:1) and there are no scholarly grounds to question it.[2] Unlike many of the churches he writes, Paul did not establish the church in Rome and had never visited Rome when he pens this letter. He probably writes it from Corinth on his third missionary journey around 57 AD (Acts 20:2–3).[3]

In obedience to his direct commission from Christ to take the Gospel to the Gentiles, he had planted churches in the provinces of Galatia, Macedonia, Achaia, and Asia, including in Iconium, Philippi, Thessalonica, Corinth, and Ephesus. He could now safely entrust their care to their respective church leaders (whom he had trained), under the Holy Spirit's direction.[4] At this point, he is probably reasonably confident these churches will sprout other churches. He believes his calling is to spread the Word into previously untapped territories, as he indicates in his second epistle to the Corinthians (2 Cor. 10:16). Likewise, he writes to the Romans, "From Jerusalem and all the way around to Illyricum I have fulfilled the ministry of the gospel of Christ; and thus I make it my ambition to preach the gospel, not where Christ has already been named, lest I build on someone else's foundation" (15:19–20).

He must first deliver aid to the Jerusalem saints (15:25) and then visit the Roman churches on his way to Spain (15:24). He has carefully organized this collection for the Jerusalem church from the Gentile converts, which he hopes will help heal any rifts between the Jewish and Gentile Christians and strengthen the bond between the founding church in Jerusalem and the churches he planted in Gentile lands.[5] He has longed to visit Rome and the flourishing church there, and possibly use it as a base of operations to launch his westward mission, just as he used the church in Syrian Antioch as a home base for his missionary journeys.

Some scholars believe that the church in Rome was founded by Jews from Italy who'd been converted at Pentecost in Jerusalem (Acts 2:10), then returned to Rome and spread the Good News of Christ in their synagogues. The church, then, would have begun as a congregation of mostly Jewish converts later joined by Gentiles.[6] But around 49 AD, the Roman Emperor Claudius banished all the Jews from Rome, an event mentioned in Acts 18 and corroborated by second-century Roman historian Suetonius.[7] After Jewish unrest spread over claims that Jesus was the Messiah, Claudius reportedly expelled the Jews to restore order. This expulsion necessarily involved Jewish Christians, including Priscilla and Aquila (Acts 18), resulting in the remaining Gentiles suddenly taking over the Roman church. Once Claudius' edict had run its course and the Jews were allowed to return to Rome, they were returning as a minority to a Gentile church, which doubtlessly led to tension—and ultimately divisions—in the church that deeply concerned Paul.[8]

As Rome is the hub of the Roman Empire, Paul knows it's vital that this church resolve its internal struggles, which would otherwise hinder its influence. For the church to be sufficiently strong, it needs to be properly grounded in doctrine, which is a central reason this letter is the most theological of Paul's epistles. So Paul writes it both to address specific problems confronting the church and to expound the Gospel. As Paul has never imparted his Christian wisdom to the Roman Christians, he is especially determined to provide his unsurpassed apostolic instruction. His difficulty in visiting Rome is God's sovereign choice. "In God's providence," writes John MacArthur, "Paul's inability to visit Rome gave the world this inspired masterpiece of gospel doctrine."[9]

From the start, most churches have experienced some degree of conflict, which is simply human nature. We just studied the problems that plagued the Corinthian church as it struggled with false leaders and other rebellious church members. But this epistle indicates that Rome is dealing with extraordinary problems. This is the very beginning of Christianity, and there is confusion over how the faith will affect Judaism. Should Jewish converts consider this a new religion, replacing their beloved faith, or simply the natural outgrowth of it? Which Jewish ceremonial laws would remain in force? The answers are not obvious; the apostles struggled with them, and some resisted the logical implications of the Christian's newfound freedom in Christ, which fully applies to Jewish converts. Uncertainty led to the Jerusalem Council, which provided needed resolution and direction. But certain questions remained unanswered, and Christians—especially Jewish Christians—needed guidance on the status of Jewish laws and practices in light of Christianity.

In this letter, Paul addresses whether Christians need obey the Mosaic Law (Romans 1:1–3:20); whether Abraham is the father of Gentile Christians as well as Jews; the interrelationship between law and sin; the impact of the Gentiles' salvation on the future of Israel and on the Jewish people; and to what extent Jewish ceremonial laws would remain in force, if at all. Paul seeks to help reduce the tensions in the church by showing that the Gospel unites all people in Christ.[10] If the churches in Rome are to serve as the operational base for Paul's mission to Spain, they must come together on these issues.[11]

For Paul to unite the church through his teachings, his readers must respect his credentials and authority. "Paul also needs to have the Romans believe that he is orthodox—that his gospel is the true gospel," says Douglas Moo, "and so he defends that gospel to them, explaining it in considerable detail so that they can be convinced in their support of Paul that they are supporting one who truly has the truth theologically on his side."[12]

Most commentators agree that the epistle's theme is captured in 1:16–17: "For I am not ashamed of the gospel, for it is the power of God for salvation to everyone who believes, to the Jew first and also to the Greek. For in it the righteousness of God is revealed from faith for faith, as it is written, 'The righteous shall live by faith.'" In no other epistle does Paul so clearly articulate the interrelationship between righteousness and salvation. Eternal salvation is available to all people—Jews and Gentiles—through faith in Jesus Christ. Through faith the sinner is declared righteous—Christ's righteousness is imputed to him in a judicial sense—and he is empowered by the Holy Spirit to become more righteous in fact. All believers are joined as one people in Christ.

The ESV Study Bible identifies eleven key themes, which I think are instructive as we begin to study the epistle chapter by chapter:

1. All people are sinners, therefore all need salvation from their sin;
2. The Mosaic Law, while holy, is powerless to save;
3. God's righteousness enables the victory over sin and the salvation of mankind;
4. Jesus brought the former age of redemptive history to a close and inaugurated a new age of redemptive history;
5. Christ's atoning death is central to His salvation plan;
6. Justification is by faith alone;
7. Christians share a hope of future glory;
8. Justification and salvation lead to righteousness in the present life;
9. God is sovereign in man's salvation;
10. God fulfills His promises to all people—Jews and Gentiles; and
11. The grace of the Gospel calls Christians to holiness and to lead the lives of Christ-like servants as an outworking of Christ's love in them.[13]

The epistle follows a straightforward structure, comprising two main sections: what God has accomplished in Christ (1:18–11:36), and

instructions for Christians to apply these truths in their lives (12:1–
15:13). The first section can be divided into four parts:

1. Everyone (Jews and Gentiles) is subject to God's judgment
   (1:18–3:20);
2. Salvation is available to everyone through faith in Christ
   (3:21–5:21);
3. Christians can live righteously in battling sin (6:1–8:39);
   and
4. Though Jews have mostly rejected Christ, the Jewish
   people are instrumental in God's redemptive work (9:1–
   11:36).

The second section (12–16), involving Christian ethics, features
Paul's instructions on how believers should put their faith into practice,
especially in working together to unify the church. This begins and ends
with believers centering themselves in Christ. Jesus not only saves us,
but he transforms our lives, empowering us to live righteously, and
Christians must obediently spread this Good News.[14] In this letter, Paul
lays out the consequences of our justification—it gives us *future hope*
(because we are saved unto eternal life), and it radically transforms our
present experience by empowering us to live a life of righteousness in
the Spirit.[15]

CHAPTER 1

You get a sense of this letter's gravity from the opening paragraph,
which is dense, substantive, and theologically rich:

> Paul, a servant of Christ Jesus, called to be an apostle, set
> apart for the Gospel of God, which he promised beforehand
> through his prophets in the holy Scriptures, concerning his
> Son, who was descended from David according to the flesh
> and was declared to be the Son of God in power according to
> the Spirit of holiness by his resurrection from the dead, Jesus

Christ our Lord, through whom we have received grace and apostleship to bring about the obedience of faith for the sake of his name among all the nations, including you who are called to belong to Christ, to all those in Rome who are loved by God and called to be saints: Grace to you and peace from God our Father and the Lord Jesus Christ.

Paul announces that He is Christ's servant, which in some contexts means "slave," but there is a distinct difference here. Paul is dedicated to Christ like a slave and subordinates himself entirely to advancing the cause of Christ; but unlike a slave, he does so voluntarily, out of love and obedience. Let's not forget Paul's counterintuitive teaching that man is not truly free until he becomes a slave to Christ. Before He accepts Christ, He is a slave to sin, but becoming a slave to Christ liberates him from sin (Gal. 5:1).

Paul is called to be an apostle—a position of authority quite different from that of a slave. The apostles have the authority (and the duty) to establish and supervise churches and to discipline them if necessary.[16] Apostles must have been chosen by Christ (Matt. 10:1–7; Acts 1:24–26; Gal. 1:1), they must have seen the risen Lord (Acts 1:22; 1 Cor. 9:1; 15:7–9), and most of them were with Christ from the beginning of His earthly ministry.[17] Christ appointed Paul to be an apostle, one of His representatives to speak on His behalf—to preach the Gospel and to write Scripture, which is God's Word, equal to the Old Testament Scriptures (1 Cor. 14:37; 2 Cor. 13:3; Gal. 1:8–9; 1 Thess. 2:13; 4:15; 2 Pet. 3:2, 15–16).[18] Every New Testament book was written by an apostle or one in close association with him, in the power of the Holy Spirit (cf. John 14:26).[19]

As we have taken special notice of Paul's abiding humility throughout the epistles we've studied, it should be obvious that he would never audaciously claim authority to speak on God's behalf if he hadn't received his commission directly from Christ. When I first became a Christian, I was moved by the arresting realization that the book I held in my hand—the Bible—is the living Word of God, and that every word in it is inspired by Him. Ever since, I have had an indescribable reverence for this holy book and every word it contains.

Paul was "set apart" for the Gospel of God; Christ specifically selected him to proclaim the Gospel and to represent Him to the Gentiles. As it happens, God chose him for this purpose before he was born (Gal. 1:15–16). The term that is translated "set apart" often means to be separated from others, but here it means he was set aside for a holy task, exclusive to him and the other apostles. "Paul had been a Pharisee (Phil. 3:5), supposing himself to be set apart from other men for the service of God," writes C. K. Barrett. "He now truly was what he has supposed himself to be—separated, not, however by human exclusiveness but by God's grace and election."[20]

When Paul says he was set apart before he was born, he is not speaking figuratively or hyperbolically. Consider the full import of this. It's not just that God chose Paul before he was born, but before He created the universe. He knew before He created mankind that we would fall into sin, and that He would send His Son to redeem us through His sacrificial death (cf. Acts 2:23; 4:27, 28; Eph. 1:4; 2 Tim. 1:9; 1 Peter 1:20). We are probably incapable of fully grasping the magnitude of God's love for humanity, shown in His decision to create mankind despite the excruciating suffering His Son would endure as a result. It must be understood in the context of the infinite bliss, love, and fellowship, the Father, Son, and Holy Spirit shared from eternity past.[21] "At the cross, we see the immensity of God's pain as He endured the sacrifice of Jesus," writes Ajith Fernando, "And God experienced that pain of the cross from the time He created the world, for the Bible describes Jesus as 'the Lamb that was slain from the creation of the world (Rev. 13:8; 1 Peter 1:20).'"[22]

God set Paul apart before time began in order that he be a messenger for His Good News of salvation in Jesus Christ, and He preannounced this Gospel through His Old Testament prophets. We've previously noted that God's promises to Israel in the Old Testament included His promise to Abraham to bless all nations through him and his descendants, and that the New Testament identifies the Gospel as that blessing. Paul tells the Galatians, "Know then that it is those of faith who are the sons of Abraham. And the Scripture, foreseeing that God would justify the Gentiles by faith, preached the gospel beforehand to Abraham, saying

'In you shall all the nations be blessed.' So then, those who are of faith are blessed along with Abraham, the man of faith" (Gal. 3:7–9).

I have previously related that when I became aware of the sheer number and specificity of the messianic prophecies and their detailed fulfillment in Jesus Christ, I could no longer pretend to resist Christianity's truth claims on "intellectual" grounds. As this realization was so pivotal in my own spiritual history, I wrote a book, *The Emmaus Code*, chronicling the countless ways the Old Testament points to Christ, hoping to highlight, however inadequately, the Scriptures Jesus must have expounded to His disciples on the Emmaus Road. In Luke's words, "And beginning with Moses and all the Prophets, he interpreted to them in all the Scriptures the things concerning himself" (Luke 24:27).

Always emphasizing the continuity of the Old and New Testaments and stressing that Christ is the promised Messiah, Paul underscores that Jesus Christ was descended from David in the flesh, and also was declared to be the Son of God in power according to the Spirit of holiness by his resurrection from the dead. Jesus is fully human and is fully divine—not half one and half the other. Concerning the "Spirit of Holiness" (Holy Spirit), Christ's power is often connected to the power and holiness of the Holy Spirit,[23] both in His earthly ministry and during the current church age inaugurated, as we've seen, at Pentecost (Acts 2).

God promised David an everlasting kingdom through his line of descendants (Samuel 7:12–17), and the Israelites relied on this promise, which was the source of their expectation of a coming Messiah (cf. Isaiah 11:1, 10; Jer. 23:5–6). They expected Him to establish His reign when He came, and the fact that Jesus didn't, and instead died, is part of the reason the Jews rejected Him as the Messiah, as we've noted. With these references to Jesus as David's descendant, Paul is plainly identifying Him as the Messiah.[24] Through His resurrection from the dead, Christ triumphed over death, which is, writes John MacArthur, "the supreme demonstration and most conclusive evidence that He is God the Son."[25]

Through Christ, Paul and the other apostles received grace—God's unmerited gift of salvation—and their appointment as apostles, to call people to the obedience that comes from faith in Him.[26] Obedience and faith are inextricably tied, such that an individual cannot have genuine faith without having obedience and vice versa.[27] Paul tells the Romans that his apostolic call to the Gentiles includes them, and he offers them grace and peace from the Father and the Son.

Paul thanks God for the Roman brothers, whose faith, emanating from the heart of the world's greatest empire, is proclaimed throughout the world. He mentions them constantly in his prayers and asks God to allow him to finally come visit them. He yearns for this encounter so that he may impart to each of them some spiritual gift to strengthen them. He longs to encourage them, and for them to encourage him. He has long wanted to visit and reap some harvest among them but has so far been prevented. He wants to help reach nonbelievers in Rome with the Gospel, and to strengthen and mature the faith of the believers.[28] We should note that Gospel preaching isn't just for nonbelievers. Christians need to hear this preaching throughout their lives, as it reinforces their faith, increases their gratitude and love God and their fellow man, and promotes their obedience.

Paul now expresses the major theme of his epistle: "For I am not ashamed of the gospel, for it is the power of God for salvation to everyone who believes, to the Jew first and also to the Greek. For in it the righteousness of God is revealed from faith for faith, as it is written, 'The righteous shall live by faith.'" Salvation is available to all who have faith in Christ, and salvation is interconnected with righteousness. Upon our conversion, we are declared righteous, and the Holy Spirit empowers us to begin living more righteously. The unusual phrase "from faith for faith" probably means that one's righteousness from God and his right standing with God is based on faith, from start to finish.[29]

After laying out his central thesis, Paul now begins to explain, methodically and brilliantly, why everyone needs the Gospel of Grace, and what that should mean for our everyday lives. He starts by proclaiming that everyone is a sinner and is rightly condemned. Verses 18–20 have been particularly meaningful to me over the years, as I have contemplated these issues and particularly the attitude of unbelievers: "For the wrath of God is revealed from heaven against all ungodliness and unrighteousness of men, who by their unrighteousness, suppress the truth. For what can be known about God is plain to them, because God has shown it to them. For his invisible attributes, namely, his eternal power and divine nature, have been clearly perceived, ever since the creation of the world, in the things that have been made. So they are without excuse."

There is no difference between the God of the Old and New Testaments. He is unchanging, though He progressively revealed Himself to man. God's wrath is real. It is not an academic device to rationalize God's justice. "The God of the Bible is a personal God," writes Clinton Arnold, "and his wrath, while just and measured, is no impersonal force."[30] We instinctively know, as beings created in God's image, that God exists, and we also know things about His attributes and His nature because He has plainly revealed Himself to us through His glorious creation, which we have the unique capacity to observe and understand. We have no excuse to deny His existence and therefore, His wrath against us for rejecting Him and for our unrighteousness is just.

Though men knew God, they didn't honor or praise Him, and their thinking became futile and pointless, which darkened their foolish hearts. When men consistently suppress, resist, and reject the truth, their ability to perceive the truth is eventually diminished.[31] Jesus affirmed this when He said, "The light has come into the world, and people loved the darkness rather than the light because their works are evil. For everyone who does wicked things hates the light and does not come to the light, lest his works should be exposed" (John 3:19–20).

Men who claimed to be wise, proclaims Paul, became fools and exchanged the immortal God's glory for idolatrous images that resembled his lowly creatures—mortal man, birds, animals, and creeping things. In turn, God gave them up to their own immorality and allowed them to dishonor their bodies among themselves. For "they exchanged the truth about God for a lie and worshipped and served the creature rather than the Creator." So "God gave them up to dishonorable passions. For their women exchanged natural relations for those that are contrary to nature; and the men likewise gave up natural relations with women and were consumed with passion for one another, men committing shameless acts with men and receiving in themselves the due penalty for their error."

Because they didn't acknowledge God, He gave them up to a debased mind to sin. They were filled with all kinds of unrighteousness, evil, covetousness, malice, envy, murder, strife, deceit, and maliciousness. They are gossips, slanderers, haters of God, insolent, haughty, boastful, inventors of evil, disobedient to parents, foolish, faithless, heartless, and ruthless. They are fully aware of God's righteous command that those who practice such things deserve death, yet they continue to do them and to approve of others who practice them.

As we noted previously, idolatry is a particularly heinous sin and an abominable affront to God, who created us in love, because it severs our relationship to Him. "Idolatry is a prevailing sin," writes Charles Spurgeon, "because man is alienated from God who is a Spirit, and in his carnal folly demands a god whom his senses can apprehend."[32] Spurgeon also argues, "The essence of idolatry is this—to love anything better than God, to trust anything more than God, to wish to have a God other than we have. . . . In some form or other this great sin is the main mischief in the heart of man."[33]

Our God is long-suffering, but after a person has repeatedly hardened his own heart to the point of no return, God will accept his rejection and give him over to his sin. He will either remove his restraint and allow sin to run its course on him or He will impose divine judgment on him.[34] "It is as if he is saying," writes R. C. Sproul, "'If you want a mind fixed on debauchery, you can have it.'"[35]

God doesn't just give people over without a long battle. This is a form of extreme rebellion that fully warrants God's judgment.[36] This "is not just any sinful mind," says James Montgomery Boice, "... but about the specifically 'depraved mind' created by continuing down this awful path for a lifetime. . . . It is a mind so depraved that it begins to think that what is bad is actually good and that what is good is actually bad. May I say it? It is the mind of the devil."[37] God is particularly intolerant of those who habitually engage in sin and fiendishly entice others onto their dark and death-bound path. "This is the lowest point of degradation," writes theologian Charles Hodge. "To sin, even in the heat of passion, is evil; but to delight in the sins of others shows that men are of set purpose and fixed preference, wicked."[38]

CHAPTER 2

Having criticized the Gentiles' sins, Paul now turns to those of the Jews. He sometimes uses the diatribe form, which involves an imaginary dialogue with opponents to raise and answer possible objections to one's arguments.[39] Most interpreters assume Paul is addressing a Jewish audience throughout this section, though some believe he's speaking to both Jews and Gentiles until verse 17, where he explicitly identifies his interlocutor as Jewish. Another view is that Paul is addressing any self-righteous person who presumes to judge other people.[40] John MacArthur argues that Paul is directing his remarks primarily to Jews, but also to moralizing Gentiles who think they are exempt from judgment because they believe themselves innocent of the offenses described in Chapter 1.

Paul makes clear in Chapter 1 that those who haven't been privy to God's special revelation of the Old Testament—Gentiles—are nevertheless subject to God's judgment. So in Chapter 2, he issues a strong warning to the Jews not to assume that their national identity and status as God's chosen people makes them immune to God's judgment.[41] Paul tells his hypothetical interlocutor he has no excuse, for when he passes judgment on another person, he is condemning himself because he is guilty of the same sins.

God's judgment is inherently true and just. No person will escape it, especially those who presume to judge others and are guilty of the same things, because in judging, they reveal that they have knowledge of why such behavior is wrong. People shouldn't presume that God's kindness, forbearance, and patience mean that he will exempt them from judgment. To the contrary, he will judge all, but His kindness is meant to lead them to repentance. Because of their hardness of heart and failure to repent, they are incurring God's wrath, which will result in the imposition of His divine judgment in the future.

God will render judgment based on man's works—He gives eternal life to those who seek glory, honor, and immortality through their well-doing, but those who are self-seeking, disobey the truth, and follow an unrighteous path will be subject to His wrath and fury. Tribulation and distress await evil-doers, whether Jew or Gentile, but those who do good will receive glory, honor, and peace. God is impartial.

Does this mean Paul is rejecting the principle of salvation by faith alone? Clearly not, as he makes expressly clear in Romans 1:16–17; 3:20; 3:28, 9:30–10:4, and other Scriptures (Gal. 2:16; 3:11; Eph. 2:8–9; Philipp. 3:9; cf. Acts 13:39). Rather, He judges the reality of our faith based on how we actually live.[42] "The good works of the redeemed," says John MacArthur, "are not the basis of their salvation, but the evidence of it."[43]

All who have sinned without the Law (Gentiles) will perish; though not under the Law, they have it written on their hearts, and they fail to live up to it as their consciences tell them. Men have an internal law—a moral conscience or compass—that informs them they are sinners.[44] All who have sinned under the Law (Jews) will likewise perish—because they fail to meet the Law. According to the Gospel that Christ revealed to Paul, all people will be judged by Christ, the Agent of divine judgment (cf. John 5:22, 27; Acts 17:31), Who will see all men's secrets and judge them accordingly.[45] Elsewhere Paul makes the same point: "Therefore do not pronounce judgment before the time, before the Lord comes, who will bring to light the things now hidden in darkness and will disclose the purposes of the heart. Then each one will receive his commendation from God" (1 Cor. 4:5; cf. 1 Cor. 3:13).

Paul now returns to the diatribe form to present his case against the Jews who boast in God and in following the Law. Will their status as God's chosen, covenant people exempt them from His judgment? They hold themselves out as experts in the Law, instructors of the foolish and teachers of children, having exclusive access to the Law, which is the embodiment of knowledge and truth. But they are hypocrites—for teaching others but not themselves, and for preaching against stealing, adultery, idolatry, and blasphemy while being guilty of those sins themselves.

Circumcision is valuable if you obey the Law, says Paul, but worthless if you don't, so circumcision is effectively uncircumcision. Conversely, if an uncircumcised man keeps the Law, his uncircumcision will be regarded as circumcision, so that the uncircumcised man will be in a position to condemn those who have the Law and circumcision but break the Law. In other words, circumcision does not make one a Jew. "For no one is a Jew who is merely one outwardly, nor is circumcision outward and physical. But a Jew is one inwardly, and circumcision is a matter of the heart, by the Spirit, not by the letter." Only God knows our hearts (1 John 3:20), therefore true praise will come not from fellow human beings but from God. Paul is introducing his argument here and only hints at salvation by faith in Christ, by which believers are deemed to have followed the Law in a judicial sense because God declares them righteous, as Christ's righteousness is imputed to them. He develops this argument later in the epistle.[46]

Under the New Covenant, one is saved by faith in Jesus Christ, not by following the Law, because no human being can follow it. Paul is using the term "Jew" to describe Abraham's spiritual descendants. In his letter to the Galatians, Paul writes, "There is neither Jew nor Greek, there is neither slave nor free, there is no male and female, for you are all one in Christ Jesus. And if you are Christ's, then you are Abraham's offspring, heirs according to promise" (Gal. 3:28–29; cr. Romans 4:16). God, in His covenant with Abraham, as we've repeatedly noted, promised Abraham He would bless all people and nations through him, and He fulfills that promise through His offer of salvation through faith in Jesus Christ, which is available to all people—Jews and Gentiles. Paul is not saying that Gentiles who are saved actually become Jews but that they become Abraham's spiritual "offspring"—his heirs according to God's promise.

CHAPTER 3

So, is there is any advantage in being Jewish? Yes, in every way. The Jews are entrusted with God's Law. If some of them are unfaithful, that doesn't nullify God's faithfulness. Paul says, "Let God be true though every one were a liar, as it is written, 'That you may be justified in your words, and prevail when you are judged.'" He is paraphrasing a portion of a psalm of David in which he confesses his sin with Bathsheba. David writes, "Against you, you only, have I sinned and done what is evil in your sight, so that you may be justified in your words and blameless in your judgment" (Psalm 51:4). Even if everyone in the world disagreed with God, He would be right and they would all be wrong. Truth inheres in God's nature and He cannot lie (Titus 1:2). God is faithful even if many people are unfaithful (cf. Psalm 116:11), and He is true even if people are not.

In the psalm, David admits that because of his sin, any judgment God imposes on him will be just. Paul applies David's confession to

Israel's sin in breaking God's covenant, concluding that God's judgment on Israel is also just. The distinction, though, is that unlike David, the nation of Israel has not owned up to its sinfulness and its breach of the covenant—so Israel feels God's judgment is unjust. But the contrary is true: God must impose judgment to be faithful to His covenant, thereby vindicating his promises and warnings.[47]

Since man's unrighteousness showcases God's righteousness, shouldn't God be pleased about it? Isn't it unfair, then, that He inflicts His wrath on man? By the same reasoning, if men lie, shouldn't God be pleased that their untruthfulness accentuates His truthfulness, to His glory? Why shouldn't they keep on sinning for the greater good and for God's glory? Paul emphatically responds in the negative, summarily dismissing these absurd inferences from his arguments. If these things were true, God couldn't judge sinners at all. How ludicrous to suggest that God's goodness and truthfulness depend on anything fallen man does. The only way for man to glorify God is to be obedient to His Word. "He who leaps over this boundary," writes John Calvin, "strives not to honor God, but to dishonor him."[48]

Are Jews, then, any better off than the Gentiles? After all, Paul has just said that Jews have an advantage. But, alas, they are not better off in terms of their salvation—because all men are under sin. Paul cites Psalms 14:1–3; 53:1–3, saying that no man is righteous, not even one. No one understands; no one seeks God. All have turned aside and become worthless; no one does good, not even one. They are all full of sin and they are on the path to ruin and misery. There is no fear of God before their eyes.

Sin has infected the entire human race and every aspect of life. Not one human being is righteous. In verses 11 and 12, Paul talks about man's broken relationship with God, and in verses 13–18 he describes sin's devastating impact on human beings and their relations with one another. In the successive verses, he mentions various human body parts: the throat, tongue, lips, mouth, feet, and eyes. All are corrupted.[49] Theologians describe sin's comprehensive devastation of human beings as total depravity. This doesn't mean man is the worst creature imaginable, but that his entire being is damaged by sin.[50]

Paul cites Psalm 36:1: "There is no fear of God before their eyes." The Bible tells us that the fear of the Lord is the beginning of wisdom

(Psalm 111:10) and of knowledge (Pr. 1:7). Man must fear God, as in holding him in awe, with deep reverence. Otherwise, he is a god unto himself, lost in moral and intellectual chaos and devoid of the greatest love in existence. "The wicked person is first revealed by his presumption: 'There is no fear of God before his eyes.' All sin flows from this," writes Donald Williams. "… Thus in Romans 3:11–18 when, from the Old Testament, Paul catalogs sin he climaxes his list with this verse. It is the final, irrefutable argument for our being transgressors."[51]

The Law applies to those under the Law, i.e., the Jews, so that every mouth may be stopped and the whole world may be held accountable to God. Though the Law applies directly only to Jews, as noted, the Law is written on Gentiles' hearts as well, so everyone is accountable to God and they are so thoroughly guilty that they cannot open their mouths in their own defense. For no human being—Jew or Gentile—can be justified in God's sight by works of the Law. It would be difficult to say more clearly that no human being can save himself through his own works. God is holy and perfect, and He demands perfection that no man can attain. The Law was given to make man conscious of his sin—and "loudly proclaims his need for the gospel."[52]

This is a perfect segue into Paul's next line of argument—that God has provided a means to justification through faith in Jesus Christ.[53] These verses (3:21–31) are some of my favorites of the Bible. Paul writes, "But now the righteousness of God has been manifested apart from the law, although the Law and the Prophets bear witness to it—the righteousness of God through faith in Jesus Christ for all who believe." I love this sentence because of the juxtaposition of its two clauses containing the term "law," each with distinctly different meanings. It highlights the difference between the Old Covenant and the Old Testament. Though it's impossible for us to satisfy the requirements of the *Law* that God gave to Moses (under the Old Covenant) on our own power, there is another way that requires nothing of us but faith in Jesus Christ, who fulfills the Law on our behalf.

We have proof of that because the *"Law and the Prophets"* (the Old Testament) affirm it. The New Covenant replaces the Old Covenant, but the Old Testament (the Law and the Prophets) remains as Holy Scripture along with the New Testament. Reading the Old Testament will reinforce our faith because, among myriad other reasons, it foretells of Jesus Christ. The Old Testament "bears witness" to Christ in countless ways, as Christ Himself explained to His disciples on the Emmaus Road.

Paul follows with another gem: "For there is no distinction: for all have sinned and fall short of the glory of God, and are justified by His grace as a gift, through the redemption that is in Christ Jesus, whom God put forward as a propitiation by his blood, to be received by faith." It doesn't matter who we are—our race, ethnicity, gender, our wonderful or miserable human qualities, or our stellar or unimpressive pedigree; in the end, when it comes to measuring up to God's perfection, we are all in the same sinking ship. This does not mean all human beings are equally sinful, but we are all infinitely deficient in meeting God's standard, and thus are powerless to achieve salvation through our own works. If that sounds like a kick in the teeth, then we should appreciate the remainder of the sentence even more. All we must do is accept God's gracious and free offer to justify and redeem us (to declare us righteous) by receiving His gift and placing our trust in Christ for the remission of our sins and eternal life. If we do this, we won't immediately become sin-free people, but when God judges believers for purposes of salvation, He sees only the righteousness of Christ, which has been imputed to us. I never tire of Charles Spurgeon's incomparable expression of this truth:

> If the Holy One of Israel shall look upon us as we are He must be displeased; but when He sees us in Christ Jesus He is well pleased for His righteousness' sake. When the Lord looks this way we hide behind the veil, and the eyes of the Lord behold the exceeding glories of the veil, to wit the person of His own dear Son, and He is so pleased with the cover that He forbears to remember the defilement and deformity of those whom it covers. God will never strike a soul through the veil of His Son's sacrifice. He accepts us because He cannot but accept His Son, who has become our covering.[54]

Paul continues, "This was to show God's righteousness, because in his divine forbearance he had passed over former sins. It was to show his righteousness at the present time, so that he might be just and the justifier of the one who has faith in Jesus." This is another densely packed declaration. Human beings lived thousands of years before Christ entered human history, and, as Adam's descendants, they were all sinners. So what happened to the people who preceded Christ? God didn't disregard their sins, but postponed His judgment until Christ's coming.[55] Christ's cross looks backward as well as forward.

Those who lived and died before His incarnation were saved by looking forward in faith to His coming—though they didn't know His name.[56] "The person who lived before Christ's time was saved by grace through faith in a redeemer who was to come, just as today a person is saved by grace through faith in the redeemer who has already come," writes James Montgomery Boice. "The Old Testament women and men looked forward to Christ. We look back. . . . The Old Testament sacrifices pointed to Jesus."[57] God's forbearance in delaying His judgment shows He is just, and His offer of salvation makes Him the "justifier of the one who has faith in Jesus."

As salvation is God's gift to believers, man cannot boast in His own works or that he has been declared righteous through faith. "One is justified by faith apart from the works of the law." God is the God of Jews and Gentiles alike, and He justifies all in the same way—through faith in Christ. Yet Paul emphatically assures us that salvation by faith does not overthrow the Law. To the contrary, faith upholds the Law.

I noted that Paul's introductory sentence for this section contains two distinct but complementary meanings of "the law." Paul ends the section by elaborating further on the concept. Salvation by faith in Christ does not nullify the Mosaic (Old Testament) Law—it upholds it. This principle comes directly from Jesus Christ, Who said, "Do not think that I have come to abolish the Law or the Prophets; I have not come to abolish them but to fulfill them. For truly, I say to you, until heaven and earth pass away, not an iota, not a dot, will pass from the Law until all is accomplished" (Matt. 5:17–18). God didn't err in giving Israel the Law and then make things right with a new dispensation. As we've noted, He planned from eternity past to send His Son because He knew before He created us that we would sin.

The Law was never intended to be a means of salvation, but it wasn't flawed in any respect. Our perfectly holy God created this perfectly holy

Law, which will always remain perfect. Its precepts still mostly apply under New Testament morality. God didn't overrule the Law with Christ—He *completed* it. This is a glorious distinction that explains a glorious truth. Christ is the end of the Law—the fulfillment of all of God's promises. He is the Savior whom God promised through His Old Testament prophets.

CHAPTER 4

Now Paul returns to a discussion of Abraham to show that although the Jews hold him up as the most righteous man, his own works did not save him. Paul quotes Genesis 15:6 to show that Abraham—who lived before Moses and thus before God gave Israel the Law—was saved by faith. Abraham couldn't have been saved by obeying the Mosaic Law, not only because no man can live up to its perfect standards, but also because he didn't have the Law—it was given centuries after he died. Salvation has always been through faith, and God's presentation of the Law didn't change it—it facilitated it, as we've earlier noted. "Abraham believed God, and it was counted to him as righteousness" (cf. Romans 4:22; Gal. 3:6; James 2:23). Salvation is not earned, because that would mean God owed man his salvation. It is solely a gift, and as David explained in his Psalm, it is God's blessing for those He counts as righteous apart from their works (Psalm 32:1–2). Moreover, Abraham was counted righteous before he had been circumcised. His circumcision was a sign that his righteousness had been sealed by faith. He was thereby made the spiritual father of all who would come to faith in Christ and be declared righteous (Gal. 3:28–29).

If Abraham's physical descendants (the Jews) were his only spiritual descendants on the basis of adhering to the Law, then God's promise of salvation through faith would have been rendered a nullity. God doesn't issue meaningless promises. But the Law identifies (and forbids) the sin that separates us from God and thereby generates His wrath. As the Law is powerless to save and declare men righteous, God's gracious provision of salvation to all who believe in His Son extends both to Jews and Gentiles, and is the only way to fulfill His promise to bless all nations through Abraham. He demonstrated his faith in relying on God's promise to give him a son (and many descendants) though he was almost a hundred years old and his wife Sarah was barren.[58] Abraham's unwavering faith saved him—and paved the way for the salvation of his spiritual offspring who are individually justified through their faith in Jesus Christ, Who God raised from the dead.

Curiously, in verse 24, Paul talks about faith in God. The usual formulation is that our saving faith must be in Jesus Christ. We must understand that all three persons of the Triune Godhead are in perfect harmony in their intentions and actions. They were all involved in the resurrection of Christ, and they are all involved in our salvation. We cannot believe in Christ without trusting God. Grant Osborne explains that in this chapter, Paul is focusing on God and His interactions with Abraham. "This is slightly unusual, as Paul normally emphasizes faith in Jesus," writes Osborne, "but the parallel with Abraham's faith in God is behind this thrust."[59] Professor Douglas Moo offers a similar insight: "It is typical for Paul to designate God as the one who raised Jesus from the dead (cf. 8:11; 10:9; 1 Cor. 6:14; 15:15; 2 Cor. 4:14), but it is somewhat unusual for him to designate God himself as the object of Christian faith. Undoubtedly, he does so here to bring Christian faith into the closest possible relationship to Abraham's faith. Not only is our faith of the same nature as Abraham's; it ultimately has as its object the same God, 'who gives life to the dead.'"[60] There is no inconsistency—Paul is stressing the continuity of God's promise to Abraham and carrying it forward to New Testament times by saying, essentially, that Abraham relied on God, and so do we.

CHAPTER 5

Paul now details the additional benefits of our salvation. We are not only declared legally righteous, but we have peace through Christ because we rejoice in the hope of God's glory. Paul has just informed us that we all fall short of the glory of God (3:23), but now he is saying that through faith in Christ, we are assured we will share in that glory. "Not only that," Paul declares, "but we rejoice in our sufferings, knowing that suffering produces endurance, and endurance produces character, and character produces hope, and hope does not put us to shame, because God's love has been poured into our hearts through the Holy Spirit who has been given to us." We know from our own experience that adversity builds character—that when we struggle through a problem, we can be stronger on the other side. Paul applies this principle to our faith walk. Though Christians in America don't usually experience the kind of persecution as Christians do in some other countries or as the saints of old did, the principle still holds: in our personal weakness, we (like Paul) grow stronger in Christ.

Following Christ through all kinds of tribulations produces abundant benefits for the believer. How can one's character not grow when he selflessly acts as Christ's servant to promote the Gospel despite the personal sacrifices it entails? As believers sacrificially serve others, they are imitating Christ and becoming more Christ-like.

Suffering enables us to persevere and ultimately builds our character, which fortifies our hope in God's promises. On a human level, we hope for certain things and may be gravely disappointed if they don't come to fruition. But God's promise of our future resurrection to eternal life with Him is a hope in which we can be certain, and will never disappoint us. (As we noted in our discussion of 1 Thessalonians, "hope" as used in the New Testament is not just longing for a future event, but a confident expectation—a firm confidence that God's promises will be fulfilled.) God also showers us with His love through the Holy Spirit, Whom He gives to us when we place our faith in Christ. So hope for the believer in Jesus, writes Bruce Barton, "includes a future worth rejoicing over and a present that will not disappoint either."[61]

While we were weak, Christ died for the ungodly. A person would most likely be unwilling to die for a righteous person, or even just a good person. But God loves us so much that Christ died for us even when we were sinners. Commentators differ on whether Paul is making a distinction between being righteous and good, or using the terms interchangeably, because the two terms translated from the Greek have slightly different meanings.[62] But in the end, it doesn't matter. The point is that people wouldn't want to die for either a good person or a righteous person, which makes God's death for sinners that much more amazing.

We are justified by Christ's sacrificial death and shedding of blood on the cross—we must never forget the agony He experienced in receiving God's wrath in our place. "The gospel is that Christ has suffered the full wrath of God for my sin," writes Timothy Keller. "Jesus Christ traded places with me, living the perfect life I should have lived, and dying the death I had been condemned to die."[63] If God reconciled people to Himself by Christ's death when they were enemies rebelling against Him, how much more will He intercede for us and preserve our salvation now that we are reconciled to Him and have ended our rebellion! Paul isn't suggesting that our salvation is in stages, or that it's uncertain once we attain it. He's just emphasizing the gloriousness of Christ saving man though man opposed Him. Just think how much more He will relish following through on our salvation now that we are united in Him! We must rejoice in our relationship with Christ because of the eternal security His reconciliation guarantees for us.

Sin came into the world through one man—Adam—and death spread to all men because all sinned. Not only was the entire human race infected with Adam's original sin; all men have sinned individually. Sin already existed from the time of Adam to the time of Moses, when God gave man His Law. This sin resulted in man's death, even though man was not disobeying God's direct commands like Adam, or defying the commands of the Law, which hadn't yet been given. The Old Testament contains many people, events, institutions, and ceremonies that fore-shadow or prefigure something or someone in the New Testament. Adam is a type of Christ in a contrasting way, being the opposite of Christ in several respects. Satan tempted him, just as he did Christ. Adam suc-cumbed while Jesus resisted. Adam, like Christ, is depicted as represent-ing all mankind and affecting all human beings through his actions. Adam's actions bring death; Christ's bring life.

Paul contrasts God's gift of eternal life to man's trespass, which resulted in his death. Many died through one man's trespass, but God's gracious gift of life is even more abundant. This gift is different from the trespass that led to death because the judgment followed just one trespass and brought condemnation, but the free gift followed many trespasses and brought justification. If death reigned through the trespass of one man, much more will grace reign among the beneficiaries of God's gift of righteousness through the one man, Jesus Christ.

Paul is revealing how much greater Christ's impact is than Adam's. Adam brought death; Christ brings life. Let's acknowledge that we are condemned not just through Adam's sin but our own. Either way, we deserve the death sentence. There is a stark contrast between our deserved death and our unmerited redemption, which God gives us through Christ as an act of His sovereign grace. So one sin led to the death of all men, and one act of righteousness—Christ's death on the cross—leads to justification for all men who have faith in Him. The one man who caused our death did so through his disobedience; the one Man who gives us life did so through His obedience.

When the Law was given, man's sins increased—because men became aware of God's direct commands and violated them even more. But as sin increased, grace abounded all the more—because, in simple terms, it takes more grace to forgive more sin. It's as if Paul is saying that no matter how much sin we commit, we can never quench God's gracious forgiveness. So, as sin reigned in death, grace reigned through righteousness, leading to eternal life in Jesus Christ.

CHAPTER 6

Paul asks whether man should sin more, since grace increases the more sin increases; but he answers by assuring us that is not the case. No one who has died to sin and been freed from its penalty and power through His faith in Christ would voluntarily return to that miserable condition. We have been baptized into Christ and therefore baptized into His death. We were buried with him by baptism into death, so that just as He was raised from the dead by the glory of the Father, we too might walk in the newness of life.

Most commentators agree that Paul isn't speaking of water baptism when he says, "baptized into Christ," but spiritual baptism. Through faith in Christ, believers are baptized, or placed into Christ and united and identified with Him.[64] This recalls Paul's statement to the Galatians, "For as many of you as were baptized into Christ have put on Christ" (Ga. 3:27; cf. Col. 3:1–4). Just like Christ came to life anew in His resurrection, believers acquire a new form of life through their faith in Him, and their identification with Him in His resurrection guarantees their own bodily resurrection.[65]

If we have been united with Christ in His death by dying to our own sin through faith in Him, we shall surely be united with Him through our resurrection to eternal life. Our old self, which was dominated by sin, was crucified with Him so that we would no longer be enslaved to sin. Upon his conversion, the believer, through the power of the Holy Spirit, is freed from the penalty and power of sin, as noted. We firmly believe that if we have died with Christ—died to our sins through faith in Him—we will also live with Him. We know that because Christ was raised from the dead, He will never die again. He conquered death, which no longer has any control over Him. In saying "we know," Paul is surely referring to His firsthand knowledge that Christ was resurrected, based on His personal encounter with Him on the Damascus Road.

Christ died to sin, but now lives to God. Christ never sinned personally, but He did take on our sins, which He'll never have to do again. Like Christ, we must consider ourselves dead to sin and alive to God in Christ Jesus. William Hendriksen contends that Paul offers the best commentary on his own verse (Romans 6:11) in his epistle to the Colossians: "If then you have been raised with Christ, seek the things that are above, where Christ is, seated at the right hand of God. Set your minds on the things that are above, not on things that are on earth. For you have died, and your life is hidden with Christ in God. When Christ Who is your life appears, then you also will appear with him in glory" (3:1–4).[66]

Paul tells the Roman brothers, "Let not sin therefore reign in your mortal body, to make you obey its passions. Do not present your members to sin as instruments for unrighteousness, but present yourselves to God as those who have been brought from death to life, and your members to God as instruments for righteousness. For sin will have no dominion over you, since you are not under law but grace." As we have died to sin, we must not allow it to regain its foothold over us. As we've discussed, our conversion does not immediately make us sin free; we will wrestle with sin on a daily basis through the power of the Holy Spirit throughout our lives. We must not allow our bodies to become instruments of sin, but dedicate them to God as instruments of righteousness. I think Paul is warning us not to become conceited and assume we are immune from sin as believers, but to always be vigilant against the temptations of the flesh. We must shift our focus to Christ and His love and make Him the Lord of our lives. As we are under grace and not Law, sin will no longer have the upper hand, as we rely on the Holy Spirit to sanctify us in Christ.

Now Paul asks a question like the one with which he began the chapter: are we to sin because we are not under Law, but under grace? The answer is still an emphatic no. The difference in verse 1 and this verse 15 is that in the former, he asks whether the surplus of forgiveness would encourage us to sin, since there would seem to be no punitive consequences. In verse 15, the question is whether the absence of Law as a restriction on our behavior would remove any reason for us not to sin.[67] "The Christian can never say, 'Sin does not matter. It will all be the same in the end,'" writes Leon Morris. "As [Emil] Brunner puts it [in his *The Letter to the Romans*], 'Freedom from the Law does not mean freedom from God but freedom for God.'"[68]

If you present yourself to anyone as an obedient slave, you will obey that master. In this context, you will either be a slave to sin, which leads to death, or to obedience, which leads to righteousness. Just as he warned us not to submit our bodies to sin, Paul is implying we have some choice in these matters, and we should not allow ourselves to become slaves to sin again. We should surrender to Christ as the Master of our lives. Paul thanks God that believers have been liberated from the bondage of sin and have become obedient to Christian teaching and slaves to righteousness. "New believers," writes John MacArthur, "have an innate and compelling desire to know and obey God's Word."[69]

Peter writes, "Like newborn infants, long for the pure spiritual milk, that by it you may grow up into salvation—if indeed you have tasted that the Lord is good" (1 Peter 2:2–3). Paul follows up by urging believers to present themselves as slaves to righteousness, which leads to sanctification—just as they used to present themselves as slaves to sin. As we've noted earlier, sanctification occurs purely through the power of the Holy Spirit working in us, but we have a choice in making ourselves available for the work of the Spirit. We must obediently exercise the spiritual disciplines (prayer, Bible study, fasting, etc.) so that we will become more Christ-like.

When we were slaves to sin, we were free concerning righteousness. That is, when one is a slave to sin, he is free from the control of righteousness.[70] In a different but analogous context, Jesus said, "No one can serve two masters, for either he will hate the one and love the other, or he will be devoted to the one and despise the other" (Matt. 6:24). The result of sin and its fruit is death. But now that believers have been liberated from sin and have become slaves of God, the fruit of the Spirit begins to manifest itself in their lives, and they grow holier. While the wages of sin is death, the free gift of God is eternal life in Christ Jesus.

CHAPTER 7

Paul addresses his introductory comments in this chapter to those who know the Law, probably meaning Jewish Christians and Gentile Christians familiar with the Old Testament. Most interpreters believe he is referring to the Mosaic Law,[71] though some say he is speaking of law in general.[72] I prefer the former view, as he has been focusing his entire discussion on the Mosaic Law.

His opening assertion is that the Law only binds a person when he is alive. So a married woman is released from her marital bonds on her husband's death and can remarry without being considered an adulteress. Likewise, Christians are released from the bonds of the Law (the written Law in the case of the Jews, and the Law written on the Gentiles' hearts) by Christ's death and now belong to Christ, so they may bear fruit for God. Christians receive the Spirit upon their conversion and begin to produce spiritual fruit—attributes of holiness, such as love, joy, peace, patience, kindness, goodness, faithfulness, gentleness, and self-control (Gal 5:22–23; cf. John 15:4–5). Before they became Christians, they were under the dominion of the flesh—their sinful nature—and the Law aroused their sinful passions to work fruit for death.[73]

As we've seen and will examine further below, the Law ironically tends to promote sin, and sin results in death (Romans 5:15, 17, 21; 6:16; 21, 23; 7:10–11, 13; 8; 2 6, 10, 13). But Christians, having died to the

Law, are released from it so they may serve in the new way of the Spirit. The Holy Spirit indwells Christians, empowers them to serve God, and helps them become more like Christ. They are motivated by love and obedience rather than the requirements of the Law.

After explaining that the Law aroused their sinful passions, Paul asks whether that means the Law itself is sin. By no means, he assures them. But there is a connection between the Law and sin, in that knowledge of the Law enables people to identify sin, because they can compare their behavior to God's divine standard.[74] Paul says, for example, that he wouldn't have understood the meaning of "to covet" if the Law hadn't forbidden it. But sin, through the commandment, produced all kinds of covetous desire in him. "Not only does the law identify sin for us," writes R. C. Sproul, "but it incites sin by functioning as an external stimulus to our own sins. That is, nothing is so attractive to us as the forbidden."[75] This is a sobering indictment of human nature, and it is undeniable, considering that the forbidden fruit played a major role in man's original sin. It occurs to me that if something that is forbidden was enticing enough to produce sin in Adam and Eve in their original state, how much more powerful a force it is working on fallen man.

Apart from the Law, sin lies dead. Paul says he was once alive and apart from the Law, but when the Law was introduced, sin came alive and he died. The very commandment that promised life resulted in his death. Paul clearly does not mean that sin didn't exist before the Law, for as he noted earlier, we know that Adam and Eve sinned long before God gave the Law to Moses. Perhaps he means that before the Law sin was latent—inactive or inert—instead of nonexistent.[76] One cannot break the Law if no law is in force. The Law doesn't save people, but it does function to establish people's guilt. It has been said that the Law is like a mirror—the mirror can show you that your face is dirty, but it can't clean your face. "Without something to rebel against," Leon Morris observes, "there could be no rebels."[77]

Nor does Paul mean he was ever technically outside the Law's requirements, because he tells us repeatedly that he was raised as an observant Jew, a Pharisee in the strictest sense of that term. He could be referring to his youthful years, before he reached the age of accountability.[78] Or he could be referring to men who live with little spiritual awareness and an untroubled conscience,[79] because the significance of the Law and of right living has yet to register in their consciousness. But when the commandment came, Paul became aware of the Law's requirements and recognized himself as a great sinner, and the self-satisfied person he had been ceased to exist.[80] Sin, working through the Law, deceived and killed him. Paul makes the same point about the lethality of the Law in his second letter to the Corinthians. "For the letter kills, but the Spirit gives light" (2 Cor. 3:6). Yet, he has also told us, and tells us again here in the very next verse (Romans 7:12), that the Law is holy, righteous, and good.

So he asks whether that which is good—the Law—brought death to him. And just as emphatically as he denied that the Law is sin, he wholly rejects that it brings death. The holy Law doesn't lead to death—sin, working through it, does. It produces evil from something that is inherently good. The Law exposes sin's truly evil nature, because people can only recognize sin, as such, through the Law. "Sin uses the commandments in the law, that are good, in order to produce death in people because people cannot keep the law in their own strength," writes Bruce Barton. "But, by using the commandments as instruments of death, sin reveals itself in all its ugliness."[81]

I must note that as further evidence that Paul is not scapegoating the Law itself, he elsewhere declares, as we've seen, that it leads us to Christ by making us aware of our inadequacies and our inability to save ourselves on our own strength and apart from Him (Gal. 3:24). "To slay the sinner is then the first use of the Law, to destroy the life and strength wherein he trusts and convince him that he is dead while he lives;" writes John Wesley; "not only under the sentence of death, but actually dead to God, void of all spiritual life, dead in trespasses and sins."[82] So no matter what negativity may flow from sin's exploitation of the Law, it is dwarfed by the glorious goodness the Law produces.

We know that the Law is spiritual—it is holy, righteous, and good. But Paul confesses that he is still of the flesh, "sold under sin":

> For I do not understand my own actions. For I do not do what
> I want, but I do the very thing I hate. Now if I do what I do
> not want, I agree with the law, that it is good. So now it is no

longer I who do it, but sin that dwells within me. For I know that nothing good dwells in me, that is, in my flesh. For I have the desire to do what is right, but not the ability to carry it out. For I do not do the good I want, but the evil I do not want is what I keep on doing. Now if I do what I do not want, it is no longer I who do it, but sin that dwells within me. So I find it to be a law that when I want to do right, evil lies close at hand. For I delight in the law of God, in my inner being, but I see in my members another law waging war against the law of my mind and making me captive to the law of sin that dwells in my members.

Commentators debate whether Paul is describing himself in his unregenerate state, i.e., before he became a believer, or as a Christian struggling with his sin nature. I believe he's speaking as a Christian. After all, he says that "the law of sin" dwells only in his "members," and that these members are waging war against the law of his mind—the new and redeemed part of him.[83] Moreover, he could hardly delight in the Law of God (verse 22)—in his inner being, no less—if he were not a believer. Paul's unfolding of the argument also fits with the progression of the book. He's now writing about sanctification of believers, not their condemnation before they were saved.

His statement in verse 16 further shows his reverence for the Law. The NLT translation is clearer: "But if I know what I am doing is wrong, this shows that I agree that the law is good." In other words, the Law informs him of his sin, and it's beneficial for a person to be aware of sin, because it could ultimately lead him to Christ—therefore, the Law is good. Paul's arguments in Chapter 7 "depict vividly the inner conflict characteristic of the true Christian," writes Charles Cranfield, "a conflict such as is possible only in the man, in whom the Holy Spirit is active and whose mind is being renewed under the discipline of the gospel."[84]

Throughout this section, Paul makes the same point from a variety of angles. He says that even in his present, redeemed state he still wrestles with his flesh. "Sin is not a power that operates 'outside' the person, making him do its bidding," Douglas Moo avers. "Sin is something resident in the very being."[85] What else is the process of sanctification if not one's daily struggle against sin under the power of the Holy Spirit? If our sinful nature had totally died upon regeneration, there would be no need for sanctification, because we would have already arrived. "This is why the secret of sanctification is to develop in our hearts a growing intensity of desire to please God, to be obedient to Christ," states R. C. Sproul. "That's why we are called to fill our minds with the Word of God that we may know more of the loveliness of God, the majesty of God, the sweetness and excellence of Christ. . . . But no Christian in this world achieves a 100% consistent desire to obey God only. There is a powerful desire left over from the fallen nature."[86]

This is the powerful force Paul admits that he's struggling with in these exceedingly personal, humble, and candid passages. The conflict within him is so intense that he says he wants to do the right things, but doesn't have the ability to do them in his own power. And if he does those things he doesn't want to do, it's not really him acting but the sin that dwells within him. Paul isn't denying responsibility for his sin but saying that sometimes his sinful nature overpowers him.

In verse 24, Paul declares, "Wretched man that I am! Who will deliver me from this body of death?" Some argue that a believer could not express such personal misery.[87] I disagree. To the contrary, Paul's acute awareness of the sinful side of his nature is strong evidence that he is saved, for the Holy Spirit operates in the believer to quicken his awareness of sin. Indeed, this is perfectly consistent with Isaiah's mortified view of himself as a deeply sinful man when he came in contact with the holiness of the pre-incarnate Christ in the Temple (Isaiah 6). As H. D. M. Spence-Jones notes about Paul, "Such a cry indicates the stirrings of Divine life within the soul."[88]

Paul ends this chapter with the uplifting message that there is a final cure for our sinful nature: Christ is the Deliverer who saves us from sin and death. It's a fitting ending to his moving discussion of the Law and its proper role in the new Church. Paul's dazzling language and passionate arguments spring from the pages straight into many believers' hearts, including mine. These chapters offer a glimpse of Paul's inner beauty that radiates with the love of Christ. This elegance continues to shine through in the second half of the epistle, which begins with Paul moving his focus to the Christian's life in the Holy Spirit.

CHAPTER TWELVE

ROMANS 8–16
CHRIST: THE HOPE OF JEWS AND GENTILES

The Book of Romans is the closest thing to a systematic theology that can be found in the New Testament. Its content is vitally important. In fact, if God has used any single book of the Bible more than any other to change lives, it is the Book of Romans.

—R. C. SPROUL[1]

CHAPTER 8

"Romans 8 is without doubt one of the best-known, best-loved chapters of the Bible," writes John Stott. "If in Romans 7 Paul has been preoccupied with the place of the law, in Romans 8 his preoccupation is with the work of the Spirit. . . . The essential contrast Paul paints is between the weakness of the law and the power of the Spirit."[2] Similarly, E. F. Harrison observes that Chapter 8 "is one of the absolutely high points in the entire corpus of Pauline literature. . . . This is high and holy ground indeed for the Christian pilgrim to read."[3]

Paul begins, "There is therefore now no condemnation for those who are in Christ Jesus. For the law of the Spirit of life has set you free in Christ Jesus from the law of sin and death." The sin nature is still inside Christians, so they still sin, but these sins are powerless to kill them.

Christ has died for their sins and they belong to Him—they are thereby freed from condemnation.[4] God accomplishes what the Law could not— He justifies human beings, delivering them from the penalty of sin and death.

"By sending his own Son in the likeness of sinful flesh and for our sin," says Paul, "he condemned sin in the flesh, in order that the righteous requirement of the law might be fulfilled in us, who walk not according to the flesh but according to the Spirit." God sent Jesus as a human being to live a sinless life and thus meet the Law's requirement, on our behalf, that we live perfect lives. Despite living a sinless life, however, Christ still received God's wrath for all our sins. As God poured out His wrath on Christ, Who stood as our substitute, He finally dealt with sin by condemning it, rendering it powerless to kill those who receive Christ in faith and appropriate His finished work on the cross. As believers who are declared righteous before God because of Christ's substitutionary sacrifice, we now live by the Spirit, not in the flesh. The Spirit indwells Christians, empowering them to walk with Christ and exhibit the fruit of the Spirit as they are sanctified.

Paul contrasts the respective mindsets of those who live in the flesh with those who live according to the Spirit. The former are oriented toward the trappings of the sinful flesh, which is hostile to God, while the latter fix their minds on spiritual things, earnestly seeking to become more Christ-like. If the Spirit dwells in a person—and He dwells in all Christians—then the person is not in the flesh. But if a person doesn't have the Spirit he doesn't have Christ—he is not a Christian. Not only does God, who raised Jesus from the dead, empower the Christian through the Holy Spirit to live by the Spirit in this life; He also assures us eternal life and will transform our mortal bodies to immortal bodies through the Spirit that indwells us.

Those who are of the flesh and live according to the flesh (their sinful passions) remain bound by death. But if they receive the Holy Spirit through faith in Christ, they are Sons of God and will live. They didn't receive the spirit of slavery (which can be translated "a slavish spirit")[5] just so they could return to the bondage of sin and fear; they received the Spirit of adoption as sons, by whom they cry, "Abba! Father!" This is a profound revelation from Paul. We are not slaves who must cower before an angry God as our Master. That's not what the fear of God means. Though we are still human beings, incomparable to our perfect God, He has graciously adopted us as His sons. "The believer is admitted to the heavenly family," writes Leon Morris, "to which he has no rights of his own. But he is now admitted and can call God 'Father.'"[6]

It's a remarkable privilege to be invited to address our infinitely Holy God by such a personal and intimate term. This familiarity would be impossible in Judaism. This is the same term Jesus, God's only Son, uses to call the Father in His agonizing prayer in the Garden of Gethsemane: "Abba, Father, all things are possible for you. Remove this cup from me. Yet not what I will, but what you will" (Mark 14:36). And this "Abba" is the same term Jesus authorized His disciples to repeat after Him (Matt. 7:7–11).[7] The Spirit bears witness with our spirit that we are children of God—heirs of God and fellow heirs with Christ. That is, the Holy Spirit confirms the believer's realization that He is saved and adopted into God's family as an adopted son and thus God's heir with Christ unto eternal salvation, which will involve his suffering with Christ, but also his future glorification.

While we will suffer during our life on earth, it will not compare with the glory that will be revealed to us in eternity. This knowledge of future glory makes our suffering much easier to endure, for we know our suffering is finite and our glorious future with God is eternal. What further demonstrates the contrast is that our suffering is caused by other men, whereas our glory comes from God.

God's creation waits with eager longing, continues Paul, for the revealing of the sons of God. The creation was cursed through man's sin (Gen. 3:17–19) and came into a state of physical decay, but we are assured that along with the children of God it will be liberated from its bondage to corruption and restored to its glory (Rev. 21:5; 22). Until now the entire creation has been groaning together as if in the pains of childbirth—and so have Christians, who have the Holy Spirit. Christians groan inwardly as they await their adoption as sons—the redemption of their bodies. The childbirth metaphor is appropriate because while it entails great suffering "it carries with it the hope of new life for all creation."[8] Christians are already adopted as sons of God, but Paul means that the process that began upon our salvation and our adoption (Eph.

1:5; Gal. 4:5–7) will be consummated with our future glorification when we are resurrected from the dead and our imperfect, mortal bodies will be transformed into perfect, immortal bodies.[9] In this hope, we are saved.

Hope that is seen is not hope, because no one hopes for what he already sees. But if we hope for what we don't yet see, we wait for it with patience. As Paul makes clear in Romans Chapter 5, the term "hope" as used here has no uncertainty. God's promise of our resurrection to eternal life with Him is a hope of which we can be certain and that will never disappoint us. We hope for our full redemption because it has not yet occurred; it will happen when Christ returns. As with many different concepts in Christianity, there is both a present and a future component. We are saved immediately upon our conversion, but we await more fulsome blessings of salvation when we are united with Christ in the future.[10]

But Christians are not left to deal with their present sufferings and groanings on their own. The Holy Spirit helps us in our weakness by interpreting and communicating prayers when we can't even understand, much less articulate, our own needs to God, which come to us only as deep groanings. The Spirit will ensure that our prayers conform to God's will. No actual words need to be uttered for this communication to occur because the Father fully understands our minds and the mind of the Spirit.

Paul provides another abiding assurance for Christians (those who love Him): "And we know that for those who love God all things work together for good, for those who are called according to his purpose." Of course, this doesn't mean bad things won't happen to Christians or that they won't endure hardship; indeed, the assurance is given to mitigate hardship, not to eliminate it. The "good" that God promises here may not always be what we think is in our best interest, but what God, in His infinite wisdom, deems will help transform us into Christ's image and attain our future glory.[11] No, God doesn't bar all bad things from coming our way, but He uses them to benefit us. As R. C. Sproul declares, "God redeems the evil that befalls us."[12]

But whom are those God called according to His purpose, asks Paul. Obviously, he is talking about all Christians, but what does it mean that they are called according to His purpose? Paul tells us that those God foreknew He predestined to be conformed to Christ's image, so that they might be the firstborn among many brothers. And those He predestined He also called, and those He called He also justified, and those He justified He also glorified.

One's interpretation of this passage depends on, or more accurately, *determines* his view on predestination. It is beyond the scope of this book to explore deeply the differing views, but in general terms, most Roman Catholics, Methodists, Arminians, and Lutherans subscribe to what can be called the prescient view of predestination.[13] That is, God is omniscient; therefore, He knows everything that will happen in the future, including who will respond to the Gospel, and He thereby elects those He knows will accept it. They point to verse 29 above—that those God foreknew he predestined. Calvinists reject this, believing that God fully elects people for the Gospel without taking a pre-creation inventory of who would be receptive to the message.

Paul assures us that those God chooses will be conformed to the image of Christ and will be justified (declared righteous and saved) and glorified—they will receive immortal resurrection bodies and be liberated from the presence of sin. God is in control; He will safely navigate us to eternity with Him. And if God is for us, who can be against us? Again, this does not mean we won't face enemies in this life, but that no one can obstruct God's divine plan for us. Since God was willing to sacrifice His own Son so that we could live, of course He will graciously give us all things—abundant present and future blessings in Christ[14]—with the gift of the Holy Spirit in this life, culminating in our salvation and all that entails.

"Who shall bring any charge against God's elect?" asks Paul. "It is God who justifies. Who is to condemn?" Again, no one can prevail against God's plan for us. God has already justified us and only He has the power to condemn, so no one else can condemn us. Christ died for us, was raised from the dead, and now sits at the right hand of God and intercedes for us. It's inconceivable that God would have implemented this elaborate plan, which involved indescribable suffering for His only Son, and allow anything to interfere with it.

Paul further asks, "Who shall separate us from the love of Christ?" His answer is one of the most beloved and reassuring passages in all of

Scripture, which speaks for itself and cannot be improved: "For I am sure that neither death nor life, nor angels nor rulers, nor things present nor things to come, nor powers, nor height nor depth, nor anything else in all creation, will be able to separate us from the love of God in Christ Jesus our Lord." Amen.

After writing one of the most profound verses of the Bible, Paul uses the next three chapters to address a nagging issue close to his heart: if everything he's saying is true, why do most of God's chosen people (the Jews) reject it? In Chapter 12, he returns to his argument, urging believers to apply all the inspiring truths he has imparted to live their lives as a living sacrifice, holy and pleasing to God. But for now, he focuses on Israel.

CHAPTER 9

Paul opens this chapter with a multi-pronged plea that his readers believe his truthfulness. He writes in an earnest tone that matches his lament over his fellow Jews, which is the main subject of this chapter: "I am speaking the truth in Christ—I am not lying; my conscience bears me witness in the Holy Spirit—that I have great sorrow and unceasing anguish in my heart. For I could wish that I myself were accursed and cut off from Christ for the sake of my brothers, my kinsmen according to the flesh." Then he itemizes all the advantages the Jewish people have with God in what Grant Osborne aptly calls "a marvelous recapitulation of her covenant privileges."[15] "They are Israelites, and to them belong the adoption, the glory, the covenants, the giving of the law, the worship and the promises," writes Paul. "To them belong the patriarchs, and from their race, according to the flesh, is the Christ, who is God over all, blessed forever. Amen."

Paul's description of Israel's unique calling is striking. God called Abraham and told him to go to a land that He would show Him, and He would make a nation out of him, make his name great, bless all nations through him and his descendants, and give them the land as their everlasting possession. In subsequent covenants, He promised He would bring forth the Messiah from King David's lineage who would reign forever. He gave the Law to Moses for his people and made the Israelites a nation of priests who would mediate God's salvation blessing to all mankind. Paul is summarizing many of these blessings, saying Israel was adopted—God bestowed on the Israelites the privilege of being His chosen people (Exodus 4:22–23; Hos 11:1). He gave them glory—He was present and dwelled with them in the tabernacle during their wilderness wanderings (Exodus 25:8; 40:34) and then at the Temple (1 Kings 8:11; Ezek. 43:2).[16] Once the tabernacle had been built, the "glory of the Lord" filled it (Exodus 4:34), and after Solomon gave his dedication prayer to consecrate the Temple, it was filled with "the glory of God" (2 Chron. 7:1, 2).

He made them His covenant people through a series of covenants to which we've alluded, including, among many others, the Abrahamic (Gen. 15; 17), the Mosaic (Exodus 19–24), and the Davidic (2 Sam. 7:1–27). He gave them the Law—the Ten Commandments at Mount Sinai; the worship—the tabernacle worship (cf. Heb. 9:6); temple worship and the system of sacrifices; and the promises, especially of the coming Messiah.[17] The great patriarchs Abraham, Isaac, and Jacob came from the Jewish people, and God made His promises to them prior to His giving of the Law.[18] The twelve tribes of Israel descend from Jacob, whose name God changed to Israel. Jacob's son Judah was an ancestor of Christ.[19] Paul finishes his list of the Jews' privileges by pronouncing that Christ is indeed God over all, stressing exactly who the Jews are rejecting. He is not just the promised Messiah, as if that weren't enough; He is the Son of God.[20]

Paul says the Jews' rejection of Christ does not mean God's promises have failed. As he has already explained, it is not Abraham's physical descendents who are the children of God; it is his spiritual descendants— those, whether Jew or Gentile, who avail themselves of God's promised blessing by placing their saving faith in Jesus Christ. Besides, Paul shows that not even all of Abraham's physical descendants are in the line of promise, which is traced only through Abraham's son Isaac, not his son Ishmael. In the same way, not all of Isaac's children are in the line of promise, as God chose the younger son Jacob over Esau. Moreover, God chose Jacob before he and his twin Esau were born, and before either had done anything good or bad, to elucidate how God's sovereignty was at work, not involving human works or merit. Paul cites the Old Testament passage, "Jacob I loved, but Esau I hated" (Mal. 1:2, 3). Most commentators agree that God doesn't mean "hate" literally, but that He rejected rather than accepted Esau. Additionally, many believe God's election of Israel here refers to a national election—He was not rejecting Esau individually but was choosing Israel, through Jacob, and rejecting the Edomites, who would descend from Esau.[21]

Paul asks whether God's salvation scheme is unjust. Absolutely not! God will have mercy and compassion on those He chooses, wholly apart from man's will or works—which is a wonderful thing, because if our salvation depended on our good works, none of us would make it. For example, God chose Pharaoh to demonstrate His power through him so that His name would be proclaimed throughout the world. "So then he has mercy on whomever he wills," observes Paul, "and he hardens whomever he wills."

Paul asks why God would fault someone He had hardened. Why would he punish someone for resisting His will when it was His sovereign choice that they resist? Paul bluntly answers, "But who are you, O man, to answer back to God? Will what is molded say to its molder, 'Why have you made me like this?' Has the potter no right over the clay, to make out of the same lump one vessel for honorable use and another for dishonorable use? What if God, desiring to show his wrath and to make known his power, has endured with much patience vessels of wrath prepared for destruction, in order to make known the riches of his glory for vessels of mercy, which he has prepared beforehand for glory—even us whom he has called, not from the Jews only but also from the Gentiles?"

People have been questioning God's fairness from the beginning. We see this theme in the Old Testament, and Paul certainly addresses it in his letters. But Paul homes in on questions particular to certain New Testament revelations—though in fairness, they involve issues similar to those addressed in Job.

If God elects some and not others, and if he hardens people's hearts, isn't he acting arbitrarily? We've already noted that God hardens the hearts only of those who have begun to do it to themselves.[22] We must not forget that all men are under sin, as Paul has shown earlier in this letter (3:9, 19) and is emphasized throughout the Bible. Therefore, by hardening men, God is not being unfair or unjust, because they are already justly condemned because of their own sin. When He chooses to save some men, He is demonstrating his mercy, which is His sovereign prerogative to administer as He wishes.[23]

What about the charge, then, that God is unfair for punishing human beings for resisting His will when His will is irresistible? Paul essentially rejects the charge, because God's will is not that we be sinful. But part of Paul's response bothers some people, for he effectively says that man has no right to question God because it's absurd for a created being (the clay) to question his Maker (the potter). The same principle is expressed in the Book of Job: "God is greater than man. Why do you contend against him, saying 'He will answer none of man's words'? (33:12–13; cf. Jeremiah 18). It seems harsh to us that our all-loving God would rebuke us for asking questions that flow from the logical minds with which He created us. John Stott points out, however, that God is not censuring people for asking questions but for their quarrelsome attitude—those who show disrespect and defiance, as opposed to genuine curiosity and an earnest desire for answers.[24] A human being must never try to make himself God or presume to put himself on His level.

Stott makes another important distinction. The potter/clay analogy is useful as far as it goes, but human beings are different from inanimate clumps of clay.[25] They are no different in terms of their infinite inferiority to God, but they are different in that unlike anything else in God's creation, inanimate or animate, they are made in God's image, and are rational, moral, spiritual, and accountable beings. They are capable of conversing with God, and He encourages us to use our minds to explore His creation. He reveals his thoughts (Amos 4:13, NLT) and mysteries (Daniel 2:28) to mankind. We are to study His Word to understand His will. We are to rightly divide His Word (2 Tim. 2:15 KJV). We are to cultivate the mind of Christ (Philip. 2:5) and arm ourselves with His way of thinking (1 Peter 4:1).

God, then, is not telling us to be incurious, but He is telling us not to be rebellious. Just as the potter has the right to mold his clay into vessels to suit his purposes, God has the right to deal with fallen man as He deems fit, exercising both His wrath and His mercy. He does not create us to punish us, but administers His punishment or pours out His mercy on people, who are already sinful beings.[26]

By choosing to be merciful to some and not to others, God is not being unjust—because He has a right to condemn everyone. And Paul offers a reason—which is not arbitrary—that God might well choose to be merciful to some and not others. He shows His wrath for some to display His glory for others, just as His prophets foretold He would. Paul cites Hosea to show that while the Gentiles were initially excluded from God's covenants with Israel, He would eventually make them spiritual heirs of His promises to Abraham: "Those who were not my people I will call 'my people' (Hosea 2:23; cf. 1 Peter 2:10). God foretold through Isaiah that though the Jews are His covenant people, many would reject Him, but a remnant would remain with Him and be saved (Isaiah 10:22, 23).

Summarizing, Paul says that the Gentiles, who did not pursue righteousness, have attained it by faith. By contrast, the Jews pursued righteousness through the Law but failed to achieve it because they pursued it through works instead of faith. The Jews have stumbled over the stumbling stone—they rejected Christ.

As for God's fairness in terms of election, I admit I don't understand everything and wrestle with certain passages. Calvinists believe in "double predestination"—that God elected certain people for salvation before time began, and that His choice had nothing to do with their decision to accept or reject Him. I understand their scriptural basis for this and respect their opinion. I agree that in eternity past, God elected those He would save, but I believe His decision was based on his foreknowledge of who would receive His offer of salvation, for which there is also scriptural support—including the Chapter 8 passage cited above, those passages assuring us that Jesus doesn't want to lose even one of His sheep, and in God's gracious and loving character shown throughout the Bible. Moreover, He promises us, "Ask, and it will be given to you; seek, and you will find; knock, and it will be opened to you. For everyone who asks receives, and the one who seeks finds, and to the one who knocks it will be opened" (Matt. 7:7–8).

Regardless of which position is correct, I don't believe our salvation depends on whether we subscribe to the Calvinist view on "double predestination." I just think the two sides should show respect for each other's positions. Ultimately, I have great comfort in knowing that our God is a perfectly just, merciful, and loving God, Who is righteous and true, and Who is the Author of life and the Author of morality. We derive our moral sensitivities and our instincts about justice and righteousness from Him, and we develop a fuller understanding of those concepts by studying His Word. Even if the Calvinist position is true, none of us knows whom God has elected, and His offer of salvation remains open to all of us, Jew and Gentile alike. I dare say that nothing would please Him more than if we accepted His offer—His freely given gift of eternal life through faith in Jesus Christ, His Son, who lived a perfect life, died a sacrificial death, and was resurrected to life to conquer sin and death to free us from both and prepare a place in Heaven for us to abide, with Him, in eternity. Thanks be to God for His infinite love and for the unmerited grace He bestows on those who place their trust in Christ.

CHAPTER 10

Paul clearly believes God wants all to be saved, which is why he opens up this chapter by declaring, "Brothers, my heart's desire and prayer to God for them is that they may be saved." If Paul thought their condemnation was a foregone conclusion I doubt he would be offering futile prayers to God. He recognizes that the Jews have a zeal for God, but it's not based on the knowledge of Jesus Christ, which God has now revealed. They try to pursue righteousness on their own by rigorously following his laws instead of submitting to God's righteousness through faith in His Son. Christ is the end of the Law—he fulfills the Law—imputing righteousness to all those who believe in Him.

For a person to become righteous based on the Law, he has to follow every precept perfectly—a sheer impossibility. But finding the righteousness based on faith doesn't require us to jump through a bunch of hoops. We needn't ascend into heaven or descend into hell looking for Christ, counsels Paul. We must just look to the Word of God, which is within our grasp, for it assures us, "If you confess with your mouth that Jesus is Lord and believe in your heart that God raised him from the dead, you will be saved. For with the heart one believes and is justified, and with the mouth one confesses and is saved. For the Scripture says, 'Everyone who believes in him will not be put to shame.' For there is no distinction between Jew and Greek; for the same Lord is Lord of all, bestowing his riches on all who call on him. For 'everyone who calls on the name of the Lord will be saved.'"

In verse 8 Paul quotes Deuteronomy 30:14: the word is near us—in our mouth and in our heart. That's probably why in verse 9 he mentions confessing with our mouth before believing in our heart. The natural order of events would be to believe in one's heart and then confess with one's mouth, which is the order he uses in verse 10.[27] What is important is that we do both. Saving faith requires more than mere intellectual assent to the proposition that Christ is the Son of God Who died for our sins—after all, "Even the demons believe—and shudder" (James 2:19). One must place one's trust in Christ for eternal salvation and truly rely on Him for it, which the ESV Study Bible describes as a "deep inward trust in Christ at the core of one's being."[28] The confession with our mouth simply means acknowledging to God that Christ is God and that you trust Him for your salvation. As J. A. Witmer points out, the heart and mouth aspects are not two separate steps to salvation.[29] They happen together, which is why the order can be stated either way. Everyone who does these things will be saved and thus not be put to shame.

Now Paul stresses the importance of preaching the Gospel and spreading the Good News to everyone. How can people believe in and confess their faith in Christ if they haven't ever heard of Him? And how can they hear about Him unless someone preaches the Gospel to them? And how can people preach to them unless they are sent and thereby given an opportunity to preach? Paul quotes Isaiah: "How beautiful are the feet of those who preach the good news!" (52:7; cf. Nahum 1:15; Eph. 6:15) Unfortunately, not all have obeyed the call to repent and believe in Christ. Paul quotes Isaiah again, "Lord who has believed what he has heard from us?" (53:1) "So faith," writes Paul, "comes from hearing, and hearing through the word of Christ." Simply put, people need to hear the Gospel—the good news of salvation in Christ—to believe it.

Paul asks whether the Jews were really given the opportunity to hear the message. Yes, he concludes, they have been given sufficient opportunities to hear because the Word has been preached throughout the known world by this time. So they heard, but did they understand? Their own Scriptures, after all, foretold that God would extend His offer of salvation to the Gentiles—pagans with no understanding—and this would make the Jews jealous and angry (Deut. 32:21). Isaiah proclaimed that God would show Himself to those who neither sought Him nor asked for Him (the Gentiles). Isaiah lamented that God had held out His hands all day long to Israel—a disobedient and contrary people. He has repeatedly offered Himself to the Jews, but they have persistently rejected the Gospel.

CHAPTER 11

Paul asks if God has actually rejected His own chosen people. By no means! Paul relates that he is an Israelite, a descendant of Abraham, of the tribe of Benjamin, and God obviously didn't reject him. God has not rejected His people, whom He foreknew. He reminds us of the prophet Elijah's plea with God against Israel for killing His prophets, demolishing His altars, and threatening Elijah's life. God replies that in His grace He preserved a remnant of seven thousand Israelites who did not bow in idolatry to the pagan god Baal. The Israelites failed to obtain righteousness, and so God hardened their hearts, except for His elect remnant among them. Again, Paul liberally quotes from the Old Testament to support his point (Isaiah 29:10; Psalm 69:22, 23).

Did they stumble beyond recovery? Emphatically not. Rather, through their rejection of Christ, salvation has come to the Gentiles so as to make Israel jealous. If their rejection leads to the blessing of salvation for the Gentiles, how much greater blessings will come when many more Jews finally receive the Gospel!

Paul addresses the Gentiles, telling them that as an apostle to the Gentiles he serves and magnifies his ministry—as opposed to deviating from it—by making the Jews jealous and thereby saving some of them. For if their rejection of the Gospel means that more people (Gentiles) will ultimately receive the message, what will their acceptance mean but life from the dead? Here, "Paul was not referring to bodily resurrection," writes John MacArthur. He was speaking of individual Jews receiving spiritual life as a result of their faith in Christ, and of the Jews in general experiencing a rebirth in the glorified millennial kingdom of God.[30]

Paul says, "If the dough offered as firstfruits is holy, so is the whole lump, and if the root is holy, so are the branches." Paul seems to be using this imagery to confirm that although not every Jew will be saved—any more than all Gentiles will be saved—God will honor His promises and many more Jews will be saved in the future. "Paul believes that Israel's refusal to accept Christ is temporary," writes Bruce Barton, "and that one day the nation will be brought back to God."[31]

Paul invokes the imagery of the root and branches, saying,

> But if some of the branches were broken off, and you, although a wild olive shoot, were grafted in among the others and now share in the nourishing root of the olive tree, do not be arrogant toward the branches. If you are, remember it is not you who support the root, but the root that supports you. Then you will say, 'Branches were broken off so that I might be grafted in.' That is true. They were broken off because of their unbelief, but you stand fast through faith. So do not become proud, but fear. For if God did not spare the natural branches, neither will he spare you.

The Jews initially rejected the Gospel and God grafted in the Gentiles, who were not part of God's covenant with Israel, nor were they privy to the Old Testament and the superintending care God gave His chosen people. God plucked them from their thoroughly pagan world and graciously presented the Gospel to them. As such, the Gentiles dare not react with pride and arrogance but fear—meaning they should be reverential and humbly grateful for God's gift. For if Gentile Christians—those grafted in—turn from the Gospel in their pride, he won't spare them any more than he's sparing the Jews who are rejecting Him.

They must be mindful of God's kindness to them and continue to accept the Gospel in humility and gratitude, and also recognize His severity toward those who have rejected Christ and fallen. The same will happen to them if they reject Him. But if the Jews turn from their unbelief and toward Him, He will graft them in just as He is now grafting in the Gentiles. For if the Gentiles were grafted in though they come from a wild olive tree, how much more will the Jews, who come from natural branches, be grafted back into their own olive tree?

Paul again warns the Gentiles against falling into pride (becoming wise in their own sight). They must be aware of the mystery he's been explaining to them: Israel has been experiencing a partial hardening, but that will end once the evangelization of the Gentiles has come to full fruition. At that time all Israel will be saved. Commentators agree that God doesn't mean every single Jew then living will be saved, but the nation as a whole—the majority of Jews—will be restored to God in the final generation before Christ's return.[32]

Paul now recapitulates what he's just explained. He says the Jews are enemies of the Gospel for the sake of the Gentiles (so that they could be grafted in), but the Jews are still God's elect—beloved for the sake of their forefathers. This is because God's gifts and His calling are irrevocable—He will always honor His promises. Just as the Gentiles used to be disobedient but have now received mercy because of the Jews' disobedience, the Jews' disobedience will indirectly lead to God's mercy on them as well because God's mercy shown to Gentiles upon the Jews' disobedience will lead to the Jews' restoration with God. What a remarkable testament to God's grace that the Jews' disobedience will lead, ultimately, to mercy for both Gentiles and Jews! God has consigned all to disobedience so that He may extend His mercy to all.

Paul concludes this chapter with another one of my favorite passages: "Oh, the depth of the riches and wisdom and knowledge of God! How unsearchable are his judgments and how inscrutable his ways! For who has known the mind of the Lord, or who has been his counselor? Or who has given a gift to him that he might be repaid? For from him and through him and to him are all things. To him be glory forever. Amen." Paul is joyfully exclaiming God's wondrous plan of salvation, which is robust with mercy and grace, but he is also paying tribute to God's unfathomable wisdom, which is too rich for words. God's plan is brilliant and perfect—beyond the capacity of the human mind to have conceived, but conceived nevertheless for our benefit. Since everything belongs to God we can't give Him anything. Since all things are from God, He deserves everlasting glory.

CHAPTER 12
‹‹‹‹‹‹‹‹‹‹‹‹‹‹‹‹‹‹‹‹‹‹‹‹‹‹‹‹‹‹‹‹‹

Chapters 1–11 deal with God's mercy toward sinners, both Jews and Gentiles, in offering them salvation through Jesus Christ, and with the rich theology surrounding His gracious acts. The remaining five chapters involve the redeemed sinner's obligation to God in return. The epistle to the Romans is often described as Paul's most theological book, and that's true, but it gives us more than theology; it exhorts us to apply these principles in our Christian living. Most religions have moral codes that contain helpful and practical guidelines, but they are often abstract and untethered to meaningful events in history. Christianity's moral standards are grounded in God's salvation history with mankind, from the Creation, to His forming of the Hebrew nation and His gracious dealing with the nation, to Christ's incarnation, life, death, and resurrection. "Christian ethics are practical specifically because they do not stand alone," writes Robert Mounce, "but emerge as unavoidable implications of an established theological base. Theology in isolation promotes a barren intellectualism. Ethics apart from a theological base is impotent to achieve its goals."[33] So what follows is Paul's exposition of what it means to live out the Gospel in our lives.

Paul begins, "I appeal to you therefore, brothers, by the mercies of God, to present your bodies as a living sacrifice, holy and acceptable to God, which is your spiritual worship. Do not be conformed to this world, but be transformed by the renewal of your mind, that by testing you may discern what is the will of God, what is good and acceptable and perfect."

In his introductory clause, Paul's use of "therefore" refers to his arguments in the preceding chapters. He is saying, "Based on the principles I've set forth and in light of God's free gift of salvation to you, this is how you must respond in Christian living." Paul exhorts us to present our bodies as a living sacrifice to God because of the abundant mercy He has shown us undeserving sinners through Jesus Christ—God asks us to sacrifice only after He has sacrificed for us. F. F. Bruce notes that "the sacrifices of the new order do not consist in taking the lives of others, like the ancient animal sacrifices, but in giving one's own."[34] Obviously, he doesn't mean we have to offer our physical bodies on the altar as the Jews did with animal sacrifices. Christ's death was the once-and-for-all sacrifice that secured eternal redemption for all who believe in Him (Hebrews 9:12). No more animal sacrifices were needed to temporarily cover sin once Christ gave Himself.

Paul is telling Christians we must offer ourselves completely to the Lord and surrender control to Him, making Him Lord of our lives. Our bodies comprise our emotions, our mind, our thoughts, and our desires, as well as their physical components that enable us to act in the world. "The body represents the total person," writes Bruce Barton. "It is the instrument by which all our service is given to God. To live for God, we must offer Him all that we are, represented by our body."[35] This sacrificial offering of our bodies, Paul explains, is to be a spiritual act of worship. It's only reasonable that we respond to Him in worship and service for what He has done for us. Paul seems to be referencing how we worship God in our everyday lives, not just during formal worship services. We must live as Christians twenty-four hours a day—in our interactions with others, in our jobs, in our families—and in all things, we must honor God.

We must not be conformed to this world but be transformed by the renewal of our minds. We are all familiar with the admonition that we should be in the world and not of the world. God placed us on earth for a reason, not just to be ascetics and withdraw from life. We are to model Christian behavior as witnesses to others, as just one part of our evangelism. But Paul is making His point in both the negative and the positive. We must consciously avoid imitating the fallen world, and we must make a deliberate effort to allow ourselves to be transformed by the renewal of our minds.

Paul minced no words when he told the Galatians that Christ died "to deliver us from the present evil age" (Gal. 1:4). This age must not serve as a model for Christian living, as its values are in direct opposition to the Christian's growth—his sanctification. As Paul later tells the Colossians, "Set your minds on things that are above, not on things that are on earth" (Col. 3:2). The world incessantly pressures us to adopt its customs and worldview. So yes, we must reject these things, but we can never achieve real spiritual change unless we experience transformation from within.[36] Peter writes, "As obedient children, do not be conformed to the passions of your former ignorance, but as He who called you is holy, you also be holy in all your conduct, since it is written, 'You shall be holy, for I am holy'" (1 Peter 1:14–16).

We must allow the Holy Spirit to change us, and that means practicing the spiritual disciplines because just as we are powerless to save ourselves, we are powerless to affect our own heart-transformation. But we can exercise our will in submitting ourselves to Christ and placing ourselves in position for the Holy Spirit to bring about real change within us. "Holiness of life rarely progresses apart from deliberative acts of the will," cautions Robert Mounce. "While sanctification is gradual in the sense that it continues throughout life, each advance depends on a decision of the will."[37] Our transformed and renewed mind will enable us to discern God's will and what is good and pleasing to Him.

We must not think of ourselves more highly than we should but should think with sober judgment, each of us according to the measure of faith that God has assigned. Likewise, Paul writes to the Philippians, "Do nothing from selfish ambition or conceit, but in humility count others more significant than yourselves. Let each of you look not only to his own interests, but also to the interests of others" (Philip. 2:3–4).

In the vernacular of today's culture, we need to get over ourselves. Pride not only obstructs our relationship with God; it distorts our self-assessment. When one of my kids or friends has had a difficult or embarrassing experience, I remind them (while reminding myself at the same time) that while it sometimes feels like the world's spotlight is on us and magnifying our troubles for all to see, in truth most people are too wrapped up in their own lives and troubles to focus on ours. We must keep things in proper perspective, beginning with ourselves. As important as we all are to ourselves, we must soberly assess our humble standing before Christ and strive to get outside ourselves—by serving others, for example.

We must serve Christ and His Church according to the "measure of faith"—the spiritual gifts—He has given us. We'll be less likely to be puffed up on ourselves if we remember we are all a united body in Christ and that each believer has valuable gifts to contribute. We couldn't begin to do all the things that need to be done on our own. There is unity in our diversity and we must each exercise our own gifts—prophecy, service, teaching, exhortation, generosity, leadership, and mercy—to the best of our ability, so that we might better serve the Church as a whole.

We must not forget that while the saving faith of each individual is a matter between him and Jesus Christ—no one else can do it for us—Christianity is a relational faith. We not only have a relationship with Christ, but we must live in community with other believers, acting in fellowship with one another. Our Triune God is a relational God—a God with distinct persons, but Who is absolutely unified. We must model our own Christian living accordingly. Paul commands us to live in harmony with one another. We must consider this in light of Jesus' summary of the Ten Commandments: to love God and to love our neighbors as ourselves, the latter flowing from the former. Similar to spokes in a wheel that converge at the hub, drawing closer to God will necessarily draw us closer to one another.[38]

Paul offers a moving description of the true Christian in one of the most sublime passages in all of Scripture. To me, these exhortations show just how superior the New Covenant is to the Old Covenant. We don't live according to the Mosaic Law, because we are no longer under Law, but under grace (Romans 6:14–15). We are now released from the Law "so that we serve in the new way of the Spirit" (Romans 7:6). "For the law of the Spirit of life has set you free in Christ Jesus from the law of sin and death" (Romans 8:1). Therefore, Paul tells us:

> Let love be genuine. Abhor what is evil; hold fast to what is good. Love one another with brotherly affection. Outdo one another in showing honor. Do not be slothful in zeal, be fervent in spirit, serve the Lord. Rejoice in hope, be patient in tribulation, be constant in prayer. Contribute to the needs of the saints and seek to show hospitality.
>
> Bless those who persecute you; bless and do not curse them. Rejoice with those who rejoice, weep with those who weep. Live in harmony with one another. Do not be haughty,

but associate with the lowly. Never be wise in your own sight. Repay no one evil for evil, but give thought to do what is honorable in the sight of all. If possible, so far as it depends on you, live peaceably with all. Beloved, never avenge yourselves, but leave it to the wrath of God, for it is written, "Vengeance is mine, I will repay, says the Lord." To the contrary, "if your enemy is hungry, feed him; if he is thirsty, give him something to drink; for by so doing you will heap burning coals on his head." Do not be overcome by evil, but overcome evil with good.

I want to repeat that we don't become more Christ-like on our own power, but through the power of the Holy Spirit. We have a responsibility, however, to turn our minds toward God—toward the Father, the Son, and the Holy Spirit—and to consciously reorient ourselves with a passion for seeking after God. We must place ourselves before the Holy Spirit and allow Him to do His work. Further, we must accept God's Word that there is pervasive evil in the world and not dismiss or minimize it for any reason, including to better fit in with a culture that is hostile to the very concepts of biblical morality and absolute truth.

Notice that Paul begins and ends this passage by starkly contrasting good and evil. We must let our love be real; we must outright hate evil, which stands in direct opposition to the Spirit life—to our duty and ability to conform ourselves to Christ. We cannot change our external behavior appreciably if we don't experience a change from within. But evil stands as both an internal (in our flesh) and external force opposing our spiritual transformation. We must consciously and actively resist and oppose evil. "In this world love must feel hate for evil," writes John Piper. "Since evil hurts people and dishonors God, you can't claim to love people while coddling evil ... Evil obscures the beauty of Christ. And Christ is our greatest good. Our greatest joy."[39]

CHAPTER 13

Paul writes, "Let every person be subject to the governing authorities. For there is no authority except from God, and those that exist have been instituted by God. Therefore, whoever resists the authorities resists what God has appointed, and those who resist will incur judgment. For rulers are not a terror to good conduct, but to bad. Would you have no fear of the one who is in authority? Then do what is good, and you will receive his approval, for he is God's servant for your good."

In this Chapter, Paul affirms God's sovereignty—He is the God of history, and that means He has established governments to promote order and to protect people from evil. Though God does not approve of tyrannical governments,[40] He has sometimes allowed them, through His permissive will (as opposed to His directive or prescriptive will), to be established[41] to impose His judgment against the world or certain nations, as when He raised up the Assyrian Empire to conquer and take the Northern Kingdom of Israel into captivity because of its persistent disobedience (2 Kings 17:6).

We are to obey governmental authorities because they derive their power from God. But there's an exception to this rule: when obeying the authorities would require disobedience to God. (Exodus 1:17; Daniel 3:16–18; 6:7, 10.)[42] You'll recall Peter and John's refusal to obey the authorities' commands to quit preaching the Gospel (Acts 4:19), and the apostles later being described as "men who have turned the world upside down" and "acting against the decrees of Caesar, saying that there is another king, Jesus" (Acts 17:6–7). And surely no Christian would fault Dietrich Bonhoeffer's resistance to Hitler's Third Reich. We can hardly blame the early Christians who refused to deny Christ in favor of any pagan or governmental quasi-deity, for they weren't rebelling against the civil society or ignoring its laws. But they rightly refused to bow down to false gods. The lines are not always clear, but as Christians, we have a right to oppose unlawful government actions and to advocate for changes in government policy or new leaders, especially through democratic means where available. We are, in reality, part of the government. We can also derive some comfort from knowing that God is ultimately in charge, and that He will judge and remove rulers in His time.[43]

A principal reason that God institutes governing authorities is to impose law and order, which is what Paul means in saying that rulers are not a terror to good conduct, but to bad conduct. Paul knows that governments sometimes abuse their authority, as he is often subjected to such abuse. On the other hand, he has just instructed us that although we cannot conform to the world, we also cannot withdraw from it, as if we are aloof and above.

We should certainly take Paul's words seriously, but not read absolutism into them. At the time he is writing, the Roman Empire has established order and peace and has yet to embark on the types of brutal persecution it is poised to commit. We must also read Romans 13 (and 1 Peter 2:13–14) in light of Revelation 13 and 18, says Walter Kaiser. "The former [Rev. 13] pictures the state as a beast opposed to God's purposes;" writes Kaiser. "The latter [Rev. 18] speaks of the downfall of any nation that becomes a modern Babylon, corrupted by wealth, materialism and injustice ... Thus a serious look at the scriptural material will prevent us from viewing the demands of society and its rulers with uncritical acceptance and automatic approval."[44]

Paul is saying it is God's will that we live in community, harmony, peace, and order under established governments that exist largely to ensure these things. We must pay taxes that are due, which recalls Jesus' words that we must "render to Caesar the things that are Caesar's, and to God the things that are God's" (Matt. 22:21). As noted, this doesn't mean we can't work lawfully to effect changes in our government, and if the governmental authorities deviate radically from their purpose and become instruments of injustice rather than justice, agents of moral decay, abusers of the weak and powerless, or thoroughly corrupt and oppressive, our duty to obey them may not be so clear.[45]

Paul next returns to the subject of love that he addressed in Chapter 12, in which he showed that love is at the heart of our life in Christ, which inspires us to obey and please God—an ethic that transcends written laws. That is, as Christians, we operate in the realm of the Law of Christ, which is defined by love. In verses 8–10, Paul cites specific commandments again and, consistent with Jesus' "Great Commandment" (Matt. 22:34–40), teaches that all of the Ten Commandments are summarized as our love for God and our neighbors. He writes, "Love does no wrong to a neighbor; therefore, love is the fulfilling of the law."

Paul closes this short chapter admonishing Christians to awake from their sleep—to avoid complacency and start living the Christian lives they are called to live, by demonstrating their faith in Christ through their love for one another and in their actions. They must cast off the works of darkness and put on the armor of light, which is another way of saying Christians must put on the full armor of God (Eph. 6:13–17; cf. 1 Thess. 5:8), realize they are engaged in a spiritual battle, and marshal God's truth and holiness as offensive and defensive weapons against their enemy. "The message is clear: we as Christians have passed from the sphere of darkness and death into the sphere of light and life," writes Jack Cottrell. "Therefore we must at once cast away from us everything associated with darkness and evil, and wrap ourselves completely and exclusively in the lifestyle of moral purity and truth (Eph. 5:8–9).[46]

We must avoid immoral behavior of all sorts as well as quarreling and jealousy among ourselves. We must avoid the allures of the flesh and put on Jesus Christ, by striving to live in a close personal relationship with Him and emulate His character and behavior.[47] As Paul has repeatedly emphasized, we must continue our sanctification process as we grow spiritually in Christ with the noble goal of being transformed into His image.

CHAPTER 14

Continuing to dispense advice on Christian living, Paul tells us to welcome the weak in faith and not to argue with them over opinions. We have all encountered Christian scolds whose harshness and legalism is counterproductive to evangelism. Let's honor the truth and correct doctrine, but let's not be too argumentative on matters that don't affect our salvation. The strong in faith are those who exhibit both freedom and obedience, and don't need lists of rules to be secure in their faith.[48] The weak Christians are probably the Jewish Christians, who could not comfortably separate themselves from their prior ceremonial practices,[49] and the immature Gentile Christians who are so reluctant to associate with pagan idols that they won't eat meat that comes from animal remains that had been sacrificed to idols.[50] The mature believer should encourage those less developed believers and not pass judgment on their present state.

Throughout his letters, Paul consistently advises us not to get hung up on the small stuff. He personally conforms to the practices of whomever he is evangelizing to avoid imposing stumbling blocks to their faith, provided those practices were not inherently sinful. Here he tells the Romans that those who follow no religiously imposed dietary restrictions mustn't despise those who only eat vegetables, and those who only eat vegetables must not pass judgment on the ones who eat freely because God welcomes both groups. Faith in Jesus Christ is the important thing.

Likewise, Christians must not pass judgment on the servants of another because it's not their prerogative; it's the servants' masters' prerogative to lead and evaluate their performance. Paul is using this analogy to instruct Christians that they should not be judgmental busybodies, especially on insignificant issues, but should defer to Christ's judgment of fellow believers. The believer will stand or fall before Christ, not before other believers.

Paul then moves on to the observance of special days—probably Jewish festivals—and imparts the same instructions. It's not that important whether people observe these days or not, so long as they're convinced before God of the propriety of their actions. Believers can dissent on issues and each still be in good standing before God.[51] The important thing is that they honor the Lord and give thanks to God. We live to the Lord and die to the Lord. Christ died so that he could be Lord of both the dead and the living. Christ's sacrificial death and His resurrection should inspire us to live for Him, not ourselves. We should show our Christian love to everyone, both the strong and the weak, for He died for us all.[52] Before we pass judgment on our brothers, we must recognize that just like them, we will stand before the judgment seat of God, Who is our Judge. As we've explained, we are saved by faith in Christ, not our works, but Christ will evaluate us for our service and bestow rewards on some (1 Cor. 3:10–17; 2 Cor. 5:10). We mustn't presume we are superior to others because we all must account to God, and our judgment of others won't help us one bit on that occasion.

Now Paul returns to familiar themes. We must not pass judgment on others, and must scrupulously avoid placing stumbling blocks in people's way. Nothing is more important than one's relationship with Christ, and it's particularly egregious for Christians to detrimentally interfere with other believers' relationships with Christ and their Christian walk. When you cause your brother to stumble, you are sinning against Christ (1 Cor. 8:12). We should encourage our brothers' security in the faith and growth in Christ. Paul reiterates his message (1 Cor. 8:7, 10) that nothing (no food) is inherently unclean, though it's unclean for those who think it's unclean—because in that case, it's a matter of their own conscience. If you insist on eating something that will grieve another Christian, you are not walking in Christian love because you're harming fellow believers for whom Christ died, and possibly even destroying their faith.[53]

Therefore, don't let what you regard as good be spoken of as evil. That is, strong Christians shouldn't insist on exercising their Christian freedom in these inconsequential ceremonial matters when it could lead weaker Christians to spurn Christian liberty. If a Christian eats certain foods in front of a weaker believer who believes these foods are forbidden, he will be hurting the faith of the weaker one. It's even worse if the strong Christian pressures the weaker one to join in against his conscience. Additionally, disputes between the two could result in an unattractive witness to nonbelievers. This principle could apply beyond food to the exercise of Christian liberty in general.

The kingdom of God isn't about eating and drinking but righteousness, peace, and joy in the Holy Spirit. Thus, anyone who serves Christ is acceptable to God and approved by men. So we should all pursue what promotes and builds one another up in Christ. As Paul writes to the Ephesians, "Let no corrupting talk come out of your mouths, but only such as is good for building up, as fits the occasion, that it may give grace to those who hear" (Eph. 4:29). And as he told the Corinthians, "When you come together, each one has a hymn, a lesson, a revelation, a tongue, or an interpretation. Let all things be done for building up" (1 Cor. 14:26).

Paul repeats that, for the sake of food, they must not destroy God's work. Everything is clean, but don't cause your brother to stumble over food or drink. It's better that you keep your opinions about such matters between yourself and God rather than use your Christian liberty in callous disregard for how it might affect others. The Christian who does not abuse his liberty and consciously avoids interfering with another's faith will be blessed. But let's not forget that even though all food itself is clean, if a weaker person eats food he doubts is clean, he condemns himself because he's going against his own conscience. Whatever does not proceed from faith—those things that our conscience forbids—is sinful.

CHAPTER 15

Strong Christians have an obligation to support and be patient toward weaker Christians rather than please themselves. They must also extend Christian charity to their neighbors to build them up. Christ served and lived for others and we should follow His example. Paul interprets Psalm 69:9 as applying to Jesus, saying, "For Christ did not please himself, but as it is written, 'The reproaches of those who reproached you fell on me.'" That is, He bore the brunt of insults and injuries that should have been directed at us. Though sinless, He absorbed all the judgment for our sin. Paul says that Old Testament Scripture was written to instruct us, as it teaches us to endure and provides us encouragement so that we might have hope.

We should take Paul's words to heart because the Old Testament is crucial to us. Some Christians tend to neglect it, thinking it is unnecessary or that the New Testament supersedes it. That couldn't be further from the truth. Again, the New Covenant supersedes the Old Covenant, but the New Testament does not supersede the Old Testament. "All Scripture is breathed out by God and profitable for teaching, for reproof, for correction, and for training in righteousness, that the man of God may be complete, equipped for every good work" (2 Tim. 3:16–17). From beginning to end, the Old Testament points to Christ, but it also provides valuable instruction that is relevant today—not just in the Proverbs and the Psalms, but in numerous other ways, including its revelations about God's historical dealings with Israel, which are recorded, in part, for our edification (see 1 Cor. 10:1–13). The Bible—the Old Testament and the New—is the Word of God, so we must read it all to better understand God's perfect nature and His will for our lives.[54]

The more we learn, the closer we become to God and the stronger our faith becomes, which encourages us and instills hope for what lies ahead. For as we read Scripture, we can't help but learn that God is a God of grace, Who is long-suffering, just, kind, merciful, and trustworthy. Scripture is self-authenticating in its remarkable unity and in its record of God's fulfillment of His promises and prophecies announced by His prophets. Our changeless God hasn't deviated from His sovereign plan, which He made before time began, to provide salvation for all who believe in His Son, Jesus Christ. He made that promise to Abraham and told us He would accomplish it through a nation of His descendants. One of these descendants would be King David, and from His line would come another Descendant who would be the Messiah, and He would bring God's promise of salvation and blessing to all nations.

The more familiar we become with the Bible, the more intimately we understand how God's magnificent plan has come together through His perfect and sovereign will. No matter what trials and tribulations we experience in life, the Bible gives us endurance, encouragement, and hope, as Paul so eloquently states. Paul prays that the God who gives us this endurance and encouragement inspires us to live in harmony with one another in Christ, so that together we may glorify God the Father. As such, we must greet and be charitable to one another for the glory of God.

Christ became a servant to the Jews in fulfillment of God's promises to Abraham and the other patriarchs. These promises, though initially made to Abraham, are for the benefit of all nations—to provide salvation for all, which leads to the Gentiles praising God for His mercy. Paul cites numerous Old Testament passages proving that God's offer of salvation to the Gentiles was not an afterthought but His plan all along. One of those passages is a messianic prophesy from Isaiah that the Messiah will come from the root of David's father Jesse (Isaiah 11:10; cf. Rev. 5:5). Paul now prays that the God of hope fill Christians with joy and peace as they believe in and trust Him, so they will be empowered by the Holy Spirit to be filled with hope.

Paul adds a word of personal encouragement to the believers in Rome, saying he is sure they're filled with goodness and knowledge and can instruct one another. He didn't plant this church, so it appears he wants to establish some personal rapport with the congregants by sharing his wisdom and instruction. He should have credibility with them because God specially chose him to preach the Gospel to the Gentiles, so they would believe in Christ and grow in Him through the power of the Holy Spirit. Therefore, Paul implores them to take his words to heart as authoritative and beneficial.

Paul is proud of the work God has done through him to bring the Gentiles to Christ and into obedience to God—in his ministry in Jerusalem and throughout the Roman Empire. Having fulfilled his charge, he will now continue to preach in places that have not yet heard the Word. Indeed, his desire to spread the word to uncharted territories is why he has been delayed so long in coming to Rome. But now that he has completed his goal, he intends to see them briefly on his way to evangelize in Spain, and he hopes the Roman brothers will help him make it there.

Before he can come to see them, however, he must return to Jerusalem to deliver the aid he has arranged for the poor there. The provinces of Macedonia and Achaia have made their contributions to the Jerusalem church—and happily so, because they owe it to them. As the Gentiles have been blessed to share in the Jews' spiritual blessings, they want to share their material blessings with them in return. Paul says that after completing his delivery in Jerusalem, he will leave for Spain and visit them on the way, bringing Christ's fullness and blessing and share it with them. In the meantime, he prays that in Christ and the Holy Spirit they join him in praying that he may be safely delivered from the unbelievers in Judea when he returns there, and that his offering will be well received by the Jerusalem church. These things will ensure that by God's will he may come to Rome joyfully and be refreshed in their company. He prays that the God of peace be with all of them.

CHAPTER 16

In this final chapter, Paul commends a great many of his friends to the Roman church. "This chapter," notes John MacArthur, "is the most extensive and intimate expression of Paul's love and affection for other believers and co-workers found anywhere in his New Testament letters."[55]

He warns them to watch out for those who cause divisions and to avoid those who preach false doctrine. Such people serve themselves rather than Jesus Christ, and they exploit naïve people through deceit and flattery. He tells the believers that they have a reputation for obedience, which makes him rejoice, but he still warns them to be wise as to what is good and innocent as to what is evil. They must continue to walk with the Holy Spirit, learn more about God, become closer to Him, and become ever more attuned to His will.

Paul is basically repeating his instruction from the beginning of Chapter 12: "Do not be conformed to this world, but be transformed by the renewal of your mind." He wants them to be innocent about evil, in the sense of avoiding it, and diligently seeking the good. The God of peace will soon crush Satan under their feet. This is probably a reference to Genesis 3:15, which is the first Messianic prophecy in the Bible, wherein God promises that the seed of the woman (Jesus Christ, the only human being ever to be sired by the Holy Spirit and not a human father) would crush the serpent's head. We know how this story ends, and Paul is simply reassuring the believers that they will be part of Christ's victory over Satan, sin, and death.

Paul praises God for the Gospel of Jesus Christ that God promised in the beginning but to some extent shrouded in mystery, and has now fully disclosed through the fulfillment of the prophetic writings, which have been shared with all nations as God has commanded so that they all might come to faith and obedience in Christ.

Many scholars regard his letter to the Romans as Paul's most profound epistle. Its wide-ranging discussions of Jewish Law, the Holy Spirit, human suffering, God's mercy, and assorted other topics, interspersed with valuable lessons derived from the Old Testament, have provided comfort and guidance to Christians everywhere for nearly two thousand years. Paul's long-standing enthusiasm to visit the Romans permeates the letter, as does his constant urge to spread the Gospel, build up local churches, and advance every believer in his faith walk. Paul is here setting forth some of the fundamental concepts of Christianity, and his insights formed a basis for the miraculous spread of the Church throughout every part of the world.

CONCLUSION

I have ended this book here only because of space limitations. I intend to complete our tour through the rest of the New Testament in my next book and can hardly wait to begin. Nothing enriches our lives more than immersing ourselves in God's Word, which is what I do when I research and write these books. I hope that in reading them you are inspired to do likewise—jump into the pages of Scripture and drink in God's wisdom.

Perhaps reading this book has reinforced your understanding of Paul's uniqueness and why God sovereignly chose Paul for this pivotal time in His salvation history. As we read the New Testament, we are dazzled by Paul's unrivaled passion, his intellect, his perseverance despite any hardship, his abundant love for the churches he founded and the believers he evangelized, his deep, abiding, unrelenting affection for his Jewish brothers, his alternating sternness and tenderness in communicating his instructions, his exemplary evangelism, and above all, his love for Christ and his fellow man. Readers of these letters can't miss Paul's determination that the congregations he established grow harmoniously in Christ. There is no mistaking his view that while saving faith is between the individual and God, Christianity is very much a relational religion. The church is vital; Christian brethren must support one another and hold one another accountable. Paul is adamant that all believers are united in the Holy Spirit as members in the body of Christ. Each member must contribute his gifts and services to the good of the body.[1]

Paul echoes Jesus' teaching that we are saved not by our works and not by adherence to the Law, but by faith in Jesus Christ. Further, he affirms that Christ is the fulfillment of the Law (Romans 10:4). While works don't earn us salvation, we will reflect our saving faith and exhibit the fruit of the Spirit through our works. Paul desperately wants his Jewish brothers to understand that Jesus is the Messiah—their Messiah Whom their Scriptures promised. Throughout his writings, we see a divinely inspired interweaving of the Old Testament with the New and come to grasp the marvelous integration of all of Scripture and the unity of God's salvation history. The more we study the Book of Acts and Paul's letters, the more fully we comprehend God's plan for our lives and His offer of free grace for our salvation through faith in Christ.

Paul underscores the role of the Holy Spirit in our salvation and in our sanctification. He makes clear that we are not only saved by faith in Christ but also begin new lives as reborn creatures, becoming more Christ-like as we rely on the power of the Spirit. We all have different spiritual gifts and must use those gifts for the benefit of the Church.

My humble wish is that you have learned or re-learned important basics about the Book of Acts and these six Pauline epistles and are excited to get back into the Bible, read these books and meditate on their message. We profit greatly each time we read Scripture and I challenge you to commit to reading the Bible from start to finish as soon as you can begin—you will never regret it.

ACKNOWLEDGMENTS

I can't say enough about Regnery Publishing as a professional and loyal partner. I express my sincere gratitude to Marji Ross for her willingness to venture with me into the faith-based genre and for her continued support and encouragement. She has always been accessible, open-minded, and an invaluable resource at all stages of the process. Harry Crocker is without peer in his field, is dedicated to his profession, and has always been there for me. Alyssa Cordova is an extraordinary publicist, and I greatly appreciate her energy and expertise. Tom Spence does a great job handling the legal side of things and makes things smooth and seamless.

My longtime editor Jack Langer has become a special friend upon whom I absolutely rely to help maximize the readability of my books. This book is no exception. No matter how much I've learned about editing through the years, especially from Jack, and no matter how clean I believe my manuscript is, he always makes it so much better. He has a special gift for word economy and clarity, and he always asks the right questions when I have something that might be misconstrued or misunderstood. He places himself in the position of the reader and helps me clear up inadvertent ambiguities or seeming contradictions. I am continually amazed by his focus. Through it all, he performs his craft without a trace of ego—with the goal of making my books the best they can be and allowing me to have my voice and to say precisely what I want to say. I am proud that we work so well together and hope our relationship continues for as long as I'm blessed to be in this business.

As I've said before, my wife Lisa, my best friend and mother of our five children, was patient and prayerful during the early years that I would come to faith in Christ, and her confidence and persistence finally paid off. Her support throughout is impossible to adequately express. She is always understanding during the time-consuming process of book writing.

Once again, my friend Frank Turek read this book as he did my other Christian-themed books, vetting it for theological accuracy and making many helpful suggestions. Frank is always solid and if he doesn't know the answer—which is rare—he'll admit it and push me in the right direction to find it. I am proud to be a board member of his organization, CrossExamined.org, which is doing amazing apologetics work on our college campuses, combating the secular message that dominates America's universities. I was blessed to go with Frank, his wife Stephanie, and his organization on my first trip to Israel last year. If you ever get a chance to visit Israel, don't pass it up. If you get a chance to go with Frank—even better.

My longtime friend Sean Hannity has always been supportive of all my books and other professional endeavors. Sean remains a humble, kind, and generous man despite his celebrity and phenomenal success. I am proud to call him my close friend and am eternally appreciative of his encouragement. I couldn't have a more loyal ally.

I greatly appreciate the friendship and steadfast support of Mark Levin, upon whom I can always depend. I am extremely grateful for his support of this project—as always.

My brother Rush is always at the top of my list. Rush is, above all, a loving brother—the best brother one could have. Again, sincere thanks to him for inspiring me, for opening doors for me directly and indirectly, and for doing wonderful work for this nation we both love from the bottom of our hearts. He has always supported me and my career pursuits, unfailingly encouraging me and cheering me on. I am blessed and grateful to have such a generous, caring, and thoughtful brother who makes a difference every day in his work to keep this nation true to its founding principles. He doesn't get nearly the credit he deserves and takes way more heat than anyone should have to endure. From the beginning of his national radio show, Rush has been the tip of the spear for the modern conservative movement and remains so today, persevering through it all and always at the top of his field.

Most of all, I am grateful to God for patiently guiding me into His truth, blessing me with His love, and steering me into the saving faith in Jesus Christ. I am blessed beyond all measure.

NOTES

INTRODUCTION

1. Paul. N. Benware, *Survey of the New Testament (Revised)* (Chicago: Moody Press, 1990), 163.

2. Elmer L. Towns & Ben Gutierrez, *The Essence of the New Testament* (Nashville: B&H, 2012).

3. Paul N. Benware, *Survey of the New Testament (Revised)* (Chicago: Moody Press, 1990), 163.

4. The 2nd and 3rd Epistles of John were written to individuals. Louis Berkhof, *New Testament Introduction* (Grand Rapids, MI: Eerdmans-Sevensma Co., 1915), 138, and M. G. Easton, In *Easton's Bible Dictionary* (New York: Harper & Brothers, 1893).

5. Irving L. Jensen, *Jensen's Survey of the New Testament: Search and Discover* (Chicago: Moody Press, 1981), 240.

6.   Crossway Bibles, *The ESV Study Bible* (Wheaton, IL: Cross-
     way Bibles, 2008), 2147.

7.   F. F. Bruce, *Paul: Apostle of the Free Spirit,* (Milton Keynes,
     UK: Paternoster, 1977).

CHAPTER 1

1.   Charles R. Swindoll, *Paul: A Man of Grace and Grit* (Nash-
     ville: Thomas Nelson, 2009).

2.   Luke wrote 37,933 words and 2,183 verses, compared to
     Paul's 32,407 words and 2,033 verses. Jeffrey Kranz, Over-
     viewBible.com 2014; Bruce H. Wilkinson & Kenneth Boa,
     Talk thru the Bible (Nashville: T. Nelson, 1983), 328.

3.   F. F. Bruce, *Paul: Apostle of the Free Spirit* (Milton
     Keynes, UK: Paternoster, 1977), 15.

4.   Ibid, 16.

5.   Ibid, 17.

6.   Ibid, 18.

7.   Ibid, 18.

8.   See the fascinating discussion of these themes in F. F.
     Bruce, *Paul: Apostle of the Free Spirit* (Milton Keynes,
     UK: Paternoster, 1977), 18.

9.   Charles R. Swindoll, *Paul: A Man of Grace and Grit*
     (Nashville: Thomas Nelson, 2009).

10. Lynn H. Cohick, *NT231 Paul of Tarsus* (Bellingham, WA:
     Lexham Press, 2015), Segment 8.

11. R. P. Lightner, Philippians. In J. F. Walvoord & R. B. Zuck
     (Eds.), *The Bible Knowledge Commentary: An Exposition
     of the Scriptures* (Wheaton, IL: Victor Books, 1985), Vol-
     ume 2, 660.

12. Charles R. Swindoll, *Paul: A Man of Grace and Grit*
     (Nashville: Thomas Nelson, 2009).

13. John B. Polhill, *Paul and His Letters* (Nashville, TN: Broadman & Holman, 1999), 5.

14. Alister E. McGrath, *Intellectuals Don't Need God & Other Modern Myths: Building Bridges to Faith Through Apologetics* (Grand Rapids, MI: Zondervan, 2010).

15. F. F. Bruce, *Paul: Apostle of the Free Spirit* (Milton Keynes, UK: Paternoster, 1977), 37.

16. Cicero *Against Verres*, in *The Verrine Orations*, trans. L. H. G. Greenwood (London: Heinemann, 1928–1935), 2.5.66, par. 170.

17. Walter A. Elwell & B. J. Beitzel, Paul, The Apostle, In *Baker Encyclopedia of the Bible*, (Grand Rapids, MI: Baker Book House, 1988), Volume 2, 1621.

18. Lyman Abbott, *The Life and Letters of Paul the Apostle* (Boston; New York; Cambridge: Houghton, Mifflin and Company; The Riverside Press, 1898), 28.

19. F. F. Bruce, *Paul: Apostle of the Free Spirit* (Milton Keynes, UK: Paternoster, 1977), 64.

20. Ibid, 71.

21. Lyman Abbott, *The Life and Letters of Paul the Apostle* (Boston; New York; Cambridge: Houghton, Mifflin and Company; The Riverside Press, 1898), 36.

22. D. J. Burrell, *The Early Church: Studies in the Acts of the Apostles* (New York: American Tract Society, 1897), 114.

23. Arno C. Gaebelein, *The Annotated Bible: Matthew to The Acts* (Vol. 6) (Bellingham, WA: Logos Bible Software, 2009), 279.

24. John G. Butler, J. G. *Paul: The Missionary Apostle* (Vol. Number Eleven). (Clinton, IA: LBC Publications, 1995), Volume 11, 40.

25. John B. Polhill, *Paul and His letters* (Nashville, TN: Broadman & Holman, 1999), 44.

26. G. Lyttelton, *Observations on the Conversion and Apostleship of St. Paul* (London, 1747), paragraph 1, cited by F. F. Bruce, *Paul: Apostle of the Free Spirit* (Milton Keynes, UK: Paternoster, 1977), 75.

27. J. D. Burrell, *The Early Church: Studies in the Acts of the Apostles* (New York: American Tract Society, 1897), 114.

28. Walter A. Elwell, In *Evangelical Dictionary of Biblical Theology* (electronic ed.) (Grand Rapids: Baker Book House, 1996), 34.

29. Ibid, 34.

30. W. J. Conybeare & J. S. Howson, *The Life and Epistles of St. Paul* (New ed.) (New York: Charles Scribner's Sons, 1893), Volume 1, 97.

31. Ray Stedman, *Adventuring Through the New Testament* (Discovery House Publishers, Kindle Edition, 2011), Kindle Locations 301–308.

32. Ibid, Kindle Locations 266–268.

33. Many scholars dispute that Mark 16:9–20, which contains the ascension account, were written by Mark and some of the earliest manuscripts do not include this section. The ESV has a note to that effect.

34. J. Vernon McGee, *Thru the Bible Commentary: Church History (Acts 1–14)* (electronic ed., Vol. 40) (Nashville: Thomas Nelson, 1991), vi.

35. Joseph S. Exell, *The Biblical Illustrator (Acts):* (Oak Harbor, WA: Logos Research Systems, Inc., 1997), 2.

36. R. C. Sproul, *Acts* (Wheaton, IL: Crossway, 2010), 18.

37. Ben Witherington III, *The Acts of the Apostles: A Socio-rhetorical Commentary* (Grand Rapids, MI: Wm. B. Eerdmans Publishing Co., 1998), 71.

38. Joseph S. Exell, *The Biblical Illustrator (Acts):* (Oak Harbor, WA: Logos Research Systems, Inc., 1997), 0.

39. John R. Stott, *The Message of Acts: the Spirit, the Church & the World* (Leicester, England; Downers Grove, IL: InterVarsity Press, 1994), 34.

40. Ibid, 34.

41. Joseph S. Exell, *The Biblical Illustrator (Acts):* (Oak Harbor, WA: Logos Research Systems, Inc., 1997), 1.

42. Ibid, 5.

43. John Foster Kent, *The Work and Teachings of the Apostles* (New York; Chicago; Boston: Charles Scribner's Sons, 1916), 8.

44. John B. Polhill, *Acts* (Vol. 26) (Nashville: Broadman & Holman Publishers, 1992), 23.

45. R. C. Sproul, *Acts* (Wheaton, IL: Crossway, 2010), 18.

46. Norman L. Geisler & Frank Turek, *I Don't Have Enough Faith to be an Atheist,* (Wheaton, IL: Crossway Books, 2004), 240.

47. Mark Water, *The Bible and Science Made Easy* (Alresford, Hampshire: John Hunt Publishers Ltd., 2001), 30.

48. Norval Geldenhuys, *Commentary on the Gospel of Luke: The English Text with Introduction, Exposition and Notes* (Grand Rapids, MI: Wm. B. Eerdmans Publishing Co., 1952), 39; Josh McDowell, *Evidence for Christianity* (Nashville, TN: Thomas Nelson Publishers, 2006). 94.

49. Associates for Biblical Research, *Bible and Spade*, Volume 3, No. 1, 7.

50. A. N. Sherwin-White, *Roman Society and Roman Law in the New Testament* (Oxford: Clarendon Press, 1963), 189.

51. Joshua Jipp, *NT326 Book Study: The Acts of the Apostles* (Bellingham, WA: Lexham Press, 2017) Segment 4.

52. J. B. Lightfoot, "Discoveries Illustrating the Acts of the Apostles," *Essays on the Work Entitled Supernatural Religion* (London, 1889), 19–20.

53. Norman L. Geisler & Frank Turek, *I Don't Have Enough Faith to Be an Atheist* (Wheaton, IL: Crossway Books, 2004), 256–259.

54. Brian Janeway, Is the Acts of the Apostles Historically Reliable? Part 2 of 2. *Chafer Theological Seminary Journal*, 1999) Volume 5, 76.

55. Crossway Bibles, *The ESV Study Bible* (Wheaton, IL: Crossway Bibles, 2008), 2075.

56. Ibid

57. Ibid.

58. Brian Janeway, Is the Acts of the Apostles Historically Reliable? Part 2 of 2. *Chafer Theological Seminary Journal*, 1999) Volume 5, 74.

59. Ronald F. Youngblood, F. F. Bruce, et al. Thomas Nelson Publishers (Eds.), In *Nelson's New Illustrated Bible Dictionary* (Nashville, TN: Thomas Nelson, Inc., 1995), Acts of the Apostles.

60. Ralph P. Martin & P. H. Davids, In *Dictionary of the Later New Testament and its Developments* (electronic ed.) (Downers Grove, IL: InterVarsity Press, 1997), 11.

61. I. Howard Marshall, *Acts: An Introduction and Commentary* (Vol. 5) (Downers Grove, IL: InterVarsity Press, 1980), 22.

62. Hans Conzelmann, *Acts of the Apostles: a Commentary on the Acts of the Apostles.* (E. J. Epp & C. R. Matthews, Eds., J. Limburg, A. T. Kraabel & D. H. Juel, Trans.), (Philadelphia: Fortress Press, 1987), xlv.

63. Ralph P. Martin & P. H. Davids, (Eds.) In *Dictionary of the Later New Testament and its Developments* (electronic ed.) (Downers Grove, IL: InterVarsity Press, 1997), 12.

64. David S. Dockery, *Holman Concise Bible Commentary* (Nashville, TN: Broadman & Holman Publishers, 1998), 498.

65. Crossway Bibles, *The ESV Study Bible* (Wheaton, IL: Crossway Bibles, 2008), 2076.

66. I. Howard Marshall, *Acts: An Introduction and Commentary* (Vol. 5) (Downers Grove, IL: InterVarsity Press, 1980), 21.

67. Ben Witherington III, *The Acts of the Apostles: A Sociorhetorical Commentary* (Grand Rapids, MI: Wm. B. Eerdmans Publishing Co., 1998), 70.

68. David S. Dockery, *Holman Concise Bible Commentary* (Nashville, TN: Broadman & Holman Publishers, 1998), 500.

69. John B. Polhill, Acts. In Donald Guthrie, *New Testament Introduction* (4th rev. ed.) (Downers Grove, IL: Inter-Varsity Press, 1996), 353.

70. Donald Guthrie, *New Testament Introduction* (4th rev. ed.) (Downers Grove, IL: Inter-Varsity Press, 1996), 354.

71. Gary M. Burge, *The New Testament in Antiquity* (Grand Rapids, MI: Zondervan, 2009), 232.

72. Michael J. Kruger, *A Biblical-Theological Introduction to the New Testament: The Gospel Realized* (Crossway. Kindle Edition 2016), 146.

73. My friend, Frank Turek, notes that this would have been an impossible assertion for Luke to make unless it was. The Jews would have known Luke was a liar if Priests had not converted. Luke would have discredited himself.

74. Michael J. Kruger, *A Biblical-Theological Introduction to the New Testament: The Gospel Realized* (Crossway. Kindle Edition 2016), 146–147.

75. Ibid.

76. John F. MacArthur, Jr., The MacArthur Study Bible (Nashville, TN: Word Pub. 1997), 1631.

77. John D. Barry, Douglas Mangum, et al., *Faithlife Study Bible*, (Bellingham, WA: Lexham Press, 2012, 2016).

CHAPTER 2

1.   J. Sidlow Baxter, *Baxter's Explore the Book*, (Zondervan. Kindle Edition), 1413.

2.   Some scholars believe Theophilus is a generic addressee because linguistically the term means lover of God or one loved by God. But some believe it refers to a specific person of that name because Luke also addresses his Gospel to Theophilus and therein prefaces it with "most excellent." Ancient writers often used that device to dedicate their works to members of the nobility. See R. C. Sproul, *Acts* (Wheaton, IL: Crossway, 1910), 18.

3.   Bruce B. Barton & G. R. Osborne, *Acts* (Wheaton, IL: Tyndale House, 1999), 2.

4.   John B. Polhill, *Acts* (Vol. 26) (Nashville: Broadman & Holman Publishers, 1992), 80.

5.   Ibid, 81.

6.   Bruce B. Barton & G. R. Osborne, *Acts* (Wheaton, IL: Tyndale House, 1999), 6.

7.   John R. W. Stott, *The Message of Acts: the Spirit, the Church & the World* (Leicester, England; Downers Grove, IL: InterVarsity Press, 1994), 60.

8.   Gordon D. Fee, *The First Epistle to the Corinthians* (N. B. Stonehouse, F. F. Bruce, G. D. Fee & J. B. Green, Eds.) (Revised Edition) (Grand Rapids, MI; Cambridge, U.K.: William B. Eerdmans Publishing Company, 2014), 668.

9. Simon J. Kistemaker & William Hendriksen, *Exposition of the First Epistle to the Corinthians* (Vol. 18) (Grand Rapids: Baker Book House, 193–2001), 89.

10. Charles C. Ryrie, *Basic Theology: A Popular Systematic Guide to Understanding Biblical Truth* (Chicago, IL: Moody Press, 1999), 399–400.

11. Bruce B. Barton & G. R. Osborne, *Acts* (Wheaton, IL: Tyndale House, 1999), 2.1

12. Millard J. Erickson, *Christian Theology* (2nd ed.) (Grand Rapids, MI: Baker Book House, 1998), 885.

13. Bruce B. Barton & D. Veerman, et al., *Luke* (Wheaton, IL: Tyndale House, 1997), 481–482.

14. Frank E. Gaebelein, Merrill Chapin Tenney & Richard N. Longenecker, *The Expositor's Bible Commentary: John and Acts* (Vol. 9) (Grand Rapids, MI: Zondervan Publishing House).

15. John B. Polhill, *Acts* (Vol. 26) (Nashville: Broadman & Holman Publishers, 1992), 93.

16. Paul Gardner, *2 Peter & Jude* (Ross-shire, Great Britain: Christian Focus Publications, 1998), 128-129; Bruce B. Barton, *1 Peter, 2 Peter, Jude* (Wheaton, IL: Tyndale House Pub., 1995), 220–221.

17. Tremper Longman, Peter Enns & Mark L. Strauss, (Eds.), In *The Baker Illustrated Bible Dictionary* (Grand Rapids, MI: Baker Books. 2013), 1297, and Leland Ryken, James C. Wilhoit, et al., In *Dictionary of Biblical Imagery* (electronic ed.) (Downers Grove, IL: InterVarsity Press, 2000), 633.

18. John B. Polhill, *Acts* (Vol. 26) (Nashville: Broadman & Holman Publishers, 1992), 95.

19. Allen C. Myers, In *The Eerdmans Bible Dictionary* (Grand Rapids, MI: Eerdmans, 1987), 966.

20. Leland Ryken, James C. Wilhoit, et al., In *Dictionary of Biblical Imagery* (electronic ed.) (Downers Grove, IL: InterVarsity Press, 2000), 391.

21. Bruce Milne, *The Acts of the Apostles: Witnesses to Him … to the Ends of the Earth* (Ross-shire, Great Britain: Christian Focus Publications, 2010), 68; John B. Polhill, *Acts* (Vol. 26) (Nashville: Broadman & Holman Publishers, 1992), 110; S. D. Toussaint, Acts. In J. F. Walvoord & R. B. Zuck (Eds.), *The Bible Knowledge Commentary: An Exposition of the Scriptures* (Wheaton, IL: Victor Books, 1985), Volume 2, 358.

22. Lloyd J. Ogilvie, *Acts* (Vol. 28) (Nashville, TN: Thomas Nelson Inc., 1983), 68.

23. John F. Walvoord, *The Prophecy Knowledge Handbook* (Wheaton, IL: Victor Books, 1990), Appendix A.

24. See also the discussion of this by Patrick Henry Reardon, *Christ in the Psalms* (Chesterton, IN: Ancient Faith Publishing, 2000), 29–30.

25. W. A. VanGemeren, Psalms. In T. Longman III & D. E. Garland (Eds.), *The Expositor's Bible Commentary: Psalms (Revised Edition)* (Grand Rapids, MI: Zondervan, 2008), Volume 5, 191.

26. F. F. Bruce, *The Book of the Acts* (Grand Rapids, MI: Wm. B. Eerdmans Publishing Co., 1988), 67.

27. Bruce B. Barton & G. R. Osborne, *Acts* (Wheaton, IL: Tyndale House, 1999), 34–35.

28. Douglas Redford, *The New Testament Church: Acts-Revelation* (Cincinnati, OH: Standard Pub, 2007), Volume 2, 18.

29. See S. D. Toussaint, Acts. In J. F. Walvoord & R. B. Zuck (Eds.), *The Bible Knowledge Commentary: An Exposition*

of the Scriptures (Wheaton, IL: Victor Books, 1985), Volume 2, 359.

30. Wayne A. Grudem, *Systematic Theology: an Introduction to Biblical Doctrine* (Leicester, England; Grand Rapids, MI: Inter-Varsity Press; Zondervan Pub. House, 2004), 981.

31. David G. Peterson, *The Acts of the Apostles* (Grand Rapids, MI; Nottingham, England: William B. Eerdmans Publishing Company, 2009), 166–167; Bruce B. Barton & G. R. Osborne, *Acts* (Wheaton, IL: Tyndale House, 1999), 47.

32. Lloyd J. Ogilvie, *Preacher's Commentary, Acts* (Nashville, TN: Thomas Nelson Inc., 1983). Volume 28, 84.

33. Ravi Zacharias, "Answering a Questioner," RZIM.org, http://rzim.org/just-a-thought-broadcasts/answering-a-questioner/.

34. David G. Peterson, *The Acts of the Apostles* (Grand Rapids, MI; Nottingham, England: William B. Eerdmans Publishing Company, 2009), 188.

35. John B. Polhill, *Acts* (Vol. 26) (Nashville: Broadman & Holman Publishers, 1992), 139–140.

36. Craig S. Keener, *Acts: An Exegetical Commentary & 2: Introduction and 1:1–14:28* (Grand Rapids, MI: Baker Academic, 2012–2013), Volume 1, 996–997; Bruce B. Barton & G. R. Osborne, *Acts* (Wheaton, IL: Tyndale House, 1999), 58.

37. Craig S. Keener, and John H. Walton Keener, *NIV Cultural Backgrounds Study Bible: Bringing to Life the Ancient World of Scripture* (Grand Rapids, MI: Zondervan, 2016), 1872.

38. Dan Bouchelle, *Acts 1–9: The Gospel Unleashed* (Joplin, MO: HeartSpring Publishing, 2005), 48.

39. Joseph Klausner, *From Jesus to Paul,* E.T. (London, 1944), 282–83, cited by F. F. Bruce, *The Book of the Acts* (Grand Rapids, MI: Wm. B. Eerdmans Publishing Co., 1988), 97.

40. F. F. Bruce, *The Book of the Acts* (Grand Rapids, MI: Wm. B. Eerdmans Publishing Co., 1988), 99.

41. Craig S. Keener, *Acts: An Exegetical Commentary & 2: Introduction and 1:1–14:28* (Vol. 1) (Grand Rapids, MI: Baker Academic, 2012–2013), 1168.

42. S. D. Toussaint, Acts. In J. F. Walvoord & R. B. Zuck (Eds.), *The Bible Knowledge Commentary: An Exposition of the Scriptures* (Wheaton, IL: Victor Books, 1985), Volume 2, 364.

43. Warren W. Wiersbe, *Wiersbe's Expository Outlines on the Old Testament* (Wheaton, IL: Victor Books, 1993).

44. John B. Polhill, *Acts* (Vol. 26) (Nashville: Broadman & Holman Publishers, 1992), 160.

45. Ibid.

46. Bruce B. Barton & G. R. Osborne, *Acts* (Wheaton, IL: Tyndale House, 1999), 78.

47. I. Howard Marshall, *Acts: An Introduction and Commentary* (Vol. 5) (Downers Grove, IL: InterVarsity Press, 1980), 122.

48. John R. W. Stott, *The Message of Acts: the Spirit, the Church & the World* (Leicester, England; Downers Grove, IL: InterVarsity Press, 1994), 113.

49. Bruce B. Barton & G. R. Osborne, *Acts* (Wheaton, IL: Tyndale House, 1999), 82.

50. The term "Hellenist" has different meanings in different contexts. In 6:1 it means "Greek-speaking Jewish Christians; in 9:29 it means Greek-speaking Jews, and in 11:20 it means Greek-speaking Gentiles. Crossway Bibles. *The*

ESV Study Bible (Wheaton, IL: Crossway Bibles, 2008), 2106.

51. I. Howard Marshall, *Acts: An Introduction and Commentary* (Vol. 5) (Downers Grove, IL: InterVarsity Press, 1980), 139.

52. John B. Polhill, *Acts* (Vol. 26) (Nashville: Broadman & Holman Publishers, 1992), 193.

53. Ibid, 197.

54. Ibid, 188.

CHAPTER 3

1. Mark Water, *The New Encyclopedia of Christian Quotations* (Alresford, Hampshire: John Hunt Publishers Ltd., 2000), 16.

2. Though Luke says all, he couldn't have meant absolutely everyone, because the church continued in Jerusalem. S. D. Toussaint, Acts. In J. F. Walvoord & R. B. Zuck (Eds.), *The Bible Knowledge Commentary: An Exposition of the Scriptures* (Wheaton, IL: Victor Books, 1985), Vol. 2, 372.

3. Bruce B. Barton & G. R. Osborne, *Acts* (Wheaton, IL: Tyndale House, 1999), 136.

4. Ibid, 139.

5. Werner Herman Franzmann, *Bible History Commentary: New Testament* (electronic ed.) (Milwaukee, WI: WELS Board for Parish Education, 1998), 1227–1228.

6. Ibid.

7. F. F. Bruce, *The Book of the Acts* (Grand Rapids, MI: Wm. B. Eerdmans Publishing Co., 1988), 172.

8. John B. Polhill, *Acts* (Vol. 26) (Nashville: Broadman & Holman Publishers, 1992), 224.

9. Arno Gaebelein, *The Annotated Bible: Matthew to The Acts* (Vol. 6) (Bellingham, WA: Logos Bible Software, 2009), 278.

10. John D. Barry et al., *Faithlife Study Bible* (Bellingham, WA: Lexham Press, 2012–2016).

11. S. D. Toussaint, Acts. In J. F. Walvoord & R. B. Zuck (Eds.), *The Bible Knowledge Commentary: An Exposition of the Scriptures* (Wheaton, IL: Victor Books, 1985), Volume 2, 375.

12. C. G. Kruse, Kruse, Persecution. In *Dictionary of New Testament Background: A Compendium of Contemporary Biblical Scholarship* (Downers Grove, IL: InterVarsity Press, 2000), 777.

13. Werner Herman Franzmann, *Bible History Commentary: New Testament* (electronic ed.) (Milwaukee, WI: WELS Board for Parish Education, 1998), 1250.

14. Thomas Hale, *The Applied New Testament Commentary* (Colorado Springs, CO; Ontario, Canada; East Sussex, England: David C. Cook, 1996), 464.

15. I. Howard Marshall, *Acts: An Introduction and Commentary* (Vol. 5) (Downers Grove, IL: InterVarsity Press, 1980), 184; Bruce B. Barton & G. R. Osborne, *Acts* (Wheaton, IL: Tyndale House, 1999), 161.

16. Charles C. Ryrie, *Acts of the Apostles* (Chicago: Moody Press, 1961), 57–58; John R. Stott, *The Message of Acts: the Spirit, the Church & the World* (Leicester, England; Downers Grove, IL: InterVarsity Press, 1994), 176; John B. Polhill, *Acts* (Vol. 26) (Nashville: Broadman & Holman Publishers, 1992), 241.

17. Bruce B. Barton & G. R. Osborne, *Acts* (Wheaton, IL: Tyndale House, 1999), 160.

18. Ibid, 161.

19. M. G. Easton, Lydda, In *Easton's Bible Dictionary* (New York: Harper & Brothers, 1893).

20. R. Jones, Sharon, Plain of. In J. D. Barry, D. Bomar, D. R. Brown, R. Klippenstein, D. Mangum, C. Sinclair Wolcott, ... W. Widder (Eds.), *The Lexham Bible Dictionary* (Bellingham, WA: Lexham Press, 2016).

21. Walter A. Elwell & Phlip W. Comfort,. In *Tyndale Bible dictionary* (Wheaton, IL: Tyndale House Publishers, 2001), 53; A. Van Selms, Gentile. In G. W. Bromiley, *The International Standard Bible Encyclopedia, Revised* (Wm. B. Eerdmans, 1979–1988), Volume 2, 444.

22. Bruce B. Barton & G. R. Osborne, *Acts* (Wheaton, IL: Tyndale House, 1999), 167.

23. John R. Stott, *The Message of Acts: the Spirit, the Church & the World* (Leicester, England; Downers Grove, IL: InterVarsity Press, 1994), 183.

24. I. Howard Marshall, *Acts: An Introduction and Commentary* (Vol. 5) (Downers Grove, IL: InterVarsity Press, 1980), 194.

25. F. F. Bruce, *The Book of the Acts* (Grand Rapids, MI: Wm. B. Eerdmans Publishing Co., 1988), 204.

26. Simon J. Kistemaker & W. Hendriksen, *Exposition of the Acts of the Apostles* (Vol. 17) (Grand Rapids: Baker Book House, 1953–2001), 380.

27. Ibid, 386.

28. F. F. Bruce, *The Book of the Acts* (Grand Rapids, MI: Wm. B. Eerdmans Publishing Co., 1988), 206.

29. Bruce B. Barton & G. R. Osborne, *Acts* (Wheaton, IL: Tyndale House, 1999), 184.

30. Ibid, 180.

31. S. D. Toussaint, Acts. In J. F. Walvoord & R. B. Zuck (Eds.), *The Bible Knowledge Commentary: An Exposition*

of the Scriptures (Wheaton, IL: Victor Books, 1985), Volume 2, 382.

32. The term "Hellenist" has different meanings in different contexts. In 6:1 it means "Greek-speaking Jewish Christians; in 9:29 it means Greek-speaking Jews, and in 11:20 it means Greek-speaking Gentiles. Crossway Bibles. *The ESV Study Bible* (Wheaton, IL: Crossway Bibles, 2008), 2106.

33. John R. Stott, *The Message of Acts: the Spirit, the Church & the World* (Leicester, England; Downers Grove, IL: InterVarsity Press, 1994), 201.

34. Simon J. Kistemaker & W. Hendriksen, *Exposition of the Acts of the Apostles* (Vol. 17) (Grand Rapids: Baker Book House, 1953–2001), 422.

35. M. G. Easton, In *Easton's Bible dictionary* (New York: Harper & Brothers), 1893.

36. Craig S. Keener & John H. Walton, (Eds.), *NIV Cultural Backgrounds Study Bible: Bringing to Life the Ancient World of Scripture* (Grand Rapids, MI: Zondervan, 2016), 1897.

37. Charles C. Ryrie, *Acts of the Apostles* (Chicago: Moody Press, 1961), 57–58; John R. Stott, *The Message of Acts: the Spirit, the Church & the World* (Leicester, England; Downers Grove, IL: InterVarsity Press, 1994), 69.

38. John F. MacArthur, Jr. *The MacArthur Study Bible: New American Standard Bible* (Nashville, TN: Thomas Nelson Publishers, 2006).

39. H. W. Hoehner. In G. W. Bromiley, *The International Standard Bible Encyclopedia, Revised* (Wm. B. Eerdmans, 1979–1988), Volume 2, 697.

40. John F. MacArthur, Jr. *The MacArthur Study Bible: New American Standard Bible* (Nashville, TN: Thomas Nelson Publishers, 2006).

41. John Chrysostom, Homilies of St. John Chrysostom, Archbishop of Constantinople, on the Acts of the Apostles. In P. Schaff, J. Walker, J. Sheppard, H. Browne & G. B. Stevens (Trans.), *Saint Chrysostom: Homilies on the Acts of the Apostles and the Epistle to the Romans* (Vol. 11) (New York: Christian Literature Company, 1889), 172.

42. *Word In Life Study Bible* (electronic ed.), (Nashville, TN: Thomas Nelson, 1996), Acts 12:12–17.

43. F. F. Bruce, *The Book of the Acts* (Grand Rapids, MI: Wm. B. Eerdmans Publishing Co., 1988), 239.

44. John R. Stott, *The Message of Acts: the Spirit, the Church & the World* (Leicester, England; Downers Grove, IL: InterVarsity Press, 1994), 209.

45. Flavius Josephus & William Whiston, *The Works of Josephus: Complete and Unabridged* (Peabody: Hendrickson, 1987), Antiquities, 19.349–351, 523–524.

46. Werner Herman Franzmann, *Bible History Commentary: New Testament* (electronic ed.) (Milwaukee, WI: WELS Board for Parish Education, 1998), 1297.

47. Thomas D. Lea & David Alan Black, *The New Testament: Its Background and Message* (2nd ed.) (Nashville, TN: Broadman & Holman Publishers, 2003), 305–306.

48. F. Dicken, F. Herod Antipas. In J. D. Barry, D. Bomar, D. R. Brown, R. Klippenstein, D. Mangum, C. Sinclair Wolcott, ... W. Widder (Eds.), *The Lexham Bible Dictionary* (Bellingham, WA: Lexham Press, 2016).

49. F. F. Bruce, *The Book of the Acts* (Grand Rapids, MI: Wm. B. Eerdmans Publishing Co., 1988), 247.

50. Werner Herman Franzmann, *Bible History Commentary: New Testament* (electronic ed.) (Milwaukee, WI: WELS Board for Parish Education, 1998), 1303.

51. Jews often had a second name, either Greek or Roman, like John Mark, and so it was appropriate for Luke to begin calling Paul by his non-Jewish name, as he was now beginning, in earnest, his mission to the Gentiles. John R. Stott, *The Message of Acts: the Spirit, the Church & the World* (Leicester, England; Downers Grove, IL: InterVarsity Press, 1994), 219.

52. John R. Stott, *The Message of Acts: the Spirit, the Church & the World* (Leicester, England; Downers Grove, IL: InterVarsity Press, 1994), 220.

53. Richard N. Longenecker, The Acts of the Apostles. In F. E. Gaebelein, *The Expositor's Bible Commentary: John and Acts* (Vol. 9) (Grand Rapids, MI: Zondervan Publishing House, 1981), 420.

54. Werner Herman Franzmann, *Bible History Commentary: New Testament* (electronic ed.) (Milwaukee, WI: WELS Board for Parish Education, 1998), 1308.

55. F. F. Bruce, *The Book of the Acts* (Grand Rapids, MI: Wm. B. Eerdmans Publishing Co., 1988), 255.

56. I. Howard Marshall, *Acts: An Introduction and Commentary* (Vol. 5) (Downers Grove, IL: InterVarsity Press, 1980), 237; S. D. Toussaint, Acts. In J. F. Walvoord & R. B. Zuck (Eds.), *The Bible Knowledge Commentary: An Exposition of the Scriptures* (Wheaton, IL: Victor Books, 1985), Volume 2, 390; F. F. Bruce, *The Book of the Acts* (Grand Rapids, MI: Wm. B. Eerdmans Publishing Co., 1988), 255.

57. Craig A. Blaising and Darrell L. Bock, *Progressive Dispensationalism* (Grand Rapids, MI: Baker Books, 1993), 166.

58. Robert D. Bergen, *1, 2 Samuel* (Vol. 7) (Nashville: Broadman & Holman Publishers, 1996), 340.

59. Richard N. Longenecker, Acts. In T. Longman III & D. E. Garland (Eds.), *The Expositor's Bible Commentary: Luke–Acts (Revised Edition)* (Vol. 10) (Grand Rapids, MI: Zondervan), 922.

60. F. F. Bruce, *The Book of the Acts* (Grand Rapids, MI: Wm. B. Eerdmans Publishing Co., 1988), 260.

61. S. D. Toussaint, Acts. In J. F. Walvoord & R. B. Zuck (Eds.), *The Bible Knowledge Commentary: An Exposition of the Scriptures* (Wheaton, IL: Victor Books, 1985), Volume 2, 390.

CHAPTER 4

1. Mark Water, *The New Encyclopedia of Christian Quotations* (Alresford, Hampshire: John Hunt Publishers Ltd.), 314.

2. Richard N. Longenecker, The Acts of the Apostles, In F. E. Gaebelein, *The Expositor's Bible Commentary: John and Acts* (Vol. 9) (Grand Rapids, MI: Zondervan Publishing House, 1981), 436.

3. Bruce B. Barton & G. R. Osborne, *Acts* (Wheaton, IL: Tyndale House, 1999), 239.

4. John B. Polhill, *Acts* (Vol. 26) (Nashville: Broadman & Holman Publishers, 1992), 316.

5. C. K. Barrett, "Theologia Crucis—in Acts," in *Theologia Crucis—Signum Crucis: Festschrift für E. Dinkler,* ed. G. Andresen and E. Klein (Tübingen, 1979), 79.

6. Wayne A. Grudem, *1 Peter: An Introduction and Commentary* (Vol. 17) (Downers Grove, IL: InterVarsity Press, 1988), 192.

7. John W. Wade, *Acts: Unlocking the Scriptures for You* (Cincinnati, OH: Standard, 1987), 153.

8. Richard N. Longenecker, The Acts of the Apostles, In F. E. Gaebelein, *The Expositor's Bible Commentary: John and Acts* (Vol. 9) (Grand Rapids, MI: Zondervan Publishing House, 1981), 442.

9. John W. Wade, *Acts: Unlocking the Scriptures for You* (Cincinnati, OH: Standard, 1987), 159.

10. John R. W. Stott, *The Message of Acts: the Spirit, the Church & the World* (Leicester, England; Downers Grove, IL: InterVarsity Press, 1994), 247; F. F. Bruce, *The Book of the Acts* (Grand Rapids, MI: Wm. B. Eerdmans Publishing Co, 1988), 295.

11. Bruce B. Barton & G. R. Osborne, *Acts* (Wheaton, IL: Tyndale House, 1999), 262.

12. F. F. Bruce, *The Book of the Acts* (Grand Rapids, MI: Wm. B. Eerdmans Publishing Co, 1988), 296.

13. Clinton E. Arnold, *Zondervan Illustrated Bible Backgrounds Commentary: John, Acts.* (Vol. 2) (Grand Rapids, MI: Zondervan, 2002), 362.

14. John R. W. Stott, *The message of Acts: the Spirit, the Church & the World* (Leicester, England; Downers Grove, IL: InterVarsity Press, 1994), 248.

15. Simon J. Kistemaker & William Hendriksen, *Exposition of the Acts of the Apostles* (Vol. 17) (Grand Rapids: Baker Book House, 1953–2001), 557.

16. John R. W. Stott, *The message of Acts: the Spirit, the Church & the World* (Leicester, England; Downers Grove, IL: InterVarsity Press, 1994), 248.

17. S. D. Toussaint, Acts, In J. F. Walvoord & R. B. Zuck (Eds.), *The Bible Knowledge Commentary: An Exposition*

of the Scriptures (Wheaton, IL: Victor Books, 1985), Volume 2, 396.

18. John F. MacArthur, Jr. *Acts* (Chicago: Moody Press, 1994), Volume 2, 85.

19. I. Howard Marshall, *Acts: An Introduction and Commentary* (Vol. 5) (Downers Grove, IL: InterVarsity Press, 1980, 276.

20. N. T. Wright, *Acts for Everyone, Part 2: Chapters 13–28* (London: Society for Promoting Christian Knowledge, 2008), 59.

21. D. A. Carson, The Gospels and Acts. In D. A. Carson, *NIV Zondervan Study Bible: Built on the Truth of Scripture and Centered on the Gospel Message* (Grand Rapids, MI: Zondervan, 2015), 2252.

22. Crossway Bibles, *The ESV Study Bible* (Wheaton, IL: Crossway Bibles, 2008), 2117.

23. Simon J. Kistemaker & William Hendriksen, *Exposition of the Acts of the Apostles* (Vol. 17) (Grand Rapids: Baker Book House, (1953–2001), 714.

24. N. T. Wright, *Acts for Everyone, Part 2: Chapters 13–28* (London: Society for Promoting Christian Knowledge, 2008), 63.

25. S. D. Toussaint, Acts, In J. F. Walvoord & R. B. Zuck (Eds.), *The Bible Knowledge Commentary: An Exposition of the Scriptures* (Wheaton, IL: Victor Books, 1985), Volume 2, 399.

26. Bruce B. Barton & G. R. Osborne, *Acts* (Wheaton, IL: Tyndale House, 1999), 283.

27. John F. MacArthur, Jr. *The MacArthur Study Bible: New American Standard Bible* (Nashville, TN: Thomas Nelson Publishers, 2006).

28. S. D. Toussaint, Acts, In J. F. Walvoord & R. B. Zuck (Eds.), *The Bible Knowledge Commentary: An Exposition of the Scriptures* (Wheaton, IL: Victor Books, 1985), Volume 2, 401.

29. Crossway Bibles, *The ESV Study Bible* (Wheaton, IL: Crossway Bibles, 2008), 2120.

30. Clinton E. Arnold, *Zondervan Illustrated Bible Backgrounds Commentary: John, Acts.* (Vol. 2) (Grand Rapids, MI: Zondervan, 2002), 379.

31. D. A. Carson, The Gospels and Acts. In D. A. Carson, *NIV Zondervan Study Bible: Built on the Truth of Scripture and Centered on the Gospel Message* (Grand Rapids, MI: Zondervan, 2015), 2255.

32. Simon J. Kistemaker & William Hendriksen, *Exposition of the Acts of the Apostles* (Vol. 17) (Grand Rapids: Baker Book House, 1953–2001), 625.

33. Charles C. Ryrie, *Ryrie Study Bible: New International Version* (Expanded ed.) (Chicago: Moody Publishers, 1994), 1700.

34. Simon J. Kistemaker & William Hendriksen, *Exposition of the Acts of the Apostles* (Vol. 17) (Grand Rapids: Baker Book House, 1953–2001), 628–629.

35. Gary H. Everett, *The Book of Acts* (Gary Everett, 2011), 194.

36. I. Howard Marshall, *Acts: An Introduction and Commentary* (Vol. 5) (Downers Grove, IL: InterVarsity Press, 1980, 305.

37. Chalmer E. Faw, *Acts* (Scottdale, PA: Herald Press. 1993), 196.

38. M. S. Beal, Corinth. In J. D. Barry, D. Bomar, D. R. Brown, R. Klippenstein, D. Mangum, C. Sinclair Wolcott,

... W. Widder (Eds.), *The Lexham Bible Dictionary* (Bellingham, WA: Lexham Press, 2016).

39. Crossway Bibles, *The ESV Study Bible* (Wheaton, IL: Crossway Bibles, 2008), 2151.

40. Walter H. Franzmann, *Bible History Commentary: New Testament* (electronic ed.) (Milwaukee, WI: WELS Board for Parish Education, 1998), 1370.

41. C. Suetonius Tranquillus, *Suetonius: The Lives of the Twelve Caesars; An English Translation, Augmented with the Biographies of Contemporary Statesmen, Orators, Poets, and Other Associates* (A. Thomson, Ed.). Medford, MA: Gebbie & Co., 1889), Chapter 25.

42. Craig A. Evans, *Ancient Texts for New Testament Studies: A Guide to the Background Literature* (Grand Rapids, MI: Baker Academic, 2005), 298.

43. I. Howard Marshall, *Acts: An Introduction and Commentary* (Vol. 5) (Downers Grove, IL: InterVarsity Press, 1980, 313.

44. Crossway Bibles, *The ESV Study Bible* (Wheaton, IL: Crossway Bibles, 2008), 2171.

45. John F. MacArthur, Jr., *The MacArthur Study Bible* (electronic ed.) (Nashville, TN: Word Pub, 1997), 1667.

46. Francis Martin & Evan Smith, *Acts* (Downers Grove, IL: InterVarsity Press, 2006), 227.

47. John Calvin & Henry Beveridge, *Commentary Upon the Acts of the Apostles* (Bellingham, WA: Logos Bible Software, 2010), Volume 2, 191.

48. Gordon J. Keddie, *You Are My Witnesses: The Message of the Acts of the Apostles* (Darlington, England: Evangelical Press, 2000), 222.

49. Walter H. Franzmann, *Bible History Commentary: New Testament* (electronic ed.) (Milwaukee, WI: WELS Board for Parish Education, 1998), 1372.

50. William M. Ramsay, *St. Paul the Traveller and the Roman citizen* (London: Hodder & Stoughton, 1907), 260.

51. Walter H. Franzmann, *Bible History Commentary: New Testament* (electronic ed.) (Milwaukee, WI: WELS Board for Parish Education, 1998), 1375.

52. Charles C. Ryrie, *Ryrie Study Bible: New International Version* (Expanded ed.) (Chicago: Moody Publishers), 1702.

53. Charles C. Ryrie, *Basic Theology: A Popular Systematic Guide to Understanding Biblical Truth* (Chicago, IL: Moody Press, 1999), 409.

54. John R. W. Stott, *The Message of Acts: the Spirit, the Church & the World* (Leicester, England; Downers Grove, IL: InterVarsity Press, 1994), 304–305.

55. John F. MacArthur, Jr. *The MacArthur study Bible: New American Standard Bible* (Nashville, TN: Thomas Nelson Publishers, 2006).

56. Crossway Bibles, *The ESV Study Bible* (Wheaton, IL: Crossway Bibles, 2008), 2097.

57. Charles C. Ryrie, *Ryrie Study Bible: New International Version* (Expanded ed.) (Chicago: Moody Publishers), 1703.

58. Joseph Addison Alexander, *The Acts of the Apostles Explained* (Vol. 2) (London: James Nisbet & Co., 1857), 193.

59. F. F. Bruce, *The Book of the Acts* (Grand Rapids, MI: Wm. B. Eerdmans Publishing Co, 1988), 366.

60. R. C. Sproul, *Acts* (Wheaton, IL: Crossway, 2010), 329.

61. John W. Wade, *Acts: Unlocking the Scriptures for You* (Cincinnati, OH: Standard, 1987), 204.

62. Bruce B. Barton & G. R. Osborne, *Acts* (Wheaton, IL: Tyndale House, 1999), 333.

63. R. D. I. Miller, Sacred Stone, In D. N. Freedman, *The Anchor Yale Bible Dictionary* (New York: Doubleday, 1992), Volume 5, 870.

64. John R. W. Stott, *The Message of Acts: the Spirit, the Church & the World* (Leicester, England; Downers Grove, IL: InterVarsity Press, 1994), 316.

65. Ibid.

66. Major Contributors and Editors, Achaia. In J. D. Barry, D. Bomar, D. R. Brown, R. Klippenstein, D. Mangum, C. Sinclair Wolcott, ... W. Widder (Eds.), *The Lexham Bible Dictionary* (Bellingham, WA: Lexham Press, 2016).

67. Charles C. Ryrie, *Ryrie Study Bible: New International Version* (Expanded ed.) (Chicago: Moody Publishers), 1705.

68. John R. W. Stott, *The Message of Acts: the Spirit, the Church & the World* (Leicester, England; Downers Grove, IL: InterVarsity Press, 1994), 317; Craig S. Keener and John H. Walter, *NIV Cultural Backgrounds Study Bible: Bringing to Life the Ancient World of Scripture* (Grand Rapids, MI: Zondervan, 2016), 1920.

69. Simon J. Kistemaker & William Hendriksen, *Exposition of the Acts of the Apostles* (Vol. 17) (Grand Rapids: Baker Book House, 1953–2001), 713.

70. John B. Polhill, *Acts* (Vol. 26) (Nashville: Broadman & Holman Publishers, 1992), 418.

71. Bruce Milne, *The Acts of the Apostles: Witnesses to Him ... to the Ends of the Earth* (Ross-shire, Great Britain: Christian Focus Publications, 2010), 398; Simon J.

Kistemaker & William Hendriksen, *Exposition of the Acts of the Apostles* (Vol. 17) (Grand Rapids: Baker Book House, (1953–2001), 717; Bruce B. Barton & G. R. Osborne, *Acts* (Wheaton, IL: Tyndale House, 1999) 343; John B. Polhill, *Acts* (Vol. 26) (Nashville: Broadman & Holman Publishers, 1992), 418.

72. John B. Polhill, *Acts* (Vol. 26) (Nashville: Broadman & Holman Publishers, 1992), 418.

73. A. M. Rodrigues, Assos, In J. D. Barry, D. Bomar, D. R. Brown, R. Klippenstein, D. Mangum, C. Sinclair Wolcott, … W. Widder (Eds.), *The Lexham Bible Dictionary* (Bellingham, WA: Lexham Press, 2016).

74. Paul W. Walaskay, *Acts.* (P. D. Miller & D. L. Bartlett, Eds.) (Louisville, KY: Westminster John Knox Press, 1998), 187; see also John B. Polhill, *Acts* (Vol. 26) (Nashville: Broadman & Holman Publishers, 1992), 421.

75. John F. MacArthur, Jr. *The MacArthur Study Bible: New American Standard Bible* (Nashville, TN: Thomas Nelson Publishers, 2006), 1672.

76. Simon J. Kistemaker & William Hendriksen, *Exposition of the Acts of the Apostles* (Vol. 17) (Grand Rapids: Baker Book House, 1953–2001), 731.

77. Bruce B. Barton & G. R. Osborne, *Acts* (Wheaton, IL: Tyndale House, 1999), 350.

78. Ibid, 353.

CHAPTER 5

1. Mark Walter, *The New Encyclopedia of Christian Quotations* (Alresford, Hampshire: John Hunt Publishers Ltd.), 315.

2.   Geoffrey William Bromiley, (Ed.) In *The International Standard Bible Encyclopedia, Revised* (Wm. B. Eerdmans, 1979–1988), Volume 3, 488.

3.   I. Howard Marshall, *Acts: An Introduction and Commentary* (Vol. 5) (Downers Grove, IL: InterVarsity Press, 1980), 359; John B. Polhill, *Acts* (Vol. 26) (Nashville: Broadman & Holman Publishers, 1992), 748.

4.   Matthew Henry, *Matthew Henry's Commentary On the Whole Bible: Complete and Unabridged in One Volume* (Peabody: Hendrickson, 1994), 2160.

5.   Simon J. Kistemaker & William Hendriksen, *Exposition of the Acts of the Apostles* (Vol. 17) (Grand Rapids: Baker Book House, 1953–2001), 750.

6.   John Calvin & Henry Beveridge, *Commentary upon the Acts of the Apostles* (Bellingham, WA: Logos Bible Software, 2010), Volume 2, 268.

7.   John B. Polhill, *Acts* (Vol. 26) (Nashville: Broadman & Holman Publishers, 1992), 433.

8.   Bruce B. Barton & G. R. Osborne, *Acts* (Wheaton, IL: Tyndale House, 1999), 362.

9.   Walter C. Kaiser, Jr., Peter H. Davids, et al., *Hard Sayings of the Bible* (Downers Grove, IL: InterVarsity, 1996), 38.

10.   Ronald F. Youngblood, et al., Thomas Nelson Publishers (Eds.), In *Nelson's New Illustrated Bible Dictionary* (Nashville, TN: Thomas Nelson, Inc., 1995).

11.   S. D. Toussaint, Acts. In J. F. Walvoord & R. B. Zuck (Eds.), *The Bible Knowledge Commentary: An Exposition of the Scriptures* (Wheaton, IL: Victor Books, 1985), Volume 2, 417.

12.   S. D. Toussaint, Acts. In J. F. Walvoord & R. B. Zuck (Eds.), *The Bible Knowledge Commentary: An Exposition*

of the Scriptures (Wheaton, IL: Victor Books, 1985), Volume 2, 417.

13. Stephen F. Olford & David Olford, *Anointed Expository Preaching* (Nashville, TN: Broadman & Holman Publishers, 1998), 277; Maxie Dunham & Lloyd J. Ogilvie, *Galatians / Ephesians / Philippians / Colossians / Philemon* (Vol. 31) (Nashville, TN: Thomas Nelson Inc., 1982), 376.

14. Clinton E. Arnold, *Zondervan Illustrated Bible Backgrounds Commentary: John, Acts.* (Vol. 2) (Grand Rapids, MI: Zondervan, 2002), 441.

15. Bruce B. Barton & G. R. Osborne, *Acts* (Wheaton, IL: Tyndale House, 1999), 380.

16. Ibid, 381.

17. John F. MacArthur, Jr. *John MacArthur Sermon Archive* (Panorama City, CA: Grace to You, 2014), *Providential Protection*, October 13, 1974.

18. Bruce B. Barton & G. R. Osborne, *Acts* (Wheaton, IL: Tyndale House, 1999), 382.

19. Flavius Josephus & William Whiston, *The Works of Josephus: Complete and Unabridged*, Antiquities of the Jews, XX, 6, 2–3; 9, 1–2, (Peabody: Hendrickson, 1987); Stewart Custer, *Witness to Christ : A Commentary on Acts* (Greenville, SC: BJU Press, 2000), 330.

20. I. Howard Marshall, *Acts: An Introduction and Commentary* (Vol. 5) (Downers Grove, IL: InterVarsity Press, 1980), 384.

21. F. F. Bruce, *The Book of the Acts* (Grand Rapids, MI: Wm. B. Eerdmans Publishing Co., 1988), 436.

22. Robert B. Hughes & Carl J. Laney, *Tyndale Concise Bible Commentary* (Wheaton, IL: Tyndale House Publishers, 2001). 504; see also John R. W. Stott, *The Message of*

Acts: the Spirit, the Church & the World (Leicester, England; Downers Grove, IL: InterVarsity Press, 1994), 360.

23. Flavius Josephus & William Whiston, *The Works of Josephus: Complete and unabridged* (Peabody: Hendrickson, 1987), The Jewish Wars, 2.12.1 Sections 228–31; 5.5.2 Section 194; Antiquities 15.11.5 Section 417; B. D. Chilton, Judaism, In J. B. Green & S. McKnight (Eds.), *Dictionary of Jesus and the Gospels* (Downers Grove, IL: InterVarsity Press, 1992), 404.

24. F. F. Bruce, *The Book of the Acts* (Grand Rapids, MI: Wm. B. Eerdmans Publishing Co., 1988), 441.

25. William H. Willimon, *Acts* (Atlanta, GA: John Knox Press, 1988), 174.

26. John R. W. Stott, *The Message of Acts: the Spirit, the Church & the World* (Leicester, England; Downers Grove, IL: InterVarsity Press, 1994), 358.

27. Ibid, 358–359.

28. Ibid, 361.

29. Werner Herman Franzmann, *Bible History Commentary: New Testament* (electronic ed.) (Milwaukee, WI: WELS Board for Parish Education, 1998), 1437.

30. John B. Polhill, *Acts* (Vol. 26) (Nashville: Broadman & Holman Publishers, 1992), 485.

31. John F. MacArthur, Jr. *Acts* (Chicago: Moody Press, 1994), Volume 2, 309.

32. Simon J. Kistemaker & William Hendriksen, *Exposition of the Acts of the Apostles* (Vol. 17) (Grand Rapids: Baker Book House, 1953–2001). 851; John B. Polhill, *Acts* (Vol. 26) (Nashville: Broadman & Holman Publishers, 1992), 486.

33. John B. Polhill, *Acts* (Vol. 26) (Nashville: Broadman & Holman Publishers, 1992), 487.

34. F. F. Bruce, *The Book of the Acts* (Grand Rapids, MI: Wm. B. Eerdmans Publishing Co., 1988), 453.

35. John B. Polhill, *Acts* (Vol. 26) (Nashville: Broadman & Holman Publishers, 1992), 491.

36. I. Howard Marshall, *Acts: An Introduction and Commentary* (Vol. 5) (Downers Grove, IL: InterVarsity Press, 1980), 405.

37. F. F. Bruce, *The Book of the Acts* (Grand Rapids, MI: Wm. B. Eerdmans Publishing Co., 1988), 454.

38. Charles Caldwell Ryrie, *Ryrie Study Bible: New International Version* (Expanded ed.) (Chicago: Moody Publishers, 1994), 1714.

39. I. Howard Marshall, *Acts: An Introduction and Commentary* (Vol. 5) (Downers Grove, IL: InterVarsity Press, 1980), 409.

40. Montague Rhodes James, *The Apocryphal New Testament: Being the Apocryphal Gospels, Acts, Epistles, and Apocalypses* (Oxford: Clarendon Press, 1924), 273.

41. S. D. Toussaint, Acts. In J. F. Walvoord & R. B. Zuck (Eds.), *The Bible Knowledge Commentary: An Exposition of the Scriptures* (Wheaton, IL: Victor Books, 1985), Volume 2, 423.

42. R. C. H. Lenski, *The Interpretation of the Acts of the Apostles* (Minneapolis, MN: Augsburg Publishing House, 1961), 1020.

43. I. Howard Marshall, *Acts: An Introduction and Commentary* (Vol. 5) (Downers Grove, IL: InterVarsity Press, 1980), 410.

44. N. T. Wright, *Acts for Everyone, Part 2: Chapters 13–28* (London: Society for Promoting Christian Knowledge, 2008), 206.

45. Charles Caldwell Ryrie, *Ryrie Study Bible: New International Version* (Expanded ed.) (Chicago: Moody Publishers, 1994), 1716.

46. Richard N. Longenecker, Acts. In T. Longman III & D. E. Garland (Eds.), *The Expositor's Bible Commentary: Luke–Acts (Revised Edition)* (Vol. 10) (Grand Rapids, MI: Zondervan, 2007), 1078.

47. John Calvin & Henry Beveridge, *Commentary upon the Acts of the Apostles* (Bellingham, WA: Logos Bible Software, 2010), Volume 2, 389–390.

48. Joseph S. Exell, *The Biblical illustrator (Acts): Or anecdotes, similes, emblems, illustrations; expository, scientific, geographical, historical, and homiletic, gathered from a wide range of home and foreign literature, on the verses of the Bible* (Oak Harbor, WA: Logos Research Systems, Inc., 1997), 378.

49. R. C. Sproul, *Acts* (Wheaton, IL: Crossway, 2010), 408.

50. Simon J. Kistemaker & William Hendriksen, *Exposition of the Acts of the Apostles* (Vol. 17) (Grand Rapids: Baker Book House, 1953–2001), 915–916.

51. John F. MacArthur, Jr. *Acts* (Chicago: Moody Press, 1994). Volume 2, 343.

52. John Calvin & Henry Beveridge, *Commentary upon the Acts of the Apostles* (Bellingham, WA: Logos Bible Software, 2010), Volume 2, 400.

53. R. C. H. Lenski, *The Interpretation of the Acts of the Apostles* (Minneapolis, MN: Augsburg Publishing House, 1961), 1083.

54. John F. MacArthur, Jr. *Acts* (Chicago: Moody Press, 1994), Volume 2, 353.

55. F. F. Bruce, *The Book of the Acts* (Grand Rapids, MI: Wm. B. Eerdmans Publishing Co., 1988), 436.

56. Ibid, 475.

57. Paul W. Walaskay, *Acts*. (P. D. Miller & D. L. Bartlett, Eds.) (Louisville, KY: Westminster John Knox Press, 1998), 239.

58. F. F. Bruce, *The Book of the Acts* (Grand Rapids, MI: Wm. B. Eerdmans Publishing Co., 1988), 501.

59. S. D. Toussaint, Acts. In J. F. Walvoord & R. B. Zuck (Eds.), *The Bible Knowledge Commentary: An Exposition of the Scriptures* (Wheaton, IL: Victor Books, 1985), Volume 2, 429.

60. Ibid, 430.

61. S. M. Miller, "Bald, Blind and Single?" *Christian History Magazine-Issue 47: The Apostle Paul & His Times*, 1995.

62. F. F. Bruce, *Paul: Apostle of the Free Spirit* (Milton Keynes, UK: Paternoster, 1977), 469–470.

CHAPTER 6

1. B. B. Barton, *Galatians* (Wheaton, IL: Tyndale House, 1994), pp. x–xi.

2. Dale Leschert, *The Flow of the New Testament* (Fearn, Great Britain: Christian Focus Publications, 2002), 22.

3. Irving L. Jensen, *Prison Epistles: Ephesians, Philippians, Colossians and 1 & 2 Thessalonians* (San Bernardino, CA: Here's Life Publishers, Inc., 1987), 10.

4. Irving L. Jensen, *Journey of the Bible: The Remarkable Story of How the Bible Came from God to You* (Minneapolis, MN: World Wide Publications, 1990), 83.

5. D. K. Campbell, Galatians, In J. F. Walvoord & R. B. Zuck (Eds.), *The Bible Knowledge Commentary: An Exposition of the Scriptures* (Wheaton, IL: Victor Books, 1985), Volume 2, 587–588.

6. Z. G. Smith, Galatians. In J. D. Barry, D. Bomar, D. R. Brown, R. Klippenstein, D. Mangum, C. Sinclair Wolcott,...W. Widder (Eds.), *The Lexham Bible Dictionary* (Bellingham, WA: Lexham Press, 2016).

7. Crossway Bibles, *The ESV Study Bible* (Wheaton, IL: Crossway Bibles, 2008), 2241; D. K. Campbell, Galatians, In J. F. Walvoord & R. B. Zuck (Eds.), *The Bible Knowledge Commentary: An Exposition of the Scriptures* (Wheaton, IL: Victor Books, 1985), Volume 2, 587–588.

8. D. K. Campbell, Galatians, In J. F. Walvoord & R. B. Zuck (Eds.), *The Bible Knowledge Commentary: An Exposition of the Scriptures* (Wheaton, IL: Victor Books, 1985), Volume 2, 587–588.

9. Douglas J. Moo, *NT341 Book Study: Paul's Letter to the Galatians* (Bellingham, WA: Lexham Press, 2015), Segment 3.

10. D. K. Campbell, Galatians, In J. F. Walvoord & R. B. Zuck (Eds.), *The Bible Knowledge Commentary: An Exposition of the Scriptures* (Wheaton, IL: Victor Books, 1985), Volume 2, 588.

11. Crossway Bibles, *The ESV Study Bible* (Wheaton, IL: Crossway Bibles, 2008), 2241; Douglas J. Moo, *NT341 Book Study: Paul's Letter to the Galatians* (Bellingham, WA: Lexham Press, 2015), Segment 3.

12. John MacArthur, Jr., *The MacArthur Study Bible* (electronic ed.) (Nashville, TN: Word Pub., 1997), 1786.

13. Elmer L. Towns & Ben Gutiὲrrez, *The Essence of the New Testament* (Nashville: B&H, 2012), Chapter 13.

14. Crossway Bibles, *The ESV Study Bible* (Wheaton, IL: Crossway Bibles, 2008), 2241; Douglas J. Moo, *NT341 Book Study: Paul's Letter to the Galatians* (Bellingham, WA: Lexham Press, 2015), Segment 3.

15. D. K. Campbell, Galatians, In J. F. Walvoord & R. B. Zuck (Eds.), *The Bible Knowledge Commentary: An Exposition of the Scriptures* (Wheaton, IL: Victor Books, 1985), Volume 2, 588.

16. Simon J. Kistemaker & William Hendriksen, *Exposition of the Epistles of Peter and the Epistle of Jude* (Vol. 16) (Grand Rapids: Baker Book House, 1953–2001), 312.

17. C. Marius Victorinus Afer, *In Galatas*, introd. (ed. A. Locher, 1), cited in F. F. Bruce, Bruce, *The Epistle to the Galatians: A Commentary on the Greek Text* (Grand Rapids, MI: W.B. Eerdmans Pub. Co., 1982), 21.

18. Elmer L. Towns & Ben GutiÈrrez, *The Essence of the New Testament* (Nashville: B&H, 2012), Chapter 13.

19. F. F. Bruce, Bruce, *The Epistle to the Galatians: A Commentary on the Greek Text* (Grand Rapids, MI: W.B. Eerdmans Pub. Co., 1982), 108.

20. Bruce B. Barton, *Galatians* (Wheaton, IL: Tyndale House, 1994), 59–60.

21. John F. MacArthur, Jr. *Galatians* (Chicago: Moody Press, 1983), 55.

22. Bruce B. Barton, *Galatians* (Wheaton, IL: Tyndale House, 1994), 62.

23. John R. W. Stott, *The Message of Galatians: Only One Way* (Leicester, England; Downer's Grove, IL: InterVarsity Press, 1986), 55.

24. John F. MacArthur, Jr. *Galatians* (Chicago: Moody Press, 1983), 58.

25. Bruce B. Barton, *Galatians* (Wheaton, IL: Tyndale House, 1994), 82.

26. William Hendriksen & S. J. Kistemaker, *Exposition of Galatians* (Vol. 8) (Grand Rapids: Baker Book House, 1953–2001), 112.

27. John F. MacArthur, Jr. *Galatians* (Chicago: Moody Press, 1983), 84.

28. Dale Leschert, *The Flow of the New Testament* (Fearn, Great Britain: Christian Focus Publications, 2002), 231.

29. D. K. Campbell, Galatians, In J. F. Walvoord & R. B. Zuck (Eds.), *The Bible Knowledge Commentary: An Exposition of the Scriptures* (Wheaton, IL: Victor Books, 1985), Volume 2, 599–600.

30. Charles H. Spurgeon, *Galatians* (E. Ritzema, Ed.) (Bellingham, WA: Lexham Press, 2013).

31. Charles H. Spurgeon, *Spurgeon's Sermons, "The Uses of the Law"* (electronic ed., Vol. 3, Albany, OR: Ages Software, 1998).

32. D. K. Campbell, Galatians. In J. F. Walvoord & R. B. Zuck (Eds.), *The Bible Knowledge Commentary: An Exposition of the Scriptures* (Wheaton, IL: Victor Books, 1985), Volume 2, 604.

33. Bruce B. Barton, *Galatians* (Wheaton, IL: Tyndale House, 1994), 163.

34. Crossway Bibles, *The ESV Study Bible* (Wheaton, IL: Crossway Bibles, 2008), 2254.

35. John R. W. Stott, *The Message of Galatians: Only One Way* (Leicester, England; Downer's Grove, IL: InterVarsity Press, 1986), 151.

36. Ibid, 153–154.

37. Crossway Bibles, *The ESV Study Bible* (Wheaton, IL: Crossway Bibles, 2008), 2255.

38. Charles H. Spurgeon, *Galatians* (E. Ritzema, Ed.) (Bellingham, WA: Lexham Press. 2013).

39. Timothy George, *Galatians* (Vol. 30) (Nashville: Broadman & Holman Publishers, 1994), 416.

40. John F. MacArthur, Jr. *Galatians* (Chicago: Moody Press, 1983), 193.

CHAPTER 7

1. William Hendrickson & S. J. Kistemaker, *Exposition of I-II Thessalonians*, (Grand Rapids: Baker Book House),Vol. 3, p. 4.
2. Irving L. Jensen, *Jensen's Survey of the New Testament: Search and Discover* (Chicago: Moody Press, 1981), 350.
3. F. F. Bruce, *1 and 2 Thessalonians* (Vol. 45) (Dallas: Word, Incorporated, 1998), xxvii.
4. Leon Morris, *1 and 2 Thessalonians: An Introduction and Commentary* (Vol. 13) (Downers Grove, IL: InterVarsity Press, 1984), 42.
5. Bruce B. Barton & G. R. Osborne, *1 & 2 Thessalonians: Life Application Commentary* (Wheaton, IL: Tyndale House Publishers, 1999), 17.
6. John R. W. Stott, *The Message of Thessalonians: the Gospel & the End of Time* (Leicester, England; Downers Grove, IL: InterVarsity Press, 1994), 29.
7. Bruce B. Barton & G. R. Osborne, *1 & 2 Thessalonians: Life Application Commentary* (Wheaton, IL: Tyndale House Publishers, 1999), 17.
8. Crossway Bibles, *The ESV Study Bible* (Wheaton, IL: Crossway Bibles, 2008), 2305.
9. Paul J. Achtemeier, Harper & Row and Society of Biblical Literature, In *Harper's Bible Dictionary* (1st ed.) (San Francisco: Harper & Row, 1985). 579.
10. R. E. O. White, Love. In *Baker Encyclopedia of the Bible* (Grand Rapids, MI: Baker Book House, 1988), Vol. 2, 1357–1360.

11. Paul J. Achtemeier, Harper & Row and Society of Biblical Literature, In *Harper's Bible Dictionary* (1st ed.) (San Francisco: Harper & Row, 1985), 579.

12. R. E. O. White, Love. In *Baker Encyclopedia of the Bible* (Grand Rapids, MI: Baker Book House, 1988), Vol. 2, 1357–1360.

13. Leon Morris, *Testaments of Love* (Eerdmans, 1981), 128, quoted in Leon Morris, *1 and 2 Thessalonians: An Introduction and Commentary* (Vol. 13) (Downers Grove, IL: InterVarsity Press, 1984), 44.

14. Paul J. Achtemeier, Harper & Row and Society of Biblical Literature, In *Harper's Bible Dictionary* (1st ed.) (San Francisco: Harper & Row, 1985), 580.

15. R. E. O. White, Love. In *Baker Encyclopedia of the Bible* (Grand Rapids, MI: Baker Book House, 1988), Vol. 2, 1357–1360.

16. Eugene E. Carpenter & Philip W. Comfort, In *Holman Treasury of Key Bible Words: 200 Greek and 200 Hebrew Words Defined and Explained* (Nashville, TN: Broadman & Holman Publishers, 2000), 305.

17. Leon Morris, *1 and 2 Thessalonians: An Introduction and Commentary* (Vol. 13) (Downers Grove, IL: InterVarsity Press, 1984), 45.

18. Augustine of Hippo, Expositions on the Book of Psalms, In P. Schaff (Ed.) A. C. Coxe (Trans.), *Saint Augustine: Expositions on the Book of Psalms* (Vol. 8) (New York: Christian Literature Company, 1888), 243.

19. Leon Morris, *1 and 2 Thessalonians: An Introduction and Commentary* (Vol. 13) (Downers Grove, IL: InterVarsity Press, 1984), 45.

20. Allen Verhey & Joseph S. Harvard, *Ephesians* (A. P. Pauw & W. C. Placher, Eds.) (Louisville, KY: Westminster John Knox Press, 2011), 93.

21. Tim Shenton, *Opening up 1 Thessalonians* (Leominster: Day One Publications, 2006), 19–20.

22. Michael D. Martin, *1, 2 Thessalonians* (Vol. 33) (Nashville: Broadman & Holman Publishers, 1995), 63.

23. Tim Shenton, *Opening up 1 Thessalonians* (Leominster: Day One Publications, 2006), 21.

24. John F. MacArthur, Jr., *The MacArthur Study Bible: New American Standard Bible* (Nashville, TN: Thomas Nelson Publishers., 2006).

25. Leon Morris, *The First and Second Epistles to the Thessalonians* (Grand Rapids, MI; Cambridge, U.K.: Wm. B. Eerdmans Publishing Co., 1991), 82.

26. Douglas J. Moo, The Letters and Revelation, In D. A. Carson, *NIV Zondervan Study Bible: Built on the Truth of Scripture and Centered on the Gospel Message* (Grand Rapids, MI: Zondervan, 2015), 2441.

27. Ibid, 2442.

28. Michael D. Martin, *1, 2 Thessalonians* (Vol. 33) (Nashville: Broadman & Holman Publishers, 1995), 101.

29. Crossway Bibles, *The ESV Study Bible* (Wheaton, IL: Crossway Bibles, 2008), 2307.

30. Leon Morris, *1 and 2 Thessalonians: An Introduction and Commentary* (Vol. 13) (Downers Grove, IL: InterVarsity Press, 1984), 69.

31. John R. W. Stott, *The Message of Thessalonians: the Gospel & the End of Time* (Leicester, England; Downers Grove, IL: InterVarsity Press, 1994), 66.

32. William Hendriksen & S. J. Kistemaker, *Exposition of I–II Thessalonians* (Vol. 3) (Grand Rapids: Baker Book House, 1953–2001), 88.

33. Gary Habermas, *The Historical Jesus: Ancient Evidence for the Life of Christ* (Joplin, MO: College Press Publishing Company, 1996), 146–152.

34. Gene L. Green, *The letters to the Thessalonians* (Grand Rapids, MI; Leicester, England: W.B. Eerdmans Pub.; Apollos, 2002), 186.

35. Bruce B. Barton & G. R. Osborne, *1 & 2 Thessalonians: Life Application Commentary* (Wheaton, IL: Tyndale House Publishers, 1999), 64.

36. Douglas J. Moo, The Letters and Revelation, In D. A. Carson, *NIV Zondervan Study Bible: Built on the Truth of Scripture and Centered on the Gospel Message* (Grand Rapids, MI: Zondervan, 2015), 2443.

37. Ibid, 2444.

38. Norman L. Geisler, *Systematic Theology, Volume Four: Church, Last Things* (Minneapolis, MN: Bethany House Publishers, 2005), 253.

39. Crossway Bibles, *The ESV Study Bible* (Wheaton, IL: Crossway Bibles, 2008), 2309.

40. John F. MacArthur, Jr., *The MacArthur Study Bible: New American Standard Bible* (Nashville, TN: Thomas Nelson Publishers, 2006).

41. Earl D. Radmacher, Ronald Barclay Allen & H. Wayne House, *The Nelson Study Bible: New King James Version* (Nashville: T. Nelson Publishers, 1997).

42. John F. MacArthur, Jr., *The MacArthur Study Bible: New American Standard Bible* (Nashville, TN: Thomas Nelson Publishers, 2006).

43. Ibid.

44. I believe the Bible teaches that the Rapture will occur
    before the seven-year Tribulation period (the pretribulation
    view), but some believe it will occur in the middle (midtrib-
    ulation view), and others at the end of the Tribulation
    (posttribulation view). Still others believe the Rapture
    won't occur at all, while some argue that it will occur, but
    will be partial—only certain believers will be raptured.
    There are also varying views as to *whether* Christ will
    return for a literal thousand-year reign (Millennial reign)
    and *when* He will do so. The premillennial view is that
    Christ's return will come before His literal thousand-year
    reign. The postmillennial view is that the Millennium will
    be a time of peace, material prosperity, and spiritual wel-
    fare on earth brought about by the Church; that Christ
    will not be on earth during this period—except in the
    hearts of believers—but that He will return after the Mil-
    lennium (not a literal thousand years) and His return will
    be followed immediately by the general resurrection and
    judgment. Ryrie, C. C. (1999), *Basic Theology: A Popular
    Systematic Guide to Understanding Biblical Truth,* Chi-
    cago, IL: Moody Press, 512; Campbell, D. K. (1991), Fore-
    word in C. Bubeck Sr., *Basic Bible Interpretation: A
    Practical Guide to Discovering Biblical Truth,* Colorado
    Springs, CO: David C. Cook and TH341, Segment 23.
    The millennial view holds that Christ is currently reigning
    in heaven along with the believers on earth as they submit
    their lives to Him and evangelize, though His reign is not a
    literal thousand-year period. The period covers the time
    between Christ's first and second comings and will be a
    mixture of good and evil, unlike the postmillennial view,
    which says it will be a time of peace and prosperity. Christ
    will not reign on earth for a thousand years, because He is

ruling from Heaven. When Christ returns, there will be a general resurrection and judgment of both believers and unbelievers, after which both will be ushered into the eternal state. Chou, A. (2016). Millennialism in J. D. Barry, D. Bomar, D. R. Brown, R. Klippenstein, D. Mangum, C. Sinclair Wolcott,... W. Widder (Eds.), *The Lexham Bible Dictionary*. Bellingham, WA: Lexham Press; Campbell, D. K. (1991). Foreword in C. Bubeck Sr., *Basic Bible Interpretation: A Practical Guide to Discovering Biblical Truth*. Colorado Springs, CO: David C. Cook, 231. See also Waymeyer, M. (2004). *Revelation 20 and the Millennial Debate*. The Woodlands, TX: Kress Christian Publications, page 3.

45. John F. MacArthur, Jr., *The MacArthur Study Bible: New American Standard Bible* (Nashville, TN: Thomas Nelson Publishers, 2006).

46. T. L. Constable, 2 Thessalonians. In J. F. Walvoord & R. B. Zuck (Eds.), *The Bible Knowledge Commentary: An Exposition of the Scriptures* (Wheaton, IL: Victor Books, 1985). Volume 2, 705.

47. Ibid, 706.

48. D. K. Lowery, D. K., 2 Corinthians. In J. F. Walvoord & R. B. Zuck (Eds.), *The Bible Knowledge Commentary: An Exposition of the Scriptures* (Wheaton, IL: Victor Books, 1985), Volume 2, 563.

49. J. A. Martin, Isaiah. In J. F. Walvoord & R. B. Zuck (Eds.), *The Bible Knowledge Commentary: An Exposition of the Scriptures* (Wheaton, IL: Victor Books, 1985), Volume 1, 1059.

50. John F. MacArthur, Jr., *The MacArthur Study Bible: New American Standard Bible* (Nashville, TN: Thomas Nelson Publishers, 2006).

51. Ibid.
52. Ibid.
53. Ibid.
54. T. L. Constable, 2 Thessalonians. In J. F. Walvoord & R. B. Zuck (Eds.), *The Bible Knowledge Commentary: An Exposition of the Scriptures* (Wheaton, IL: Victor Books, 1985), Volume 2, 705.
55. Scholars differ widely in their interpretation of end-time events. The following is a rough outline of major end-time events prophesied in the Bible from the pretribulation/premillennial perspective: 1) the Rapture (John 14:1–3; 1 Cor. 15:51–52); 1 Thess. 4:16–18; Rev. 3:10); 2) the seven-year period of Tribulation (Daniel 9:27); 3) Christ's Second Coming at the end of the Tribulation period, leading the armies of heaven to victory over His enemies (Zech. 14:1–11; Matt. 24:27–31; Rev. 19:11–16); after which the Antichrist and the false prophet are thrown into the lake of fire (Rev. 19:20); 4) Satan is cast into the abyss (Rev. 20:1–3); 5) Christ begins His millennial reign on earth (Psalm 72:8; Isaiah 9:6–7; Daniel 2:14–35; 44; 7:13–14; Zech. 9:10; Rev. 20:4); 6) Christ releases Satan from his imprisonment after His millennial reign (Rev. 20:7); 7) Christ destroys Satan by fire in the final battle (Rev. 20:9) and casts him into the lake of fire (Rev. 20:10); 8) the existing heavens and earth are destroyed (Rev. 21:1) and the new heavens and new earth are created (Peter 3:10; Rev. 21:1); 8) Christ rules forever in His eternal kingdom with all believers being part of his kingdom (Isaiah 9:6–7; Ezek. 37:24–28; Daniel 7:13–14; Luke 1:32–33; Rev. 11:15). Most of this is borrowed from a comprehensive, detailed outline in C. H. Dyer, Ezekiel in J. F. Walvoord & R. B. Zuck (Eds.), *The Bible Knowledge Commentary: An Exposition of the*

Scriptures (Wheaton, IL: Victor Books, 1985), Volume 1, 1318–1321.

56. Michael D. Martin, *1, 2 Thessalonians* (Vol. 33) (Nashville: Broadman & Holman Publishers, 1995), 181.

57. Ibid.

58. Crossway Bibles, *The ESV Study Bible* (Wheaton, IL: Crossway Bibles, 2008), 2269.

59. Gary V. Smith, *Isaiah 40–66* (Vol. 15B) (Nashville, TN: Broadman & Holman Publishers, 2009), 672.

60. John F. MacArthur, Jr., *The MacArthur Study Bible: New American Standard Bible* (Nashville, TN: Thomas Nelson Publishers., 2006).

61. Jeffrey A. D. Weima, *Baker Exegetical Commentary on the New Testament: 1–2 Thessalonians* (R. W. Yarbrough & R. H. Stein, Eds.) (Grand Rapids, MI: Baker Academic. 2014), 47.

62. Crossway Bibles, *The ESV Study Bible* (Wheaton, IL: Crossway Bibles, 2008), 2314.

63. Charles C. Ryrie, *Ryrie Study Bible: New International Version* (Expanded ed.) (Chicago: Moody Publishers, 1994), 1846.

64. Jeffrey A. D. Weima, *Baker Exegetical Commentary on the New Testament: 1–2 Thessalonians* (R. W. Yarbrough & R. H. Stein, Eds.) (Grand Rapids, MI: Baker Academic, 2014), 48.

65. Robert H. Gundry, *A Survey of the New Testament* (Fourth Edition) (Grand Rapids, MI: Zondervan, 2003), 367–368.

66. William Hendriksen & S. J. Kistemaker, *Exposition of I–II Thessalonians* (Vol. 3) (Grand Rapids: Baker Book House, 1953–2001), 154.

67. John F. MacArthur, Jr., *1 & 2 Thessalonians* (Chicago: Moody Press, 2002), 229.

68. Tim Shenton, *Opening up 1 Thessalonians* (Leominster: Day One Publications, 2006), 22.

69. John R. W. Stott, *The Message of Thessalonians: the Gospel & the End of Time* (Leicester, England; Downers Grove, IL: InterVarsity Press, 1994), 146.

70. Leon Morris, *1 and 2 Thessalonians: An Introduction and Commentary* (Vol. 13) (Downers Grove, IL: InterVarsity Press, 1984), 117.

71. T. L. Constable, 2 Thessalonians. In J. F. Walvoord & R. B. Zuck (Eds.), *The Bible Knowledge Commentary: An Exposition of the Scriptures* (Wheaton, IL: Victor Books, 1985), Volume 2, 716.

72. John F. MacArthur, Jr., *1 & 2 Thessalonians* (Chicago: Moody Press, 2002), 233.

73. Douglas J. Moo, The Letters and Revelation, In D. A. Carson, *NIV Zondervan Study Bible: Built on the Truth of Scripture and Centered on the Gospel Message* (Grand Rapids, MI: Zondervan, 2015), 2451.

74. P. S. Johnston, Hell. In T. D. Alexander & B. S. Rosner (Eds.), *New Dictionary of Biblical Theology* (electronic ed.) (Downers Grove, IL: InterVarsity Press, 2000), 543.

75. D. K. Lowery, 2 Corinthians, In J. F. Walvoord & R. B. Zuck (Eds.), *The Bible Knowledge Commentary: An Exposition of the Scriptures* (Wheaton, IL: Victor Books, 1985), Vol. 2, 562.

76. William Hendriksen & S. J. Kistemaker, *Exposition of I–II Thessalonians* (Vol. 3) (Grand Rapids: Baker Book House, 1953–2001), 161.

77. Ibid.

78. Most scholars maintain that Paul's reference to Christ's coming and the gathering of all believers to Himself concerns the Rapture (1 Thess. 4:13–18, etc.), because that is when believers will be transported to meet Him. The reference to the Day of the Lord in the same sentence, however, is referring to Christ's Second Coming (and not the Rapture), when He will judge the world. F. F. Bruce, *1 and 2 Thessalonians* (Vol. 45) (Dallas: Word, Incorporated, 1998). 163; T. L. Constable, 2 Thessalonians in J. F. Walvoord & R. B. Zuck (Eds.), *The Bible Knowledge Commentary: An Exposition of the Scriptures* (Wheaton, IL: Victor Books, 1985). Volume 2, 717; John F. MacArthur, Jr., *The MacArthur Study Bible: New American Standard Bible* (Nashville, TN: Thomas Nelson Publishers., 2006).

79. T. L. Constable, 2 Thessalonians. In J. F. Walvoord & R. B. Zuck (Eds.), *The Bible Knowledge Commentary: An Exposition of the Scriptures* (Wheaton, IL: Victor Books, 1985), Volume 2, 718.

80. Bruce B. Barton & G. R. Osborne, *1 & 2 Thessalonians: Life Application Commentary* (Wheaton, IL: Tyndale House Publishers, 1999), 125.

81. T. L. Constable, 2 Thessalonians. In J. F. Walvoord & R. B. Zuck (Eds.), *The Bible Knowledge Commentary: An Exposition of the Scriptures* (Wheaton, IL: Victor Books, 1985), Volume 2, 718.

82. F. F. Bruce, *1 and 2 Thessalonians* (Vol. 45) (Dallas: Word, Incorporated, 1998), 167.

83. William Hendriksen & S. J. Kistemaker, *Exposition of I–II Thessalonians* (Vol. 3) (Grand Rapids: Baker Book House, 1953–2001), 169.

84. T. L. Constable, 2 Thessalonians. In J. F. Walvoord & R. B. Zuck (Eds.), *The Bible Knowledge Commentary: An*

Exposition of the Scriptures (Wheaton, IL: Victor Books, 1985). Volume 2, 719.; Bruce B. Barton & G. R. Osborne, 1 & 2 Thessalonians: Life Application Commentary (Wheaton, IL: Tyndale House Publishers, 1999), 130.

85. Bruce B. Barton & G. R. Osborne, *1 & 2 Thessalonians: Life Application Commentary* (Wheaton, IL: Tyndale House Publishers, 1999), 131.

86. Charles C. Ryrie, *Ryrie Study Bible: New International Version* (Expanded ed.) (Chicago: Moody Publishers, 1994), 1965.

87. William Hendriksen & S. J. Kistemaker, *Exposition of I–II Thessalonians* (Vol. 3) (Grand Rapids: Baker Book House, 1953–2001), 186.

88. Gene L. Green, *The letters to the Thessalonians* (Grand Rapids, MI; Leicester, England: W.B. Eerdmans Pub.; Apollos, 2002), 323–324.

89. G. K. Beale, *1–2 Thessalonians* (Downers Grove, IL: Inter-Varsity Press, 2003), 222–223.

90. Richard Mayhue, *1 & 2 Thessalonians: Triumphs and Trials of a Consecrated Church* (Fearn: Christian Focus Publications, 1999), 194. Dr. Charles Ryrie writes, "God's activity (the Holy Spirit's work of regeneration) and man's responsibility (faith) are equally necessary in salvation." Charles C. Ryrie, *Ryrie Study Bible: New International Version* (Expanded ed.) (Chicago: Moody Publishers, 1994), 1849.

91. T. L. Constable, 2 Thessalonians. In J. F. Walvoord & R. B. Zuck (Eds.), *The Bible Knowledge Commentary: An Exposition of the Scriptures* (Wheaton, IL: Victor Books, 1985), Volume 2, 721.

92. Jon A. Weatherly, *1 & 2 Thessalonians* (Joplin, MO: College Press Pub. Co., 1996).

93. John R. W. Stott, *The Message of Thessalonians: the Gospel & the End of Time* (Leicester, England; Downers Grove, IL: InterVarsity Press, 1994), 191.

94. T. L. Constable, 2 Thessalonians. In J. F. Walvoord & R. B. Zuck (Eds.), *The Bible Knowledge Commentary: An Exposition of the Scriptures* (Wheaton, IL: Victor Books, 1985), Volume 2, 722–723.

95. John F. MacArthur, Jr., *1 & 2 Thessalonians* (Chicago: Moody Press, 2002), 302.

96. Ibid, 302–303.

97. William Hendriksen & S. J. Kistemaker, *Exposition of I–II Thessalonians* (Vol. 3) (Grand Rapids: Baker Book House, 1953–2001), 202.

98. Ibid, 203.

CHAPTER 8

1. Mark Water, *The New Encyclopedia of Christian Quotations* (Alresford, Hampshire: John Hunt Publishers Ltd., 2000), 230.

2. John D. Barry, Douglas Mangum et al., *Faithlife Study Bible* (Bellingham, WA: Lexham Press, 2012–2106).

3. Paul N. Benware, *Survey of the New Testament (Revised)* (Chicago: Moody Press, 1990), 190; Charles C. Ryrie, *Ryrie Study Bible: New International Version* (Expanded ed.) (Chicago: Moody Publishers, 1994), 1751.

4. Crossway Bibles, *The ESV Study Bible* (Wheaton, IL: Crossway Bibles, 2008), 2187.

5. Ibid.

6. Paul N. Benware, *Survey of the New Testament (Revised)* (Chicago: Moody Press, 1990), 192.

7. Bruce B. Barton & G. R. Osborne, *1 & 2 Corinthians* (Wheaton, IL: Tyndale House, 1999), 6.

8. Ibid.

9. Craig L. Blomberg, *NT334 Book Study: Paul's First Letter to the Corinthians* (Bellingham, WA: Lexham Press, 2017), Segment 2.

10. David K. Lowery, 1 Corinthians. In J. F. Walvoord & R. B. Zuck (Eds.), *The Bible Knowledge Commentary: An Exposition of the Scriptures* (Wheaton, IL: Victor Books, 1985), Volume 2, 506.

11. Leon Morris, *1 Corinthians: An Introduction and Commentary* (Vol. 7) (Downers Grove, IL: InterVarsity Press, 1985), 30.

12. Marcus Dods, *The First Epistle to the Corinthians* (New York: Hodder & Stoughton; George H. Doran Company, not dated), 6.

13. Craig L. Blomberg, *NT334 Book Study: Paul's First Letter to the Corinthians* (Bellingham, WA: Lexham Press, 2017), Segment 6.

14. Gordon D. Fee, *The First Epistle to the Corinthians* (N. B. Stonehouse, F. F. Bruce, G. D. Fee & J. B. Green, Eds.) (Revised Edition) (Grand Rapids, MI; Cambridge, U.K.: William B. Eerdmans Publishing Company, 2014), 65.

15. See Duane Liftin, *Paul's Theology of Preaching* (Downer's Grove, Ill.: Intervarsity, 2015).

16. David K. Lowery, 1 Corinthians. In J. F. Walvoord & R. B. Zuck (Eds.), *The Bible Knowledge Commentary: An Exposition of the Scriptures* (Wheaton, IL: Victor Books, 1985), Volume 2, 509.

17. William Sailer, J. Creighton Christman, et al., *Religious and Theological Abstracts*, "Sanctification and Justification: A Unity of Distinctions" (Myerstown, PA: Religious and Theological Abstracts, 2012).

18. Charles C. Ryrie, *Basic Theology: A Popular Systematic Guide to Understanding Biblical Truth* (Chicago, IL: Moody Press, 1999), 343.

19. William Sailer, J. Creighton Christman, et al., *Religious and Theological Abstracts,* "Sanctification: The Work of the Holy Spirit and Scripture" (Myerstown, PA: Religious and Theological Abstracts, 2012); Charles C. Ryrie, *Basic Theology: A Popular Systematic Guide to Understanding Biblical Truth* (Chicago, IL: Moody Press, 1999), 442.

20. See a more thorough discussion of these concepts in my book, *Jesus on Trial, A Lawyer Affirms the Truth of the Gospel* (Washington, D.C.: Regnery Publishing, 2014), 76–80.

21. Millard J. Erickson, *Christian Theology,* (2nd ed.) (Grand Rapids, MI: Baker Book House, 1998), 1011.

22. Simon J. Kistemaker & William Hendriksen, *Exposition of the First Epistle to the Corinthians* (Vol. 18) (Grand Rapids: Baker Book House, 1953–2001), 59.

23. Mark Taylor, *1 Corinthians.* (E. R. Clendenen, Ed.) (Vol. 28) (Nashville, TN: B&H Publishing Group, 2014), 71.

24. Simon J. Kistemaker & William Hendriksen, *Exposition of the First Epistle to the Corinthians* (Vol. 18) (Grand Rapids: Baker Book House, 1953–2001), 65.

25. Dale Leschert, *The Flow of the New Testament* (Fearn, Great Britain: Christian Focus Publications, 2002), 258.

26. C. K. Barrett, *The First Epistle to the Corinthians* (London: Continuum, 1968), 56.

27. Crossway Bibles, *The ESV Study Bible* (Wheaton, IL: Crossway Bibles, 2008), 2193.

28. Simon J. Kistemaker & William Hendriksen, *Exposition of the First Epistle to the Corinthians* (Vol. 18) (Grand Rapids: Baker Book House, 1953–2001), 63.

29. Crossway Bibles, *The ESV Study Bible* (Wheaton, IL: Crossway Bibles, 2008), 2193.

30. Mark Taylor, *1 Corinthians.* (E. R. Clendenen, Ed.) (Vol. 28) (Nashville, TN: B&H Publishing Group, 2014), 73.

31. Alan F. Johnson, *1 Corinthians* (Vol. 7) (Downers Grove, IL: InterVarsity Press, 2004), 62.

32. Anthony C. Thiselton, *The First Epistle to the Corinthians: A Commentary on the Greek text* (Grand Rapids, MI: W.B. Eerdmans, 2000), 208–209.

33. David E. Garland, *1 Corinthians* (Grand Rapids, MI: Baker Academic, 2003), 82.

34. Ibid, 84.

35. Crossway Bibles, *The ESV Study Bible* (Wheaton, IL: Crossway Bibles, 2008), 910.

36. Walter C. Kaiser, Jr., A Neglected Text in Bibliology Discussions: 1 Corinthians 2:6–16 (*Westminster Theological Journal, 43* (2), 301–319, 1980).

37. Robert Gromacki, *Called to Be Saints: An Exposition of I Corinthians* (The Woodlands, TX: Kress Christian Publications, 2002), 42.

38. Bruce B. Barton & G. R. Osborne, *1 & 2 Corinthians* (Wheaton, IL: Tyndale House, 1999), 46.

39. Wendell Lee Willis, "The 'Mind of Christ' in 1 Corinthians 2, 16," *Bib* 70 (1989): 110–22; quoted in William Hendrickson & S. J. Kistemaker, *Exposition of the First Epistle to the Corinthians* (Vol. 18) (Grand Rapids: Baker Book House, 1953–2001), 94.

40. Wendell Lee Willis, "The 'Mind of Christ' in 1 Corinthians 2, 16," *Bib* 70 (1989): 118; quoted in David E. Garland, *1 Corinthians* (Grand Rapids, MI: Baker Academic, 2003), 102.

41. Steve Moyise, *Paul and Scripture* (London: SPCK, 2010), 90.

42. David Guzik, *1 Corinthians* (Santa Barbara, CA: David Guzik, 2013).

43. A. W. Tozer, *Reclaiming Christianity: A Call to Authentic Faith*, (J. L. Snyder, Ed.) (Ventura, CA: Regal, 2009), 120.

44. Ibid, 129–130.

45. Mark Taylor, *1 Corinthians*. (E. R. Clendenen, Ed.) (Vol. 28) (Nashville, TN: B&H Publishing Group, 2014), 98.

46. Morna Hooker, "Hard Sayings: 1 Cor. 3:2," *Theology* 69 (1966): 21; cf. 19–22, cited in Anthony C. Thiselton, *The First Epistle to the Corinthians: A Commentary on the Greek text* (Grand Rapids, MI: W.B. Eerdmans, 2000), 291–292.

47. Gordon D. Fee, *The First Epistle to the Corinthians* (N. B. Stonehouse, F. F. Bruce, G. D. Fee & J. B. Green, Eds.) (Revised Edition) (Grand Rapids, MI; Cambridge, U.K.: William B. Eerdmans Publishing Company, 2014), 125.

48. Richard B. Hays, *First Corinthians* (Louisville, KY: John Knox Press, 1997), 51.

49. Ibid.

50. Ibid, 53.

51. David K. Lowery, 1 Corinthians. In J. F. Walvoord & R. B. Zuck (Eds.), *The Bible Knowledge Commentary: An Exposition of the Scriptures* (Wheaton, IL: Victor Books, 1985), Volume 2, 512.

52. Richard B. Hays, *First Corinthians* (Louisville, KY: John Knox Press, 1997), 55.

53. D. R. Sunukjian, Amos. In J. F. Walvoord & R. B. Zuck (Eds.), *The Bible Knowledge Commentary: An Exposition of the Scriptures* (Wheaton, IL: Victor Books, 1985), Volume 1, 1437.

54. Bruce B. Barton & G. R. Osborne, *1 & 2 Corinthians* (Wheaton, IL: Tyndale House, 1999), 54.

55. David Prior, *The Message of 1 Corinthians: Life in the Local Church* (Leicester, England; Downers Grove, IL: InterVarsity Press, 1985), 59.

56. Richard B. Hays, *First Corinthians* (Louisville, KY: John Knox Press, 1997), 51.

57. Ibid.

58. Ben Witherington, III, *Conflict and Community in Corinth: A Socio-Rhetorical Commentary on 1 and 2 Corinthians* (Grand Rapids, MI: Wm. B. Eerdmans Publishing Co., 1995), 134–135.

59. Richard B. Hays, *First Corinthians* (Louisville, KY: John Knox Press, 1997), 56–57.

60. Ibid, 57.

61. Ben Witherington, III, *Conflict and Community in Corinth: A Socio-Rhetorical Commentary on 1 and 2 Corinthians* (Grand Rapids, MI: Wm. B. Eerdmans Publishing Co., 1995), 133.

62. Gordon D. Fee, *The First Epistle to the Corinthians* (N. B. Stonehouse, F. F. Bruce, G. D. Fee & J. B. Green, Eds.) (Revised Edition) (Grand Rapids, MI; Cambridge, U.K.: William B. Eerdmans Publishing Company, 2014), 166–167.

63. Simon J. Kistemaker & William Hendriksen, *Exposition of the First Epistle to the Corinthians* (Vol. 18) (Grand Rapids: Baker Book House, 1953–2001), 122.

64. Gordon D. Fee, *The First Epistle to the Corinthians* (N. B. Stonehouse, F. F. Bruce, G. D. Fee & J. B. Green, Eds.) (Revised Edition) (Grand Rapids, MI; Cambridge, U.K.: William B. Eerdmans Publishing Company, 2014), 167.

65. Scot McKnight, *The Letter of James* (Grand Rapids, MI; Cambridge, UK: William B. Eerdmans Publishing Company, 2011), 272.

66. David E. Garland, *1 Corinthians*. Grand Rapids, MI: Baker Academic, 2003), 127.

67. Bruce B. Barton & G. R. Osborne, *1 & 2 Corinthians* (Wheaton, IL: Tyndale House, 1999), 59.

68. Simon J. Kistemaker & William Hendriksen, *Exposition of the First Epistle to the Corinthians* (Vol. 18) (Grand Rapids: Baker Book House, 1953–2001), 133.

69. Crossway Bibles, *The ESV Study Bible* (Wheaton, IL: Crossway Bibles, 2008), 2196.

70. John MacArthur, Jr., *The MacArthur Study Bible* (electronic ed.) (Nashville, TN: Word Pub, 1997), 1734.

71. Marcus Tullius Cicero, *The Orations of Marcus Tullius Cicero, literally translated by C. D. Yonge, B. A.* (C. D. Yonge, Ed.) (Medford, MA: Henry G. Bohn, York Street, Covent Garden, 1856), Clu. 5.14–6.15; William R. G. Loader, *The New Testament on Sexuality* (Grand Rapids, MI; Cambridge, U.K.: William B. Eerdmans Publishing Company, 2012), 162.

72. Craig Blomberg, *1 Corinthians* (Grand Rapids, MI: Zondervan Publishing House, 1994), 106.

73. Douglas J. Moo, The Letters and Revelation, In D. A. Carson, *NIV Zondervan Study Bible: Built on the Truth of Scripture and Centered on the Gospel Message* (Grand Rapids, MI: Zondervan, 2015), 2335.

74. Gordon D. Fee, *The First Epistle to the Corinthians* (N. B. Stonehouse, F. F. Bruce, G. D. Fee & J. B. Green, Eds.) (Revised Edition) (Grand Rapids, MI; Cambridge, U.K.: William B. Eerdmans Publishing Company, 2014), 226.

75. Ibid, 225.

76. Simon J. Kistemaker & William Hendriksen, *Exposition of the First Epistle to the Corinthians* (Vol. 18) (Grand Rapids: Baker Book House, 1953–2001), 172.

77. Gordon D. Fee, *The First Epistle to the Corinthians* (N. B. Stonehouse, F. F. Bruce, G. D. Fee & J. B. Green, Eds.) (Revised Edition) (Grand Rapids, MI; Cambridge, U.K.: William B. Eerdmans Publishing Company, 2014), 228.

78. Crossway Bibles, *The ESV Study Bible* (Wheaton, IL: Crossway Bibles, 2008), 2198.

79. Larry Richards, *Every Angel in the Bible* (Nashville: T. Nelson, 1997), 200.

80. Mark Taylor, *1 Corinthians*, (E. R. Clendenen, Ed.) (Vol. 28) (Nashville, TN: B&H Publishing Group, 2014), 148.

81. John F. MacArthur, Jr. *1 Corinthians* (Chicago: Moody Press, 1984), 141.

82. Ibid.

83. W. Harold Mare, 1 Corinthians. In F. E. Gaebelein, *The Expositor's Bible Commentary: Romans through Galatians* (Vol. 10) (Grand Rapids, MI: Zondervan Publishing House, 1976), 224.

84. Craig Blomberg, *1 Corinthians* (Grand Rapids, MI: Zondervan Publishing House, 1994), 126.

85. Leon Morris, *1 Corinthians: An Introduction and Commentary* (Vol. 7) (Downers Grove, IL: InterVarsity Press, 1985), 101.

86. Alan F. Johnson, *1 Corinthians* (Vol. 7) (Downers Grove, IL: InterVarsity Press, 2004), 103.

87. Bruce B. Barton & G. R. Osborne, *1 & 2 Corinthians* (Wheaton, IL: Tyndale House, 1999), 91–92.

88. Simon J. Kistemaker & William Hendriksen, *Exposition of the First Epistle to the Corinthians* (Vol. 18) (Grand Rapids: Baker Book House, 1953–2001), 210.

89. John F. MacArthur, Jr. *1 Corinthians* (Chicago: Moody Press, 1984), 156.

90. Ibid, 155.

91. D. F. Wright, Sexuality, Sexual Ethics. In G. F. Hawthorne, R. P. Martin & D. G. Reid (Eds.), *Dictionary of Paul and his letters* (pp. 871–875) (Downers Grove, IL: InterVarsity Press, 1993).

92. Ibid.

93. Mark Taylor, *1 Corinthians*. (E. R. Clendenen, Ed.) (Vol. 28) (Nashville, TN: B&H Publishing Group, 2014), 166.

94. Gordon D. Fee, *The First Epistle to the Corinthians* (N. B. Stonehouse, F. F. Bruce, G. D. Fee & J. B. Green, Eds.) (Revised Edition) (Grand Rapids, MI; Cambridge, U.K.: William B. Eerdmans Publishing Company, 2014), 280.

95. Ibid.

96. Charles C. Ryrie, *Ryrie Study Bible: New International Version* (Expanded ed.) (Chicago: Moody Publishers, 1994), 1762.

97. Ibid.

98. Bruce B. Barton & G. R. Osborne, *1 & 2 Corinthians* (Wheaton, IL: Tyndale House, 1999), 104.

99. Ibid.

100. Roy E. Ciampa & Brian S. Rosner, *The First Letter to the Corinthians* (Grand Rapids, MI; Cambridge, U.K.: William B. Eerdmans Publishing Company, 2010), 323.

101. Norman L. Geisler & Thomas A. Howe, *When Critics Ask : A Popular Handbook on Bible Difficulties* (Wheaton, Ill.: Victor Books, 1992), 510.

102. Walter C. Kaiser, Jr., et al., *Hard sayings of the Bible* (Downers Grove, IL: InterVarsity), 593.

103. Charles C. Ryrie, *Ryrie Study Bible: New International Version* (Expanded ed.) (Chicago: Moody Publishers, 1994), 1762.

104. Crossway Bibles, *The ESV Study Bible* (Wheaton, IL: Crossway Bibles, 2008), 2202.

105. D. A. Carson, Weekend: When Knowledge Is Not Enough. (R. C. Sproul Jr., Ed.) *Tabletalk Magazine, March 1996: All God's Children*, 1996, 42.

106. Craig L. Blomberg, *NT334 Book Study: Paul's First Letter to the Corinthians* (Bellingham, WA: Lexham Press, 2017), Segment 45.

CHAPTER 9

1.   Mark Water, *The New Encyclopedia of Christian Quotations,* (Alresford, Hampshire: John Hunt Publishers Ltd., 2000), 487.

2.   Roy E. Ciampa & Brian S. Rosner, *The First Letter to the Corinthians* (Grand Rapids, MI; Cambridge, U.K.: William B. Eerdmans Publishing Company, 2010), 402.

3.   Bruce B. Barton & G. R. Osborne, *1 & 2 Corinthians* (Wheaton, IL: Tyndale House, 1999), 123.

4.   John Chrysostom (1889), Homilies of St. John Chrysostom, Archbishop of Constantinople, on the First Epistle of St. Paul the Apostle to the Corinthians. In P. Schaff, H. K. Cornish, J. Medley & T. B. Chambers (Trans.), *Saint Chrysostom: Homilies on the Epistles of Paul to the Corinthians* (Vol. 12) (New York: Christian Literature Company, 1889), Hom. 1 Cor. 21.7, page 122.

5.   Mark Taylor, *1 Corinthians* (E. R. Clendenen, Ed.) (Vol. 28) (Nashville, TN: B&H Publishing Group, 2014), 217.

6. Roy E. Ciampa & Brian S. Rosner, *The First Letter to the Corinthians* (Grand Rapids, MI; Cambridge, U.K.: William B. Eerdmans Publishing Company, 2010), 411.

7. Craig L. Blomberg, *NT334 Book Study: Paul's First Letter to the Corinthians* (Bellingham, WA: Lexham Press, 2017), Segment 40. Of course, Paul firmly believes the Gospel fulfills the hopes of Israel. He utilizes the same practice when evangelizing Gentiles.

8. Bruce B. Barton & G. R. Osborne, *1 & 2 Corinthians* (Wheaton, IL: Tyndale House, 1999), 129–130.

9. Mark Taylor, *1 Corinthians* (E. R. Clendenen, Ed.) (Vol. 28) (Nashville, TN: B&H Publishing Group, 2014), 224; Bruce B. Barton & G. R. Osborne, *1 & 2 Corinthians* (Wheaton, IL: Tyndale House, 1999), 132.

10. Leon Morris, *1 Corinthians: An Introduction and Commentary* (Vol. 7) (Downers Grove, IL: InterVarsity Press, 1985), 138.

11. John F. MacArthur, Jr. *1 Corinthians* (Chicago: Moody Press, 1984), 214–215.

12. David K. Lowery, 1 Corinthians. In J. F. Walvoord & R. B. Zuck (Eds.), *The Bible Knowledge Commentary: An Exposition of the Scriptures* (Wheaton, IL: Victor Books, 1985), Volume 2, 526.

13. Bruce B. Barton & G. R. Osborne, *1 & 2 Corinthians* (Wheaton, IL: Tyndale House, 1999), 138.

14. Craig L. Blomberg, *NT334 Book Study: Paul's First Letter to the Corinthians* (Bellingham, WA: Lexham Press, 2017), Segment 45.

15. Richard B. Hays, *First Corinthians* (Louisville, KY: John Knox Press, 1997), 234–235.

16. Roy E. Ciampa & Brian S. Rosner, *The First Letter to the Corinthians* (Grand Rapids, MI; Cambridge, U.K.: William B. Eerdmans Publishing Company, 2010), 479.

17. Craig L. Blomberg, *NT334 Book Study: Paul's First Letter to the Corinthians* (Bellingham, WA: Lexham Press, 2017), Segment 45.

18. Roy E. Ciampa & Brian S. Rosner, *The First Letter to the Corinthians* (Grand Rapids, MI; Cambridge, U.K.: William B. Eerdmans Publishing Company, 2010), 469.

19. Douglas J. Moo, The Letters and Revelation, In D. A. Carson, *NIV Zondervan Study Bible: Built on the Truth of Scripture and Centered on the Gospel Message* (Grand Rapids, MI: Zondervan, 2015), 2345.

20. John F. MacArthur, Jr. *1 Corinthians* (Chicago: Moody Press, 1984), 253.

21. Ibid.

22. Craig L. Blomberg, *NT334 Book Study: Paul's First Letter to the Corinthians* (Bellingham, WA: Lexham Press, 2017), Segment 48.

23. Ibid, Segment 50.

24. Simon J. Kistemaker & William Hendriksen, *Exposition of the First Epistle to the Corinthians* (Vol. 18) (Grand Rapids: Baker Book House, 1953–2001), 373.

25. Bruce B. Barton & G. R. Osborne, *1 & 2 Corinthians* (Wheaton, IL: Tyndale House, 1999), 157.

26. Gordon D. Fee, *The First Epistle to the Corinthians* (N. B. Stonehouse, F. F. Bruce, G. D. Fee & J. B. Green, Eds.) (Revised Edition) (Grand Rapids, MI; Cambridge, U.K.: William B. Eerdmans Publishing Company, 2014), 560.

27. Paul Barnett, *1 Corinthians: Holiness and Hope of a Rescued People* (Ross-shire, Scotland: Christian Focus Publications, 2000), 209.

28. Anthony C. Thiselton, *The First Epistle to the Corinthians: A Commentary on the Greek text* (Grand Rapids, MI: W.B. Eerdmans, 2000), 889.

29. James Montgomery Boice, *Romans: God and History* (Vol. 3) (Grand Rapids, MI: Baker Book House, 1991), 1210.

30. Wayne A. Grudem, *Systematic Theology: An Introduction to Biblical Doctrine* (Leicester, England; Grand Rapids, MI: Inter-Varsity Press; Zondervan Pub. House, 2004), 1016.

31. Bruce B. Barton & G. R. Osborne, *1 & 2 Corinthians* (Wheaton, IL: Tyndale House, 1999), 168–169.

32. *New Living Translation Study Bible*, (Carol Stream, IL: Tyndale House Publishers, Inc., 2008).

33. David Prior, *The Message of 1 Corinthians: Life in the Local Church* (Leicester, England; Downers Grove, IL: InterVarsity Press, 1985), 210.

34. Arnold Bittlenger, *Gifts and Graces* (Hodder & Stoughton Ltd, 1967), 53.

35. Jonathan Edwards, *Ethical Writings* (P. Ramsey & J. E. Smith, Eds.) (Vol. 8) (New Haven; London: Yale University Press, 1989), 185.

36. Paul W. Barnett, *1 Corinthians: Holiness and Hope of a Rescued People* (Ross-shire, Scotland: Christian Focus Publications, 2000), 245.

37. Crossway Bibles, *The ESV Study Bible* (Wheaton, IL: Crossway Bibles, 2008), 2052.

38. R. L. Wilken & J. L. Kovacs, (Eds.), *1 Corinthians: Interpreted by Early Christian Commentators.* (J. L. Kovacs, Trans.) (Grand Rapids, MI; Cambridge, UK: William B. Eerdmans Publishing Company, 2005), 219.

39. Anthony C. Thiselton, Glossolalia. In *The Thiselton Companion to Christian Theology* (pp. 344–345) (Grand Rapids, MI; Cambridge, U.K.: William B. Eerdmans Publishing Company, 2015), 344; see also Paul J. Achtemeier, Harper & Row and Society of Biblical Literature, In *Harper's Bible dictionary* (1st ed.) (San Francisco: Harper & Row, 1985), 1082.

40. Wayne A. Grudem, *Systematic Theology: An Introduction to Biblical Doctrine*, (Leicester, England; Grand Rapids, MI: Inter-Varsity Press; Zondervan Pub. House, 2004), 1071.

41. V. D. Verbrugge, 1 Corinthians. In T. Longman III &. Garland, David E., *The Expositor's Bible Commentary: Romans–Galatians (Revised Edition)* (Vol. 11) (Grand Rapids, MI: Zondervan, 2008), 381.

42. Douglas J. Moo, The Letters and Revelation, In D. A. Carson, *NIV Zondervan Study Bible: Built on the Truth of Scripture and Centered on the Gospel Message* (Grand Rapids, MI: Zondervan, 2015), 2351; Simon J. Kistemaker & William Hendriksen, *Exposition of the First Epistle to the Corinthians* (Vol. 18) (Grand Rapids: Baker Book House, 1953–2001), 490.

43. Richard Oster, *1 Corinthians* (Joplin, MO: College Press Pub. Co., 1995).

44. C. K. Barrett, *The First Epistle to the Corinthians* (London: Continuum, 1968), 320.

45. Craig L. Blomberg, *NT334 Book Study: Paul's First Letter to the Corinthians* (Bellingham, WA: Lexham Press, 2017), Segment 63.

46. V. D. Verbrugge, 1 Corinthians. In T. Longman III &. Garland, David E., *The Expositor's Bible Commentary:*

Romans–Galatians (Revised Edition) (Vol. 11) (Grand Rapids, MI: Zondervan, 2008), 382.

47. Mark Taylor, *1 Corinthians.* (E. R. Clendenen, Ed.) (Vol. 28) (Nashville, TN: B&H Publishing Group, 2014), 341.

48. Crossway Bibles, *The ESV Study Bible* (Wheaton, IL: Crossway Bibles, 2008), 2212.

49. Leon Morris, *1 Corinthians: An Introduction and Commentary* (Vol. 7) (Downers Grove, IL: InterVarsity Press, 1985), 189.

50. John MacArthur, Jr. (Ed.) *The MacArthur Study Bible* (electronic ed.) (Nashville, TN: Word Pub, 1997), 1753.

51. David E. Garland, *1 Corinthians* (Grand Rapids, MI: Baker Academic, 2003), 665–666; Richard B. Hays, *First Corinthians* (Louisville, KY: John Knox Press, 1997), 247.

52. Richard B. Hays, *First Corinthians* (Louisville, KY: John Knox Press, 1997), 247.

53. Bruce B. Barton & G. R. Osborne, *1 & 2 Corinthians* (Wheaton, IL: Tyndale House, 1999), 213.

54. Paul W. Barnett, *1 Corinthians: Holiness and Hope of a Rescued People* (Ross-shire, Scotland: Christian Focus Publications, 2000), 266.

55. Ben Witherington, III, *Conflict and Community in Corinth: A Socio-Rhetorical Commentary on 1 and 2 Corinthians* (Grand Rapids, MI: Wm. B. Eerdmans Publishing Co., 1995), 287.

56. David K. Lowery, 1 Corinthians. In J. F. Walvoord & R. B. Zuck (Eds.), *The Bible Knowledge Commentary: An Exposition of the Scriptures* (Wheaton, IL: Victor Books, 1985), Volume 2, 541.

57. David E. Garland, *1 Corinthians* (Grand Rapids, MI: Baker Academic, 2003), 673.

58. John F. MacArthur, Jr. *1 Corinthians* (Chicago: Moody Press, 1984), 392.
59. Warren W. Wiersbe, *Wiersbe's Expository Outlines on the New Testament* (Wheaton, IL: Victor Books, 1992), 462.
60. John D. Barry, Douglas Mangum, et al., *Faithlife Study Bible* (Bellingham, WA: Lexham Press, 2012, 2016).
61. L. M. McDonald, 1 Corinthians. In C. A. Evans & C. A. Bubeck (Eds.), *The Bible Knowledge Background Commentary: Acts–Philemon* (First Edition, pp. 255–366) (Colorado Springs, CO: David C Cook, 2004), 354.
62. William G. T. Shedd, *A History of Christian Doctrine* (Minneapolis: Klock & Klock Christian Publishers, n.d.), Vol. 2, page 403.
63. Norman L. Geisler, *The Battle for the Resurrection* (Eugene, OR: Wipf & Stock Publishers, 1992), 30.
64. N. T. Wright, *The Resurrection of the Son of God* (London: Society for Promoting Christian Knowledge, 2003), 278.
65. Gary R. Habermas, Experiences of the Risen Jesus: The Foundational Historical Issue in the Early Proclamatino of the Resurreciton, *Dialog: A Journal of Theology*, Vol. 45; No. 3 (Fall, 2006), pp. 288–297; published by Blackwell Publishing, UK. http://www.garyhabermas.com/articles/dialog_rexperience/dialog_rexperiences.htm.
66. W. Harold Mare, 1 Corinthians. In F. E. Gaebelein, *The Expositor's Bible Commentary: Romans through Galatians* (Vol. 10) (Grand Rapids, MI: Zondervan Publishing House, 1976), 282.
67. Mark Taylor, *1 Corinthians*. (E. R. Clendenen, Ed.) (Vol. 28) (Nashville, TN: B&H Publishing Group, 2014), 374.

68. Paul W. Barnett, *1 Corinthians: Holiness and Hope of a Rescued People* (Ross-shire, Scotland: Christian Focus Publications, 2000), 278.

69. Norman L. Geisler, Resurrection, Evidence For. In *Baker encyclopedia of Christian apologetics* (Grand Rapids, MI: Baker Books, 1999), 651–656.

70. David K. Lowery, 1 Corinthians. In J. F. Walvoord & R. B. Zuck (Eds.), *The Bible Knowledge Commentary: An Exposition of the Scriptures* (Wheaton, IL: Victor Books, 1985), Volume 2, 543.

71. Paul W. Barnett, *1 Corinthians: Holiness and Hope of a Rescued People* (Ross-shire, Scotland: Christian Focus Publications, 2000), 282–283.

72. Ibid, 285.

73. Got Questions Ministries, *Got Questions? Bible Questions Answered* (Bellingham, WA: Logos Bible Software, 2002–2013).

74. S. J. Wellum, The Deity of Christ in the Apostolic Witness, In C. W. Morgan & R. A. Peterson (Eds.), *The Deity of Christ* (Wheaton, IL: Crossway, 2011), 131.

75. Bruce B. Barton & G. R. Osborne, *1 & 2 Corinthians* (Wheaton, IL: Tyndale House, 1999), 230.

76. W. Harold Mare, 1 Corinthians. In F. E. Gaebelein, *The Expositor's Bible Commentary: Romans through Galatians* (Vol. 10) (Grand Rapids, MI: Zondervan Publishing House, 1976), 288.

77. Crossway Bibles, *The ESV Study Bible* (Wheaton, IL: Crossway Bibles, 2008), 2215.

78. Charles C. Ryrie, *Ryrie study Bible: New International Version* (Expanded ed.) (Chicago: Moody Publishers, 1994), 1776.

79. Douglas J. Moo, The Letters and Revelation, In D. A. Carson, *NIV Zondervan Study Bible: Built on the Truth of Scripture and Centered on the Gospel Message* (Grand Rapids, MI: Zondervan, 2015), 2356.

80. David Guzik, *1 Corinthians* (Santa Barbara, CA: David Guzik, 2013).

81. John MacArthur, Jr., *The MacArthur Study Bible* (electronic ed.) (Nashville, TN: Word Pub, 1997), 1757.

82. David Prior, *The Message of 1 Corinthians: Life in the Local Church* (Leicester, England; Downers Grove, IL: InterVarsity Press, 1985), 274.

83. George Eldon Ladd, *I Believe in the Resurrection of Jesus* (Grand Rapids: William B. Eerdmans Publishing Company, 1975), 115, 117.

84. W. Harold Mare, 1 Corinthians. In F. E. Gaebelein, *The Expositor's Bible Commentary: Romans through Galatians* (Vol. 10) (Grand Rapids, MI: Zondervan Publishing House, 1976), 290.

85. Gordon D. Fee, *The First Epistle to the Corinthians* (N. B. Stonehouse, F. F. Bruce, G. D. Fee & J. B. Green, Eds.) (Revised Edition) (Grand Rapids, MI; Cambridge, U.K.: William B. Eerdmans Publishing Company, 2014), 891.

86. We explore this in greater depth in the Chapter on Romans.

87. Craig L. Blomberg, *NT334 Book Study: Paul's First Letter to the Corinthians* (Bellingham, WA: Lexham Press, 2017), Segment 76.

88. Gordon D. Fee, *The First Epistle to the Corinthians* (N. B. Stonehouse, F. F. Bruce, G. D. Fee & J. B. Green, Eds.) (Revised Edition) (Grand Rapids, MI; Cambridge, U.K.: William B. Eerdmans Publishing Company, 2014), 892.

89. Paul Barnett, *1 Corinthians: Holiness and Hope of a Rescued People* (Ross-shire, Scotland: Christian Focus Publications, 2000), 299.

90. Roy E. Ciampa & Brian S. Rosner, *The First Letter to the Corinthians* (Grand Rapids, MI; Cambridge, U.K.: William B. Eerdmans Publishing Company, 2010), 860.

CHAPTER 10

1. W. W. Wiersbe, *Wiersbe's Expository Outlines on the New Testament*, (Wheaton, IL: Victor Books, 1992), 475.

2. Crossway Bibles, *The ESV Study Bible* (Wheaton, IL: Crossway Bibles, 2008), 2219.

3. Bruce B. Barton & Grant R. Osborne, *1 & 2 Corinthians* (Wheaton, IL: Tyndale House, 1999), 265.

4. Edward E. Hindson & Woodrow Kroll (Eds.) *KJV Bible Commentary* (Nashville: Thomas Nelson, 1994), 2334.

5. Ibid.

6. David S. Dockery, The Pauline Letters. In D. S. Dockery, *Holman Concise Bible Commentary* (Nashville, TN: Broadman & Holman Publishers, 1998), 561.

7. Bruce B. Barton & Grant R. Osborne, *1 & 2 Corinthians* (Wheaton, IL: Tyndale House, 1999), 258.

8. Murray J. Harris 2 Corinthians. In F. E. Gaebelein, *The Expositor's Bible Commentary: Romans through Galatians* (Vol. 10) (Grand Rapids, MI: Zondervan Publishing House, 1976), 302.

9. Crossway Bibles, *The ESV Study Bible* (Wheaton, IL: Crossway Bibles, 2008), 2220.

10. Murray J. Harris 2 Corinthians. In F. E. Gaebelein, *The Expositor's Bible Commentary: Romans through Galatians* (Vol. 10) (Grand Rapids, MI: Zondervan Publishing House, 1976), 303; Edward E. Hindson & Woodrow

Kroll (Eds.) *KJV Bible Commentary* (Nashville: Thomas Nelson, 1994), 2334.

11. Murray J. Harris 2 Corinthians. In F. E. Gaebelein, *The Expositor's Bible Commentary: Romans through Galatians* (Vol. 10) (Grand Rapids, MI: Zondervan Publishing House, 1976), 302–303.

12. John F. MacArthur, *2 Corinthians* (Chicago: Moody Publishers, 2003), 1.

13. Ibid, 2.

14. William R. Baker, *2 Corinthians* (Joplin, MO: College Press Pub, 1999), 66.

15. Bruce B. Barton & Grant R. Osborne, *1 & 2 Corinthians* (Wheaton, IL: Tyndale House, 1999), 271.

16. David E. Garland, *2 Corinthians* (Vol. 29) (Nashville: Broadman & Holman Publishers, 1999), 85.

17. David Guzik, *2 Corinthians* (Santa Barbara, CA: David Guzik, 2013).

18. David K. Lowery, 2 Corinthians. In J. F. Walvoord & R. B. Zuck (Eds.), *The Bible Knowledge Commentary: An Exposition of the Scriptures* (Wheaton, IL: Victor Books. 1985), 556.

19. Bruce B. Barton & Grant R. Osborne, *1 & 2 Corinthians* (Wheaton, IL: Tyndale House, 1999), 284.

20. Ibid, 290.

21. Simon J. Kistemaker & William Hendriksen, *Exposition of the Second Epistle to the Corinthians* (Vol. 19) (Grand Rapids: Baker Book House, 1953–2001), 79.

22. John G. Butler, *Analytical Bible Expositor: I & II Corinthians* (Clinton, IA: LBC Publications, 2009), 180.

23. David Abernathy, *An Exegetical Summary of 2 Corinthians* (2nd ed.) (Dallas, TX: SIL International, 2008), 78.

24. Geoffrey W. Grogan, *2 Corinthians: The Glories and Responsibilities of Christian Service* (Ross-shire, Great Britian: Christian Focus Publications, 2007), 71.

25. John Calvin & John Pringle, *Commentaries on the Epistles of Paul the Apostle to the Corinthians* (Bellingham, WA: Logos Bible Software, 2010), Volume 2, 152.

26. Crossway Bibles, *The ESV Study Bible* (Wheaton, IL: Crossway Bibles, 2008), 2226.

27. John Calvin & John Pringle, *Commentaries on the Epistles of Paul the Apostle to the Corinthians* (Bellingham, WA: Logos Bible Software, 2010), Volume 2, 153.

28. William R. Baker, *2 Corinthians* (Joplin, MO: College Press Pub, 1999), 118.

29. Murray J. Harris, 2 Corinthians. In F. E. Gaebelein, *The Expositor's Bible Commentary: Romans through Galatians* (Vol. 10) (Grand Rapids, MI: Zondervan Publishing House, 1976), 337.

30. Simon J. Kistemaker & William Hendriksen, *Exposition of the Second Epistle to the Corinthians* (Vol. 19) (Grand Rapids: Baker Book House, 1953–2001), 143–144.

31. William MacDonald, *Believer's Bible Commentary: Old and New Testaments*. (A. Farstad, Ed.) (Nashville: Thomas Nelson, 1995), 1837.

32. Douglas J. Moo, *The Epistle to the Romans* (Grand Rapids, MI: Wm. B. Eerdmans Publishing Co., 1996), 503.

33. Geoffrey W. Grogan, *2 Corinthians: The Glories and Responsibilities of Christian Service* (Ross-shire, Great Britain: Christian Focus Publications, 2007), 136.

34. John MacArthur, Jr. (Ed.) *The MacArthur Study Bible* (electronic ed.) (Nashville, TN: Word Pub, 1997), 1770.

35. William MacDonald, *Believer's Bible Commentary: Old and New Testaments* (A. Farstad, Ed.) (Nashville: Thomas Nelson, 1995), 1839.

36. Paul W. Barnett, *The Second Epistle to the Corinthians* (Grand Rapids, MI: Wm. B. Eerdmans Publishing Co., 1997), 276.

37. William R. Baker, *2 Corinthians* (Joplin, MO: College Press Pub, 1999), 223.

38. David E. Garland, *2 Corinthians* (Vol. 29) (Nashville: Broadman & Holman Publishers, 1999), 284.

39. Bruce B. Barton & Grant R. Osborne, *1 & 2 Corinthians* (Wheaton, IL: Tyndale House, 1999), 355.

40. David E. Garland, *2 Corinthians* (Vol. 29) (Nashville: Broadman & Holman Publishers, 1999), 300.

41. David Guzik, *2 Corinthians* (Santa Barbara, CA: David Guzik, 2013).

42. John MacArthur, Jr., *The MacArthur Study Bible* (electronic ed.) (Nashville, TN: Word Pub, 1997), 1772.

43. N. T. Wright, *Paul for Everyone: 2 Corinthians* (London: Society for Promoting Christian Knowledge, 2004), 66–67.

44. David E. Garland, *2 Corinthians* (Vol. 29) (Nashville: Broadman & Holman Publishers, 1999), 304.

45. John MacArthur, Jr., *The MacArthur Study Bible* (electronic ed.) (Nashville, TN: Word Pub, 1997), 1773.

46. J. Philip Arthur, *Strength in Weakness: 2 Corinthians Simply Explained* (Darlington, England: Evangelical Press, 2004), 149.

47. Crossway Bibles, *The ESV Study Bible* (Wheaton, IL: Crossway Bibles, 2008), 2233.

48. D. A. Carson,, *NIV Zondervan Study Bible: Built on the Truth of Scripture and Centered on the Gospel Message* (Grand Rapids, MI: Zondervan, 2015), 2371.

49. Ibid.

50. John MacArthur, Jr., *The MacArthur Study Bible* (electronic ed.) (Nashville, TN: Word Pub, 1997), 1776.

51. Mark A. Seifrid, *The Pillar New Testament Commentary: The Second Letter to the Corinthians* (D. A. Carson, Ed.) (Grand Rapids, MI; Cambridge, U.K.; England: William B. Eerdmans Publishing Company; Apollos, 2014), 356.

52. Bruce B. Barton & Grant R. Osborne, *1 & 2 Corinthians* (Wheaton, IL: Tyndale House, 1999), 407.

53. David E. Garland, *2 Corinthians* (Vol. 29) (Nashville: Broadman & Holman Publishers, 1999), 410.

54. Simon J. Kistemaker & William Hendriksen, *Exposition of the Second Epistle to the Corinthians* (Vol. 19) (Grand Rapids: Baker Book House, 1953–2001), 316.

55. George W. Clark, *Romans and I and II Corinthians: Commentary* (Philadelphia: American Baptist Publication Society, 1897), 384–385.

56. Crossway Bibles, *The ESV Study Bible* (Wheaton, IL: Crossway Bibles, 2008), 2235.

57. Chad Owen Brand, Charles Draper, et al. (Eds.) Meekness. In *Holman Illustrated Bible Dictionary* (Nashville, TN: Holman Bible Publishers, 2003), 1098.

58. J. C. Connell, Meekness. In D. R. W. Wood, I. H. Marshall, A. R. Millard, J. I. Packer & D. J. Wiseman (Eds.), *New Bible Dictionary* (3rd ed.) (Leicester, England; Downers Grove, IL: InterVarsity Press, 1996), 747.

59. Simon J. Kistemaker & William Hendriksen, *Exposition of the Second Epistle to the Corinthians* (Vol. 19) (Grand Rapids: Baker Book House, 1953–2001), 334.

60. J. Philip Arthur, *Strength in Weakness: 2 Corinthians Simply Explained* (Darlington, England: Evangelical Press, 2004), 183.

61. Ibid.

62. Linda L. Belleville, *2 Corinthians* (Vol. 8) (Downers Grove, IL: InterVarsity Press, 1996).

63. William R. Baker, *2 Corinthians* (Joplin, MO: College Press Pub, 1999), 415.

64. Crossway Bibles, *The ESV Study Bible* (Wheaton, IL: Crossway Bibles, 2008), 2238.

65. Ibid.

66. C. K. Barrett, *The Second Epistle to the Corinthians* (London: Continuum, 1973), 311.

67. Mark A. Seifrid, *The Pillar New Testament Commentary: The Second Letter to the Corinthians* (D. A. Carson, Ed.) (Grand Rapids, MI; Cambridge, U.K.; England: William B. Eerdmans Publishing Company; Apollos, 2014), 444; John MacArthur, Jr., *The MacArthur Study Bible* (electronic ed.) (Nashville, TN: Word Pub, 1997), 1783.

68. J. Philip Arthur, *Strength in Weakness: 2 Corinthians Simply Explained* (Darlington, England: Evangelical Press, 2004), 222.

69. John G. Butler, *Analytical Bible Expositor: I & II Corinthians* (Clinton, IA: LBC Publications, 2009), 253.

70. Linda L. Belleville, *2 Corinthians* (Vol. 8) (Downers Grove, IL: InterVarsity Press, 1996).

71. David J. MacLeod, Surprised by the Power of the Spirit, *Emmaus Journal*, Volume 10, 121, 2001.

72. Mark A. Seifrid, *The Pillar New Testament Commentary: The Second Letter to the Corinthians* (D. A. Carson, Ed.) (Grand Rapids, MI; Cambridge, U.K.; England: William B. Eerdmans Publishing Company; Apollos, 2014), 463.

73. David E. Garland, *2 Corinthians* (Vol. 29) (Nashville: Broadman & Holman Publishers, 1999), 533.

74. Ibid, 536.

75. Crossway Bibles, *The ESV Study Bible* (Wheaton, IL: Crossway Bibles, 2008), 2239.

76. Paul W. Barnett, *The Second Epistle to the Corinthians* (Grand Rapids, MI: Wm. B. Eerdmans Publishing Co., 1997), 598–599.

77. David K. Lowery, 2 Corinthians. In J. F. Walvoord & R. B. Zuck (Eds.), *The Bible Knowledge Commentary: An Exposition of the Scriptures* (Wheaton, IL: Victor Books, 1985), 553.

78. John F. MacArthur, *2 Corinthians* (Chicago: Moody Publishers, 2003), 6.

79. Paul W. Barnett, *The Second Epistle to the Corinthians* (Grand Rapids, MI: Wm. B. Eerdmans Publishing Co., 1997), 598–599.

80. D. A. Carson, *NIV Zondervan Study Bible: Built on the Truth of Scripture and Centered on the Gospel Message* (Grand Rapids, MI: Zondervan, 2015), 2359–2360.

81. R. C. H. Lenski, *The Interpretation of St. Paul's First and Second Epistle to the Corinthians* (Minneapolis, MN: Augsburg Publishing House, 1963), 795.

82. James Luther Mays, *Harper's Bible Commentary* (San Francisco: Harper & Row, 1988), 1202.

CHAPTER 11

1. Mark Water, *The New Encyclopedia of Christian Quotations*, (Alresford, Hampshire: John Hunt Publishers Ltd., 2000), 896.

2. Douglas J. Moo, *The Epistle to the Romans* (Grand Rapids, MI: Wm. B. Eerdmans Publishing Co., 1996), 1.

3. David S. Dockery, The Pauline Letters. In D. S. Dockery, *Holman Concise Bible commentary* (Nashville, TN: Broadman & Holman Publishers, 1998), 541.

4. F. F. Bruce, *Romans: An Introduction and Commentary* (Vol. 6) (Downers Grove, IL: InterVarsity Press, 1985), 19.

5. Ibid, 20.

6. Douglas J. Moo, *NT331 Book Study: Paul's Letter to the Romans* (Bellingham, WA: Lexham Press, 2014), Segment 1.

7. A. F. Walls, Aquila and Prisca, Priscilla. In D. R. W. Wood, I. H. Marshall, A. R. Millard, J. I. Packer & D. J. Wiseman (Eds.), *New Bible Dictionary* (3rd ed.) (Leicester, England; Downers Grove, IL: InterVarsity Press, 1996), 61.

8. Douglas J. Moo, *NT331 Book Study: Paul's Letter to the Romans* (Bellingham, WA: Lexham Press, 2014), Segment 1.

9. John F. MacArthur, Jr., *The MacArthur Bible Handbook* (Nashville, TN: Thomas Nelson Publishers, 2003), 364.

10. Crossway Bibles, *The ESV Study Bible* (Wheaton, IL: Crossway Bibles, 2008), 2152.

11. Ibid.

12. Douglas J. Moo, *NT331 Book Study: Paul's Letter to the Romans* (Bellingham, WA: Lexham Press, 2014), Segment 4.

13. Crossway Bibles, *The ESV Study Bible* (Wheaton, IL: Crossway Bibles, 2008), 2154.

14. John D. Barry, et al. *Faithlife Study Bible* (Bellingham, WA: Lexham Press, 2012–2016).

15. *The Holy Bible: English Standard Version* (Wheaton: Standard Bible Society, 2016).

16. Everett F. Harrison, Romans. In F. E. Gaebelein, *The Expositor's Bible Commentary: Romans through*

Galatians (Vol. 10) (Grand Rapids, MI: Zondervan Publishing House, 1976), 14.

17. Steve Bond, Apostle. In C. Brand, C. Draper, A. England, S. Bond, E. R. Clendenen & T. C. Butler (Eds.), *Holman Illustrated Bible Dictionary* (Nashville, TN: Holman Bible Publishers, 2003), 88.

18. Crossway Bibles, *The ESV Study Bible* (Wheaton, IL: Crossway Bibles, 2008), 2157.

19. Even the unknown writer of Hebrews meets these apostolic criteria, based on the rich content of his letter.

20. C. K. Barrett, *A Commentary on the Epistle to the Romans* (London: Adam & Charles Black, 1967), 17.

21. John Piper, J. Taylor, and P. K. Helseth, *Beyond the Bounds: Open Theism and the Undermining of Biblical Christianity* (Wheaton, IL: Crossway Books, 2003), 108; S. J. Lawson, Foundations of Grace (Lake Mary, FL: Reformation Trust Publishing, 2006), 47.

22. Ajith Fernando, *The Supremacy of Christ* (Wheaton, IL: Crossway Books, 1995), 218.

23. Crossway Bibles, *The ESV Study Bible* (Wheaton, IL: Crossway Bibles, 2008), 2157.

24. John D. Barry et al., *Faithlife Study Bible* (Bellingham, WA: Lexham Press, 2012, 2016).

25. John MacArthur, Jr., *The MacArthur Study Bible* (electronic ed.) (Nashville, TN: Word Pub., 1997), 1691.

26. Colin G. Kruse, *Paul's Letter to the Romans.* (D. A. Carson, Ed.) (Cambridge, U.K.; Nottingham, England; Grand Rapids, MI: William B. Eerdmans Publishing Company; Apollos, 2012), 50–51.

27. William Hendriksen & S. J. Kistemaker, *Exposition of Paul's Epistle to the Romans* (Vol. 12–13) (Grand Rapids: Baker Book House, 1953–2001), 45.

28. Douglas J. Moo, *The Epistle to the Romans* (Grand Rapids, MI: Wm. B. Eerdmans Publishing Co., 1996), 61.

29. Crossway Bibles *The ESV Study Bible* (Wheaton, IL: Crossway Bibles, 2008), 2158; John MacArthur, Jr., *The MacArthur Study Bible* (electronic ed.) (Nashville, TN: Word Pub., 1997), 1693.

30. Clinton E. Arnold, *Zondervan Illustrated Bible Backgrounds Commentary: Romans to Philemon* (Vol. 3) (Grand Rapids, MI: Zondervan, 2002), 12.

31. J. A. Witmer, Romans. In J. F. Walvoord & R. B. Zuck (Eds.), *The Bible Knowledge Commentary: An Exposition of the Scriptures* (Wheaton, IL: Victor Books, 1985), Volume 2, 443.

32. Charles H. Spurgeon, *Spurgeon's Sermons*, "The Choice of a Leader," (electronic ed., Vol. 21, Albany, OR: Ages Software, 1998).

33. Charles H. Spurgeon, *Spurgeon's Sermons* "Idols Abolished," (electronic ed., Vol. 23, Albany, OR: Ages Software, 1998).

34. John MacArthur, Jr., *The MacArthur Study Bible,* (electronic ed.) (Nashville, TN: Word Pub., 1997), 1694.

35. R. C. Sproul, *Romans* (Wheaton, IL: Crossway, 2009), 52.

36. J. A. Witmer, Romans. In J. F. Walvoord & R. B. Zuck (Eds.), *The Bible Knowledge Commentary: An Exposition of the Scriptures* (Wheaton, IL: Victor Books, 1985), Volume 2, 444.

37. James Montgomery Boice, *Romans: Justification by Faith* (Vol. 1) (Grand Rapids, MI: Baker Book House, 1991), 182.

38. Grant R. Osborne, *Romans* (Downers Grove, IL: InterVarsity Press, 2004), 58.

39. Craig S. Keener, *Romans* (Eugene, OR: Cascade Books, 2009), 42.

40. John R. W. Stott, *The Message of Romans: God's Good News for the World* (Leicester, England; Downers Grove, IL: InterVarsity Press, 2001), 81.

41. Robert H. Mounce, *Romans* (Vol. 27) (Nashville: Broadman & Holman Publishers, 1995), 88.

42. Ibid, 91.

43. John MacArthur, Jr., *The MacArthur Study Bible*, (electronic ed.) (Nashville, TN: Word Pub., 1997), 1695.

44. Grant R. Osborne, *Romans* (Downers Grove, IL: InterVarsity Press, 2004), 69.

45. J. A. Witmer, Romans. In J. F. Walvoord & R. B. Zuck (Eds.), *The Bible Knowledge Commentary: An Exposition of the Scriptures* (Wheaton, IL: Victor Books, 1985), Volume 2, 446.

46. Clinton E. Arnold, *Zondervan Illustrated Bible Backgrounds Commentary: Romans to Philemon* (Vol. 3) (Grand Rapids, MI: Zondervan, 2002), 19.

47. Grant R. Osborne, *Romans* (Downers Grove, IL: InterVarsity Press, 2004), 82.

48. John Calvin & John Owen, *Commentary on the Epistle of Paul the Apostle to the Romans* (Bellingham, WA: Logos Bible Software, 2010), 122.

49. Everett F. Harrison, Romans. In F. E. Gaebelein, *The Expositor's Bible Commentary: Romans through Galatians* (Vol. 10) (Grand Rapids, MI: Zondervan Publishing House, 1976), 39.

50. Ibid.

51. Donald Williams & L. J. Ogilvie, *Psalms 1–72* (Vol. 13) (Nashville, TN: Thomas Nelson Inc., 1986), 288.

52. Everett F. Harrison, Romans. In F. E. Gaebelein, *The Expositor's Bible Commentary: Romans through Galatians* (Vol. 10) (Grand Rapids, MI: Zondervan Publishing House, 1976), 40.

53. John D. Barry, et al. *Faithlife Study Bible* (Bellingham, WA: Lexham Press, 2012–2016).

54. Charles H. Spurgeon, *Christ in the Old Testament: Sermons on the Foreshadowing of our Lord in Old Testament History, Ceremony, and Prophecy* (electronic edition.) (Chattanooga, TN: AMG Publishers, 1998), 370.

55. D. M. Gurtner, Romans. In C. A. Evans & C. A. Bubeck (Eds.), *The Bible Knowledge Background Commentary: Acts–Philemon* (First Edition, pp. 203–244) (Colorado Springs, CO: David C Cook, 2004), 213.

56. Bruce B. Barton, D. Veerman & N. S. Wilson, *Romans* (Wheaton, IL: Tyndale House Publishers, 1992), 76.

57. James Montgomery Boice, *Foundations of the Christian Faith: A Comprehensive & Readable Theology* (Downers Grove, IL: InterVarsity Press, 1986), 256.

58. William Hendriksen & S. J. Kistemaker, *Exposition of Paul's Epistle to the Romans* (Vol. 12–13) (Grand Rapids: Baker Book House, 1953–2001), 164.

59. Grant R. Osborne, *Romans: Verse by Verse* (Bellingham, WA: Lexham Press, 2017), 130.

60. Douglas J. Moo, D. *The Epistle to the Romans* (Grand Rapids, MI: Wm. B. Eerdmans Publishing Co., 1996), 288.

61. Bruce B. Barton, D. Veerman & N. S. Wilson, *Romans* (Wheaton, IL: Tyndale House Publishers, 1992), 103.

62. R. C. Sproul, *Romans* (Wheaton, IL: Crossway, 2009), 98.

63. J. D. Greear & Timothy Keller, *Gospel: Recovering the Power that Made Christianity Revolutionary* (Nashville: B&H, 2011).

64. J. A. Witmer, Romans. In J. F. Walvoord & R. B. Zuck (Eds.), *The Bible Knowledge Commentary: An Exposition of the Scriptures* (Wheaton, IL: Victor Books, 1985), Volume 2, 461.

65. Ibid, 462.

66. William Hendriksen & S. J. Kistemaker, *Exposition of Paul's Epistle to the Romans* (Vol. 12–13) (Grand Rapids: Baker Book House, 1953–2001), 201.

67. Jack Cottrell, *Romans* (Vol. 1) (Joplin, MO: College Press Pub. Co., 1996).

68. Leon Morris, *The Epistle to the Romans* (Grand Rapids, MI; Leicester, England: W.B. Eerdmans; Inter-Varsity Press, 1988), 261.

69. John MacArthur, Jr., *The MacArthur Study Bible* (electronic ed.) (Nashville, TN: Word Pub., 1997), 1704.

70. Robert H. Mounce, *Romans* (Vol. 27) (Nashville: Broadman & Holman Publishers, 1995), 158.

71. Douglas J. Moo, The Letters and Revelation. In D. A. Carson, *NIV Zondervan Study Bible: Built on the Truth of Scripture and Centered on the Gospel Message* (Grand Rapids, MI: Zondervan, 2015), 2303; Crossway Bibles *The ESV Study Bible* (Wheaton, IL: Crossway Bibles, 2008), 2168; Grant R. Osborne, *Romans* (Downers Grove, IL: InterVarsity Press, 2004), 166.

72. Jack Cottrell, *Romans* (Vol. 1) (Joplin, MO: College Press Pub. Co., 1996); John MacArthur, Jr., *The MacArthur Study Bible* (electronic ed.) (Nashville, TN: Word Pub., 1997), 1704.

73. R. C. H. Lenski, *The Interpretation of St. Paul's Epistle to the Romans* (Columbus, Ohio: Lutheran Book Concern, 1936), 452.

74. John MacArthur, Jr., *The MacArthur Study Bible* (electronic ed.) (Nashville, TN: Word Pub., 1997), 1705.

75. R. C. Sproul, *Romans* (Wheaton, IL: Crossway, 2009), 121.

76. Grant R. Osborne, *Romans* (Downers Grove, IL: InterVarsity Press, 2004), 199; Crossway Bibles *The ESV Study Bible* (Wheaton, IL: Crossway Bibles, 2008), 2168; Grant R. Osborne, *Romans* (Downers Grove, IL: InterVarsity Press, 2004), 2169.

77. Leon Morris, *The Epistle to the Romans* (Grand Rapids, MI; Leicester, England: W.B. Eerdmans; Inter-Varsity Press, 1988), 280.

78. R. C. Sproul, *Romans* (Wheaton, IL: Crossway, 2009), 122.

79. Leon Morris, *The Epistle to the Romans* (Grand Rapids, MI; Leicester, England: W.B. Eerdmans; Inter-Varsity Press, 1988), 281.

80. William Hendriksen & S. J. Kistemaker, *Exposition of Paul's Epistle to the Romans* (Vol. 12–13) (Grand Rapids: Baker Book House, 1953–2001), 221.

81. Bruce B. Barton, D. Veerman & N. S. Wilson, *Romans* (Wheaton, IL: Tyndale House Publishers, 1992), 139.

82. Ray Comfort, *The Evidence Bible: Irrefutable Evidence for the Thinking Mind, Notes.* (K. Cameron, Ed.) (Orlando, FL: Bridge-Logos, 2003), 1464.

83. John F. MacArthur, Jr., *Romans* (Chicago: Moody Press, 1991), Volume 1, 383.

84. Charles E. B. Cranfield, *A Critical and Exegetical Commentary on the Epistle to the Romans* (London; New York: T&T Clark International, 2004), 341.

85. Douglas J. Moo, *The Epistle to the Romans* (Grand Rapids, MI: Wm. B. Eerdmans Publishing Co., 1996), 458.

86. R. C. Sproul, *The Gospel of God: An Exposition of Romans* (Great Britain: Christian Focus Publications, 1994), 125.

87. Grant R. Osborne, *Romans: Verse by Verse* (Bellingham, WA: Lexham Press, 2017), 217.

88. H. D. M. Spence-Jones, *The Pulpit Commentary: Romans* (London; New York: Funk & Wagnalls Company, 1909), 200.

CHAPTER 12

1. R. C. Sproul, *Before the Face of God: A Daily Guide for Living the Book of Romans, Book 1* (Grand Rapids: Baker Book House; Ligonier Ministries, 1992).

2. John R. W. Stott, *The Message of Romans: God's Good News for the World* (Leicester, England; Downers Grove, IL: InterVarsity Press, 2001), 216.

3. E. F. Harrison & D. A. Hagner, Romans. In T. Longman III &. Garland, David E., *The Expositor's Bible Commentary: Romans–Galatians (Revised Edition)* (Vol. 11) (Grand Rapids, MI: Zondervan, 2008), 127.

4. Jack Cottrell, *Romans* (Vol. 1) (Joplin, MO: College Press Pub. Co., 1996).

5. Leon Morris, *The Epistle to the Romans* (Grand Rapids, MI; Leicester, England: W.B. Eerdmans; Inter-Varsity Press, 1988), 314.

6. Leon Morris, *The Epistle to the Romans* (Grand Rapids, MI; Leicester, England: W.B. Eerdmans; Inter-Varsity Press, 1988), 315.

7. The Sermon on the Mount by Joachim Jeremias (the Ethel M. Wood Lecture delivered before the University of London on 7 March 1961: University of London, Athlone Press, 1961), 96, 97, as quoted in John R. W. Stott, *The Message of the Sermon On the Mount* (Matthew 5–7): Christian Counter-culture (Leicester; Downers Grove, IL: InterVarsity Press, 1985), 185.

8. F. F. Bruce, *Romans: An Introduction and Commentary* (Vol. 6) (Downers Grove, IL: InterVarsity Press, 1985), 174.

9. John MacArthur, Jr., *The MacArthur Study Bible*, (electronic ed.) (Nashville, TN: Word Pub., 1997), 1708.

10. Bruce B. Barton, D. Veerman & N. S. Wilson, *Romans* (Wheaton, IL: Tyndale House Publishers, 1992), 162.

11. Douglas J. Moo, The Letters and Revelation. In D. A. Carson, *NIV Zondervan Study Bible: Built on the Truth of Scripture and Centered on the Gospel Message* (Grand Rapids, MI: Zondervan, 2015), 2307.

12. R. C. Sproul, *The Gospel of God: An Exposition of Romans* (Great Britain: Christian Focus Publications, 1994), 147.

13. Ibid, 152.

14. Grant R. Osborne, *Romans* (Downers Grove, IL: InterVarsity Press, 2004), 226.

15. Ibid, 235.

16. John D. Barry, et al. *Faithlife Study Bible* (Bellingham, WA: Lexham Press, 2012–2016).

17. J. A. Witmer, Romans. In J. F. Walvoord & R. B. Zuck (Eds.), *The Bible Knowledge Commentary: An Exposition*

of the Scriptures (Wheaton, IL: Victor Books, 1985), Volume 2, 476.

18. E. F. Harrison & D. A. Hagner, Romans. In T. Longman III &. Garland, David E., *The Expositor's Bible Commentary: Romans–Galatians (Revised Edition)* (Vol. 11) (Grand Rapids, MI: Zondervan, 2008), 103.

19. John D. Barry, et al. *Faithlife Study Bible* (Bellingham, WA: Lexham Press, 2012–2016).

20. Grant R. Osborne, *Romans* (Downers Grove, IL: InterVarsity Press, 2004), 240.

21. Leon Morris, *The Epistle to the Romans* (Grand Rapids, MI; Leicester, England: W.B. Eerdmans; Inter-Varsity Press, 1988), 357.

22. Ibid, 361.

23. But again, some commentators see this chapter not as pertaining to individual salvation concerning Pharaoh or anyone else. They believe that God hardened Pharaoh's heart and used his rebellion to accomplish His will on earth.

24. John R. W. Stott, *The Message of Romans: God's Good News for the World* (Leicester, England; Downers Grove, IL: InterVarsity Press, 2001), 271.

25. Ibid.

26. Ibid, 272.

27. J. A. Witmer, Romans. In J. F. Walvoord & R. B. Zuck (Eds.), *The Bible Knowledge Commentary: An Exposition of the Scriptures* (Wheaton, IL: Victor Books, 1985), Volume 2, 481.

28. Crossway Bibles, *The ESV Study Bible* (Wheaton, IL: Crossway Bibles, 2008), 2175.

29. J. A. Witmer, Romans. In J. F. Walvoord & R. B. Zuck (Eds.), *The Bible Knowledge Commentary: An Exposition*

of the Scriptures (Wheaton, IL: Victor Books, 1985), Volume 2, 481.

30. John J. MacArthur, Jr., *Romans* (Chicago: Moody Press, 1991), 111.

31. Bruce B. Barton, D. Veerman & N. S. Wilson, *Romans* (Wheaton, IL: Tyndale House Publishers, 1992), 217.

32. R. C. Sproul, *The Gospel of God: An Exposition of Romans* (Great Britain: Christian Focus Publications, 1994), 191; Bruce B. Barton, D. Veerman & N. S. Wilson, *Romans* (Wheaton, IL: Tyndale House Publishers, 1992), 222–223.

33. Robert H. Mounce, *Romans* (Vol. 27) (Nashville: Broadman & Holman Publishers, 1995), 230.

34. F. F. Bruce, *Romans: An Introduction and Commentary* (Vol. 6) (Downers Grove, IL: InterVarsity Press, 1985), 223.

35. Bruce B. Barton, D. Veerman & N. S. Wilson, *Romans* (Wheaton, IL: Tyndale House Publishers, 1992), 230.

36. Robert H. Mounce, *Romans* (Vol. 27) (Nashville: Broadman & Holman Publishers, 1995), 232.

37. Ibid, 231.

38. Ibid, 240.

39. John Piper, *Sermons From John Piper,* "Abhor What is Evil; Hold Fast to What is Good," (Minneapolis, MN: Desiring God, 2004).

40. R. C. Sproul, *The Gospel of God: An Exposition of Romans* (Great Britain: Christian Focus Publications, 1994), 212.

41. George Thomas Kurian, In *Nelson's New Christian Dictionary: the Authoritative Resource on the Christian World* (Nashville, TN: Thomas Nelson Publishers, 2001).

42. John MacArthur, Jr., *The MacArthur Study Bible,* (electronic ed.) (Nashville, TN: Word Pub., 1997), 1718.

43. Grant R. Osborne, *Romans* (Downers Grove, IL: InterVarsity Press, 2004), 343.

44. Walter C. Kaiser, et al., *Hard Sayings of the Bible* (Downers Grove, IL: InterVarsity, 1996), 574.

45. Ibid, 575–576.

46. Jack Cottrell, *Romans* (Vol. 2) (Joplin, MO: College Press Pub. Co., 1996).

47. Crossway Bibles, *The ESV Study Bible* (Wheaton, IL: Crossway Bibles, 2008), 2180.

48. David L. Bartlett, *Romans* (P. D. Miller, Ed.) (Louisville, KY: Westminster John Knox Press, 1995), 122.

49. Douglas J. Moo, *The Epistle to the Romans* (Grand Rapids, MI: Wm. B. Eerdmans Publishing Co., 1996), 447.

50. David L. Bartlett, *Romans* (P. D. Miller, Ed.) (Louisville, KY: Westminster John Knox Press, 1995), 123.

51. Bruce B. Barton, D. Veerman & N. S. Wilson, *Romans* (Wheaton, IL: Tyndale House Publishers, 1992), 264.

52. John D. Barry, et al. *Faithlife Study Bible* (Bellingham, WA: Lexham Press, 2012–2016).

53. John R. W. Stott, *The Message of Romans: God's Good News for the World* (Leicester, England; Downers Grove, IL: InterVarsity Press, 2001), 366.

54. As I've noted throughout, I'm not suggesting that every Old Testament law is still applicable to Christians or that all the so-called prosperity promises of the Old Testament apply to Christians, but every word of the Old Testament, like the New Testament, is the inspired Word of God.

55. John MacArthur, Jr., *The MacArthur Study Bible,* (electronic ed.) (Nashville, TN: Word Pub., 1997), 1723.

CONCLUSION

1. F. F. Bruce, *Paul: Apostle of the Free Spirit*, (Milton Keynes, UK: Paternoster, 1977), 210.

INDEX

A

Abbott, Lyman, 5, 7
Abraham, 29–30, 39–41, 50, 67–68,
    102, 107, 112–13, 135–137, 251,
    261, 265–66, 272, 277–78, 294–95,
    298, 301, 315
    saved by faith, 27, 79, 88, 93, 100,
        128, 132–34, 138, 162, 170–71,
        263, 272, 276–77, 312, 320
    spiritual descendants, 272, 277, 295
Abrahamic Covenant, the, 30, 135,
    137, 295
abstinence, 187, 240
Achaia, 86, 90–91, 148, 167, 223, 259,
    316
Achaicus, 168, 223

Acts, Book of
    and the indispensability of the
        Christian witness, 17
    as a bridge between the gospels and
        the epistles, 11–12
    important speeches in, 17
    outlines of, 18
    title of, 13
    writing of, 14
Adam (first man), 108, 187, 204, 219–
    21, 276, 280–81, 285
Adriatic Sea, 91, 118
Aegean Sea, 93
Aeneas, 52–53
Agabus, 58, 98, 130

Agrippa, King, 8, 17, 49, 59, 111–12, 114–17
Alexander, 90
Alexander the Great, 97
Alexandria, 58, 86, 117, 121
Amorites, 66
Amos (book), 67, 75, 154, 178, 297
Amphipolis, 80
Ananias (from Damascus), 24, 33–34, 102
  encounter with Saul of Tarsus, 10, 49–51
Ananias (Jewish priest), 103, 104, 106
Anatolia, 93
angels, 23, 36, 37, 42, 105, 120, 159, 181, 185, 204, 208, 216, 248, 294
Anselm, 160
Antichrist, the, 153, 161–62
Antioch, 17–18, 57–59, 62–64, 66, 72–74, 76, 84, 86, 126, 131, 247, 260
Antipatris, 106
Aphrodite (pagan deity), 167–68
Apollonia, 80
Apollos (evangelizer), 86–87, 168, 177–78, 180–81, 204, 215, 223
apologetics, 82, 322
Aquila, 84, 86–87, 168, 204, 215, 223, 260
Aramaic (language), 101
Aratus, 82
Areopagus, the, 72, 81
Aristarchus, 90
Arminians, 293
Artemis (pagan deity), 90–91, 228
Arthur, J. Philip, 248
Asia Minor, 3, 15, 78, 97, 126
Assos, 93

Assyrian Empire, 309
Assyrians, 154
Athens, 17, 72, 81–83, 143, 150, 168
atonement, 29, 208
Augustine, Saint, 147, 160, 209
authority, 24, 26–29, 32, 36, 43, 48–49, 54, 106–107, 111–12, 127–30, 143, 161, 165, 178, 181, 185, 188, 190, 195–96, 203–204, 219, 223, 227, 232, 247, 249–50, 253–54, 256, 261, 264, 308–309
Azotus (Ashdod), 48

B

Baal (pagan deity), 199, 301
Babylon, 69, 154, 310
baptism, 28, 87–88, 102
  by water, 170, 281
  of the Holy Spirit, 22
  infant baptism, 27
  whether it is necessary for salvation, 27, 170
Bar-Jesus (magician, a.k.a. Elymas), 64
Barnabas, 34, 51, 58, 62–64, 69–77, 127, 130–31, 195
Barnett, Paul, 208, 213, 237
Barrett, C. K., 73, 265
Barry, John, 215
Barsabbas, 23, 76
Barton, Bruce, 56, 96, 125, 131, 189, 213, 219, 279, 286, 302, 305
Bathsheba, 272
Beale, G. K., 163
Benjamin (tribe of Israel), 3, 301
Berea, 81, 92, 143, 242
Bithynia, 78
Black Sea, 78
blasphemy, 31, 38, 42

Blomberg, Craig, 183, 201, 222

boasting, 4, 86, 114, 148, 172–73, 182–83, 227, 229, 244, 253

Boice, James Montgomery, 206, 269, 276

Bonhoeffer, Dietrich, 309

Bosnia-Herzegovina, 91

Bruce, F. F., 1, 7, 26, 53, 91, 106, 121, 123, 161, 305

Brunner, Emil, 71, 283

Burrell, D. J., 8–9

Butler, John G., 8

C

Caesarea, 48, 51, 53–54, 57–60, 86, 97–98, 100, 105–106, 109–111

Caligula (emperor), 59

Calvin, John, 85, 98, 115, 120, 231, 273

Calvinists, 293, 298

Campbell, D. K., 137

Canaanites, 41, 66, 183

Carson, D. A., 192, 243

Castor (pagan deity), 121

Catholicism, Catholics, 293

Cauda, 117

charity, 52, 54, 243, 245, 246, 314

Chios, 93

Chloe, 168–69

Christian, "carnal Christians," 176–77

Christianity
    as a relational faith, 307, 320
    biblical Christianity, 29
    Christian living, 11, 13, 126, 158, 304–305, 307, 311
    Christians ethics, 263, 304
    the self-sacrificial nature of Christian love, 208

factions within, 168–69, 177
    Resurrection as the lynchpin of Christianity, 29

Christians
    as adopted sons of God, 137–37, 291
    all Christians need prayers, 164
    charitable from the beginning, 58
    engaged in a spiritual war, 247
    and hardship, 228, 292
    as instruments of God's grace, 246
    must not be conformed to this world, 304–305, 317
    and sin nature, 141, 185, 287
    spiritual Christian, 176
    unequally yoked with unbelievers, 240
    weaker Christians, 192, 202, 313–14
    will suffer persecution on earth, 73

Chrysostom, John, 60, 196

Church, the
    community oriented, 34
    different gifts within the, 320
    early debates on circumcision, 74
    as God's building, 177–78
    as God's field, 177–78
    as God's temple, 177, 179

Cicero, 4, 183

Cilicia, 3, 51, 58, 76, 106, 117, 129

Clark, George, 246

Claudius (emperor), 58, 84, 260

Claudius Lysias, 103, 105

Clement of Rome, 14

Cnidus, 117

Colosse, 89

communion, 16, 201, 211

community, 16, 28, 33–35, 43, 53, 58, 76, 88, 99, 111, 166, 169, 177, 179, 184, 198, 307, 310, 367, 375

conscience, 103, 107, 123, 180, 192, 198, 202, 234, 271, 286, 294, 313–14

conversion, 2–3, 5, 7–10, 22, 28, 37, 45–46, 48–42, 56–59, 65, 70, 80, 88, 102–103, 113, 123, 129, 145, 148, 190, 212, 267, 282, 284, 292

Corinth, 83–87, 91–92, 143–44, 158, 168, 193, 199, 226–27, 229, 255, 257, 259

importance of the city, 167

Corinthians (epistles), 9, 11, 84, 90, 93, 108, 140, 144

1 Corinthians, 125, 153, 166–68, 175, 178, 195, 225

2 Corinthians, 125, 225–227, 255–256, 260, 286

Cornelius, 17, 53–57, 59, 131

Cottrell, Jack, 311, 388

Council at Jerusalem, 62, 75–76, 78, 100, 127, 197, 261

Cranfield, Charles, 287

Crete, 82, 117–18

Crispus, 84, 92

Croatia, 91

Cyprus, 57, 62, 64, 76, 100, 117

D

Damaris, 83

Damascus, 1, 7–10, 48–52, 102, 113–114, 129, 179, 195, 217, 251, 282

David (Old Testament figure), 11, 24, 26, 30, 32, 41, 66–68, 75, 263, 266, 272–73, 277, 294, 315

promised an everlasting kingdom, 266

Davidic Covenant, 67, 295

Day of the Lord, the, 26, 143, 153–55, 158–59, 161

Demetrius, 90–91

demons, 89, 116, 147, 182, 187, 201, 248, 300

Derbe, 62, 71, 73, 77, 126

Destroyer, the (Angel of Death), 199

Deuteronomy (book), 66, 300

Dionysius the Areopagite, 83

doctrine, 70, 79, 126, 128, 138, 143, 152 177, 178, 201, 205, 216, 238, 240, 248, 253, 260, 261, 311, 317

Dods, Marcus, 169

Drusilla, 109

E

Edwards, Jonathan, 160, 208–209

Egnatian Way, 80

Egypt, Egyptians, 39–42, 66, 97, 101, 117, 199

Elijah (prophet), 92, 301

Elisha (prophet), 92

Emmaus Code, The (Limbaugh), 47, 266

Emmaus Road, the, 47, 266, 275

Ephesians (epistle), 95, 125, 191, 247, 313

Ephesus, 16–17, 85–87, 90–91, 93, 167, 220, 222, 226, 259

Epicurean, 81

Epimenides of Crete, 82

Erastus, 90–91

Erickson, Millard, 23, 171

Esau, 295–96

ESV Study Bible, 88, 262, 300

Eutychus, 19, 92–93

evangelism, evangelization, 13, 70, 75, 81–82, 84, 123, 131, 148–49, 303, 311

Exell, Joseph, 12–13, 116

exorcism, exorcists, 46, 79, 89, 248

Ezekiel (prophet), 98

F

Faw, Chalmer, 83

Fee, Gordon, 177, 180, 188, 204, 222

Felix (Roman governor), 17, 105–109

Fernando, Ajith, 265

Fair Havens, 117

Fortunatus, 168

Forum of Appius, 122

Franzmann, Werner, 50, 62

G

Gaebelein, A. C., 8

Gaius, 59, 90

Gallio, 85–86, 92

Gamaliel, 3, 37, 102

Garden of Gethsemane, 291

Garland, David, 174, 214, 239, 246

Gaza, 47–48

Geisler, Norman, 16, 153, 216–17

Genesis (book), 47, 187, 204, 235, 277, 317

Gentiles, the, 4, 8, 10, 17–20, 24, 30, 33, 48–49, 52–53, 55–58, 62, 65, 70–76, 80, 89, 93, 98, 100–103, 113–114, 123, 127, 130–31, 147–50, 168, 171, 197, 202, 207, 228–229, 235, 247, 249, 251, 259–63, 265, 267, 269–74, 276–77, 284, 289, 296, 298, 301–304, 315–16

Girgashites, 66

glorification, 138, 170–71, 291–92

glossolalia (speaking in tongues), 210

"Great Commandment," the, 310

Great Commission, the, 12, 70, 228

Greece, 83, 90–93, 143, 148, 204, 227

greed, 34, 94, 109, 123, 184–85

Greek (language), 4, 16, 25, 34, 46, 51, 57, 101, 145, 150, 279

Grudem, Wayne, 27, 73, 210

Guthrie, Donald, 18

Guzik, David, 239

H

Hagar, 137

Harrison, E. F., 289

Hays, Richard, 179

head coverings, 203–204

healing, 16, 19, 28–29, 31–32, 36–37, 52–53, 72, 121, 206–207, 231

Hellenists, the, 38, 51, 57

Hendriksen, William, 133, 143, 160, 282

Hermes, 72

Herod Agrippa I, 59

Herod Antipas the tetrarch, 63

Herod the Great, 48, 59

Hierapolis, 89

Hitler, Adolf, 309

Hittites, 66

Hivites, 66

Hodge, Charles, 167, 269

homosexuality, 199, 204

Hosea (book), 221–22, 246, 298

humility, 100, 133, 163, 167, 175, 182, 227, 247, 256, 264, 302, 306

I

Iconium, 62, 70–73, 78, 126, 259
idolatry, 35, 42, 54, 81, 84, 138, 200,
    240–41, 269, 271, 301
Illyricum, 91–92, 226, 260
inheritance, 135–36, 147, 154, 236
Isaac, 29, 39, 41, 50, 102, 107, 112,
    137, 295
Isaiah (prophet), 23, 28, 47, 56, 67, 82,
    85, 98, 122, 154, 156–57, 163, 173,
    175, 181, 185, 221, 222, 246, 252,
    288, 298, 300–301, 315
Iscariot, Judas, 24
Ishmael, 137, 295
Israel, 5, 17, 23–24, 27, 33, 35–36,
    39–41, 47, 49, 53–55, 66–67, 72,
    96, 98, 113, 122, 135, 156, 184,
    198–201, 233, 240, 261, 265, 273,
    275–77, 294–296, 298, 301–303,
    309, 314
Italy, 2, 84, 117, 260

J

Jacob (Israel), 29, 39–41, 50, 102, 107,
    112, 295–96
James (apostle), 59–61, 89, 119, 129–
    31, 197, 217
James (book), 55, 64, 89, 120, 156, 277,
    300
James (Jesus' half-brother), 14, 75–76,
    100
Janeway, Brian, 16
Jason, 80–81
Jebusites, 66
Jeremiah (book), 181, 297, 161, 180
Jeremiah (prophet), 98, 233, 249

Jerusalem, 3, 6–7, 9–10, 12, 16–20,
    22–24, 31, 35–36, 41, 45–49,
    51–52, 55–62, 65, 71, 74–76, 78,
    86, 88, 90–91, 93–94, 96–102, 105–
    107, 109–111, 114, 127, 129–30,
    137, 144, 168, 179, 197, 222, 226,
    243–44, 246–47, 253, 260–61, 316
Job, 23, 55, 171, 174–75, 180–81, 296–
    97
Joel, 25–26, 215
Johnson, Alan, 186
John the Baptist, 22, 55, 57, 65, 67
Joppa, 52–54, 57
Joseph (patriarch), 40, 42
Josephus (historian), 14, 16, 61, 104,
    106, 109
"Judaizers," 74–76, 78, 127, 134, 141
Judea, 2, 8, 10, 12, 19–20, 23, 31, 45,
    51, 53, 55–60, 62, 86, 94, 98, 114,
    122, 149, 316
Jude, 128, 161, 185
Julius the centurion, 117, 120–21
justification, 27, 133, 138, 169–70, 263,
    274, 280–81
    by faith alone, 128, 262

K

Kaiser, Walter, 191, 310
Kent, Charles Foster, 14
Kings (books)
    1 Kings, 82, 92, 295
    2 Kings, 92, 309
Kistemaker, Simon, 203, 231
Klausner, Joseph, 32

L

Ladd, George Eldon, 221

Laodicea, 89

Lasea, 131

Last Supper, the, 22

Law of Moses, 2, 68–69, 74, 100, 127

Lenski, R. C. H., 120, 256

Leschert, Dale, 135

Leviticus (book), 25, 29, 96, 183, 218, 232

Lightfoot, J. B., 15

Lord's Supper, the, 92, 168, 201, 204–206, 226

Lowery, David K., 170

Lucius of Cyrene, 63

Lutherans, 293

Lycia, 117

Lydda, 52

Lydia, 78–80

Lystra, 62, 71–73, 77–78, 83, 126

Lyttelton, George, 8

M

MacArthur, John, 119–120, 127, 154, 165, 185, 213–14, 221, 227, 239, 244, 256, 261, 266, 270–71, 283, 302, 316

Macedonia, 78, 84, 90–92, 143–44, 148, 222, 226, 229, 232, 242–43, 245, 250, 259, 316

Malta, 121

Manaen, 63

Marius Victorinus, 128

marriage, 96, 187–88, 190–91
Christian marriage, 168

Martin, Ralph, 17, 211

Mary, 60–61

Matthias, 24

McDonald, William, 237

McGee, J. Vernon, 12

McGrath, Alister, 4

Mediterranean, the, 48, 52–53, 58

Menander, 220

mercy, 43, 69, 147–48, 200, 231, 234, 296, 297–98, 303–304, 307, 315, 317

Methodists, 293

Miletus, 93, 97

miracles, 6, 26, 28, 32, 35, 41, 46, 65, 71, 89, 162, 207–208, 253

Mnason of Cyprus, 100

Montenegro, 91

Moo, Douglas, 150, 237, 261, 278, 287

moral codes, 304

Morris, Leon, 144, 147, 159, 169, 186, 198, 283, 291

Mosaic Law, the, 75, 85, 100, 137, 261–62, 276–77, 284, 307

Moses, 2, 7, 38, 40–42, 74–75, 84, 100, 114, 127, 135, 137, 140, 157, 199–200, 233, 266, 274, 277, 280, 285, 295

Mounce, Robert, 304, 306

Mount Gerizim, 46

Mount Sinai, 25, 40–41, 137, 295

Myasia, 93

Myra, 117

Mysia, 78

N

Nahum (book), 300

Nathan (prophet), 66

Neapolis, 78

Nero, 14

New Covenant, the, 233, 239, 272, 274, 307, 314

New Living Translation (NLT), 89, 204, 245, 287, 297

New Testament in Antiquity, 18
New Testament, the, 1, 7, 15, 23, 25, 34, 47, 67, 93, 94, 98, 123, 128, 144–46, 152, 154, 161, 191, 203, 208, 217, 225, 232, 252, 264–66, 274, 277–80, 296, 314, 316
Nicodemus, 25
North Galatian Theory, 126

O

obedience, 7, 13, 18, 27–28, 36, 114, 116, 154, 165, 175, 181, 184, 197, 231, 242, 245–46, 249, 259, 264, 266, 267, 281, 283, 285, 303, 311, 316–17
Old Covenant, the, 233–34, 274, 307, 314
Old Testament, the, 6, 17–18, 23–25, 30, 35, 39, 47, 54–55, 66, 69, 75, 81–82, 85, 92, 94, 98, 107, 112–14, 122, 126, 134, 137, 154, 156–57, 171, 173, 175, 196, 198, 201, 212, 215, 246, 233, 240, 245, 246, 252, 254, 264–66, 270, 274–77, 280, 284, 296, 301–302, 314–315, 317, 320
Osborne, Grant, 278, 294

P

paganism, pagans, 18, 35, 82, 84, 91, 135, 149, 152, 167, 169, 181, 183, 191–92, 197, 199, 201–202, 206, 214, 218, 241, 254, 301–302, 309, 311
Pamphylia, 73, 76, 117
Paphos, 64–65
Parthenon, the, 82, 90

Pauline Epistles, the, 125
    Missionary Epistle, the, 125
    Pastoral Epistles, the, 125
    Prison Epistles, the, 125
peace, 8, 19, 31, 51, 55, 61, 76, 80, 107, 129, 139, 154, 156, 166, 189–90, 213, 223, 254–55, 264, 267, 270, 278, 284, 310, 313, 315–17
Peloponnesian peninsula, 167
Pentecost, 8, 16, 18, 22, 24–26, 56–57, 68, 88, 90, 154, 210, 222, 260, 266
Pentecost Festival, 93
Perga, 62, 65–66, 73
Perizzites, 66
Pharisees, the, 6, 31, 37, 54, 74, 104–105, 108, 113
Philemon (epistle), 125, 190
Philippi, 60, 78, 80, 92–93, 149, 242, 259
Phoenicia, 57, 74
Phoenix, 117
Piper, John, 308
Pisidia, 62
Pisidian Antioch, 17–18, 66, 72–73, 84, 126
Pliny, 110
pluralism, 129
Polhill, John, 35, 40–42, 93, 98, 109
Pollux (pagan deity), 121
Pontius Pilate, 33
Porcius Festus, 109
predestination, 293, 298–99
pride, 3–4, 11, 109, 115–16, 132–33, 141, 147, 172, 192, 241–42, 249, 302–303, 306
Prior, David, 178, 207
Priscilla, 84, 86–87, 168, 204, 215, 223, 260

Promised Land, the, 35, 39

prophecy, 17, 26, 33, 98, 113, 157, 206–210, 212, 214–15, 307, 317

Psalms, the, 23, 273, 314

Ptolemais, 97

Publius, 121

Puteoli, 122

R

Ramsay, William, 15, 86

Rapture, the, 153–55, 159, 161, 219

Red Sea, the, 41

Revelation, Book of, 33, 47, 67, 95, 155–56, 160–162, 185, 219, 252, 265, 291, 310, 315

Rhegium, 122

rhetoric, 170, 173

Rhoda, 74

Roman Empire, the, 2, 4, 58, 64, 189, 260, 310, 316

Rome, 4, 11, 14, 19, 58–59, 62, 84–85, 90–91, 94, 96, 105, 107, 110–11, 116–17, 119, 121–23, 125, 143, 249, 259–61, 264, 267, 315–16

Ryrie, Charles, 59, 162

S

Sabbath, the, 6, 66–67, 69, 75, 78, 80, 84, 92, 128, 165

Sadducees, the, 31, 36–37, 59, 104–105, 113

Salmone, 117

Samaria, Samaritans, 10, 12, 19–20, 23, 45–46, 51–52, 57, 59, 62, 74, 98

Samos, 93

Samothrace, 78

Samuel (book)

1 Samuel, 3, 23

2 Samuel, 67

Samuel (prophet), 66

sanctification, 234, 283, 287–88, 305–306, 311, 320

Sanhedrin, the, 6, 31–32, 36, 38, 59, 102–103, 105–108

Sapphira, 33-35

Sarah (wife of Abraham), 137, 278

Satan, 11, 23, 34, 49, 113, 133, 150-51, 162, 164, 183

Sceva, 89

Seifrid, Mark, 245

Seleucia, 64

selfishness, 34

selflessness, 146, 176

Sergius Paulus, 64–65

Sharon, 52

Shedd, William G. T., 216

Sherwin-White, A. N., 15

Sicily, 121

Sidon, 61, 117

Silas, 76, 79-81, 84, 143, 158

Silvanus (Silas), 143, 158

Simeon (Niger), 63

Simon (sorcerer), 46

Simon (tanner), 53, 203

slavery, 42, 69, 130, 137, 189, 190, 237, 290

Smith, Gary, 157

Solomon, 28, 35, 41, 64, 66, 82, 170, 295

sophism, 173

Sosthenes, 85, 92, 169

Spain, 249, 260, 316

speaking in tongues, 56, 88, 210–215

Spence-Jones, H. D. M., 288

spiritual gifts, 168, 206–208, 320

spiritual warfare, 95, 248

spouses, 187–88, 190, 240

Sproul, R. C., 285, 288-89, 292

Spurgeon, Charles, 135, 269, 275

Stoics, 82

Stott, John, 13, 22, 35, 65, 88, 139, 145, 159, 165, 289, 297

Straight Street, 49

Suetonius, 84, 260

summary statements outline, 19

Swindoll, Chuck, 1, 3

Synagogues, 48, 50–51, 64, 75–76, 260

Syracuse, 122

Syria, 129, 131

Sytris, 118

T

Tabitha (Dorcas), 19, 52–53

Tarsus, 3, 43, 51, 58, 101, 126

taxes, 310

temptation, 140, 152, 187–88, 200

Ten Commandments, 54, 201, 209, 233, 295, 307, 310

Tertullian, 160

Tertullus, 106–107

Thais (Greek comedy), 220

theology, 138, 158, 168, 201, 289, 304

Theophilus, 14, 15, 145–54

Thessalonians (epistle), 93, 144, 159–60

　　1 Thessalonians, 125, 143, 158, 219, 279

　　2 Thessalonians, 125, 143, 152, 157

Thessalonica, 80, 81–82, 92, 143-144, 149–51, 242, 259

Third Reich, the, 309

Thiselton, Anthony, 173

Three Taverns, the, 122

Thru the Bible (series), 12

Thyatira, 79

Tiberius (emperor), 59

Timothy (epistles), 95

　　1 Timothy, 125, 187, 191

　　2 Timothy, 125

Timothy (friend of Paul), 77–78, 81, 84, 90, 143, 150

Titius Justus, 84

tolerance, 45, 129, 231

Tozer, A. W., 176

Tribulation, the, 271, 279, 307, 315

Trinity, 162, 206, 219

Troas, 78, 92, 126, 226, 231

Trophimus, 101

Troy, 78

Tubingen school theory, 15

Turek, Frank, 16, 115, 322

Turkey, 58, 78, 126

Tuttle, Bob, 246

Twitter, 47

Tyrannus, 89

Tyre, 61, 97

W

Wesley, John, 159, 286

Wiersbe, Warren, 33, 215, 225

Williams, Donald, 274

Willis, Wendell, 175

Witherington, Ben, 13, 214

Witmer, J. A., 300

worldliness, 226

Wright, D. F., 187–88

Wright, N. T., 216, 239

Z

Zeus, 72, 82

Zacharias, Ravi, 30

Zophar, 175